To: _____

From: _____

Date: _____

Kicking the Habit

Submit yourselves, then, to God. Resist the devil, and he will flee from you.

JAMES 4:7

I read somewhere that it takes at least two solid weeks of repetition before a habit is established, and I used that theory when I tried (for the third time in my life) to quit smoking. I decided that every time the craving swooped in, I would replace it with a prayer and a replacement taste; I landed on a lip-pursing can (or two) of diet orange soda and a Scripture to which I could cling: "Resist the devil, and he will flee from you."

For the first week, you could have sliced cheese on my razor-sharp nerves, and I'm sure beverage stock went up as I consumed soda after soda. But I just kept at it, promising myself that the cravings would flee. Eventually. One day. Please, God.

Halfway through the second week, however, I couldn't stand it any longer. I got into my car, drove to the nearest convenience store, and bought a pack of cigarettes. I couldn't wait until I got home, so I peeled the package open before I even started the car. I held the package to my nose and breathed in deeply. There it was! The familiar draw of nicotine.

I rummaged through my purse and was horrified to discover that I'd tossed out my last disposable lighter in a moment of perceived resolution. The spot once-upon-a-time occupied by a cigarette lighter on the dashboard was now a wide open O next to the radio. Trying to decide between sprinting back into the store for a light and driving home for one, I caught a glimpse of myself in the rearview mirror. My unlit enemy sagged from my tight lips, and the scowl spread over my entire face like an angry Halloween mask. I looked myself in the eyes for a full minute before I pulled the cigarette from my mouth and crushed it in my hand. With frustrated resolve, I stalked to the trash can on the curb and deposited my purchase into it.

It wasn't until I floated into the third week on an orange-carbonated sea that I began to glimpse hope on the horizon beyond my nicotine fantasies. On the nineteenth day of my battle, I'd already had breakfast and headed for the office before I realized I hadn't yet given a single thought to a cigarette—or a can of orange soda, for that matter. I remember laughing right out loud at the discovery, and the guy next to me at the stoplight looked at me as if I'd escaped from the asylum. Which, in a way, I suppose I had. * SDB

Lone Wolf

*He is my loving God and my fortress, my stronghold and my deliverer,
my shield, in whom I take refuge, who subdues peoples under me.*

PSALM 144:2

I'm crazy about wolves.

My favorite sanctuary spans acres of tree-lined hills, where nearly fifty wolves, rescued from abuse and neglect, were brought to live with as much dignity as can be achieved in such a scenario.

Five packs live there, and each is led by a strong, capable alpha pair. They keep order and demand obedience even while at play. You'd think my first stop during visits would be the cubs, but although they're cuter than the Gerber baby, it's the lone wolves that lure me closest.

If you've ever owned a dog, you know that their faces can express joy, fear, and disappointment; I've seen the lone wolves express sadness as they pace the outskirts of pack activity. They understand what we humans can't: they will never be invited into the family circle.

They know, too, that meals will consist of what's left after the others' bellies are full. They're forced to dash in and steal biscuit crumbs, and the crumbs of human affection doled out by caretakers had better be stolen too… if they don't want to pay a painful price. Loners are not allowed to participate in the fun of rowdy roughhousing. They're forbidden from nestling for warmth on cold, dark nights and from cuddling close for comfort when thunder and lightning crash around them.

Even a powerful animal like the wolf can take only so much rejection, and before long, the loners skulk into the forest, starved for food and companionship. And as much as my heart aches for a pack's lone wolves, it's even harder to think of lone wolves of the wilderness, who will never know the kindness and care of human hands.

I think that sometimes we feel a little bit like the sanctuary's lone wolves. When we've suffered the death of a loved one, gone through a divorce, or experienced a job loss, we feel separate and apart from friends and family. Just as the wolves don't trust their own kind, we erroneously convince ourselves that no one can possibly understand what we're going through, and so we skulk off to a forest of our own making: work, alcohol or drugs, the Internet or television. We hide from our spouses, neglect our children, stop walking the dog. We no longer feel like doing good deeds, because we've lost heart.

The wolves don't know to ask God for help. *But we do!*

If only we'd remember that in times of our greatest need, we are cradled in His loving hands, and although we didn't do a thing to earn His tender, merciful care, it's there for the taking.

He has promised that we never need to live on the outskirts, alone and afraid, hungry for compassion and love. Isn't that a miracle? Isn't that a blessing. * *LL*

Do Not Pull!

We love because he first loved us.
1 JOHN 4:19

If you have ever talked to a mother about how she felt when her first child was born, you'll hear words like, "I never knew I could love anyone this much."

Generally speaking, love for our children is expansive and unconditional, even when others question our devotion. Once, when…ahem!…*someone's* three sons were all under five years of age, our new church decided to have its first-ever Christmas brunch before the service to celebrate our first holiday season as a "family" with fellowship and food.

What a beautiful picture of Christ's love, right?

Now, imagine, if you will, a five-year-old boy who sees a pretty red plate on the wall and can read the sign that says DO NOT PULL. His four-year-old brother also understands the meaning of *red*. Both brothers know instinctively that, if they pull this lever, they will be in big trouble.

However, *if they talk their darling little two-year-old brother into pulling it*, that wouldn't be so bad, would it? And here's the win-win: they'd get to see what would happen and not be responsible. What could go wrong?

Just as people sat down, brunch was interrupted by the piercing wail of the fire alarm, which did not stop until the fire department arrived twenty minutes later and charged their mother $150 to turn off the alarm. And by then everyone had evacuated the first, and incidentally *the only*, Christmas brunch.

Let me just say that the organizers of this brunch were not happy. My family was not feeling the unconditional love of Christ in those moments; instead, they were feeling the consequences of sinful actions. And trust me, those boys knew what they were doing was wrong, or they wouldn't have talked their little brother into doing it for them!

Times like this inspire me to think about how God must want to drop His head into His hands at my foibles. He must think, "I know she knows better!" And He probably shakes His head and wonders if I'm ever going to get it. Just like I know that my older son's great ability to lead others can have a dark side, God knows my own weaknesses. I like to believe He cheers for me when I do the right thing and pass it on to my own children.

Sometimes the ability to love is not easy, but I think that's why God shows us what it looks like. When we see the good and the bad in others—and sometimes in ourselves—we are seeing people as God sees them: in love. Not perfect, but worthy of love. * *KB*

The C Word

For I know the thoughts that I think toward you, says the LORD,
thoughts of peace and not of evil, to give you a future and a hope.
JEREMIAH 29:11 NKJV

There are a few words in the English language that just seem to take folks by surprise. People don't want to say the words, and they don't want to hear them. At the top of that vocabulary list is the most terrible one of all: *cancer.*

My mom used to whisper the word, as if saying it quietly would take away a bit of its punch.

"His wife passed away last year," she would say. And then, cupping her hands around her mouth, she would whisper, "Breast cancer."

There was one Sunday afternoon, years after my mom had died, that I found myself wishing she had taught this fine art of whispering to my doctor.

"I'm so sorry," she told me. "It's stage III ovarian cancer."

There was more, I think. Something about the best course of treatment and surgery to be scheduled right away, but I didn't hear most of it. Cradling the phone under my chin, I wondered, *If she'd whispered it, would it have been stage II instead?*

Over that one weekend, my life went from meetings, sales figures, and workshops to one small, dark tunnel in the shape of a *C.* My job and writing career were a thing of the past, replaced in an instant by the three surgeries that followed the diagnosis and then five weeks of daily radiation treatments, medications that made me sick, and headaches that could make a grown woman cry "Uncle."

I remember a particular day about four weeks into my treatments....I'd climbed up onto the table and nurses buzzed around me, lining up the radiation machine with the tattoos they'd placed on my pelvis a month earlier—and suddenly I was wiping tears from my face. I hadn't even realized I was crying! But as I wiped my cheek and sniffed back the next wave, it occurred to me that I was screaming. Not out loud, but from the inside. *Scrrreeeeeeaming!*

All those weeks of surgeries and treatment, and the reality of the situation had never really set in until that very moment. And just about the time I was an instant away from flying off that table and out the front door of the center, my heart fluttered and a Scripture came softly to mind:

"I know the thoughts that I think toward you, says the Lord, thoughts of peace and not of evil, to give you a future and a hope."

In that strange and surreal moment, in the dark room of my cancer treatment center, I realized that the medical professionals flitting around me had very little to do with my diagnosis. It was up to my God whether I would live or die, and for the first time in a very, very long time, I knew with clear certainty that I was going to live. * *SDB*

The Right Note

I will praise the name of God with a song, and will magnify him with thanksgiving.
PSALM 69:30 KJV

This morning when I woke, my sleep-deprived brain was serenading me with, "When I woke up this morning, you were on my mi–i–i–ind...." Which got me to thinking about all the other times I've opened my eyes and almost instantly started humming one tune or another. I've come to the conclusion that it's God's way of starting my day on the right note, literally. Even before I sit down at the kitchen table, with pen in hand to craft my latest to-do list, He has prepared my mind for the busy day ahead. Better still, He's prepared my heart, because, let's face it...with all that singing and humming, how can I help but leap into my chores with a happy spirit?

Like millions of other Christian women, demands on my time come from so many angles that I've often jokingly referred to my overcrowded calendar as the Diamond—because it has so many "facets." It doesn't matter if it's the vacuum cleaner, the dishwasher, or the laundry machine that's humming, because peripheral vision shows me a kitchen floor that needs to be washed, a dog to let out, a grocery list as-yet unshopped, and appointments to be made...or canceled. There are menus to plan and meals to prepare, bills to pay and a checkbook to balance. Cookies to bake for the church bazaar and my promise to visit Children's Oncology to paint cartoon characters on little bald patients.

Oh, but isn't it amazing how well the Lord knows me. Allowing me to start my days with song, even before my feet hit the floor, is such a gift that it brings tears to my eyes!

If your demanding schedule is growing heavy and burdensome, here's my advice to you:

As you whisper your bedtime prayers, ask the Father to wake you with a song. You'll find, as I do, that throughout the day, as you stop to catch your breath or wonder where you'll find that extra ounce of energy to check off yet another item from your too-long to-do list, the melody will echo in your head...and your heart won't be able to help but sing along.

And God doesn't care if you sing off-key! * *LL*

Daily Miracles

Is any one of you in trouble? He should pray. Is anyone happy?
Let him sing songs of praise.

JAMES 5:13

What's the deal about praying, anyway? Why is it important to God that we pray continually, as we're told in 1 Thessalonians 5:17?

I knew a college student who kept his dog so constantly with him that they developed an uncanny level of communication. The dog understood his master's every mood and intent. The student even brought the dog with him to his classes, telling the dog to wait outside the building for him. Sure enough, the dog would settle in for the duration and be waiting when class let out. There wasn't much the student could do that the dog didn't notice.

Not to equate us with dogs, but something similar happens when we pray. The communication goes two ways, and continual prayer refines our awareness of when God answers us. We don't pray into a void. If I'm in trouble, I should tell Jesus about it. If I'm happy, I should tell Jesus about that too. I should *sing* my prayers. I should understand that my thoughts are going directly to God, not just bouncing around within my own noggin. Because not only do we communicate our needs, happiness, and every thought to God when we pray, He communicates right back. It's the *answers* we sometimes fail to recognize. And sometimes the answers are miracles. When you think of it, the very idea that God communicates with us—*that's* a miracle. I'd like to experience that and appreciate it every day.

Recently I had a sudden expenditure that took me $5,000 outside of my monthly budget. I had the money available in savings, and I reluctantly planned to withdraw that amount. But I happened to receive several small payments for some writing work I had done over the past six months, and they all came in on the same day. The amount? $5,002. Two dollars extra! It actually took me awhile to recognize the miracle God had sent me that day, but when I did, it was like a reminder that He's aware of me, of my needs, of everything that happens in my life. As busy as He is, He notices me. He's involved.

It's not that God needs us to pray. We're the needy ones. Like that college student and his dog, if we stay constantly with Him, there won't be much He does that we won't notice. * *TP*

A Life of Victory

*For whatever is born of God is victorious over the world; and this is
the victory that conquers the world, even our faith.*

1 JOHN 5:4 AMP

I've witnessed a battle that was as hard-fought and heroic as any epic recorded in history. This battle will never be on the news, never celebrated by throngs in a parade. There are thousands of battles like it being won—and thousands lost—that may go unnoticed by the world. It is a battle of the heart.

My sister-in-law, René, found she was pregnant with her third child. She and my brother were thrilled.

Around that same time, one of her good friends shared the news that she, too, was expecting. They began to plan and dream about these new lives they would soon bring into the world. Sharing stories of fatigue and unusual cravings, it seemed a special blessing that they were able to experience this journey together.

Then one day René had a strange feeling that something wasn't right. She told herself it was okay, that this pregnancy was just different, but over the course of several days more things happened that fueled her inner sense of danger. At eight weeks, she was ready for her first doctor's appointment. "It will be good to hear the heartbeat," she told me, and I wholeheartedly agreed.

Alone at her first appointment, René waited expectantly, lying on her back as the doctor did a sonogram. She looked from the screen to his face and back again, watching for a sign.

After what seemed to be an eternity, the doctor spoke. "It looks like the baby stopped growing at five weeks," he said

gently. There was no heartbeat.

In *Wuthering Heights*, a character named Cathy Linton declares her love for her adopted brother, Heathcliff, in this very famous line: *"I am Heathcliff!"* The idea behind that line is that Cathy cannot separate herself from Heathcliff. His joys are her joys, and his sorrows are hers, as well. If he prospers, she prospers; and if he is destroyed, then she cannot survive. A biblical example of this would be David and Jonathan, whose souls were knit together.

Though my soul is *knit* with hers, I cannot claim to understand the depth or intensity of René's experience with miscarriage. As much as a fellow soldier can share in a comrade's wounds, I suffered with her. I searched the Scriptures for answers. I cried with her. I battled with her and for her in prayer. But the heart of a person is a place no other can truly go. The Bible says we can't even fully know our own hearts.

In the months to come, I saw Jesus defend René's heart, drive the enemy back, and begin to heal her. With each emotional conflict, God delivered her the victory, one battle at a time. I never saw her give in to bitterness or envy.

René hosted a shower in honor of her friend and her new baby boy. As I watched my sister-in-law move around the room, filling glasses and making people feel welcome with her warm smile and luminous eyes, I had to fight down a lump that rose in my throat. This is what victory looks like. * *GF*

Go for It...No One's Looking

*Now the serpent was more crafty than any of the wild animals the LORD God had made.
He said to the woman, "Did God really say, 'You must not eat from any tree in the garden'?"*

GENESIS 3:1

From the minute I wake up until I close my eyes at night, I find myself tempted by all kinds of things I shouldn't have. Some of them are blatantly wrong for me, while others seem innocent. A convincing argument can be made for almost everything I want that I shouldn't have, and there are a lot of things I probably shouldn't have that I want.

I put myself in the place of Eve when Satan came to her in the form of a serpent. I can just imagine what that crafty little bugger would say to entice me. "Go for it.... Who'll know if you have just one little taste? No one's looking," and "What's God gonna do? Punish you just for eating a little apple?"

Um...*yeah*. Satan was the first advertising exec in the world. He not only knew his market, but he was able to strip away objections before they were even raised. He took a truth and turned it into a question, creating doubt about the status quo for his target audience. Now, I'm not saying that advertising is evil, but the temptation to tell untruths is always there...just like it is with anything. It's one thing to get the word out there about a product, but it's another to present it falsely—which is exactly what Satan did. He created doubt in Eve's mind about God's authority.

Fortunately for all humanity, God had enough love for us to override the evil from Satan by sending His Son to make us right in His eyes. How amazing is that! After Satan wreaked havoc with his false advertising campaign, he slithered away and left Adam and Eve to get themselves out of the mess he'd created. And what a mess! No way would these two mortals have been able to turn things around for the world if God hadn't fixed things.

Before my feet hit the floor in the morning, I need to immerse myself in prayer—because temptation will be around every corner and in every situation I'll face during the day. And they won't all be "obviously evil" temptations; sometimes they'll seem harmless or like the right thing to do. It's not always easy to be discerning in a work environment or even on the commute to work when someone behind you is honking, gesturing obscenely, and getting all worked up because he left five minutes later than he should have. I just have to remember God's Word and His promises to get me through.
* DM

True Thirst

*O God, you are my God, earnestly I seek you; my soul thirsts for you, my body longs for you,
in a dry and weary land where there is no water.*

PSALM 63:1

Food and drink have no control over me whatsoever. Absolutely none. At least that's what I thought until they told me I had to "fast" for twelve hours before a medical test.

It's not as though I am a stranger to fasting. I have fasted many times for matters of prayer and drawing closer to the Lord but, admittedly, it has been awhile. Funny how the passing of time can change things.

What was it about knowing I couldn't have something that made me want it all the more? The minute they told me I couldn't have anything to eat, I was starving. No drink? These were medical people. Didn't they realize I could get dehydrated?

By the morning, my mouth was so dry that my lips stuck to my gums and refused to cover my teeth. Lovely mental picture, huh? Coffee called out my name with the lure of a half-price sale at Macy's. I resisted—but not without attitude.

The thing was, I could skip the food, the drink, all that, if I didn't know I had to. It was the knowing I had to do it that made me feel as though I'd been walking through a desert for days without food or drink. The air smelled of chocolate, and every billboard seemed to tease my senses and heighten my need for nourishment.

Which brings to mind my next question: Have I ever longed for Jesus in the same way? So hungry, so thirsty for Him that I can think of nothing else? Does He consume me to the point that my spiritual hunger and thirst will not be quenched until I spend time with Him?

I heard a story once where a man asked his friend how he could truly find God. The friend took the man to a nearby lake, and once they were shoulder-deep in the water, he said, "You're sure you truly want to find God?"

The man answered, "Yes."

So the friend dunked the man in the water and held his head down to the point where the man thought he would drown. When the friend pulled him back up, the man gasped, coughed, and sputtered, all the while desperately trying to pull air into his burning lungs.

Finally the friend said, "When you want to find God as much as you desired your breath, you will find Him."

I'm not sure where this story originated, but I heard it years ago and never forgot it. As much as I long to know God more, I've never longed for Him with that kind of desperation.

Have you? * *DH*

The Awesomest!

God is jealous.... The LORD is slow to anger and great in power....
The LORD has his way.... He rebukes the sea.... The LORD is good....

NAHUM 1:2–7 NKJV

I couldn't see the road ahead of me. The falling snow had covered it like a heavy drape. I couldn't tell where the road ended and the gravel shoulder began. I did, however, make out the ditch's location, since another vehicle had spun out and landed in it. The car's taillights flashed as its driver waited for a tow truck.

I clenched the steering wheel, and my shoulders tightened with tension. I prayed I wouldn't meet the same fate.

Illuminated by my headlights, white flakes zoomed in at me. I began to feel dizzy, like I'd gotten sucked into a snow globe and someone had just given it a good shake. I wondered if I'd make it home unharmed and with my minivan intact.

To quell my rising panic, I turned on the radio. I searched the FM band before finding the only Christian station whose signal was strong enough to reach me on this stormy night. An upbeat tune sung by Rich Mullins filled my vehicle. The words went something like: "When He rolls up His sleeves, He ain't just puttin' on the ritz.... There's thunder in His footsteps and lightning in His fists. Our God is an awesome God."

As I listened, I was reminded of what a Superhero Jesus Christ really is and how the Bible describes His awesomeness. God is jealous—He created us for fellowship with Him. He is slow to anger. He is of great power. He rebukes the sea (and blizzards too!). He has His way (Thy will be done). The Lord is good (Nahum 1:2–7).

Our God is an awesome God.

God is faithful and just to forgive... (1 John 1:9). God is love (1 John 4:8).

Our God is an awesome God.

My death grip on the steering wheel had loosened and my shoulders had relaxed. I wished I had started on this trek remembering that God is in control always. He would see me through this storm.

I thought of another Scripture verse: "God is our refuge and strength, a very present help in trouble" (Psalm 46:1 KJV).

Our God is an awesome God.

I came to an intersection and eased on the brake, slowing my van. I attempted a complete stop, but the road was too slippery and I slid right past the stoplight instead. The driver of a pickup truck, coming toward me on the right, miraculously saw me and swerved just in time.

Our God is an awesome God.

At long last, I left the country highway and turned onto my street. Moments later, I pulled into my driveway—safe from the storm.

Our God is most definitely an awesome God! * *AKB*

Sticks and Stones

Death and life are in the power of the tongue.
PROVERBS 18:21

Sticks and stones may break my bones, but names will never hurt me."

When backed up with solid belief, this old adage is true. However, the sting of certain names can stay with us for our entire lives if we let it. Every time an accusation is hurled at us and we allow ourselves to ponder the authenticity of the label, we're building up a solid agreement to it, like adding stones to a foundational wall.

I've heard it said that children take on the role within their family that they most easily fit into. In my case, I was raised with an older brother who was an academic genius. He knew from a very young age that he was going to be a scientist of some kind, and everything he did revolved around his academic pursuits. My grades could never compete, so the role of Brainiac was taken. Who was I going to be?

My brother and his friends started early with the references to my being the "slow sister" and the one who could never keep up. By the time I was in junior high, they'd nicknamed me "Flash," and much of my persona was wrapped up in being the wide-eyed, naive little sister of that brilliant science student. It became who I was. I even sometimes wore the black T-shirt they'd given me for Christmas that had a silver glitter thunderbolt across it reading FLASH! On the off chance that I knew the answer to a science question in class, I almost never let on. By the time I reached college, I'd learned how to master the persona I'd adopted over those years. But it was by no means an indication of who I really was.

I was fortunate enough to meet and fall in love with a man who recognized someone smarter hiding behind the thunderbolt, and he was having no part in continuing to build upon it. He was the first one to point out to me the importance of realizing that we can create either death or life by the words we speak, and he taught me that we are easily snared by the words of our mouth. When I would make a joke at my own expense, he would speak to it with encouragement, canceling it out with truth.

If I hadn't had this amazing man come into my life at such a young age, there's no telling who I would have turned out to be. Perhaps, like some of my friends over the years, I'd have taken on the role of The Diva, The Athlete, or The Rebel and never discovered who I really was at the very core: *The Creative Spirit.*

Writing is a lifeline to me in my adult life. Telling a story, turning a phrase, finding a way to say something that will inspire others...these are the life's blood of who I really am. I might never have found this road if I'd allowed those early seeds to blossom and continue to take root.

So when children tell me they can't do something, I always try to be the one to tell them that, yes, they can. If they can't figure something out, I remind them that there's always another way to look at it. If they insinuate that they are ignorant or afraid or inept, I counteract those words with truth, the way my first love did for me.

And every morning, I begin by reminding myself, "If life and death are in the power of the tongue, I choose to speak life over my body, soul, spirit, and surroundings." * *SDB*

The Strength of Sacrifice

But Hannah did not go, for she said to her husband, I will not go until the child is weaned, and then I will bring him, that he may appear before the Lord and remain there as long as he lives.

1 SAMUEL 1:22 AMP

One Sunday my husband pretended to be Samuel and told the story of how his mother, Hannah, prayed for a child and when God answered her prayer, she dedicated her son to Him at the temple.

That afternoon my son, Harper, looked me earnestly in the eyes. "Momma, would you ever take me to the temple and leave me there, like Hannah did?"

I had to answer him in honesty. "I don't know."

We explained to the kids that Hannah believed that was what God wanted her to do. Samuel was safe at the temple, and he was learning how to serve God. He became a great spiritual leader for Israel. That seemed to satisfy them.

In my mind I kept going back to Harper's question, though. Sometimes we read stories like Hannah's or Abraham's, or we've heard them all of our lives, and they feel sort of distant to us. Something that happened a long time ago to people who were different than us. What struck me about Harper's question was the freshness of perspective. He immediately related it to him and me, and that made it so much more real. No longer was it just that Bible story about Hannah and Samuel. It was, *What if God asked me to make a sacrifice like that with my own son?* I realized what a huge sacrifice it must have been for Hannah. She accepted God's will and obeyed Him even when it cost her everything. My gut reaction was that I could never be like her. I could never do that.

I have to admit that I have problems with a story like Hannah's. It's almost as difficult for me to grasp as the story of Abraham and Isaac. I believe God is sovereign and completely loving. But in the natural, neither one of these stories makes sense. Surely other honest people read them and think, *Huh? God asked these people to do what? Just like today when someone is suffering with a disease or we lose someone we love—it's hard to accept.*

Hannah—and Abraham, for that matter—waited so long for a child. She had prayed and longed for Samuel. She loved him like I love my children. It would never be possible for me to willingly give up one of them, to only see them once a year. No matter how many other children I had, I would not want to part with a single one. Yet that's what Hannah did. She turned Samuel over to Eli the priest to raise.

But sacrifices don't always have to be huge. My sacrifices lately come more in the form of preferences—something I want to do, somewhere I want to go, something I want to own. Or maybe it's just having my selfish way about things. What if God comes along and says to lay it down? To give it up? Could I do it?

Not in my own strength. In my own strength I'm not good at sacrificing anything.

But 1 Samuel 2:1–2 lets us in on a secret Hannah knew, "My heart exults in the LORD; my strength is exalted in my God…. I rejoice in my victory." It is not my strength, but the strength He gives me that matters. * *GF*

It's Not Where We Are, It's Where We're Going

"Because the poor are plundered and the needy groan, I will now arise,"
says the Lord. *"I will protect them from those who malign them."*

PSALM 12:5

Rosemary called me last summer to ask if I might be available for a chat. "I don't know what to do," she told me later that day over lattes. "I'm at the end of my rope. I really felt God's leading last year, urging me to get out of debt. The strides I made in the beginning were small, but at least I was progressing toward the goal. This year, it seems like every time I take a step forward, something happens and I'm shoved two steps back."

Isn't that the way? We get a clear picture of the destination, but it seems like all our good intentions are squashed as we make the journey.

It occurs to me, what if I was one of those enemy spirits assigned to trip up the efforts of God's people? I wouldn't just stand at the finish line, waiting for one big battle. As in all things in my life, I would make a game plan. I'd look at the big picture and fill in the gaps with strategies and obstacles to stop the progression. In my friend's case, for instance, I would start early and strike often: a medical bill here, a car problem there, until I finally squandered whatever funds I could get my hands on, setting her back from her ultimate goal.

The good news is that there seems to be a supernatural sort of grace that occurs in those times, and we find the ability to stand up, dust off the frustration and disappointment, and simply carry on.

Last week, Rosemary told me that she is in the home stretch toward her goal. She grinned as she told me, "I have no delusions about it. Someone may slash all four tires on my car next week, or the hot water heater could inexplicably explode. But you know what? I'm going to keep my eyes fixed on where I'm going, not on where I am. When I need Him, that's when God will rise up and do something extraordinary."

I'm encouraged by my friend's ongoing journey, and I find myself remembering her struggles as I wage my own battles toward goals that often seem unreachable. I can hardly wait to rejoice with her when she reaches that destination. Will it be this year that Rosemary declares her victory? Maybe not. But I'm inclined to believe that she'll reach her goal the same way the rest of us will: one step forward and two steps back this week, three steps forward the next. * SDB

I Just Can't Cut It Alone, Lord

Create in me a pure heart, O God, and renew a steadfast spirit within me.

PSALM 51:10

Today's verse brings to mind a memory from grade school that is as vivid as if it happened yesterday, which is very weird, considering how insignificant it is. The teacher asked two other girls and me to cut out shapes from construction paper for an upcoming class event. I don't remember the event or even the shape we were creating, but it involved cutting straight lines.

It didn't take more than an effort or two for me to realize that my straight lines were hurting in a big way compared to those of my cohorts. And then the teacher helpfully pointed it out. "Try to be more careful on the rest of them and get them straighter," she said.

Honestly, I tried. I'm sure the tip of my tongue protruded from my pursed lips and my brows furrowed in concentration while I cut my next shape. But it turns out I was straight-line challenged.

And like King David, the author of Psalm 51, I remain straight-line challenged to this day. David wrote this psalm after the prophet Nathan convicted him of his involvement with Bathsheba and his nasty little front-lines setup to get rid of her cuckolded husband. I don't struggle with adultery or murder, but I have yet to go to bed at night knowing I've made it through the day without going outside the lines of whom God created me to be.

Yes, I know that, as a follower of Christ, I'm a new creation in the eyes of God. Thanks to Christ's standing in for me and paying the price for my sins, God accepts me as clean and blameless—all ready for stepping into heaven at a moment's notice.

But what about today, here on earth, from the moment I spaz awake at the alarm clock to the moment I doze off in bed, praying and occasionally apologizing to the Lord for however I botched up the whole "representing Christ" thing that day? God may consider my eternal heart clean, but today? How can my heart be clean if I'm rolling around in envy, anger, impatience, gossip, selfishness, and unwholesome thoughts and words? I may be saved, but I never make it through the day without sinning. I'm not losing my salvation with my daily behavior, but neither am I winning souls to Christ or even living life as fully as He would love for me to live it.

Could get mighty depressing if not for verses like today's. If David did what he did and then stopped to consider how far outside the lines he had strayed and fell humbly to his spiritual knees, pleading, "Create in me a pure heart, O God, and renew a steadfast spirit within me," I suppose that option remains open to me too. Even if I think I've been Miss Perfect Christian today, this prayer should make the cut. * *TP*

Be Prepared

And He said to me, "My grace is sufficient for you, for My strength is made perfect in weakness." Therefore most gladly I will rather boast in my infirmities, that the power of Christ may rest upon me.

2 CORINTHIANS 12:9 NKJV

When I first got married, my husband resisted wearing seat belts for short jaunts—like to the store or the golf course. He reserved the car restraint for longer trips, with the notion that his risks were greater when he spent more time in the car. It took me awhile to convince him, but armed with research on how much more likely people were to get into accidents close to home than on long trips, he started clicking his seat belt every time he got in the car.

I think many of us live with the notion that precautions should only be taken under certain conditions—like saving seat belts for long trips or carrying an umbrella only when it's already pouring outside. When we start the day with sunny skies, we don't think about the importance of protection. However, when we walk out of our office at the end of a long day and it's pouring buckets, that umbrella sure would come in handy.

When life is going according to our plan, why do we need protection? I can't make many guarantees, but one thing I can promise is that eventually something will happen and you won't feel all smug about how nice and perfect things are. One of these days, you'll be glad you thought to click your seat belt or toss your umbrella into your bag before leaving the house.

This reminds me of how I used to live my Christian life. When things were going well, it was easy to leave Jesus on the back burner. I've even heard people say that they didn't "need" Him because they had a good life. The problem is, things happen. Imperfect people drive imperfect cars, and even if we don't get into an accident, seat belts can protect us when we have to slam on the brakes. If we have that umbrella in the car at all times, we're always protected. If we're armed with the gospel during the good times and the bad, we have the greatest protection of all. * DM

Forever…That's a Mighty Long Time

For he is the living God and he endures forever;
his kingdom will not be destroyed, his dominion will never end.

DANIEL 6:26

Time is a hard concept for me. The image of forever? Almost impossible to fathom. My day is cut into tiny chunks. Work has to be scheduled into time slots between dropping off kids for school, soccer, and playdates; dinner; laundry; homework; doctors' appointments; and the rest. Work is actually a luxury—and it leaves me thinking, how did I get here?

Life was meant to be savored, enjoyed, but the reality of day to day gets in the way of that. It's easy to think about God in terms of "He'll be there later. I'll get to Him." But the Bible tells us to seek first His kingdom and all shall be added. I've found that to be true—that if I give God the first part of my day, He will honor the rest by making me more productive and better able to function with all that's on my schedule that day.

But forever… What could I do with forever?

Sometimes I think the only thing I want to do with forever is sit down! With three boys, that kind of forever just doesn't happen. It's then that I need to remember God's version of forever—eternity…that the small things in life matter, they make up the whole. Sure, furniture comes and goes, socks are lucky if they make it through the first washing, and don't even get me started on the groceries that barely seem to make it into the house, but if we can take that time to focus on God's version of forever, the daily tasks are easier.

God only asks for a small portion of our day. In return, He gives us forever. Isn't that huge? It's like us asking our kids to do their homework and pick up their socks. In return, we'll give them three square meals a day, an education, a roof over their heads, and clean underpants. It's not a bad deal. So they should take it, right? Well, I should too, but all too often, I'm guilty of getting busy first and crying out to God for relief next.

When I think of eternity, I love to picture a ring, because it is without end. God loves us without end, but wouldn't it be nice if we engraved something on that ring this morning? What if we told God how much He means to us or how much He gives us while He expects so little in return?
* KB

The Definition of a Really Bad Day

A cheerful heart is good medicine, but a crushed spirit dries up the bones.
PROVERBS 17:22

My mom and I had a bad period that lasted from the time I was a teenager until my late thirties. We found ways to butt heads in very creative ways, even when thousands of miles stretched between us. Then she became ill, and I made a decision that was either going to bridge the considerable gap between us…or it was going to explode in my face. I moved from Los Angeles to Tampa to provide care for her.

My mom and I bonded in awesome ways during those few years after I moved to Florida. Oh, make no mistake, we still butted heads. However, I had the opportunity to get to know her, woman to woman, and I really fell in love with her. We forged out a second relationship where she was *Mom* again, and I was the child who adored her.

When she passed away, the grief was just about the most profound mountain I've ever faced. Sitting in the limousine behind the hearse carrying her casket, my emotions took the shape of a tsunami threatening in the distance. I had no idea how I would cope with walking into that church and saying good-bye to this woman who had unexpectedly (and miraculously) become my closest friend.

Please, Lord. Help me. I can't take it.

A car cut in front of the hearse, and the hearse's driver slammed on the brakes, as did the driver of the limousine carrying my brother and me. In that moment of recovery afterward, something phenomenal happened. I started to giggle. Softly at first…and then I tumbled into full-fledged laughter as I remembered a particular moment with my mom.

Munching popcorn and watching one of those really awful movies on television on a Saturday afternoon, the film plot involved a hearse with squealing brakes followed by the back doors opening and the casket sliding out and thumping to a stop in the middle of the road. My mom turned to me and said, "Now *that* is the definition of a really bad day."

Everyone in the funeral limo looked at me as if I'd lost my mind. I tried to explain myself, but the laughter rolling out of me challenged the effort.

By the time I reached the church, my dried and crushed spirit had been revived, soothed over with the balm of a cheerful heart. An unlikely healing had been brought about by a single memory and ten solid minutes of subsequent, almost uncontrollable, laughter.

* SDB

What the Rain Left

Let my teaching fall like rain and my words descend like dew,
like showers on new grass, like abundant rain on tender plants.

DEUTERONOMY 32:2

When the warm rain cleared that summer afternoon, the grandkids and I dodged (for the most part) the puddles in the driveway as we crossed to the damp but freshly washed grass. The yard had corners yet unexplored, adventures to discover. At four and three, the boys were harder to herd than balls of mercury. My grammie eyes darted to the dangers—barbed-wire fence, pond, traffic on the county road, cockleburs and thistles at the edge of the woods.... But their inquisitive gazes, following their big sister, landed on a minuscule movement among the decorative rocks near the house.

Toady frogs.

The kids named them that. Frog-shaped but toad-colored and smaller than the average peanut M&M, the toady frogs held their convention in our yard that day. There were hundreds of them. I had a brief thought about Pharaoh and plagues, but these little gems of creation caused hours of pleasure rather than distress.

Fast but kid-friendly, the toady frogs tolerated capture and investigation by sweaty kid palms. Perfectly camouflaged, they hid among the stones in the landscaping. Squatting like pro golfers lining up a putt, we stared at the rocks until we saw something hop. One-inch toady frogs don't hop far, but the grandchildren's rapt attention registered the motion and sent them scurrying after with cupped hands.

The kids knew capture was temporary. As their for-the-moment science teacher, I explained about how delicately they need to be handled, what toads need to survive, about keeping the noise level low and respecting how God made them and how He wants us to be careful of all the amazing creatures He made. You can't learn about toady frogs without seeing them up close. But they belong in their own environment, not in a glove.

A glove. That's right. While I scoured the outdoor toys and garden shed for a suitable temporary toad haven, one of the boys found his own creative answer. A translucent garden glove. He found he could fit four or five of the miniature amphibians in each finger. Like dorm rooms centered around a palm-sized main lounge.

There's something about a four-year-old carefully tending a toad-filled glove then gently setting each toad free that makes me smile.

It must have been the warm, tender rain that brought the toads in such numbers. I pray my impromptu science lesson fell like gentle rain too. That's often how the Lord sends His lessons to my heart.

Like a hand on my shoulder saying, "Hold that more tenderly. You can't keep that forever, you know; we'll have to set it free. Here, let Me show you something amazing about what you've just found."

Sometimes the Lord has to yank me back from the edge of danger. But I'm grateful He also kneels beside me to show me His wonders and whisper His lessons with the tenderness of dew on new grass. * CR

The Rock-Star Life

*That you also aspire to lead a quiet life, to mind your own business,
and to work with your own hands, as we commanded you.*

1 THESSALONIANS 4:11 NKJV

As I sit here on a Saturday night, typing this devotion, I'm thinking about how unexciting my life is. Paris Hilton and Jessica Simpson would be bored to tears, but I'm actually very content. While they're bar-crawling and party-hopping, I'm sitting at the kitchen table in my daughter and son-in-law's house, praying every few minutes for my little granddaughter's jaundice to go away. Someone more exciting from the world's view might feel sorry for me, but the simple life suits me just fine.

Don't get me wrong. There are some aspects to the rock-star life that appeal to me. I enjoy travel, interesting people, designer handbags, and great food. An occasional party is fun, too, but I need to be home by midnight or my brain turns to pie filling.

Mick Jagger sings, "You can't always get what you want." That's a good thing in my book. If I had everything I wanted, I also wouldn't ever be *satisfied*, another theme of one of his songs. Hmm. Perhaps Mick knows more than he lets on.

A rock star's life appears exciting on the surface. However, if you think about it, they have their own routines and mundane tasks. While touring, they spend most of their days on tour buses. Then they get on stages that basically all look alike, playing to crowds who shout and scream the same things. When they're home, they fall back into another routine. Even if it's partying all night, it's still a routine. The one thing that sets a rock star apart from the real world is that they depend on other people's attention.

Obviously, I don't live a rock-star life. My days are spent doing peaceful, mundane tasks that I've learned to appreciate over the years. First thing each morning, I sip my coffee and reflect on God's Word before I turn my thoughts to what I need to do that day. Once in a while, I shake things up and have lunch with friends or speak to groups who think I have something interesting to say about writing. But for the most part, my life wouldn't suit a rock star who needs constant adulation and thrills. I feel that I'm just as blessed as they are, but in a much deeper, more real way. What I have can't be dashed by fans who have turned their attention elsewhere. My faith in Christ gives me more of a rush than standing before thousands of screaming fans. * *DM*

Victory in Jesus

*For the Lord takes pleasure in His people; He will beautify the humble
with salvation and adorn the wretched with victory.*

PSALM 149:4 AMP

When I was in college, I led a little band of believers from the Honors program in a nursing home ministry. It sounds rather lofty, as I read the words of that last sentence, but the truth is that it wasn't. What it amounted to was a group of kids going into one of the nearby nursing homes about once a week and talking to the people who lived there. We'd also try to coax them into the social hall, where we gathered around the piano for a few hymns.

My favorite person to visit during these times was a lady named Elizabeth Byrd. I knocked on the door of her room one day at random, and she called for me to come in. She was sitting in her wheelchair, ankles crossed, hands folded in her lap. Her hair was neatly combed back, clothes tidy, and her skin the color of rich, dark caramel. She wore a dab of wine-colored lipstick, and her teeth gleamed like new piano keys in a wide smile as I sat down beside her.

The group who regularly assembled for music had their favorite hymns. Elizabeth liked "Amazing Grace," and a woman named Lily always asked for "The Old Rugged Cross." Another popular one was "In the Garden." They'd clap their hands and smile, some belting out the words, while others merely hummed along with the piano.

A man named Perry made a great impression on me during singing times. He was tall with silver hair and a high forehead.

Perry was in a wheelchair and had to be strapped in it with a wide black belt or he would slide out onto the floor.

His speech was unclear. He carried pictures with him that were torn out of Sunday school quarterlies. He'd hold them up during the hymns.

Perry's favorite song was "Victory in Jesus." The first time he requested it, I have to admit, it seemed ironic. The question crept into my mind: *What could possibly be victorious about Perry's state?* But I played and sang it anyway. To please Perry, we always sang all of the verses week after week.

We would always save that song for the last. It became kind of a game with Perry—he would wait with anticipation to see if we would remember, his mouth fixed in a crooked smile. He'd get all excited when I played the introduction, shaking his head to an unheard rhythm. Half the time we couldn't understand what he was saying, but he sang at the top of his voice.

The last time I saw Perry, he was singing that song. Instead of the pictures, he held up both of his arms in a big *V* and formed little *V*s with the fingers of both of his hands. Triple *V* for victory. The next week he was gone.

Now, whenever I play that song, I think of Perry. I think of a man in a ruined body whose spirit still remembered how to soar.

Victory is not in ourselves, whether we're in a pitiful state or a prideful one. Victory is in Jesus. I bet Perry sings that song even louder in heaven. * *GF*

Always Secure

We all have different gifts, each of which came because of the grace God gave us.

ROMANS 12:6 NCV

Whether or not you hold higher degrees of education or years of experience, you will eventually find yourself in the company of someone by whom you feel dwarfed in terms of intellect or ability. Some people respond to this feeling by over-reaching, attempting to cover for their insufficiency with lofty words or arrogance, though the cover-up never works. Others seem to flounder, losing their nerve completely, failing to operate even at their normal capacity. And still others seethe with envy and resentment, wasting precious energy on unproductive emotions.

It's likely that the problem is a simple misunderstanding. We may fail to realize that God grants to each of us certain strengths that resonate with His eternal purposes for our lives. Rather than feeling inferior or insecure, we should rejoice in the gifts of others, realizing that in truth we are simply different—what we lack in one area, we make up for in another. It isn't about one person being better, but rather God's deep desire that we realize our need for each other.

Don't hesitate to admire someone for the gifts God has given. Doing so does not diminish you in any way. As you spend time alone with God, your own special gifts and abilities will shine forth. * *SGES*

Ewww!

To console those who mourn in Zion, to give them beauty for ashes, the oil of joy for mourning, the garment of praise for the spirit of heaviness; that they may be called trees of righteousness, the planting of the Lord, that He may be glorified.

ISAIAH 61:3 NKJV

I am not much of a cook. I never have been. Bake some cookies or mix up a cake? I'm your girl. But the fine art of planning and executing a healthy, satisfying meal has traditionally been left to better women (and men, in some cases) than me.

For example, whenever I was hungry for yams, I went to the store, bought a can of them, and heated them up on the stove. So imagine my surprise when a friend invited me to dinner at her house and I saw her produce this huge, ugly, kidney-shaped thing out of the crisper in her refrigerator.

"What is that?" I asked her, and she stared at me as if my hair had caught on fire.

"What do you mean?" she asked.

"That. What is it?"

"It's a yam."

Interesting how something so ugly and misshapen could end up to be the beautiful dish she set out on the table an hour later. Peeled, cubed, and baked until soft with butter and brown sugar, that ugly yam had become delicious.

It occurred to me recently—I'm like that yam. Misshapen, to be sure; I'm no Jennifer Aniston! But what I have in common with that yam is *potential*.

On the occasions that I've suffered a devastating loss, even though at times I couldn't see it, there was recovery ahead. I would go on to live again, to smile, even to laugh. When I didn't think I had a song left in my heart, somehow I was able to hear the soft hum in the distance, the promise of music on my horizon.

The more often we experience His willingness to turn our mourning into joy and our ashes into something beautiful, the easier it is the next time to believe that we will survive. Like a muscle we've begun to exercise, our faith in what God will do in our lives is strengthened with its use.

I haven't bought a can of yams in years now. I love buying an ugly old yam and seeing if I can turn its "ashes" to something beautiful. Preferably with brown sugar! * *SDB*

Nocturnal Freak-Out

So do not fear, for I am with you; do not be dismayed, for I am your God.
I will strengthen you and help you; I will uphold you with my righteous right hand.

ISAIAH 41:10

The only full-night's sleep I've had recently was when I was under anesthesia for an appendectomy. Apparently, that's what a middle-aged woman has to do to get a proper rest—I say this because I've talked with every woman I know about female sleep issues.

As a child, I enjoyed the slumber of the innocent, the clueless, the pampered. When I got married and had children of my own, that fell apart. Newborns needed feeding, toddlers needed dry sheets, and teens needed to remember curfews so Mom could relax once her offspring were safe at home.

After my teenagers became responsible adults, I graduated to a new phase in life. I started to experience a little thing I like to call "nocturnal freak-out." I know it's all tied to the lovely changes a woman's body goes through as she ages, but that knowledge doesn't help at three o'clock in the morning. I don't need to have a crisis in my life. I simply awaken to answer nature's call.

And then, regardless of how hard I try to remain groggy, it's as if someone pulled the ignition cord on my brain's lawn mower. My neurons become heat-seeking missiles, determined to find a target to stress about. Within seconds of awakening, I latch onto a number of issues that absolutely must be solved before I can sleep again. Will the sale of my daughter's house go through? Will my son get his term paper turned in on time? Was that little noise my microwave made something I need to address? Did I gain weight from that decadent chocolate cake last night? Did I forget to compliment last night's hostess about her awesome chocolate cake? Will I meet my book deadline? How is my heroine going to solve the problem I threw at her yesterday? Why is my hair falling out? Why didn't I work out yesterday?

You get the picture.

I don't claim to have found a miracle cure for this kind of freak-out, whether it happens in the middle of the night or smack in the middle of the day. But recently the Lord did see fit to bless me with today's verse, and I'm telling you, its effects are immediate. I just have to remember its promise.

I haven't read commentaries on this verse. I haven't studied it in any devotional. But it has become my refuge in times of worry. It has settled in my mind to combat my nocturnal freak-outs. I like to think that God was referring to Jesus when He mentioned His "righteous right hand." God will uphold me through His righteous Right Hand. My Savior. Jesus.

No matter what worries whir in my mind in the middle of the night or in the bustle of the day, with that kind of promise, I know it's all going to work out. * *TP*

You Are What You Say (and Do)

And as ye would that men should do to you, do ye also to them likewise.

LUKE 6:31 KJV

You've heard it said that reputation is what others think you are, but character is who you are.

Two of my favorite quotes come to mind when mulling over that one.

The first is the one my grandfather quoted when one of us grabbed a cookie before dinner, crossed the street without looking both ways, or snooped in his attic without permission...and stretched the truth when he caught us red-handed at any of those things:

"Your thoughts," he'd say, pointing at each of us in turn, "become words. Words become actions. Actions become character. And character is everything."

I don't imagine any of his little cookie thieves knew what in the world he was talking about...until we grew older and spent some serious time in the real world. Then the hazy meaning of the adage became clearer, and we began to understand that it's synonymous with my other favorite, the Golden Rule.

"Do unto others as you'd have them do unto you" has long been the center point for morality, ethics, religion, and politics. It's the worldwide litmus test for fairness and decency. And Matthew and Luke weren't the only Bible scholars who believed in the concept. Quite the contrary!

Mark, John, James, Paul, and Jonah cited it, and similar passages can be found in Proverbs, Leviticus, Deuteronomy, and others, as well.

More than twenty world religions have adopted some version of its intent and meaning as doctrine. Confucius touted it as a moral truth, and in 1963, President Kennedy reminded citizens of its intent in an anti-segregation speech. "The heart of the question," he said, "is whether we are going to treat our fellow Americans the way we want to be treated." To apply it, we must first try to identify with our brothers and sisters and, as my American Indian ancestors would have said, be willing to walk a mile in their moccasins.

I try to remember these famous sage-isms when a driver cuts me off in traffic, people at the grocery store dump whole cartloads of merchandise on the conveyor belt in the Fifteen Items or Less line, or someone says something to hurt my feelings. Instead of an in-kind knee-jerk reaction, I recite Luke 6:31 and Grandpa's maxim, too.

Because I hope that by living by the Golden Rule, my reputation as a woman of Christian character will precede me...and follow me...everywhere. * *LL*

Words: Friend or Foe?

You are the most excellent of men and your lips have been anointed
with grace, since God has blessed you forever.

PSALM 45:2

I've always loved words. Reading them, speaking them, hearing them…I just love the language. A creative turn of phrase can stop me in my proverbial tracks, and I consistently strive to string words together in unexpected ways for the greatest impact. Since words are so important to me, you may ask yourself how in the world I recently found myself drowning in an attempt to take a few of them back for tailoring!

A friend who knows that I used to collect vintage jewelry often sends me a box of pieces she's picked up at flea markets or consignment shops. Some of them knock me out, others not so much—the latter of which, I usually put aside to give away. My best girlfriend and I had planned to meet at a conference I was set to attend in Indianapolis, and I wanted something very special for her birthday that same week. When I couldn't find anything just right after a dedicated search, I decided to have a look at my stash of vintage pieces. There was a stunning butterfly necklace in a clean white box that just jumped right out at me. I immediately thought of Marian, and I slipped it into my suitcase on my way to see her.

With very pretty and heartfelt words, I told my friend what she meant to me and how exceptional and special she is, closing with, "I saw this and immediately thought of you!" When she opened the box and saw the necklace, her flawless face dropped like a stone in a clear, still lake. "I'll bet," she replied.

It turned out that the butterfly necklace reminded me of Marian for a very good reason. It hadn't come in a box with a dozen other pieces. In fact, it had been one of several other gifts Marian had given me for my own birthday just a few months prior. Apparently it had been a very snug fit around my throat, and I'd placed it with the other pieces to give away. When the memory finally came back to me, my apologies seemed hollow. And I think I was more disappointed than Marian.

We didn't speak of the necklace again during our trip, but amid a later phone conversation I attempted to tell her how sorry I was. The more I tried to explain it, the worse it sounded, even to me.

However, here's the best thing about friends you've known forever: they tend to give you grace. Even though I'd obviously disappointed her, she extended the grace of understanding. In fact, when she flew in to celebrate my birthday this year and gave me several gifts, I told her, "Hey, I have something for you too. It's this beautiful butterfly necklace." And the two of us were—thank the Lord!—able to have a good laugh over it. * *SDB*

Necklace of Contrasts

Let the one who is wise heed these things and ponder the loving deeds of the LORD.
PSALM 107:43

Something's wrong if my jewelry can move seamlessly from my bedroom to the grandkids' dress-up box. I admit, most of my jewelry comes from clearance racks. The good news is that none of it has to be insured and our house isn't a target for high-end jewel thieves. Other than a couple of pieces I bought at a local art fair, there's little "real" gold, "real" silver, or "real" whatever that milky-purple stone is.

I splurged, though, on a beautiful jade-green necklace with a story behind it. The artist takes broken pieces of pottery and china and retools them.

If I ever become a jewelry designer—right after I fly solo over the North Pole, which will be right after I swim the English Channel, which will be right after I dust my baseboards, become a better swimmer, and learn how to fly—I'm going to design a necklace I saw once in a dream.

Black as onyx but rough and unpolished, one stone is coal, followed by a light-catching, expertly cut round diamond. Then another lump of coal, another diamond, coal, diamond, coal, diamond. Coal on its own would leave dusty smudges on anyone wearing the necklace, so they're dipped in…something. Polyurethane?

Coal, diamond, coal, diamond.

The classic black-and-clear alternating pattern would go with anything. It *does* go with anything. It's the pattern of consequences (rough coal) and grace (light reflected in all directions). A gem of grace for every dark consequence.

That's the life we're offered. The rough, sharp-edged, smudging chunks of coal that represent the consequences of our choices are threaded on the sterling chain of life with matching graces.

Lord, I have regrets from childhood.

"I know. I have a grace for that."

I'm still conscious of how that decision in college left me with gaps in my education.

"I have a grace for that."

I wasn't always patient with my kids.

"Grace for that."

Or my husband.

"And that."

Despite my good intentions, I made a couple of bad choices about time usage yesterday.

"Grace."

And I forgot sunscreen more than I remembered it.

"Another gem of grace."

And a consequence?

"Both."

Coal. Diamond. Coal. Diamond.

"Exactly."

There's a grace to match my every need.

"In a way."

A way?

"Do the math."

As I take another look at the imaginary but very much real necklace of consequences, I notice a distinct imbalance. The array of stones both begins and ends with grace. Grace will always outnumber consequences. His grace is more than sufficient. * CR

To Do or Not to Do Is a Pretty Stupid Question

A man's heart deviseth his way: but the LORD directeth his steps.

PROVERBS 16:9 KJV

As I sat scribbling my to-do list this morning, I was reminded of an ancient adage that goes something like, "Man plans while God laughs." It's times like these when I sense God whispering, "Loree, what is your hurry?"

Since I write (mostly) fiction for a living, it won't surprise you that on days like those, I imagine this conversation between God and me:

"What will happen if you don't scrub the kitchen floor or make the beds? Who would notice if the carpets aren't vacuumed or the end tables don't sparkle? Would anyone care if a few weeds sprout among the roses or fallen leaves collect on the welcome mat? And who'd point out that your ironing basket was full...or empty?"

"Well, for starters, my mother-in-law, that's who! And then there's my sister, and—"

"But I made your days to last twenty-four hours and not a moment more. How do you want to spend those hours? Ticking items off that to-do list of yours? Or setting aside time and energy to guarantee that you'll listen, really listen, to the cares of your hard-working husband at the end of the day?"

And my sweet daughters and grandkids, too, I thought. "But...but what will people think if they drop by and find dust bunnies on the hardwood or dishes in the sink?"

"They'll think you value the people who share your life more than those who might judge you 'less than perfect' if a few chores go undone."

(Now, really, how's a hard-workin' gal like me—who clocks sixty hours a week of housework, yard work, and *work*-work—supposed to react to that?)

And because of *course* He can hear my thoughts, He said, "By admitting that while hard work is a good thing, it can be addictive...."

"Hmm...is that why You inspired me to choose 'Good enough never is' and 'Do or do not; there *is* no try' as my life mottos?"

"Loree, my hardheaded daughter, put down your pen and pick up my Word. Five minutes there will change your mind and your thoughts—"

"—and ensure I'll smile, even if my mother-in-law shows up unexpectedly!" * *LL*

Even on Bad Hair Days

Delight yourself in the LORD.
PSALM 37:4 NASB

Are you old enough to remember when Marlo Thomas's character on *That Girl* came back for a new fall season with no bangs? I don't know about you, but I was appalled!

I always identified with Ann Marie. She was the first television character that I wanted to be. During the initial season of *That Girl*, I begged my mom for bangs just like hers, but Mom wouldn't budge. So when I felt I was old enough to make hair decisions on my own, around fourteen, I cut them myself with a teeny pair of manicure scissors. Mom had no choice but to pretty them up, and a banged Sandie was born! I've worn them ever since, and they're an odd little part of who I am, even now.

Recently I had a particularly stellar week. I got the news that a devotional I was writing was a done deal, I had several wins on the day job, and I completed a manuscript days before it was due. In celebration, I decided to pamper myself a little. I made an appointment to get my hair cut and colored and have a relaxing facial, and I ordered Chinese takeout for dinner. Before the delivery arrived, I gave the Lord an enthusiastic shout-out, expressing my joy and gratitude for everything He'd done in my life recently.

But the Chinese food that followed sent me tumbling into a deep sleep. My dreams, I'm sorry to report, were quite tragic and filled with hair angst.

Despite the fact that just a year earlier I'd frightened my hairstylist with my reaction to her overzealous "trim" of my bangs, could the poor thing have actually had the misfortune to repeat her mistake? I sat there with my jaw in my lap, staring at my reflection in the mirror. I hadn't seen bangs that short since Julia Roberts played Tinkerbell. It was horrifying. Before I could add lyrics to the symphony of my emotions, my nervous stylist, in a desperate attempt to gloss over the damage, asked, "So, umm, what's the name of your new book?"

The question the stylist asked me just as my eyes popped open hadn't been answered. I never had the chance to tell her: *Delight Yourself in the Lord…Even on Bad Hair Days.*

But just in case the Lord was trying to tell me something through that dream, I canceled my hair appointment and rebooked with a friend's stylist, knowing full well that I would have to find a way to be "delighted" even if I walked away looking like a friend of Peter Pan. * *SDB*

Obviously!

*May these words of my mouth and this meditation of my heart be pleasing
in your sight, LORD, my Rock and my Redeemer.*

PSALM 19:14

Some things are just obvious. Like sunshine. I've seen sunshine often enough to know it's out there, even on a cloudy day. Believe me, I have the age spots to prove it.

And the stars are obvious too. I don't often consider the stars during the day, but they're in the sky, regardless of the fact that I can't see them.

The physical heavens are all part of God's majestic creation, and everyone in the world is witness to them. In Psalm 19, David says it doesn't matter where you plant your feet or what language you speak; you see these obvious wonders. They're easy to spot and identify.

He says something similar about God's laws. We may not always be sure about God's will for our future, but because God's laws are spelled out in the Bible, His will with regard to our behavior is obvious. "The law of the Lord is perfect," David says. "More precious than gold" and "sweeter than honey." Yep, this psalm includes those famous words too.

Granted, some Old Testament laws are confusing. In 2005, A. J. Jacobs, senior editor of *Esquire* magazine, attempted to follow as many of the Old Testament laws as he could for one year. Some he simply found hard to understand—the ban against mixing particular fibers when making cloth; the ban on shaving one's beard; the ban on certain moves by a wife fighting on behalf of her husband.

Imagine—they had Jerry Springer moments back then!

Jacobs understood other laws but found them hard to obey consistently—as most of us do. No gossiping, cursing, lying, or working on Sunday (or whatever day one honors as the Sabbath).

Confusing laws aside, God's will about most of our moral dilemmas is clear, thanks to the Ten Commandments. I needn't look far to know that He wants to be my only god. He doesn't want me to murder or commit adultery. He wants me to honor Mom and Dad. Like the sun and the stars, His laws exist whether I acknowledge them or not.

So. God's creation? Obvious!

God's laws? Obvious!

My faults? Uhh. David says those can get a little fuzzy, and I have to agree. Sometimes I fool even myself about what's going on in my heart. In Psalm 19, David asks God to forgive his "hidden faults," and he didn't mean that those faults were hidden from *God*. I have the ability to ignore my own selfish motives, my jealous innermost thoughts, and my true angry feelings. Like David, I need to continually ask for God's grace and guidance—to say, "May these words of my mouth and this meditation of my heart be pleasing in your sight." * *TP*

A Life of Hope

Hope deferred makes the heart sick; but when dreams come true at last, there is life and joy.

PROVERBS 13:12 TLB

Jane grew up in a Christian home and received the Lord at a young age. In her twenties she met Ted, and they were married. Ted was a Christian, too, but neither one of them was very committed. They went to church, but Jane says that apart from church they had a pretty wild lifestyle.

One of Jane's biggest dreams was to become a mother.

She always wanted children and so did Ted, and they were devastated when it didn't happen after a few years of marriage. They pursued fertility treatment, spending years and countless dollars on testing, fertility drugs, surgery, and finally in-vitro fertilization. Nothing worked.

After a few visits to a new clinic, her name was put on a donor list to receive an egg from a younger woman that would be combined with Ted's sperm and implanted in Jane's womb.

Jane says she drove home from her last visit feeling soul-exhausted. Instead of being hopeful that the donor would be the answer, she was discouraged. "I just felt I had come to the end of the road."

In her living room that day, Jane sat down and pored over all their options—all the things she and Ted had tried that had ended in failure and the few choices they had left. It seemed there was no hope, and she felt her dream slipping away. It was in those moments that Jane heard an inaudible voice. Like sunlight through a window came these words into her heart: *Seek ye first the kingdom of God…and all these things shall be added unto you.*

Jane had been doing things her own way, searching everywhere for the solution except the Source. "God wanted to be my Provider. He wanted me to go to Him for what I needed. I realized that nothing else was going to work."

As she surrendered her heart to the Lord that day, recommitting her life to Him, He began to do a work in her. Listening to His voice and following His leading, Jane felt her connection with the fertility clinic begin to dry up. She removed her name from the donor list. She began to sense the urge to adopt a child and found an organization whose vision for international adoption inspired her.

"It was a long process," Jane sighs. "Lots of red tape to go through and many setbacks." But as she and Ted trusted in the Lord to provide for them, they found the strength to persist.

Finally the day came when Jane and Ted would meet their little boy, who was seventeen months old by then and coming from an orphanage in India.

Phillip Arfan arrived barefoot, in an ugly T-shirt and ragged black corduroy pants. He peered sheepishly at his new mother and clung to the chaperone, who was familiar. Jane pitched him a little ball she'd brought and held out a stuffed animal. Soon Phillip was snuggled in her arms, warm and safe, and drifting into a peaceful sleep.

In the days to come, as Jane nurtured her son, her body began the change of life. "It was as if the Lord said, *'This is finished.'*" She explains, "I became totally satisfied; my desire to become a mother was completely fulfilled. I never wanted for anything more." A few years later she had a hysterectomy. Jane says her life is a testimony to the truth of Psalm 37:4: *"Delight yourself in the LORD and He will give you the desires of your heart."*

Phillip is twelve now. Saved a few years ago, he followed Jesus in baptism this past Sunday at church. His mother held her own breath as Phillip was immersed in the water. Then, when her son came up smiling, Jane applauded through tears of joy. * *GF*

Everyday Wisdom

And to man He said, "Behold, the fear of the Lord,
that is wisdom, and to depart from evil is understanding."
JOB 28:28 NKJV

A coworker tried to convince me why it was all right for her to live with her "fiancé," a man who wasn't a believer. It was none of my business, and I told her so, but she persisted in justifying herself to me each time we went on a break at work. She considered herself my "sister in Christ," and, knowing I was a trained life coach, she trusted me. So I listened.

"Derek and me...well, we've made a commitment to each other. We were together before I became a Christian. It's like we're married. God knows my heart. We're married in His eyes."

In reply, I merely suggested that she read God's Word so she'd learn His heart, but my words seemed to fall on deaf ears.

As the days passed, I longed to share God's truth with her. I considered Lisa a friend. I wanted her to understand that living in a sexual relationship apart from marriage, while socially acceptable today, is by God's standards unacceptable. The Bible refers to it as "fornication." What's more, the Lord warns us in His Word that "no fornicator...has any inheritance in the kingdom of Christ and God" (Ephesians 5:5 NKJV). That's strong language—and I didn't think Lisa would appreciate my preaching to her, even though she sought out my opinions. I felt that God needed to speak to Lisa personally.

So I began to pray.

About a month later, she approached me and said that she and Derek had split. She'd been reading her Bible and began talking about God and the two of them going to church—even getting married. "For whatever reason," she told me, "Derek flipped out. He got really mad, said I was trying to trap him, and he threw stuff around our apartment. Then he packed up and left. He said he never wants to see me again."

I held my tongue but thought, *Good thing you didn't marry the jerk!* Instead, I asked, "So are you two really finished, or are you going to try to win him back?"

"Win him back?" Lisa laughed. "No way. He's history. I mean, I don't think he ever intended to marry me. He used me. I paid the rent and the bills, bought groceries, and made dinner. I cleaned the apartment and decorated it, and he sat back and sponged it all up...but all the while he allowed me to think we'd get married someday."

My heart broke for my friend, but at the same time I knew the breakup was for the best—her best. "I'm sorry you got hurt."

"Actually, I'm relieved. I'll never make that mistake again. I've learned that commitments go beyond mere words. The prerequisite for the next guy I date is that he has to be a serious Christian who plays by God's rules, and I'll have to see his faith in action to believe it. Know what I mean?"

I nodded. "I think so."

"I really care what God thinks. I want His blessing, not His curse."

Her reply was my answered prayer! Lisa now had a healthy fear and a solid respect for the Lord and His Word.

I smiled. "You're a wise woman, Lisa." * *AKB*

Stage Fright

Now go; I will help you speak and will teach you what to say.
EXODUS 4:12

People who know me well may be surprised to find out what an introvert I truly am. With close friends, I can be myself and let go of my insecurities and shortcomings, resulting in a gregarious side that mere acquaintances never see.

Consequently, as a result of my shyness, when my first book came out and I had a scheduled radio interview, I began to sweat. A lot.

On that fateful day, my heart thumped hard against my chest with every tick of the clock. The countdown was on as I waited for the call. How could I talk about my first book? I'd moved on to writing other books and could barely remember what I had written in the first one. What if I drew a blank? Hey, it happens to menopausal women. Trust me. I know this from personal experience. I prayed and ransacked the house in search of chocolate.

I wanted this interview to be about the book, about the Lord's faithfulness, not about me. But I was at the interviewer's mercy. The questions she shot at me would be answered off-the-cuff.

I don't *do* "off-the-cuff."

The time came and passed. No phone call. My stomach coiled and rolled. Still no phone call. It occurred to me that someone might have told her about my phobia with interviews. I prayed she'd call soon—I was quickly slipping into a chocolate coma.

An hour or so later, the interviewer called. She apologized for being late. She'd had chemotherapy that morning and was running behind. What? *Chemotherapy?* I was worrying about a silly interview while she was dealing with chemotherapy?

All fear left me.

My heart ached to know how to console her in her journey. We discussed her situation and how God was getting her through. We even laughed together. By the time we got to the actual interview, I wasn't the least bit nervous. We had bonded over something far more important than a book review. We were "sisters in the faith," traveling an uncertain road, with the Lord by our side.

As I forgot *myself*, the Lord gave me the words to encourage my sister. My concern for her made me forget the less important matters. I never had to consider where my words would come from; they were just there because He was there, to heal, encourage, and strengthen—both of us.

So whether you have a radio interview or a coffee meeting with a neighbor, keep your eyes fixed on Jesus. He will give you the words to say, and His words make all the difference.
* DH

Standing in the Storm

*A thousand may fall at your side, ten thousand at your
right hand, but it will not come near you.*

PSALM 91:7

The inner workings of Corporate America are most definitely not for the faint of heart. Although I'm grateful beyond measure for my day job as an editor, there are so many things about working for a worldwide corporation that rattle the nerves in ways that operating one's own small public relations firm did not.

One of those things is corporate performance. Business decisions must be made based on the whole bucket, not on the individual splashes of water that fill it; and so when economic difficulties come along, everyone hunkers down and waits for the fallout to see how it might unexpectedly affect them.

Rumblings about layoffs and budget cuts had been echoing for weeks. One morning, as we all fetched our coffee and chatted about our weekends as we set about starting the day, the fallout began. One of my favorite coworkers was summoned to human resources, and an hour later, he was clearing out his desk. Then I signed on to the conference bridge for a meeting, and one of the key players failed to show up. Later that day, I was told she'd been let go.

Although my heart wept for them, I couldn't stop my mind from going inward. What if I was next? What would I do without my job? While most everyone else at least had the second income of a spouse to rely upon, I had nothing more than the small, sporadic stipends of a freelance author. My savings might cover a couple of months, but beyond that, what would I do?

Between meetings, I went into a stall in the ladies' room and began to pray. I prayed for my friends who had been laid off, and for their families. I told the Lord that I knew He would take care of me no matter what occurred; then I took a breath and asked Him to spare me and the rest of the folks around me anyway.

The following week, a list was released to us, naming all our peers who were no longer employed by the company. It was a long list, consisting of very familiar names, but not one person on my immediate team appeared on it. The next day, while spending time in the Word, I came across today's familiar Scripture. I thought of the "thousands" that had fallen at my side, and I cried with gratitude as I realized it had not come near me…because of the Lord's good grace.

* SDB

Confessions of a Cookie-Cutter Christian

Let your eyes look straight ahead,
and your eyelids look right before you.

PROVERBS 4:25 NKJV

Do you ever feel like you're walking in your sleep most of the time? I do.

I wake up every morning, turn on the computer, start the coffee, get the newspaper—and this is how my day begins. As I accomplish each task on my to-do list, I check it off—and then it's time for dinner. After the dishes are done I complete the rest of my daily routine—and then it's time for bed. On Sundays I get up, shower, get dressed for church, sit through the service, smile at folks as I walk out, and drive home to get ready for the workweek. How exciting, right? Um…not. More like bor–ing!

Sometimes it's so mundane, it all seems pointless. I feel like a cookie-cutter Christian. Everything is so repetitive that I don't bother to think about my actions. I'm easily distracted when I go through the repetitive motions of everyday life. Unfortunately, many of the world's most interesting distractions take my eyes off God.

By allowing myself to fall into the rut of living a cookie-cutter life, I'm not fulfilling my goal of walking in His light every single second of every single day. My daily schedule has taken over, and I'm not using the potential He gave me. Although not obviously evil, my attitude isn't right with God.

So what should I do? Find excitement for the sake of shaking things up? Or continue to go through life with the same routine until Jesus calls me home? Neither. I think I need to adjust my mind-set and attitude…and my routine. I should find more opportunities to serve Him and to reflect on His Word.

Rather than look at my tasks as boring and mundane, I should do them with joy while I focus on the light of His Word. Before I even get out of bed, I can read a single Scripture verse to give me focus for my day. I think I might even add a few God-pleasing and interesting things to my to-do list to keep myself motivated. Not only will it help me walk in His path, but it will prevent me from straying into areas that I know aren't right for me. Varying the routine is fine as long as the purpose is to bring glory to God through Christ. * *DM*

Little Ol' Me

*The LORD did not set his affection on you and choose you because you were
more numerous than other peoples, for you were the fewest of all peoples.*

DEUTERONOMY 7:7

Fame is a funny thing. Despite the obvious annoyance of paparazzi, a publicist's dream is an increase in media exposure for her clients. One of the points of achieving fame is to appeal to the crowd mentality: if everyone's rushing to experience this (person, band, actor, film), there must be something special there! Of course we can all come up with at least one example of that crowd mentality showing itself wrong. Milli Vanilli comes to mind. Sir Mix-a-Lot. *Jersey Shore. The Real Housewives of Anywhere.*

But we do tend to put value in numbers that way.

The verse above points out yet another way God sees things differently than the world. "Powerful" people or big numbers have never impressed Him. After all, when He first set apart the Israelites as His chosen people, Abraham, Sarah, and Isaac were the only members of that particular in-crowd. And although the Israelites slowly grew in number, many other ethnic groups were far larger and more powerful.

Historically, the point of today's verse was to bolster the spirits of the Israelites before they faced a mass of larger foes—the Hittites, Amorites, and a lot of other "ites." In essence, God told them, "Don't worry about the size of your enemy. I'm going to be there for you—not because you're big and powerful but because you're Mine. I chose you because I love you—that's why I redeemed you from slavery."

I see much to embrace about this verse today as well.

God extended that "chosen" status to "a thousand generations of those who love him and keep his commandments" (Deuteronomy 7:9). A thousand generations. Now there's a big number worth considering, because it eventually included us. Jesus came to earth with our redemption from slavery in His heart. Not because we're big shots or numerous, but because He loves us, on an individual basis.

I tend to go through life with a rather healthy confidence and optimism, but on my worst days I might feel very small. I might doubt my real value to anyone. Maybe no one remembered my birthday or my favorite book idea got rejected. Perhaps someone gave a particularly negative book review or some smart-mouthed kid called me an old lady. Plenty of people might question their value for more serious reasons, like an unfaithful spouse, an abusive parent, negligent and estranged kids, chronic illness, or financial hardship.

It's easy enough to recognize God's love when everything is going our way. When appreciative friends and family surround us. When we're successful, maybe even achieving a modicum of fame. When our health is good and our accounts are in order. But God didn't set His affection on us and choose us for any of those reasons.

He *did* choose us, though, and He does love us—regardless of what the crowd might say. * *TP*

Here, Wear My Armor!

Saul replied, "You are not able to go out against this Philistine and fight him;
you are only a young man, and he has been a warrior from his youth."

1 SAMUEL 17:33

It took a lot of talking for David to convince King Saul that he could slay the giant. Even then, nervous Saul placed his tunic around the boy and added a suit of armor and a bronze helmet. But when David tried to walk around, he kept falling over from the weight of it. He rejected it all and went after Goliath armed with just a sling and some stones.

How many times have we faced challenges that look as big as that giant? We stand there, with our sling and stones, wishing we had a king to stand behind us and some armor or a helmet to protect us.

I often equate David's story to my own battle against ovarian cancer—although, when that phone call came to identify it as the Goliath standing before me, my attitude was far more Saul than David. I yearned for dependable armor or a big old helmet! When I pulled back the band of my sling, I realized I had no stone to load into it.

Then God's grace sent Dr. Alison Calkins, who was beautiful, smart, and compassionate. She looked me straight in the eyes and answered every one of my six thousand questions. She let me cry without judgment, and when my weight was more than the radiation machine would allow, she even figured out how to build a support. Through her and her team, God fashioned the little stone I needed to take one brazen shot at cancer.

I'll never forget the day Dr. Calkins told me, many weeks later, that the giant wasn't getting back up again. "You and I are going to be together for the rest of your life," she said with a smile, as she explained how she envisioned my post-cancer care. "And I'm happy to tell you…that will be a very long time."

Even now, more than six years later, I still feel queasy when I wait at the light at Martin Luther King Boulevard to turn into St. Joseph's Hospital for my annual checkup. At first, I remember the loneliness of those treatments, the fear and the anxiety and the desperation. But as I park in a spot marked RADIATION THERAPY PATIENTS ONLY and the glass door slides open and I spot Connie or Alex or Ann Marie, my heart starts to beat again. Excitedly, I anticipate seeing Dr. Calkins, knowing she'll be the reminder God brings that the giant has been slain.

I'll bet, every now and then, David spotted a small stone at the side of the road and couldn't help but smile, remembering what he and God had done. If only I could tuck Dr. Calkins into my pocket and carry her with me as a reminder: *By the grace of God, giants are slain! * SDB*

And the Award Goes to...

Nor did we seek glory from men, either from you or from others,
when we might have made demands....

1 THESSALONIANS 2:6 NKJV

I can't think of a single person who isn't at least *a little bit* competitive.

Andy Warhol wasn't just whistlin' "Dixie" when he declared that no matter who we are or what we do, we crave our fifteen minutes of fame.

It isn't sinful, after all, to want some recognition when we accomplish something. In fact, it's part of human nature to work *toward* earning awards, accolades, and praise.

Tiger Woods wants another green jacket. Andy Murray yearns for a tennis Grand Slam. The Steelers will "Terrible Towel" teams that try to keep them out of the Super Bowl, while the Phillies dream of repeating their World Series win. Brad Pitt can almost feel that Oscar in his hands, and Robert Plant can already hear his name being called at the Grammys.

And on less world-renowned stages, everyday mortals picture themselves at the podium, thanking everyone from their maiden aunt Olive to the mailman for whichever laurels have been bestowed. Authors hope that their novels will appear on bookstore shelves, and parents long to accept PTA presidential nominations. Members of the Ladies' Auxiliary secretly want credit for every dollar raised to buy the church a new organ.

I repeat: it isn't a sin to desire a bit of honor for a job well done. *Bu–u–ut...*

Personally, I get into trouble when I put "respect my deed" ahead of the deed itself...and forget who is responsible for my ability to compete in the first place! Working all day, every day, at a job that demands solitude makes it doubly pleasurable when others sing my praises, and it doesn't much matter whether they come in the form of rave reviews or certificates or letters from my readers!

For me, zeroing in too tightly on what comes *after* the work is done distracts me. And that's why I quickly file away the physical evidence of that stuff and grab my Bible.

It's amazing how quickly I feel invigorated and inspired once I've reminded myself that none of it—the work or the awards—belongs to me, but to Him who blessed me with the talent to do it and the drive to achieve it. * *LL*

It Is What It Is

And the Word became flesh and dwelt among us,
and we beheld His glory, the glory as of the only begotten
of the Father, full of grace and truth.

JOHN 1:14 NKJV

What do you think Elizabeth Barrett Browning really thought about her husband?" my college poetry professor asked.

I tentatively lifted my hand. "When she said, 'How do I love thee, let me count the ways,' she meant she loved her husband."

"Look for the symbolism," he argued. "Was she starved for affection? Was she looking for affirmation of who she was as a woman? Did she have a secret? What was really going on with her?"

I disagreed with his theory that if poets wanted to tell it like it was, they'd do it in prose.

Sometimes it is what it is. I know that many poets use symbolism, metaphors, and irony to express themselves. However, I like to think that some verse is straightforward and honest.

It's like Christ's love for us. Yes, there are some poetic devices in the Bible, but there's never any doubt that His love for us is true. We don't have to guess or figure out what He means when He tells us He loves us. His Word is truth. I wanted to believe that my favorite romantic poetry was written about true love. Yet it's nothing like the most amazing and powerful love Christ has for us. * DM

Earning Grace...and Other Horror Stories

Out of his fullness we have all received grace in place of grace already given.
For the law was given through Moses; grace and truth came through Jesus Christ.

JOHN 1:16–17

I'm one of those people who remembers dreams, and usually in great detail. For many years I've tried to figure out what messages my dreams might have for me in hopes that God will use them to communicate with me, like He did with certain men and women of the Bible. Unfortunately, years of dark hallways, growling giraffes, automobile-producing gardens, and missed social studies tests have blown by, unanalyzed, without any deciphered meaning. But the other morning I woke up with a throbbing back after dreaming that I'd been forced to carry my past sins in heavy wineskins over a rocky mountain range. It wasn't too hard to figure out the "hidden message" there as I wobbled toward the beautiful blue lake where I was allowed to deposit them. I remember thinking that I felt like one of the contestants on *The Biggest Loser.*

I love that show—partly because I've been fighting the weight battle for my whole life, but also because the brave participants inspire me. Late in each season, the producers set up a challenge for the contestants involving a race where they carry their old weight on their backs. For instance, if one of them has lost a total of 120 pounds, 120 pounds' worth of weighted packs are piled on them in the increments in which they lost it. At intervals throughout the course, they get to drop the packs in the order in which they lost the weight over the weeks.

Every time those incredible shrinking bodies add on the weight they'd been carrying through their lives before arriving at the Biggest Loser campus, I shrink into the sofa and cringe. How horrible! But as they move along the course and drop the first week's loss of twelve pounds, the second week's ten, and so on, viewers can't miss the change in their countenance.

What if we were forced to carry our sins around that way? What if our offenses and mistakes stayed with us in big weighted packs and we had to earn the right to drop them, one by one? What if the forgiveness of sin had to be bought, perhaps by racing others on a course and competing for forgiveness?

The fullness of God's grace is astounding, isn't it? We don't have to carry those sins on our backs, groaning beneath the weight of them until we've been punished enough, earned enough "grace points," or made a strong enough case for probation. Instead, with one act of utterly unselfish love, we were cleared of all charges. Punishment? Not necessary. Jesus tells us, "I've got this," as He has already taken the beatings and condemnation and shed all the blood on our behalf, leaving behind a steady supply of clean and shiny grace for whenever we need it. * *SDB*

Here Is Our King

But you are a forgiving God, gracious
and compassionate, slow to anger and abounding in love.
Therefore you did not desert them.

NEHEMIAH 9:17

David Crowder, my favorite worship singer, wrote a song called "Here Is Our King." In it, he likens God to an ocean's tide. I love the passion and feeling of this song, but the visual is so immense and powerful. God keeps coming back. He's as dependable as the ocean's waves. Sometimes the tide goes out. There is more sand and the ocean feels further away, leaving one on the dry sand to wonder if it's not coming back this time—but its power and dependability can be counted upon. Like our majestic God.

As a writer, one faces a lot of rejection, and it's important to be grounded in what you're doing—to know *why* you're doing it. First, there is the constant rejection of trying to get something published. Most writers could wallpaper their entire office with rejection letters.

Second, there's the rejection that editing brings. Though ultimately this will make your book better and ready for the real world, it's still difficult to see all those red markings on a manuscript. No easier than it was in school.

Finally, there is the book's entry into the world and the worst of the rejection. Now it's public, posted on websites. The rejection may read something like, "I don't know how this woman can call herself a Christian! A real Christian would never write this!"

During those times, it feels like the tide—like God our Comforter is so far away, that we are alone. This time, the tide is going to stay out; we just know it. But then…God comes rolling back in, with drops of encouragement and a sign that we are not forgotten. God is so faithful. He will not forget to return.

When we don't deserve it.

When we reject Him as often as Israel did.

When we dethrone Him to be our own god or to worship some ridiculous idol.

If you grew up in a household where parents weren't slow to anger, be reminded of God's gracious heart and of His love, which surpasses anything we will know on this earth. If you're a parent, think of your own child and how many times you would return for him or her. Now add supernatural love and miraculous abilities, and you will know—God is coming back for you, because you are worth it. He created you to be you. Maybe you're not the perfect Christian by the world's standards, but you are the perfect child to Him, and He's the perfect parent.

Like a wave, His love will overwhelm and encompass you. * KB

You Want Me to Do What? When?

Each of you should look not only to your own interests,
but also to the interests of others.

PHILIPPIANS 2:4

Sadly, that's usually my response when God asks me to do something I don't want to do.

I love people. I really do. But when it comes to making food, calling people, or helping in some way, I come up with a million excuses for why I can't do it. "I'm not a good cook." "I shouldn't call and bother them; they might be sleeping." "If I go to their home, what will I say?"

Moses has nothin' on me.

For me, it seems to be more of an inferiority complex than an uncaring attitude, but it's one I have to overcome just the same.

Now, granted, there are times I don't understand why I should do something. Case in point: a long time ago, I felt a gentle nudge in my spirit to give a lady a ham. It made no sense to me, but I did it just the same. Her response? "I don't know why you gave me this, but thanks."

Years later, when I shared the story with another friend, she said, "Maybe God wanted you to give her a *hand* and you thought He said *ham*."

Oh, well. I was obedient and she got a ham. It was a win-win situation.

It helps to remember that God sees the whole picture. In obedience, we trust that God will use our efforts for His glory.

My neighbors are excellent examples of people who serve others. They both were teachers who retired a couple of years ago. Since that time, we have seen them travel for missions, help others with remodeling, prepare meals, make phone calls, plan visits—you name it, they've done it. It doesn't matter if it's backbreaking work or as simple as picking up a phone, they serve without hesitation.

They are my heroes.

It's true enough that serving doesn't come easily to everyone, but the fact of the matter is, we're all called to look to the interests of others. So I've tried to start making a list each morning (yes, I'm one of those) to help me remember to do something for someone during the day I'm given. (You do realize every day is a gift, right?)

How do you remember to reach out to others? Does it come naturally to you? Do you make a list of some kind? Do you allow your day to plan itself and reach out only if someone calls you with a need?

I'm not saying there is any right or wrong way. The important thing is that we do it. Is there someone right now who needs you? * *DH*

A Life of Joy

The King's daughter is all glorious within.
PSALM 45:13 NASB

A few years ago, the book *Captivating* by John and Stasi Eldredge struck a chord among thousands of women. The thesis of that book is that women need to know they are "captivating" to the Lord—that He finds us not only acceptable, but wonderful, beautiful, and appealing. The authors note that this can be difficult to believe when one has not been nurtured as a little girl by her father. In fact, many women have wounds from their earthly fathers that only God can heal.

I'm blessed to have a father who has always made me feel loved. His nickname for me is "Pretty," and he's shown me all my life that he sees me that way—on my best and worst days. Another man in my life who taught me my value was a Sunday school teacher I had as a child who was also a friend of our family. He'd always ask the girls in our class, "How'd you get so beautiful?" And we'd have to say, "God made us that way." No other answer was acceptable.

One time I questioned my teacher about saying that God made me beautiful. "Isn't that like bragging?"

He looked at me and smiled. "You're not bragging on yourself. You're bragging on God."

Another thing both he and my daddy always told me as a child is that I was a daughter of the King. There are moments when I can still hear both of their voices in my head, declaring that truth when I need to hear it most—in those moments when happiness flees and I don't feel anything like beautiful or royalty.

I'm trying to pass this truth along to my own Sunday school class. I meet with the teenage girls at my church once a week, and this past month we made two life-sized paper dolls. One is named "Iman Object," and she is decorated in a collage of pictures we cut out of magazines. She's glitzy and glamorous, sexy and sophisticated. She wears lots of makeup, skimpy clothes, and has perfect hair and teeth. On the outside she represents the world's definition of beauty.

Our other paper doll is a little plainer. Her name is Val U'Daughter, and we're not decorating her according to what she looks like on the outside, but by what's in her heart. God is showing us what beauty means as we study people like Esther, Lydia, Anna, and Ruth. We're writing down qualities like courage, patience, kindness, and love. The person that's emerging has a deep inner life—a life of true beauty. I hope we're all becoming more like her.

What I want to teach those girls, and what I want to learn myself, is that we *are* highly valued daughters of the King. Our beauty is not based on something we can do or even the looks or brains we've been given. It doesn't come in a bottle we can buy or pass away with age. Beauty, like joy, is so much deeper than that. It's based on who our Father is. And He doesn't change. * *GF*

Muddy Shoes and the Bagel Boys

For the grace of God has appeared that offers salvation
to all people. It teaches us to say "No" to ungodliness and worldly passions,
and to live self-controlled, upright and godly lives in this present age.

TITUS 2:11–12

My gal pals and I were chatting at a corner table in the bagel shop when a well-dressed young fellow walked up to the cashier. Not particularly handsome, he was soft-spoken, polite, and looked shipshape in his polished loafers, silk tie, and crisp white shirt.

"That reminds me," Chrissy said, "of the tie I bought John for our last anniversary…that he never wears."

"And it reminds *me*," groaned Joy, "that since Pete went on a diet, he needs new clothes."

The next man in line left a trail of mud from the door to the counter and then barked out his order so loudly that the people way in back probably heard it too. As I waited to see which of my friends would comment on his rude behavior, Louise piped up with, "For two cents, I'd ask if he's single. He'd be *perfect* for my youngest daughter!"

Back home, I couldn't help but wonder why Louise hadn't seen the quieter, more courteous man as potential son-in-law material, instead of the handsome, inconsiderate one. *So much for that "clothes make the man" rule,* I thought.

Which sparked an idea for my next Sunday school lesson: I'd tell the bagel boys' story exactly as it had happened, with the good-looking loudmouth tracking in mud and the not-so-pretty fellow behaving like a gentleman.

Next, I'd run down the list memorized in business school: Shake hands with confidence. Dress with respect for yourself *and* those around you. Think before you speak, and then speak softly. Stand tall and sit up straight, so your demeanor sends the message that you are a person of good character.

Then I'd back it all up with Scripture references— John 13:34–35 and 1 Corinthians 1:10—and hand out a questionnaire, to make them *think*:

What do you want others to think of you?

What do you want other Christians to think of you?

What do *you* think of you?

Have you missed out on a friendship because you judged someone's outward appearance or the way they behaved during that very first meeting?

I'd remind my students of how 1 Samuel 16:7 says that human beings look at what's on the outside, but God looks at our hearts. If we take care of the inside, the outside will take care of itself.

That gave me pause *and* second thoughts because, unless I wanted to teach the kids that I'm a self-righteous jerk, I'd better admit how often I forget it's by God's grace that I have faith. Oh, I'll teach the lesson…someday. In the meantime, the next time I see someone like the handsome loudmouth, I won't judge him ill-bred for not taking off his cap or wiping his feet. * *LL*

Nothing Ventured

*The generous soul will be made rich,
and he who waters will also be watered himself.*

PROVERBS 11:25 NKJV

"What do you get out of that?" "Why should I bother with him?" "What did he ever do for me?"

These are questions people often ask when they feel imposed upon to do something nice for someone else. But what else can we expect with the self-focused lives we lead? From commercials that try to convince us we "deserve" something merely because we exist to the common mantra "If it feels good, then it must be right."

Ever since I became an adult, I've worked hard. I'm also somewhat of a risk taker, evidenced by the fact that I resigned from my full-time job to be a freelance writer and teacher. I feel like I need to try new things—but I have to admit, most of my risks are well-thought-out and taken only after I've worked through the downside in my mind... and feel confident that I can live with it.

I also enjoy doing community service. One of the things I love about working on my own is making my own hours so I can choose when and where to volunteer. And I know the place I should go.

In my last job, we were encouraged to spend two days per year "volunteering," which is a misnomer since the company paid us for our time. The most difficult yet rewarding day for me was when I helped out at the local food bank. At home, the very thought of reorganizing shelves and putting everything in order sends a shiver of dread down my spine. However, knowing that organization was critical to feed the masses made it tolerable. All morning I worked with about twenty other volunteers, pulling apart sacks and putting canned beans in the bean boxes and hams in the canned meat boxes. That afternoon, they split us into groups: some to distribute the food, some to work in the toy room, and others to interview clients. I went with the last group.

As I spoke to each person who needed food, I realized how richly blessed I was for being able to do this. My venture into this world of need gave me a new perspective. Now if I see a food bank bin when I shop for groceries, I often purchase something to put in there. It feels wonderful to do something for someone else—even though I don't know the people who will be on the receiving end. The Lord has blessed me by allowing me to feed and clothe my family. But He's blessed me even more by allowing me to help others. My true gain is much greater than theirs. * *DM*

The Love Lavished on You

The amazing grace of the Master, Jesus Christ,
the extravagant love of God, the intimate
friendship of the Holy Spirit, be with all of you.

2 CORINTHIANS 13:14 MSG

Have you ever spent time just thinking about the love God has lavished on you? It can be utterly overwhelming to meditate on the love of God, especially when you realize just how undeserved His love is. In the presence of His love, you confront the feebleness of your love for Him.

But God wants you to meditate on His love, particularly when you feel least deserving of it, because He wants you to understand—to the extent that anyone on earth can—how deep and profound His love is. He knows that flawed humans have a flawed grasp of genuine love, but by sitting quietly in His presence and reflecting on nothing but His awesome love for you, you can catch a glimpse of the great and magnificent love that He will pour out on you throughout eternity.

Accept God's generous love for you without hesitation and without question. He knows you're undeserving of that love, and He knows you can't possibly return an equal measure of love to Him. But that's what His grace is all about. He chooses to lavish an abundance of undeserved, unrequited love on every one of His people—including you. * *SGES*

"Good Enough" Never Is

*But since you excel in everything—in faith, in speech, in knowledge,
in complete earnestness and in the love we have kindled in you—
see that you also excel in this grace of giving.*

2 CORINTHIANS 8:7

Like most kids, I once had a love/hate relationship with Saturdays, because that's when Dad doled out allowances and Mom distributed the weekly chores list. And, like most kids, it didn't take long before I adopted a "whatever" attitude.

If a halfhearted flap didn't shake every lint ball from the scatter rugs, oh well, no one would care, right? Those lumps and bumps under my blankets? Hardly visible under a couple dozen carefully positioned stuffed animals!

When Mom pointed out that I hadn't dusted *under* the knickknacks, I wondered who (besides her) would notice. And every time Dad frowned at the quickly folded handkerchiefs I'd stacked on top of his dresser, I wanted to say, "You're only gonna blow your nose on 'em, anyway…."

So it was that "Good Enough" became my mantra (even before I knew what a mantra was), and when I held out a sticky hand to collect my allowance, I didn't even have the good grace to feel guilty. And that, of course, inspired "Do Your Best" speeches from my parents, like:

Haste Makes Waste. ("You don't need that much furniture polish!")

Finish What You Start. ("You forgot to drain the dishwater. Again.")

Take Pride in Your Work. ("Is this your best work?")

To further compound things, our pastor tucked those very same adages into his sermons on Sunday mornings. One service in particular felt as though it had been written specifically for me, and thinking that my parents had put him up to it, I went into full preteen pout mode and stayed that way, even as I washed the dinner dishes. As it happened, it was my sister's turn to dry, and when a still-greasy glass I'd haphazardly "washed" slipped from her hand, she cut her finger while trying to pick up the pieces. A dozen parental lectures echoed in my head, and I grudgingly admitted that if I'd done my job properly, Claudia wouldn't have dropped the glass in the first place.

Finally, I "got" the message. By repeating my parents' lessons, the pastor had provided proof that the Lord wanted me to learn these things and intended to use every voice at His disposal to make sure I heard Him.

My mantra changed that day, from "Good Enough!" to "Good Enough Never Is."

As I guided my daughters through mundane chores and homework, I shared lessons from my own childhood, and, as my parents and pastor had, I added Scripture to back up every word. "Everything you do and say," I told them, "echoes God's grace in you…

"…so I pray—and you should, too—that you'll always make a beautiful sound!" * *LL*

Why Isn't My Faith Enough?

And He said to her, "Daughter, your faith has made you well.
Go in peace, and be healed of your affliction."

MARK 5:34 NKJV

For years I prayed that God would heal me from my fibromyalgia. But instead of complete wellness, I developed other health issues, including small fiber neuropathy (SFN), something that preempts diabetes. I've changed my diet and now include exercise. I'm maintaining; however, there are still "down days" when I struggle with pain issues. It can get depressing sometimes.

So when I first heard the latter diagnosis leave my neurologist's mouth, I felt more than a little discouraged. I wondered why God didn't heal me.

My supervisor urged me to apply for a special program at my employer's occupational health department so if I was absent because of one of my chronic issues, I wouldn't lose my job. I filled out the paperwork and sent it to my MD. When I received the completed list from my physician, I stared at it in amazement. Eight chronic illnesses were listed.

"And you're working almost full-time?"

I looked up at the woman in Occ Health. I'm sure she normally wouldn't remark on an employee's personal information, but I knew her somewhat from coming into the office so many times. We had chatted here and there.

"That's amazing," she said. "And you write books, too? How do you manage it all? I mean, I know people with one or two illnesses on your list who are completely disabled. You've got eight."

"God's grace, I suppose."

"Then there really must be a God."

Now, I didn't know where this woman stood spiritually, but I realized in that moment that the Lord had just used my health issues to prove His sovereignty, love, and grace. He'd worked through me, and I wondered if that's why the Lord hadn't miraculously healed me— just like the apostle Paul who suffered with "infirmities" and learned that God's strength is made perfect in our weakness (2 Corinthians 12:9).

In her devotional book called *God of All Comfort*, Judy Gann writes: "God can remove our illnesses and change our circumstances in an instant—the moment they are no longer needed for His divine purposes. Until then, or until He takes us home, we can rest in the fact that our illnesses are part of His good purpose for our lives. God truly uses all things."

I slowly came to realize that there is purpose in my pain and it's not a question of my faith: It's a matter of God's will. * *AKB*

The Truth Hurts…At First

Whoever rebukes a person will in the end gain favor rather than one who has a flattering tongue.
PROVERBS 28:23

My friend Jemelle doesn't mess around. If you're a person prone to fishing for compliments, Jemelle is the wrong side of that fishhook. If you ask her about the outfit you have on, you'd better be sure you really want to know! That new haircut feeling questionable to you? Don't ask her about it unless you're braced and ready for the reply.

I made what initially felt like a very big mistake one night when I whined to her over dinner about my struggles with weight loss. "It seems like I just can't make any progress," I told her. "One step forward and two steps back."

I suddenly had the feeling she'd been holding back her feelings on the subject for a long time and I'd just handed over the key to the lecture room.

"That's because you're only half committed," she began. "You need to really look at what you're eating. Your food choices just aren't healthy. You're never going to reach your goal doing it this way." A half hour later, her lecture left me feeling a little like a waterlogged bystander caught up in a flood.

But that night after she left my house, I couldn't sleep. I blamed the caffeine in the Diet Cokes I'd consumed. Then I blamed Jemelle. Who did she think she was? What did this gorgeous woman know about a weight problem like mine?

The next day, her words danced around in my head like one of those songs you just can't shake. I grabbed some chocolate, curled up in a chair, and really worked on being mad at her all afternoon. It went on like that for nearly a week…until the voice of God in my spirit told me what I already knew.

I called Jemelle and opened with, "If I ask you a question, will you promise not to hold it against me later?" It was no surprise when she replied, "No."

"I need your help," I told her—four little words that set into motion an avalanche of support, encouragement, tips, and advice that I rely upon heavily to this day, years later.

Next to other friends—*wonderful friends!*—willing to help me make my excuses, who play down my concerns with polite courtesy or uncomfortable silences, she can seem pretty harsh at times. But the truth is this: Jemelle has no interest in flattering me or making me feel comfortable in my own skin. Her concern is having me around; she wants me to be present at her children's birthday parties and at family gatherings (which always include me). She wants us to enjoy our lives together.

No, it isn't always easy to hear what Jemelle has to say. But I've come to believe that every person—male or female, fat or thin, old or young— absolutely must have a Jemelle in their life to tell them the truth when no one else can or will. I wouldn't trade this woman for all the chocolate in the Ghirardelli factory. And that's sayin' somethin'! * *SDB*

You Needed Me

And who knows but that you have come to
royal position for such a time as this?

ESTHER 4:14

One of my best friends lost her husband to cancer a few years ago. Matt was a sweetheart, but he wasn't a believer until it was almost too late. God was patient with him, though, and so was his wife, Val. Their marriage was no cakewalk (what marriage is?), and Matt's lack of interest in salvation couldn't have been easy for Val to accept. Had I been in her shoes, I think I would have henpecked for Jesus, and we all know how effective that is. But Val carried on as a believer, a churchgoer, a women's Bible study leader, and most importantly for her husband, an ever-patient wife who evangelized by example.

Very shortly before his death, Matt quietly accepted the Lord into his heart. Obviously, that event brought great comfort to Val in the midst of her grief after he died.

As she drove around town running errands several months later, the old Anne Murray song "You Needed Me" came on the radio. Although Val had always loved the song, the lyrics were especially poignant to her now and reminded her of how much she had needed Matt in her life. He had wiped away her tears and given her strength and held her when she was cold. Despite the conflicts they'd experienced in their life together, Val realized what a gift God had given

her, to create Matt for such a time as that which he spent with her. And she felt God blessed her at that moment in her car, to draw her attention to a song suggesting what Matt had done for her.

Oddly, the next day the old song came on again. After years of not playing, it played for Val two days in a row. "Okay, Lord," she said, "what are You trying to show me?" And it was as if the lyrics changed to remind her of what she had done for Matt by representing Christ to him all those years. The lyrics spoke about the buying back of one's soul, about turning lies into truth, about putting one on a pedestal high enough that he could see eternity. She understood she had been created for such a time as that which she spent with Matt. Again, God blessed her then by drawing her attention to a song suggesting what He had done for Matt and how she had been His instrument.

As believers, we're all His instruments, whether we realize it or not. He puts each of us in "royal positions" for specific moments in time. It's up to us to seek our purpose and to serve Him well. Who knows? Maybe today you'll fulfill His purpose for you. * *TP*

I'm Not Scared of the Dark...Much!

He setteth an end to darkness, and searcheth out all perfection.

JOB 28:3 KJV

My neighborhood went completely dark this morning. No phone, no lights, no coffeepot, no computer. The power company's recorded message (retrieved thanks to a fully-charged cell phone) promised to return service by suppertime. If not for the delicate newborn grandchild I was babysitting, lack of creature comforts wouldn't be a problem.

As dads up and down the street tried to heft their garage doors without power openers, the elderly woman on the corner came to mind. Confined to a wheelchair, her television and radio are like friends who came to visit and never went home. Some of her medications require refrigeration, and she relies on electricity to keep her oxygen machine humming, too. A year or so ago, her kids gave her a generator for Christmas...but who would make sure there was enough gas in the tank to power it until the lights came back on? Who would run the cord to connect it to her life-saving machine? And how would I find out, when, without electricity, her phone wasn't working?

After bundling the baby, I headed up the street to check things out, praying, as the stroller squeaked over bumps and cracks in the sidewalk, that I'd get there in time to assure and calm her before taking care of things.

As I climbed the brick steps leading to her front door, her porch light flashed on and I heard the drone of the TV weatherman, who was promising a bright and sunny day. My elderly neighbor opened the door for us and, dragging a dozen feet of flexible clear tubing behind her, sang, "Come in! Sit down! And introduce me to that perfect little grandbaby of yours!"

While she crooned to the baby, I fixed us both a cup of tea and said a quiet prayer to the Father, who had known even before I left the house that the dear woman wouldn't need my help in hooking up her generator. What she needed that morning, as it turned out, was the living, breathing proof that the neighbors who so often said, "If you need anything, just call!" were thinking of her.

There were tears in her eyes when I returned to her living room with that tray of tea and cookies. "Just looking into a baby's innocent face is sure to start the waterworks," she said into a lace-trimmed hanky.

But I knew better. Oh, the baby might have inspired a little of the dampness, but the tears sparkling in her hazel eyes had been put there by joy and gratitude, and it humbled me to the soles of my sneakers.

I promised myself, even before handing her a teacup, that I'd make a point to visit her more often. Not just when the lights went out, but for no reason other than to help her pass an hour or two in that big, lonely house of hers.

And they say God works in mysterious ways! * *LL*

Little Mary

Give, and it shall be given unto you; good measure, pressed down, and shaken together, and running over, shall men give into your bosom. For with the same measure that ye mete withal it shall be measured to you again.

LUKE 6:38 KJV

It's been said that I should have been born a century ago, mostly because I'm so fond of the Wild West and its cowboys. In all honesty, I'm quite content with paved roads, electronic gadgets, and the miracles of modern medicine. It's the simple, straightforward way of the cowboy that I so admire, along with the down-to-earth terms they used to describe every element of life.

Take, for example, the term "Little Mary," the name given the fellow charged with driving the blatting cart—a vehicle designed to carry newborn calves unable to keep up with the herd. The guy holding the reins probably wasn't always tickled pink at his title, but he took it on the chin, knowing that someone had to look out for those babies.

Cowboy life often mirrored biblical principles. Those rowdy, dusty trail riders could have adopted a "survival of the fittest" mind-set, sparing the Little Mary driver's ego... and an equine team the grueling job of pulling the wagon. Instead, the cowboys looked to the future, knowing that every day the newborns grew more steady-legged and that by the time they reached the end of the trail, most of the calves would have the strength to stand on their own and keep up with the herd. So the riders outfitted the rig and turned a deaf ear to the chronic "blatting" of the young'uns, who were terrified by the rough ride that separated them from their mamas.

Cynics might say the efforts could be explained by a stoic realization that, eventually, each calf would deliver dollars by the pound. But that doesn't explain why the crusty cowpokes tenderly loaded and off-loaded critters hardly bigger than my clumsy dog at the start and finish of every parching day. Or why they crooned soft and low to calm them as the moon rose in the vast and inky sky. Or why those dog-tired men painstakingly fashioned "bottles" of leather gloves and hand-fed those li'l calves whose mothers couldn't—or wouldn't—provide nourishing milk and affection.

I believe we can all benefit by their example. The next time I see a brother or sister in need, I'll study them hard to find out what I can do to soothe them.

Fortunately for me, I won't have to bear the Little Mary moniker or clomp around on "yelpin' puppies," blistered and chafed by the grit and heat of a long, hard ride. Lucky me...I can ease on over and deliver comfort on well-padded Reeboks! * *LL*

Dry Your Tears

You number my wanderings; put my tears into Your bottle.
PSALM 56:8 NKJV

I'm convinced that every woman has that one guy in her past: the one who made her cry until she didn't think she had a tear left to shed; the one who fooled her once and then fooled her twice but, despite it all, she leapt over the old adage to open the door and let him in to fool her yet again.

Mark was that guy for me. Our relationship spanned many years, but we never seemed to have more than a month of happiness before another bump in the road threw us off course. By the time that last breakup klunked along, it wasn't a thrill to ride the roller coaster anymore; it was just exhausting. I'd learned not to trust in the love I felt for him, because every time I leaned against it for a few minutes, it gave way and I went tumbling.

We'd agreed on a birthday gift for his mother, a beautiful gold locket we'd had engraved. I carefully placed photos of Mark and his sister inside and eagerly sprinted up the sidewalk toward his front door. His mom was going to love it!

My hand was poised and I was ready to give the screen door a couple of raps when I noticed that the front door was cracked open. When I looked inside, I saw Mark on the sofa with another woman in his arms. I stood there like a statue, my hand still raised and ready to knock, my mouth gaping open in a perfect round *0*, and my eyes so wide I couldn't even blink.

It was like a scene out of a really bad movie. He looked up at me over her shoulder and our eyes met, but he didn't say a word. When I finally found my breath, I dropped the velvet box with the locket on the porch and spun around, rushing away from his house. It wasn't until much later that I realized he hadn't even bothered to follow me. The other woman in his embrace didn't even know what had occurred. I looked in my rearview mirror to see if his front door had at least opened. It hadn't. I was heartbroken.

The phone calls started coming two hours later, and they kept coming for three straight days. On the second day came the lavender roses, my favorites, followed that night by the first of a dozen e-mails that I deleted without reading. All the ploys that had been successful in reuniting us in the past just cascaded on my deaf ears and numb heart. I cried on the first night, but after that my tear ducts had at last gone dry.

I prayed and asked the Lord many times in those days why, this time, it felt different, and about a week later I opened my Bible and began to read the first Scripture that caught my eye: "You number my wanderings; put my tears into Your bottle...."

So that was it, I realized. Mark had made me cry so often and so violently, so many times. Over those years, the Lord had no doubt saved up my tears, and now I had a credit coming. I e-mailed Mark that night and asked him not to contact me again. I told him I was finished with the roller coaster, and I haven't ridden one since. Literally or figuratively. * *SDB*

A Life of Wisdom

Older women [should] be reverent and devout...as becomes those engaged
in sacred service.... They are to give good counsel and be teachers of what is right
and noble, so that they will wisely train the young women.

TITUS 2:3–4 AMP

I met Vena when my husband started working with the youth at her church. She was the elegant older lady who came to every service and had wise things to say during open discussions. I was pregnant with our first child and fresh out of the restaurant business. We moved into the parsonage of the church.

The parsonage, which was vacant because the pastor had his own house, was a huge blessing to us. It was right next door to the church, and so in those years home with my small children, I got to know several members well who also lived nearby. Vena was one of those.

Our second child, Harper, had severe acid reflux disease. It was like colic, but it lasted twenty-four hours a day, seven days a week, for the first six months of his life. I remember well all the sleepless nights I walked the floor with him, trying to give him some relief from the pain. When we did sleep, it was upright in a recliner—me sitting and holding him in that position—so he'd be more likely to keep the milk down.

This went on for months. If this story was about me, I could tell you how I came close to the brink of insanity. I never slept, and I felt very inadequate to care for Harper and my two-year-old Grace's needs. Poor Stone, when he wasn't helping with the kids, had to fend for himself. Our lives were completely consumed.

One day in the midst of all the madness, I heard a knock on my front door. There were toys all over the floor and dishes in the sink, and dirty laundry spilled out of the doorway of my utility room, which was just off the kitchen. I wasn't expecting anyone and might have panicked at the thought of someone seeing my messy house, except that I was too bone-tired to care. It was Vena.

"Uh, hi, Mrs. Vena," I remember saying, running a hand through my greasy hair. My shirt was stained with trails of spit-up. "Come in if you can get in."

She climbed over baby dolls and puzzle pieces to give me a hug. "How are you doing, hon?"

I told her the truth, which was that I was half nuts.

"Well, I've come to get your laundry."

Amid my halfhearted protests, Vena sacked up load after load of clothes. We dragged them to her car, and she left.

The next day there was another knock on the door, and Vena was back, with everything cleaned and folded and pressed. Even Stone's T-shirts were on hangers.

I started to cry. "How can I ever repay you, Mrs. Vena?"

Her big brown eyes twinkled. "One day, many years from now, the Lord will give you the chance to help a young mother. When that day comes, remember me." * *GF*

Addicted to...Fear?

For the battle is the LORD's.
1 SAMUEL 17:47

I'm watching the news. The anchorman is talking about tough economic times ahead. He refers to them as "an economic tsunami" that wipes out everyone. He predicts unemployment rates plummeting to lows not seen since 1945. I imagine a scene out of the novel *The Grapes of Wrath.* Would it really come to that?

Lifting the remote, I mute the TV. Next I pick up the phone and call my brother, a successful businessman. "What do you think, John?" I ask.

He replies with practical money-saving tips, but my fears aren't assuaged. I worry. I fret. My stomach hurts. My temples begin to throb.

Then I hear God's voice: "Be still, and know that I am God" (Psalm 46:10). "'Therefore I say to you, do not worry... which of you by worrying can add one cubit to his stature?' " (Luke 12:22–25 NKJV).

"Lord, I believe Your Word is true," I say, "but what if Dan's business fails? What if I lose my job? What if—"

"'Do not fear...for it is your Father's good pleasure to give you the kingdom' " (Luke 12:32 NKJV).

The kingdom. So even if I lose every earthly possession, I'll still have a mansion in heaven awaiting me.

The truth sinks in. "Thank You, Jesus." My emotions begin to settle. I reach for the remote control so I can finish watching the television show. What other speculations would they make about these tumultuous times ahead?

Then I wonder: Am I addicted to fear? Didn't God just tell me not to worry?

I want to be informed about current events and yet I fret over that which I have no control. Does that make sense? Not hardly! Sure, I vote, I write to my congressmen and senators about issues that are important to me, but the end result belongs to God. No situation rocks Him off His heavenly throne. After all, like David said before he killed the giant Goliath, "The battle is the Lord's." And guess what? God is always victorious!

I turn off the TV and decide to leave my worries for the future there—in God's most capable hands. * AKB

With You, There Is Forgiveness

If you, LORD, kept a record of sins, Lord, who could stand? But with you there is forgiveness, so that we can, with reverence, serve you.

PSALM 130:3–4

The night was full of laughter, marked as one of the best adult fellowships on record for our church: Tacky Night.

Imagine a fellowship hall filled with fifty so-called adults dressed in the tackiest outfits they could find. I told my husband he could just pull one of his everyday flannel shirts from the closet and be okay. But he managed to "tacky" it up—or down—even more. I don't know what it says about us, but we adults rose to the challenge with a passion usually reserved for teen fads. No offense intended, teen fashionistas, but paying *extra* for holes in your jeans?

On Tacky Night, we wore things backward, inside out, upside down, layered to the point of insanity, garish, smudged, ripped, mismatched (good to know that's back in fashion), outdated, and old things that missed as fashion statements the first time around.

My husband and I looked at each other in the full-length mirror as we prepared to head to the event. Hmm. Not tacky enough. It was, after all, a competition for Tackiest Costume.

Ah! I had the answer. I hiked my seventies' granny skirt above my ankles and ran upstairs. I yanked open my dresser drawer, and there they were—the perfect accessories for my ensemble. My band medals.

What's tackier than a grown woman wearing a vest with her junior high and high school music competition medals pinned all over it?

"Thanks for asking. This one is a blue ribbon/gold medal for taking first place for my bassoon solo in eighth grade. And this one? Yes, that's for our woodwind quintet. First place at the state competition. And these three are for vocal awards—our double sextet, show choir, and duet. These six are from—"

Yeah. That's tacky all right.

I don't remember who won the competition for Tackiest Costume. The challenge brought out a talent for tacky most of us didn't realize we had.

Fun night. Lots of laughs.

But what if…?

What if the Lord made us publicly wear our offenses against Him, in a *Scarlet Letter* sort of way—all of them? What if I had to pin a hunk of metal on my vest for every potato chip I sneaked? What if I had to add more for every time I voiced my impatience? What if each misuse of time was marked in a visible way? What if all my mistakes as a child, as a mate, as a parent, as an employee formed individual "medals" I was forced to wear—all of them at once, every day, with every outfit? I'd be doubled over with the weight—the ultimate "fallen and I can't get up!"

Lord, if You marked our transgressions, who could stand? * *CR*

There's No Place Like Home

Lord, you have been our dwelling place throughout all generations.
PSALM 90:1

I let out a deep sigh as I turned onto my street after conducting an all-day workshop with three other authors. The weeks of planning showed, and the day had been a success, but I was exhausted—and I couldn't wait to kick off my shoes, get out of my business clothes, and slip into some shorts and a T-shirt.

My preparation for the day involved more than the workshop. I'd spent a couple of afternoons organizing and cleaning so I could walk back into my tidy house after the workshop and relax. With weary enthusiasm, I shoved the key into the lock, turned it, and pushed open the door. The instant I took my first step inside, I felt like the floor had fallen out from beneath me.

I blinked, hoping it was a bad dream, but it wasn't. As I looked around, I saw toilet paper strewn from one side of the house to the other. One living room lamp lay on its side, and the other one was leaning haphazardly against the wall.

My husband and daughters had been gone all day and they still weren't back, so there was no one to blame but my dog and two cats, all of them lined up and looking at me with fake innocence. I narrowed my eyes and glared at them. If they'd had opposable thumbs, I would have ordered them to help me clean up.

I numbly made my way to my bedroom, glancing at the kitchen on the way—where I saw an even bigger mess. An empty, ripped bread bag hung over the edge of the counter. The trash can lay on its side, with coffee grounds smeared over the brand-new tile floor and smooshed into the grout that I hadn't yet sealed. Obviously, the cats and dog had tag-teamed.

"Bad dog," I mumbled as I backed away from the mess. "Bad kitties." I went into my bedroom that I'd thankfully remembered to close off to the animals, dropped my handbag onto the bed, and changed into something comfortable to clean up the mess. Instead of relaxing like I'd hoped, I went on a cleaning frenzy to straighten up my home and work off the frustration. As I cleaned, I thought about the messes I've made in life and how God's sacrifice was much greater than mine. The perspective quickly cooled me down.

My husband and daughters arrived home shortly after I finished getting everything back into shape. The girls flopped onto the sofa to watch TV, while my husband joined me in the kitchen. "So how was your day?" he asked. "Did the workshop go well?" * DM

A Little Brasso Goes a Long Way

*Listen, my dear brothers and sisters: Has not God chosen those
who are poor in the eyes of the world to be rich in faith and to inherit
the kingdom he promised those who love him?*

JAMES 2:5

My dad served as an usher at church, helping folks find seats, passing collection plates, making sure the hymnals and pencils were tucked away, and walking elderly parishioners to their cars once services ended. He was so dedicated that the pastor presented him with a brass badge. In bold, black letters above his name, it said HEAD USHER.

Blushing, Dad endured the hand-shaking congratulations of the other ushers and thanked them all—the good reverend in particular—and tucked the badge into his pocket. As he was a former soldier, they believed him when he said there wasn't time to put it on "good and straight."

Well, Dad never put it on, good and straight or any other way. When the preacher and his fellow ushers asked why, he'd chuckle and say, "Forgot to buff off the Brasso!" and "Must have left it in my loose-change tray."

After dinner one Sunday, I asked Dad why he refused to wear the bright and shiny name tag.

"Well," he began, "you know how I've always said that when we donate old clothes, we must never let anyone see us deliver the bags to the church?" I nodded. "Because it might embarrass the poor people."

"That, and because a good deed never makes you feel as good as when it's done in private."

"You mean, like when Mrs. Smitherman taught us that God wants us to pray in the closet so people won't think we're being all show-offy with our fine and fancy words."

Laughing, he said, "Exactly! The reward isn't in the admiration of others, but in knowing you've done the right thing for the right reason."

That made sense. But what did it have to do with his refusal to wear the badge?

"Service to the church is like praying…or putting my weekly tithe into an envelope before dropping it into the collection plate. I don't help out so that the pastor and others will think better of me. I do it so I'll think better of me."

I still didn't get it and said so.

"God knows when our hearts are right, and mine feels right when I'm in service to Him."

"So…the reward isn't in the admiration of others," I echoed, tacking on my own ending. "It's in heaven."

"Exactly," he repeated. Then he reached into his pocket, withdrew the name tag, and pressed it into my palm. He didn't say a word, but I got the message loud and clear.

I'll treasure that badge all the days of my life, not because it's made of polished brass, but because it's a shiny reminder that with a "right heart," we can please the Father, who has graced us with so many blessings, great and small! * *LL*

A Promise Kept

Behold, the former things have come to pass, and new things I declare;
before they spring forth I tell you of them.
ISAIAH 42:9 NKJV

The accident wasn't my fault. A black Toyota Camry flew between moving traffic and headed straight for me. In an effort to swerve out of his way, I slammed directly into the car beside mine. To make matters worse, that Camry was long gone by the time the police arrived.

"Were you on your cell phone?" the stern officer asked me. "What else would make you swerve out of the lane and into this other car? Don't you know how dangerous it can be to talk on your cell phone while driving?"

"I don't even own a cell phone!" I objected, and they looked at me as if my hair were on fire.

I could see the question in the officer's eyes: *What kind of American doesn't own a cell phone?* One like me at the time, but I didn't have the opportunity to tell him so.

"It wasn't her fault. She was forced off the road."

Relief flooded over me! This complete stranger had seen the accident happen, and he stepped forward to speak up on my behalf. And when the insurance company of the other driver summoned me to court a few months later, the same stranger promised that he would appear there as well. I had no way of knowing if he would follow through. He was an unknown to me, after all. How did I know if his word was good? What was I going to do if he left me hanging?

But he showed up. He told the judge what had happened and helped to exonerate me from accusations of reckless driving.

One of the coolest things about God is how He does everything He says He'll do. When He told Mary that she was going to give birth to His Son, despite the fact that she was still pure, sure enough! Nine months later...a Savior. And when He told Noah to start building that ark so that he and his family were ready when the rains came, He wasn't fooling around. Can you imagine Noah's relief when, after months of ridicule from those around him, the sky actually opened up and started to pour relentlessly for the very first time?

The Word is brimming with blotted stains of sin, promises about the future, and repentant new beginnings, each of them foretold by the very mouth of a loving God. Like Mary and Noah and so many others, we know that a promise made by the mouth of God is certain to be a promise kept. So when our Father tells us that He has plans for us, to bring us a future and a hope...or when He declares the cleansing of our sins because of what Jesus has done for us and He promises a place for us in heaven...thankfully, it's a done deal. * *SDB*

Not All News Is Spam

And the Lord passed before him and proclaimed, "The Lord, the Lord God, merciful and gracious, longsuffering, and abounding in goodness and truth, keeping mercy for thousands, forgiving iniquity and transgression and sin, by no means clearing the guilty, visiting the iniquity of the fathers upon the children and the children's children to the third and the fourth generation."

EXODUS 34:6–7 NKJV

The first thing I do every morning is turn on the computer and let it boot up while I get my first cup of coffee ready. Then I sit down and delete all my spam e-mail before I read any of the relevant messages and news—something sent just to me.

I find most spam to be very annoying, and I grumble about its intrusion. Why would ABC Bank want me to "click here" to validate personal information on an account I never had? Why would I want to buy a college degree online after I spent long hours studying and boatloads of my parents' money for a real one? How can I win a lottery I didn't even enter?

We get spam in various forms; however, one place you won't find spam is the Bible.

As I read today's Scripture verse, I think about the impact of God's proclamation. All other news pales compared to this holy broadcast. Every single word of it is important; there is absolutely nothing that should be deleted. In other words, there's not a bit of spam in the Bible. * *DM*

Hazards

Though I walk in the midst of trouble, you preserve my life.
PSALM 138:7

With the agility of a woman half my age—okay, a third. *Let's give that woman a true advantage*—I nimbly stepped over the trip wire, then pivoted to avoid the camouflaged danger designed to maim. I pulled out my Lamaze breathing to slow my heart rate. *Stay calm. Stay…calm.*

Balancing on one foot, I leaned forward, my arms a tightrope-walker's pole. I made an adjustment. Steady… Whew. Safely over another obstacle. But there was no relaxing yet. Metal and ball bearings—a dangerous combination—lay between me and an oasis of relative safety.

What was that? Quicksand? Great. *Resist the urge to struggle. Slow movements.* Muscles taut, I grabbed the arm of the couch with one hand and the end table with the other. Yes! Free from the gauntlet of dangers, I scraped Play-Doh off the bottom of my Nikes and headed for the kitchen to make lunch for the grandkids.

I'd successfully dodged Matchbox cars, marbles, Legos, and Mr. Potato Head parts.

But the kitchen wasn't the safe haven for which I'd hoped. And hopped.

One grandson knelt on all fours on the floor, eating Cheerios from a bowl he pretended was a dog dish.

Another grandson had found the ice cream pail of birdseed. The gallon size. He's grown so clever, that boy. I didn't know he'd learned how to pop the lid off an ice cream pail—or that he was so skilled at pouring. In some cultures, the pattern of birdseed piles on the hardwood floor would count as art. But birdseed is slippery, piled up like that. One more obstacle to navigate. Distracted from the danger, I briefly wondered if the blue jays and goldfinches at the birdfeeder would mind if their dinner was first swept off the floor.

The sound of the river swelled to a roar. *Wait a minute. There's no river in the bathroom.* My mistake. There was now.

Some days, life's obstacles are no more threatening than hidden Legos and Play-Doh land mines. Other times, the ring of the telephone is the emotional equivalent of a tornado warning or tsunami alert. *The tests don't look good. We'll have to schedule a biopsy. This is the last resort. If rehab doesn't work for her this session, she'll face jail-time. Sorry, but we're laying off people with far more seniority than you. I'm sorry we couldn't do more for your mother. All we can do now is try to keep her comfortable.*

Those calls have come, with varying outcomes, too many times in the last few years.

Always, they were accompanied by miracles. We either skirted the danger or were carried through it. What a rush it is to feel the grip of grace around us as God dodges threats we can't even see. We may be dizzied by His maneuvers, but we're held. *CR*

Forever Young

*Even to your old age and gray hairs I am he, I am he who will sustain you.
I have made you and I will carry you; I will sustain you and I will rescue you.*

ISAIAH 46:4

At the drugstore, while I was trying to decide between a musical birthday card and one of its less-noisy cousins, a lively lady stepped up beside me and said, *"You* look like a friendly gal…."

A pink-painted fingernail tapped a box of Light Golden Blond. "I've been wearing this shade since high school," she whispered, "but I *sooo* need a change!" Giving Lightest Ash Blond a shake, she arched an eyebrow. "Now, be honest, honey—which looks best?"

As if scripted by Spielberg, the song "Forever Young" wafted from the ceiling speakers. Ignoring the irony, I said, "With your pretty blue eyes and pale complexion, the lighter color will look very flattering."

She thanked me with a card-crushing hug. "Buy the Popeye card," she suggested. "My nephew loved it!"

I turned back to the greeting cards and caught a glimpse of myself in the mirror atop the sunglasses rack. My dark roots and smile lines sent me directly to the hair-color aisle…and then the skin care department. (An ounce of balm is worth a pound of wrinkles, right?) Last stop, the makeup aisle, for a tube of concealer that, according to TV commercials and magazine ads, would camouflage the telltale signs of my peculiar schedule. On my way to the checkout, I stared at the products in my cart. *Lord,* I prayed silently, *what'll this cost, not only in dollars, but in time spent applying it? And what makes me think any of it will keep me forever young?*

His gentle answer came in the form of the elderly woman who shuffled across my path, reminding me of my years working for a nursing home, where white hair, thinning skin, and age spots were tributes to lives well lived. Every wrinkle, a line connecting them with a moment from the past; each silvery hair, proof of a lesson learned. And behind farsighted lenses, eyes that sparkled with wisdom as arthritis-gnarled fingers followed lines of Scripture in worn Bibles.

Once, over the lunchtime din in the dining room, I overheard a woman whimper about being confined to a wheelchair. "Try to be more like King David," said her tablemate. "He didn't focus on the size of the obstacles he faced, but on the saving grace of his Maker."

"Now that," the Almighty seemed to be telling me, *"is how to grow old gracefully."* I realized that the ravages of time can't mar the *outside* of me, because through the grace of the Father, I'm forever changed *on the inside.*

At home, while unpacking my purchases, the Popeye card opened and blasted me with a hearty "I Am What I Am."

And this time, I didn't ignore the irony. * *LL*

Get Real, Cinderella

Or do you not know that your body is the temple of the Holy Spirit who is in you,
whom you have from God, and you are not your own?

1 CORINTHIANS 6:19 NKJV

Some days I get out of bed feeling frumpy and ugly. I suspect hormones play a role in that, but seriously, no matter how hard I try, I can't seem to get rid of those ten or twenty pounds that keep me from wearing my favorite jeans.

Where is my fairy godmother? Did someone hijack her on her way to rescue me from thunder thighs, a flabby belly, and saggy boobs? I've watched all the style shows that demonstrate how to hide "problem areas," but what happens if my problem area is head to toe?

Why do men never worry about body image? My husband can stand in front of a mirror without a shirt and actually come away from it happy. There are days when I avoid mirrors or clean windows, no matter how far out of my way I have to go. For once, I'd like to be able to stand in front of a mirror, look at myself without being critical, and stop worrying about every single imperfection gawking back at me.

The female body is constantly being measured—either favorably or as an example of how not to be—throughout life. We're put on a pedestal, ogled, and discussed as though we're a commodity, which is all wrong. I know that, but I still often feel as if everyone belongs at the royal ball but me. Pick up any women's magazine and you'll see what I'm talking about.

As Christian women, our bodies no longer belong to us. Christ lives in us, so we should respect who we are without all the disturbing worldly messages tearing us down. Being of strong, moral character is much more attractive to believers in Christ than the sexual objects portrayed by Hollywood. No amount of plastic surgery, Botox, or collagen can give us the inner beauty that glows from the love of Christ. Deep down we know what's important, and honey, the Cinderella story is nothing compared to the true love God showed us through His Son, Jesus Christ. * *DM*

Peace of Mind: Not Just for Greeting Cards

Then he returned to his disciples and found them sleeping.
"Couldn't you men keep watch with me for one hour?"

MATTHEW 26:40

Recently, I went through a rough time. I received a lot of online and snail-mail greeting cards from wonderful friends that spoke to finding "peace of mind" and "resting in God's arms." But peace hadn't been easily found in recent months. God felt distant and far-off.

"Please," I beseeched Him often. "I need some grace. Mercy."

One afternoon, with the television blaring and my third cup of coffee brewing in the Keurig, it suddenly occurred to me that I was starved for some silence. From the time the alarm sounded in the morning until the moment I drifted off to sleep to the hum of the late-evening news, some form of noise had kept me company for weeks.

So I turned off the television, and I sat down in my favorite chair and closed my eyes.

"I miss You, Lord," I whispered. "Please. I need You."

The twelve-year-old next door dribbled his basketball and plunked it against their garage door. His mother set the alarm on her SUV for the umpteenth time. A motor revved. The coffee pot belched. Another neighbor's toddler began to wail.

"Shh," I told my environment. "Please."

The phone rang, and I ignored it. My cell phone jingled with a text. The dog tossed a squeaky toy at me.

"Lord, *please*. I can't think over all the noise."

I heard a sweet, slightly sarcastic reply, deep down in my spirit. "Gee, I wonder how *that* feels."

I set my Bible on my knee and began to read. It took me several minutes before I realized that it had been at least two weeks since I'd cracked it open. And aside from a few "please"-oriented sentences tossed upward, when had I last sat down at His feet and truly prayed?

I spent the next hour talking to Jesus. I laid out the events of recent weeks before Him as if He hadn't been there to experience it all. I cried so hard that my ears plugged up when I blew my nose afterward. I slid open the glass door to the backyard, and a warm Florida breeze kissed my face. I closed my eyes and enjoyed an undercurrent of blissful silence that was marred only by the lyrical music of a song that no one but me could audibly hear:

"I love you.... I am with you.... You are the apple of My eye.... You are not alone."

From that afternoon on, I have made it a point to devote some time each day to being quiet before God. Even if it's only for fifteen minutes in my car or in my bedroom or in the garage while waiting for the dryer to stop, I breathe, I am quiet, and I listen. Sometimes my thoughts are interrupted by the noise of the day, but always I draw nearer to God. And those few minutes belong just to us. They are the most exquisite few minutes of every single day. * *SDB*

God's Strength for Your Weakness

*"My grace is...all you need. My strength comes into its own
in your weakness." Once I heard that...I quit focusing on the
handicap and began appreciating the gift.*

2 CORINTHIANS 12:9 MSG

What do you consider your greatest strength? How does this strength of character correspond to your most obvious weakness? Typically, your most glaring insufficiency bears a direct and inverse relationship to your greatest strength. For instance, someone who has an uncommon sensitivity to justice will sometimes come up short on mercy, even lean toward being legalistic. On the other hand, someone with deep compassion might lack discernment about how compassion can turn into an unhealthy form of coddling.

The good news is that God's strength supplies what you are lacking. The key to accessing His strength is consistent prayer. Your relationship with God must be kept in good repair in order to fall back on His strength when yours fails.

How does it work? It happens as you learn what it means to rely upon God in your daily walk. That is simply another way of saying that you carry His principles for living into your life—into the work place, into your home life, and into your relationships. It works when you stay in conversation with God throughout the day, so that when you need to call upon His counsel in your weakness, you may.

God's sufficiency will complete whatever is insufficient in you. * SGES

Saving Cash

*But the fruit of the Spirit is love, joy, peace,
longsuffering gentleness, goodness, faith....*

GALATIANS 5:22 KJV

My husband and I adopted a dog seven years ago. Not a cute little sit-in-your-lap, follow-at-your-heels puppy, but a ninety-pound, drooling, lumbering, clumsy beast that we call Cash.

To say that his former owner mistreated him would be the proverbial understatement of the year. Thanks to regular beatings and general neglect, Cash and his littermates endured broken bones that healed on their own, infections that went untreated, and conditions like heartworm and Lyme disease that were ignored. They lived outside, regardless of the weather, with just enough food and barely enough water to sustain them. When neighbors complained about the nonstop whimpering and whining coming from the owner's property, he was forced to choose: Give up the dogs or face fines and jail time.

Enter Larry and Loree, who, months earlier, buried the pet cat that had lived with them for nearly nineteen years. It took a few months, but Cash helped us to learn that "having a cat" and "being owned by a dog" are vastly different things!

He started out behaving like he was afraid of just about everything—like flashlights (one tool used by his former owner to torture him), thunderstorms, cameras, 99 percent of the men who visited us, and bugs...especially those with wings. Slowly his skittish behavior disappeared and was replaced by doggy games like "Scare the Delivery Boy!" and "Terrify the Meter Reader!"

I'm always amazed at how this enormous lumbering beast who, with a mere look, can flatten a burly six-foot-tall repairman against a wall but who becomes a meek little lamb when children are around. Newborns, toddlers, kindergarteners...he loves them all, and he happily greets each with a gentle (if not wet-and-sloppy) kiss.

He's a lesson in opposites, this magazine-shredding, hair-shedding, muddy-paw-print-making dog of ours. Instead of the once-abused/now-abusive mutt people warned us he might become, Cash is a shining example of what can happen when one is open to love, kindness, understanding, and compassion.

And he was more than open to ours!

If I could figure out how to get this Transformation Information from Cash to my two-legged peers, wouldn't the world would be a happier place!

So the real question is—did we save Cash, or did *he* save us? * *LL*

A Life of Transformation

The Truth will set you free.

JOHN 8:32 AMP

It was one of those moments. A moment of splendor that comes to us in the commonplace. A moment when eternity injects itself into the present. When something everyday, mundane, is suddenly transformed into something holy and wherever you are becomes a temple of God.

I was standing at my kitchen sink with my arms up to the elbows in sudsy dishes. Grace, my daughter, was sitting on the potty in the powder room right off the kitchen, kicking her legs and singing her little heart out. This scene in itself was a classic, and I laughed to myself at the hilarity of it. Then I registered the words to her song:

O victory in Jesus, my Savior, forever!
He sought me and bought me
With His redeeming blood!
He loved me ere I knew Him,
And all my love is through Him…

Bam. It struck me right through the heart. I love that song, and her innocent change to the lyrics—from the top of her lungs while sitting on the potty—seemed somehow very profound. The sink became a sanctuary, and light shone forth in my heart as I scrubbed the bottom of a greasy pot.

I am not good at love. Sure, we all have our moments when it comes easy, like when others are lovable. I'll admit that I've been given the most lovable people in the world to practice on. But even with them I find it challenging. I am a selfish being. And often loving another—really loving—requires so much more than what I have to give.

First Corinthians 13 defines love. It says, "Love is patient, love is kind. It does not envy, it does not boast, it is not proud. It is not rude, it is not self-seeking, it is not easily angered, it keeps no record of wrongs. Love does not delight in evil but rejoices with the truth. It always protects, always trusts, always hopes, always perseveres. Love never fails" (1 Corinthians 13:4–8 NIV).

If I am trying to accomplish this on my own, it may as well say "Love is impossible." But my daughter's modifications to that old hymn reveal the truth that makes it possible. All my love is *through* Him, who is the very essence of love.

This truth sets me free. I cannot love, but He can. I cannot be patient, but He can. I cannot be kind; I cannot help but envy; I cannot swallow my pride or control my anger or forgive or trust again or keep on giving. But He can. Jesus can and does love others. Through Him it is possible for me. * *GF*

Take a Deep Breath

Let us then approach God's throne of grace with confidence, so that we may
receive mercy and find grace to help us in our time of need.

HEBREWS 4:16

I took a deep breath and blew out the flames. Flames. My car was on fire. And my toddler kids were inside.

How it happened, we're still not sure.

The trip home from Grandma's started simply enough. The first few miles were uneventful. The next few revealed the reason why I didn't consider my kids the world's best travelers. Singing an endless litany of songs to toddlers strapped into kid prison (car seats) against their will and too close to one another in the backseat, I dodged road hazards and sibling disagreements. If I'd had any, I'd have dug into my purse for blood-pressure pills. Instead, I dug for more mom-grace and patience.

From above, the highway must have looked like an asphalt amusement ride—steep inclines, tight curves, warnings to hang onto the safety bar, er, steering wheel....

The miles crawled by. As moms do, I focused what I hoped was equal attention on maneuvering the deteriorating relationship in the backseat with the narrow shoulders and sprinkling of dead animals beyond the windshield. Skunks. Racoons. Deer.

An unmistakable odor seeped into the car's interior. Yes, I'd have to change the youngest's diaper at our next stop. But there was some otherworldly smell that had nothing to do with roadkill.

Burning rubber. Like flip-flops too close to a bonfire.

Fire?

No, kids, I will not sing another round of "The Wheels on the Bus." One of ours is on fire at the moment. Give Mommy a minute.

I pulled the car onto a wide stretch of cement—the lot of a gas station. Now that I think about it, flames and thousands of gallons of gasoline don't make great neighbors. Next time, I'll choose a less-flammable location when my car's on fire.

My heart racing, I bounded out of the car and traced the smoke and flames to the left front wheel. A tire should not crackle and snap like a birch log in a fireplace. But maybe that's just my opinion.

The sight of the flames—appreciably more pronounced than the birthday-candle variety—and the nearness of my children made me forget I couldn't do it. So I did. I took a quick, deep breath accompanied by a quick, deep prayer and blew out the flames.

I don't think that's even possible...but I did it.

The safety of my kids was at stake. I found superhuman-lung-capacity-grace to help in time of need. I approached the front of the car boldly, even if less than confidently, and found grace to help in time of—I don't think that's exactly what the writer of the book of Hebrews meant when he penned the words we lean on. But I understand the concept better since the fire. * CR

Warmer by the Fire

So you will be my people, and I will be your God.
JEREMIAH 30:22

Lately, I've been a little overwhelmed—not so much by what's going on in my own life, but by the struggles of many of my friends and acquaintances. That's one of the by-products of our easy access to communication with people all over the world. Any one of us only needs to be on a prayer loop or Facebook, let alone watch the news, to understand how hard life is for many people.

It's gotten to the point that, each time I come across another prayer request, I have to simply stop what I'm doing and offer up a prayer right there and then. Otherwise, I know those requests and needs will get lost on my ever-growing list.

And I've had my own share of turmoil to deal with. Who hasn't, right?

"'So you will be my people, and I will be your God.'" God made this promise quite a number of times to the Israelites in the Old Testament. And thanks to Christ's sacrifice for us, believing Gentiles have been given the same promise.

So how do we rectify the two situations? Why do so many of us suffer hardships in life if we've been given the blessing of being God's people? When I truly stop to consider the promise in that verse, it doesn't say a doggone thing about my life being easier or free of unemployment, illness, or heartache. It merely says I'm one of God's people.

Merely.

Just imagine facing whatever you face or have faced without the unbelievable honor of being His. When I think of how events might have unfolded in my own life—especially the tougher parts of it—without His looking after me? It makes me shiver.

That makes me think about dark and bitter winter nights—I'm most definitely *not* a winter person—and that feeling of sitting with my back to the fireplace to fight the cold. I mean, I'm spoiled by the comfort of my home and the availability of heat—I know that. But still. When I'm cold, I feel tension down to my bones and all up through my shoulders and neck—just full-body tension. But sitting near that fire…ah, coziness, peace, comfort… And then there's that reluctant moment when I have to get up and walk away from the fire and I feel the cold envelop me again. It's always warmer by the fire.

No matter what I might face today or in the future, I hope I will always remember the words right before today's verse. "'For who is he who will devote himself to be close to me?' declares the LORD" (Jeremiah 30:21). Surely any loss, pain, battle, or fear that comes along will be easier to endure, the closer I am to Him.

As much as I can, I want to devote myself to getting as close to Him as possible. And that's what I'll pray for others. * TP

Armed and Dangerous

Elijah was a human being just like us. He prayed that it would not rain, and it did not rain on the land for three and a half years! Then Elijah prayed again, and the rain came down.

JAMES 5:17–18

The world has always underestimated the power of the children of God.

Eva Barker was a soft-spoken, four-foot-ten-inch woman who lived in rural southwestern Wisconsin not far from the Mississippi River. Born in 1896, she was seventeen before she saw her first automobile. In her later years, with her long, white hair in a bun, she looked the part of a grandma. She liked to set "a little lunch" in front of whoever came into her tiny cottage, and then disappear into the background, invisible, like the angels, while her guest took center stage.

She wasn't sophisticated. Most of her life she wasn't even allowed to attend church. But whenever she thought no one was listening, you could hear her praying in Norwegian, her mother tongue. She was powerfully connected to her God, and drew her sustenance from His presence.

She lived to be 102. She saw the rise and fall of Nazi Germany and the Soviet Empire. Hitler, Lenin, Stalin—she outlasted them all. True, she was unknown except to a few. But only God knows how much damage this small, harmless woman did to the domain of evil through her many prayers. To the forces of evil, she was armed and dangerous. You can be too! * *SGES*

Guard Your Heart...

Keep your heart with all diligence, for out of it spring the issues of life.
PROVERBS 4:23 NKJV

A few years ago, I started to notice an alarming trend in my circumstances. A morning trip to the gym was more like a stroll down a model's catwalk where interested parties scrutinized the goods, deciding whether or not I was worthy. Conversations, musings, and gripe sessions started to wear on my heart like sandpaper. On the way home from work, the car radio pumped out seductive rhythms with lyrics that made me, a grown woman never accused of being a prude, actually blush. And at the end of the day, television characters were swearing and scheming and sleeping with their best friends' spouses on every cable and network channel I flipped to.

By the time we climb into our beds at night, our hearts and minds have been exposed to so much friction that there is no alternative, if we're sensitive to the Holy Spirit: This world wears on us. We're like stones planted in a stream, and the rushing water of the most powerful current around us eventually changes us. That realization was the catalyst for me to make a commitment to the Lord that I would guard my heart more diligently.

Not a popular choice in a world gone slightly mad.

Have you ever noticed that the minute you take a stand, adversities immediately encroach? For instance, as soon as you say something like "I'm not going to eat any more chocolate this month!"...every square of chocolate in a sixty-mile radius suddenly races across your path. On a coworker's desk, at the bottom of your purse, in the kitchen cabinet behind the granola...*chocolate*!

That's the way it was after I decided to become more aware of what I took into my spirit. I set the car radio to contemporary Christian music and started reading at night instead of watching television, but it seemed like the war around me kicked it up a notch in response. I had to make a decision to continue in the battle, to *keep on keeping on* in the fight.

If, like me, you aren't the least bit interested in becoming one of a million other smooth stones lining the stream bed and would prefer instead to be the salt that seasons your environment, I encourage you to stand against the battle that rages on.

Despite the continuous barrage from the outside world in the form of well-meaning friends, media, and general temptation, the effort to guard your heart is a worthy one. Start small. Raise your custom-made Harry Winston shield of faith, and get yourself fitted for your Jimmy Choos of peace. With the helmet of salvation and belt of truth already in place, you're far less likely to be washed away by the raging waters headed toward you. * SDB

The Wolf and His Shadow

But they measuring themselves by themselves, and comparing themselves among themselves, are not wise.

2 CORINTHIANS 10:12 KJV

If you play an audiotape of someone and ask that same person whose voice it is, nine out of ten will say they have no idea. Point out a habit or personality quirk and chances are good you'll be treated to a "Who, *me?*" expression. Why? Simple! We rarely see ourselves the way others do.

If someone asked me to name my biggest flaw, I'd say "Impatience." Asked which character trait is my most positive, I'd answer "Hardworking," "Bighearted," or "Self-sacrificing,"...depending on the mood or circumstance I'm in.

But if I'm truly hardworking, why can't my husband see it and accept as fact that the time I spend updating Facebook is a legitimate promotional effort? If I'm so big-hearted, why does my dog look so wounded after I snarl, "You were outside five times in the past hour, so leave me alone"? When I spout a quick and firm "Can't!"—do the people who ask me to bake cupcakes, Hike for a Cure, or donate $75 so innercity kids can attend the circus really think I'm self-sacrificing?

Unless we're clones of Mother Teresa, we're all guilty of duplicity like that from time to time, and it doesn't make us inherently dishonest. Or mean. Or horrible Christians. All it makes us is *human*.

I'm reminded of Aesop's fable, "The Wolf and His Shadow." As the story goes, the wolf's shadow made him appear a hundred times his actual size, making him feel stronger and braver than he had a right to feel. So when a powerful lion happened along, the wolf believed he could become king of the beasts. And as he strutted, still admiring his shadow, the lion flattened him with a single blow. The moral of the story? Do not let self-flattery make you forget who—and what—you truly are.

I'm in as much danger of becoming "lion prey" as any full-blown narcissist—if I allow myself to measure my worth by my own benchmarks. * LL

Living Life at Warp Speed

My brethren, count it all joy when you fall into various trials,
knowing that the testing of your faith produces patience.

JAMES 1:2–3 NKJV

With life demanding so much of our time these days, we have thirty hours' worth of things to do in a twenty-four-hour day. Who has time to relax and regenerate?

There's nothing like an accident, injury, or sickness to slow us down. On my early morning commute to work about two years ago, I sat at a red light, grinding my teeth about how bad the traffic was and how irritating it was that I'd missed the green light. Suddenly I felt a quick jolt and heard a popping sound. A quick glance at my rearview mirror let me know that the woman who'd been tailgating me for the past mile had miscalculated the distance between us, and she hadn't been able to stop before our cars made contact.

As I got out to check on the damage, I was amazed by the woman's skill at being able to juggle coffee in one hand and her cell phone in the other. And she was still jabbering into the phone, too, saying words I won't repeat! She tossed me a look of annoyance, but until I told her I was calling the police, she didn't flip her phone shut. Finally, she let me know she was late for an appointment and she didn't have time for this. I had to bite my tongue to prevent me from saying what was on my mind. Instead, I took a deep breath, ran my hand over the small nicks her bumper had made in mine, and told her that I was okay if she didn't want to bother with the police since my car seemed all right. She squinted as she studied her own bumper that had a little more damage than mine, before snorting and heading back to her own car. I stood there for a moment, stunned that she didn't have the decency to say another word before she gunned her engine and left. The one other person who'd stopped said he had her license plate number if I needed it in the future. I accepted it, thanked him, and went on to work.

After that incident, I changed my attitude toward the whole daily commute. Rather than fretting over getting to work on time, I gave myself more time by leaving five or ten minutes earlier. The Lord gave us twenty-four-hour days with at least a third of that time meant for sleep. He knows what we need better than we do, so why push for something we can't have? I've always been production-driven, so this is difficult for me, but I'm working on it. * DM

Send in the Angels

He himself went a day's journey into the wilderness, and came and sat down under a juniper tree; and he requested for himself that he might die, and said, "It is enough; now, O Lord, take my life, for I am not better than my fathers."

1 KINGS 19:4 NASB

Many years ago my son came home from kindergarten singing a little ditty that went something like this: "Nobody loves me. Everybody hates me. Let's just go eat worms."

It wasn't until years later that I saw how relevant those words might seem to someone with hopelessness.

A woman came to work in my department at the hospital. She felt totally lost among all the tasks she'd been assigned. She felt like others in the department weren't nice to her because she was new and didn't know what she was doing yet. No matter how hard she tried, it all seemed useless. She wanted to quit. But another coworker and I (both Christians) noticed what was happening, and we took her under our wings and coached her along.

To this day Deb (who is still working in that department, quite successfully) tells me that I was one of her "angels" during that time.

In the prophet Elijah's case, he had Queen Jezebel threatening to kill him. He got tired of running and fighting and wanted to give up. He wanted God to take his life because he felt he hadn't made any more difference to the Lord than the generations that had come before him. But in the next passage, the Bible tells us: "He lay down and slept under a juniper tree; and behold, there was an angel touching him, and he said to him, 'Arise, eat'" (1 Kings 19:5 NASB).

In other words, God's angel gave Elijah a little TLC when he needed it most.

This passage is a wonderful example of how God works in those hours when we feel like giving up on our jobs, our families, our friends—maybe even on life. He sends an angel, perhaps in the form of another one of God's children, to carry words of hope and encouragement—and maybe even chocolate chip cookies! (Better than eating worms, that's for sure!)

Who knows…maybe God will use you as an angel in disguise to bring His love and mercy to another hurting soul. * *AKB*

A Life of Restoration

I am the resurrections, and the life: he that believeth in me,
though he were dead, yet shall he live.

JOHN 11:25 KJV

When I was in college, I dated a guy I thought I was going to marry, and when our relationship ended, something in me died. It was a dark time. I went through several months of searching—for meaning, purpose, direction—for hope.

One day I went on a drive by myself in the country. I had a fast red sports car, and I opened up the top and just drove. I drove several miles, praying, listening to music, and feeling the vibration of my car around me.

I stopped at a church beside the road and parked in the small parking lot. The church was very tiny, and the grounds were as neat as a pin. I'd never been there before. I turned off my car and flipped open my Bible to a random place.

The page I landed on was in Song of Solomon. Great, I thought. *The book of love.* Something nudged me to read it anyway, and as I opened my heart, words I don't ever remember reading before began to leap off the page:

My beloved responded and said to me,
"Arise, my darling, my beautiful one,
And come along. For behold, the winter is past,
The rain is over and gone.
The flowers have already appeared in the land;
The time has arrived for pruning the vines,
And the voice of the turtledove has been heard in our land.
The fig tree has ripened its figs,
And the vines in blossom have given forth their fragrance.
Arise, my darling, my beautiful one,
And come along!"

SONG OF SOLOMON 2:10–13 NASB

The reality is that the Word of God is eternally true for everyone. But there's also a concept called *ramah*, which means that the Lord can quicken His Word in our hearts in a specific moment today, and that word, in that moment, is for us personally. It's a living thing.

That's exactly what happened to me in my car as I read those words. It was as if Jesus was speaking them directly to me, calling me His darling. *His beautiful one.*

At the time I felt washed out and used up. I certainly didn't feel beautiful, and I wasn't anyone's darling (except maybe my daddy's). But the Lord came and ministered to me that day and filled me with a sense of His love, of how precious we are to Him. I believe He was calling to me to come out of my sadness, out of the death of winter, and into the spring. He was calling me to trust and to place my hope in Him. And it's strange now, but at the time this call had nothing to do with any man. It was a call to arise and walk with Him alone in resurrection life.

The reason that's strange now is that it was that very day when I returned to campus that I connected with my husband-to-be. I had no idea, of course, and neither did he. We both had lots of growing to do, I guess, before the time would be right. But we "bumped" into each other at a meeting, and then the following fall when we saw each other again, he asked me out on a date. We were married a year after that.

When Stone proposed, he dropped to his knees and quoted Song of Solomon 2:10–13. I'll never forget the beauty of that moment, the love on his face. Like often happens in the kingdom of heaven, the restoration in my heart was now manifested before my eyes. * GF

Fear of Falling

If I say, "My foot slips," Your mercy, O LORD, will hold me up. In the multitude of my anxieties within me, Your comforts delight my soul.

PSALM 94:18–19 NKJV

I've never been fond of heights. When I look down from what I consider an unnatural height, I get a swirling, light-headed sensation that keeps me far away from the edge of balconies and cliffs. I enjoy going to big cities, but I have to force myself to think happy thoughts as my hotel elevator lifts me to a double-digit floor and deposits me far enough up in the building that if I fell out a window, I'd be in a world of hurt.

I'm one of those people who has falling dreams that startle me awake. Then I have a hard time going back to sleep for fear of a recurring dream.

From a very early age, most people have some degree of a fear of falling. Some psychologists believe that babies respond well to swaddling because it gives them a sense that they're secure and safe from being dropped.

Next time you take your kids to the park, watch them cross the monkey bars. Most of them hold on very tight, and those who have the biggest fears want their parents nearby to catch them in case they fall. Yes, there are exceptions; some children don't seem to mind falling on their heads. They just hop back up on those bars like nothing ever happened. But they're in the minority.

As people grow older, they show this fear in other ways—like by holding onto rails and banisters when climbing stairs. Of course, there are some people who defy that fear, while others watch them in awe as they skydive, bungee jump, or do any other death-defying act that involves falling.

This fear is logical because we instinctively know that if we fall, we're likely to get hurt. Even the expression *falling in love* implies that we lose control, and it can be quite painful.

In Psalm 94:18–19, the Lord promises to hold you up if you slip. This gives me comfort to know that He is there and that I can let go of my anxieties and be assured that I'm well taken care of. I can lean on Him for comfort and not fear falling into evil, as long as I'm being swaddled by His Word. * *DM*

The World on a Silver Platter

I am the Alpha and the Omega, the First and the Last.
REVELATION 1:11 NKJV

There are a lot of people who will attest to the adage that "money isn't everything." It's true. None of us can buy love or happiness or eternal salvation. Only God can meet those innermost needs.

One evening at church we sang an old hymn that reminded me of this very truth.

Take the world, but give me Jesus—
All its joys are but a name;
But His love abideth ever,
Thru eternal years the same.
O the height and depth of mercy!
O the length and breadth of love!
O the fullness of redemption—
Pledge of endless life above.

FANNY J. CROSBY (1820–1915)

We live in a time where shopping is a pastime to cure things like loneliness and unhappiness. Acquiring things is a status symbol, and yet none of those items can bring the kind of joy Christ freely offers. All you have to do is think of some famous people who seemed to have it all at one time. Greats like writer Oscar Wilde, actor Bela Lugosi, and singer/actress Judy Garland are reported to have died penniless; however, they'd lived the high life for part of their life. Their temporary wealth was just…well, temporary.

Someone once told me, "This is life and there's just one way out." How true. Every human being on this earth is destined to face his or her mortality one day, although for those who know Christ, it'll be the beginning of a new, wonderful, and perfect eternal existence with Him.

So put away the dollar bills and credit cards. The real treasure that Jesus Christ offers is totally free! * AKB

Jesus, Your Friend

No longer do I call you servants for a servant does not know what his master is doing; but I have called you friends.

JOHN 15:15 NKJV

In a culture in which the word "friend" can be used as a verb and defined to include the complete strangers who follow you on Facebook, it's no wonder that the concept of friendship has been diluted. But when tragedy, grief, or adverse circumstances strike your life, you know full well who will be there to offer a comforting hug and a helping hand. It will be the flesh-and-blood people who enhance the quality of your life through their genuine friendship.

In one of the many great paradoxes of your life with God, the closest friend you have isn't one of those flesh-and-blood people, nor is it one of your online buddies. It's Jesus Himself. He's the most faithful and trustworthy friend you'll ever have, and what's more, He's always with you. He will never leave you.

No matter how impressive it may seem to have thousands of online friends, having Jesus as your friend is one fact of your life that can be accurately described as awesome. As with any friendship, your relationship with Jesus depends in part on commitment and communication. By spending time with Him and engaging in conversation with Him, listening to Him as well as talking to Him, you show Jesus your dedication to your friendship with Him. * *SGES*

It Isn't a Stick!

*That person is like a tree planted by streams of water, which yields its fruit
in season and whose leaf does not wither—whatever they do prospers.*

PSALM 1:3

Isn't it amazing how easily the maple trees' "whirly-birds" take root? Not long ago, I transplanted one that had grown into a magnificent red-leafed sapling. When the digging was done, I sat back to admire the Lord's handi-work while sipping lemonade and reading the mail, which included a home-improvement catalog. There on page ten was a full-color, 5 x 7 photo of a shiny green-and-yellow, ultra-quiet, mulching lawn mower. With a padded handle. And chrome spokes. *Be still my heart!*

That evening when my hubby asked, "What do you want for your birthday this year?" I pointed to the mower of my dreams, which came as no surprise to the man who has ful-filled past birthday, Christmas, and anniversary requests with compound miter saws, hammer drills, ratchet sets, and plumb bobs. "Let's take a little drive after supper," he said, "and we'll get your fancy mower." *Thank You, Lord, for blessing me with a husband who understands me!* The next morning I rolled my new mower from the shed.

Now seems as good a time as any to admit that I'm a bit impatient—and a symptom of my impatience is an aver-sion to reading directions. *It's a lawn mower,* I thought, pull-ing the START cord. How different could it be from others I'd owned and loved?

Suffice it to say, the manufacturers weren't kidding when they stamped Self-Propelled on the handle. The minute I fired it up, that baby took off like a rocket, and in the blink of an eye, my newly relocated red-leafed maple went from five feet to a mere six inches in height.

I said my apologies—to the tree and its Creator—for the demolition my "who needs directions?" mind-set had caused, and pledged to bring it back. Every moment thereafter spent watering, fertilizing, pruning, and stak-ing reminded me of the destructive aftereffects of my impatience. As I prayed for God to save the little tree, I also prayed He'd rid me of the arrogance that feeds my impatience.

His grace is stunning, indeed, for just as He saved my sinful soul with the promise of salvation I had not earned, He healed that little tree. Within days, it grew an inch, and emerald sprouts peeked from the mower-scratched bark! One evening my husband noticed the still-spindly stalk. "Whatever possessed you to plant a stick in the middle of the yard?" he asked.

"It isn't a stick," I said. "It's my newest tool, and I'm using it to measure my personal growth."

As he walked away scratching his head, I smiled and sent a silent *Thank You* heavenward. Because I know that tomor-row, when I fire up my nifty new lawn edger, I intend to read the directions! * *LL*

Jordan, Jericho, and Just My Own Stuff

Have I not commanded you? Be strong and courageous. Do not be afraid; do not be discouraged, for the LORD your God will be with you wherever you go.

JOSHUA 1:9

In a few months, my financial situation is going to undergo a significant change. That doesn't make me different from many other people, especially in these days of crazy financial fluctuation in our country. At least I have forewarning, which is proving to be both a blessing and a curse. On one hand, I know exactly when I need to take on the new financial burden, so I'm taking as many steps as I can to secure my nest egg and increase my income. On the other hand, I often wake in the middle of the night stressing over how I'll handle it. *Whether* I'll handle it.

What I'm experiencing is probably a teeny-tiny version of what Joshua felt when he knew he had to take over for Moses and get the Israelites across the Jordan and into the Promised Land. At least I don't have throngs of people leaning on me. Nor do I have an icon like Moses to live up to.

In this first chapter, God commands Joshua four times to "be strong and courageous." Well, okay, I can do that. Until a little later, when I again think about the future and break out in a sweat over how slowly I'm preparing, despite my best efforts. Then I need to toughen up once more, remember Joshua's challenge, and exhort myself to be strong and courageous.

But what if that's just not my nature? I mean, I have courage in certain things, and I'm thankful for it. Birthin'

babies certainly wasn't for sissies. Neither was raising them to be healthy in mind, body, and spirit. Surviving a pretty scary marital relationship required fortitude and courage on many occasions.

Still, I think of the challenges that friends, acquaintances, and entire nations of people face—cancer, loss of loved ones, war, famine—and realize their call to courage is far more daunting than mine. How do they *do* it?

How did Joshua do it? Once he led the Israelites across the Jordan, he had to overthrow kingdoms already established in the Promised Land. And he succeeded at all of his God-commanded tasks by taking one step at a time and trusting God's guidance with unshakable obedience, right down to marching around an enemy fortress seven times and tooting horns in order to make it fall down.

We all have our Jordans to cross. We all face fortresses of varying sizes at points in our lives. While my trials may pale in comparison to someone else's, they're still my trials. Or maybe I face a task more overwhelming than someone else's. God knows all about it. If I can remember to keep putting Him at the center of each day, each effort—to pray, search His Word, and seek His will—I'll cross that river. I'll win whatever battle I see on my own personal horizon. He'll be with me, wherever I go. * *TP*

Pulling Down Strongholds

*For the weapons of our warfare are not carnal but mighty
in God for pulling down strongholds.*

2 CORINTHIANS 10:4 NKJV

I believe that God uses the hidden things of life to bring us to Him (or closer to Him) and to pull down our strongholds.

About thirteen years ago, shortly after I became a Christian, I received a phone call from a man who wanted to help with the foreclosure of our home. Soon I discovered that my husband, Daniel, had been gambling away the mortgage money for months—and I didn't have a clue. My husband was also an alcoholic. I doubted my marriage would last. I worried what would happen to my three young sons.

On my knees, pouring out my heart to God, I prayed that He would change my husband. Instead of changing my husband, God worked on me! As I prayed and prayed and worked at becoming a godly wife, my husband soon made decisions that honored Christ, which, in turn, changed his life and ours.

Today, Daniel is free from the bondages of alcohol and gambling. Jesus Christ set him free and pulled down those strongholds. Our sons saw the power of God in their father, which increased their faith.

Prayer is a mighty weapon that God uses to eliminate strongholds in our lives and the lives of those we care about.
* AKB

Loving the Unlovable

*A new commandment I give to you, that you love one another;
as I have loved you, that you also love one another.*

JOHN 13:34 NKJV

I'd been looking forward to this particular Saturday afternoon for weeks: my two favorite girlfriends and me, three bottomless cappuccinos, a bistro table by the window, and a whole afternoon to catch up. But we'd no sooner exchanged greetings and stirred our coffee when...

"Sandie! How are you, darlin'?"

The hair on the back of my neck stood up and saluted, the way it always did when this particular woman called me "darlin'." We'd worked together for three years, sat in cubicles only a few feet apart, and had the same lunch break schedule. Five days a week, fifty weeks per year, this woman was right in my face! When we were told that our office was being closed down for fiscal reasons and everyone else was crying and worrying about their futures, I was basking in an odd sense of relief. It wasn't that I never wanted to see her again; I just didn't want to see her every single day.

Or on this one.

"Can I join you guys?"

What was I going to say? I could tell from my girlfriends' expressions what they wanted me to say, but I just couldn't do it. And so I uttered the two most unexpected, unfortunate words in the English language: "Of course."

It was admittedly not the most pleasant hour of my life, sitting at that table with my two friends and my former coworker. I wanted to be talking about Jenny's adoption experience and Diana's recent trip to Ecuador. I wanted to hear about all the things I'd missed in the weeks when we'd been too busy to get together. But the truth is...it really wasn't so horrible, either.

This woman contributed to our conversation; she even cracked us up a time or two. A few weeks later, Diana suggested including her on a night out for dinner and a movie. It was only then that I fully realized how much I might have missed by excluding her from our group on that Saturday afternoon, how much my friends might have missed by not having the opportunity to get to know her. And what about how she would have felt if I'd turned her away?

Love one another. It's such a simple command that our Lord left us with, asking us to just love others the way we've been loved. But how many times a day do we miss the opportunity to do just that? How many times do we deprive someone else of the love we have to give?

What's even more important, though, is this: How many times do we deprive ourselves of the opportunity to love someone else for no other reason than to follow the command we were given, the Great Commission, to spread the love around? * *SDB*

It's a Jungle Out There

Have no fear of sudden disaster or of the ruin that overtakes the wicked,
for the LORD will be at your side and will keep your foot from being snared.

PROVERBS 3:25–26

When I turned on the news a few minutes ago, I saw a five-car pileup between my house and where I used to work. I'm not surprised, because traffic in my area has gotten out of hand. I'm happy to be home working in my now-married daughter's old bedroom-turned-office.

Commuting to work has become a problem. What used to be a pleasant half-hour drive listening to a favorite CD or radio station has turned into a road-rage-filled free-for-all to the office, where other people sit at their desks snarling after a similar experience. This is not a good way to start or end the day.

It's been more than a year since I worked full-time and had to drive in rush-hour traffic, but I haven't forgotten what it's like. And if I ever did forget, all I'd have to do is listen to my husband or daughter Lauren and they'd remind me; they still have to deal with it.

I had some harrowing experiences while commuting. I saw road rage on a daily basis. People cut each other off, tailgated, and made obscene gestures. At times, I wondered if these people were always this way or if they acted out only when they were behind the wheel. Once I was rear-ended while stopped at a traffic light. Fortunately, there was minimal damage to both cars. I have to admit to a little fear after that. I held my breath at each light, watching in the rearview mirror and praying that the car behind me would stop.

There are so many things that can get us into trouble—things much worse than fender benders—and we constantly need to remember who we are as Christians. Focusing on the big picture of our desire for eternal life with our Father in heaven should be enough. When people offer that crude, all-too-familiar hand sign as they blow past us on the road, we need to take a few seconds and pray for them rather than get as upset as they are. If we're keeping Christ at the center of our lives, all the traffic in the world shouldn't rattle us. It's just a small, insignificant blip on the screen. * DM

Life of Fullness

Let your light so sine before men, that they may see your good works,
and glorify your Father which is in heaven.

MATTHEW 5:16 KJV

When I first met Leota Campbell, she was tall and gaunt, and in appearance she could have passed for a woman of a century earlier. She didn't wear makeup. Her gray hair was combed back from her forehead and gathered in a bun at the nape. Her garments were plain. As long as she was clean and neatly dressed, she took no interest in the latest styles. Yet after I spent several days following her footsteps, I realized that her lifestyle exemplified inner beauty. She personified the saying "Beauty is as beauty does."

Leota was a beautiful woman to those who knew her, because her inner beauty glorified the works that she performed. A native of Kentucky, Leota came to West Virginia to teach in the public schools, but she is best known for her many years of service as a Baptist missionary in the southern counties of the state.

In 1985 I was privileged to compile a biography of Leota, which was sold by the American Baptist Women of West Virginia and the proceeds used to establish a trust fund in Leota's honor. Interest on the original investment continues to further the education of young people from the area where Leota served. Even after her death, Leota's beauty lives on in the achievements of those she influenced.

I interviewed several people as I worked on that project and found that those who knew Leota best were good at describing her beauty. Here are some quotations taken from the biography:

Cathy Blankenship, a young woman whom Leota led to the Lord, remembers that, "At Easter, she wears the oldest things she has, for if someone comes to church who doesn't have anything new, she doesn't want them to feel out of place."

A close friend, Emma Eastes, said, "Leota is more like Jesus than anybody I've ever known. She lives in a little trailer, doesn't care to keep up with the Joneses, and doesn't worry about meals. Her main concern is her ministry."

People learn to pray by hearing her pray.

New Christians learn the way a Christian should live by watching Leota. In word and deed, she is an example.

Her ministry is to the poor, the hurt, the downtrodden. So was His. As His, her ministry is caring for people no one else would care for.

Mrs. Ernest Gardner, a pastor's wife, recalled the witness of Leota in the aftermath of a flood in the southern part of West Virginia in 1977 when the Tug Fork River flooded and numerous residents lost their homes. "Leota gave Bibles, storybooks, and literature to the children. At one place, a child picked up some jelly beans off the floor and gave them to us. I didn't eat mine, but Leota popped them in her mouth and ate them, rather than hurt the child's feelings. And the floor never gets too messy for her to get down on her knees. She probably doesn't even notice that the house is dirty or the furnishings out of place—she sees the person."

Leota had many fears, worries, and frustrations, and when I first knew her I considered these to be incongruous with her strong faith and belief in prayer. However, I finally realized that her triumph over those fears made her more of a blessing than if she had no inhibitions or doubts.

She always described herself as "only a clay vessel," but that vessel was a beautiful one because the lump of clay was molded by the Master's hand.

In one of her poems, Leota summed up her life:

Only an earthen lamp
No beauty of design
Come, fill me, Holy Spirit,
Let Christ's glory shine.

* GF

Give Me a Sign!

He rescues and he saves; he performs signs and wonders
in the heavens and on the earth.

DANIEL 6:27

Did you ever notice how the Lord sets up road signs along the highways of our lives? I think this was one of my earliest revelations about my faith walk: Pay attention, and God will lead.

I'm one of those people who gets lost pretty much everywhere I go. I'm sort of known for it. For this reason, one of my closest friends has taken on the role of GPS in my life. If I'm headed somewhere new, he'll often send me an email with written directions that read something like this: "Take a left at Robertson Avenue. The street sign there is obscured, so it sneaks up on you, but you'll know it by the Shell station on the corner." David knows that the little details can make or break me.

Jesus knows this about me too.

Early on in my writing career, I only knew that I wanted to write. I had a very clear vision of the day my Creator crafted me for future life, whispering into my ear what He would have me do: "Writer." But that's where the clarity ended. I took a disorganized cluster-bomb approach, tossing everything I had at the wall to see if anything might stick. I tried writing sexy romance novels, scary suspense, screenplays, short stories, magazine articles, even advertising copy. If an opportunity arose to put words on a page, I engaged.

How many times have you asked, "Why did You put this desire and ability in me only to have it waste away without success?" After a gazillion instances where I asked that very question, it occurred to me that He is not a God who wastes words. If He'd really breathed *"Writer"* into me, He may have actually had a plan for me to accomplish it.

With that revelation, I began to watch the signs more closely. If an opportunity arose, I prayed, weighed, considered, asking, "What is my final destination?" *To serve God through my writing.* "How do I get there?" *By watching for the signs that lead me down that specific road.* For many writers, magazine articles and jingles make sense as part of their journey. For me and my path, however, that isn't the case. It was a long, messy road to this focus, but two years after I reached it, I sold my first romantic comedy to the inspirational market. WELCOME TO YOUR DESTINY. *At last.*

Situations often arise that require me to unfold the map again, measuring opportunity against final outcome: "Does this contribute to my journey?" If so, great! If not, I have to find a way to do what we women often have a hard time doing—I must say "No, thank you; that's not for me" and be on my way. With this kind of focus about where I'm headed, I'm able to make solid decisions that won't waste precious time and energy or break my stride. * SDB

Even Muddy Water?

But Jesus said to him, "Do not forbid him, for he who is not against us is on our side."

LUKE 9:50 NKJV

I happened to overhear a singer on TV belting out something about being baptized in muddy water. Curious, I paused at making dinner.

After all, it's not often you hear about getting washed clean in amazing grace on primetime.

"This is way too electric for me," my husband complained from his recliner. He held up the remote, intending to change the channel.

"Hold on. I want to hear."

"It's bad music."

"Listen to the words," I argued. "It's a redemption song." He grudgingly acquiesced.

The singer, who I later learned was Trace Adkins, crooned in his deep, rusty voice about how he hadn't been living like he "oughta" and how he wanted to drown that part of him in "muddy wata" (i.e., get baptized in the river behind his hometown's country church).

When Mr. Adkins and his band finished playing the tune (which, I thought, had quite the moving melody), I felt rather inspired. A second later, four people who are exceptionally near-and-dear to me came to mind. I knew they listened to country music on a regular basis. I'd been praying for them for years. They had walked away from God and lost their faith.

But there's always a way back. It just takes a rotation of the thought process. But how does that start? How does a person begin changing his or her thinking? I know how it happened for me—and keeps happening—but what about my loved ones?

Hearing the song, I wondered what would happen if these four special people heard this tune and realized they needed a little muddy water, too? Could God really use a country-western hit that was "way too electric" for my husband to reach them?

Immediately I was reminded that nothing is impossible for God (Luke 1:37). He can use people, places, songs, and inanimate objects as a sort of loving tap on the shoulder to say, "Follow Me.... My yoke is easy and My burden is light.... I am the way, the truth, and the life..." (Luke 5:27, Matthew 11:30, John 14:6 NKJV).

I felt encouraged. It's true: God can use whatever He pleases...

Yep, even muddy water! * AB

A Quiet Place

Then, because so many people were coming and going that they did not even have a chance to eat, he said to them, "Come with me by yourselves to a quiet place and get some rest."

MARK 6:31

Now that I've reached my fifties, I truly understand the meaning of a quiet place. When my kids were young, this place of complete and utter silence was a magical land of which I merely dreamed. Many of you can identify with that. You haven't experienced quiet since 1995.

Life is noisy. Kids, cars, barking dogs, the hustle-and-bustle of life—all noisy. Even in Jesus's day, this was the case. I can imagine the sounds of bleating sheep, people negotiating in the marketplace, camels stirring, the *clip-clop* of donkeys' hooves, mothers warning young children to stay close, children squealing and laughing, the thump of sandals upon hard ground.

Crowds followed Jesus and His disciples. Scores of people crushed them on every side, eager to hear the Good News. The people had needs. Some were curious. Some were hungry for Truth. Some were spies. No doubt the disciples were emotionally drained and physically spent.

Jesus called them to a quiet place for rest.

We have a small courtyard in front of our house that I have filled with plants and flowers that burst with blooms in May. A wooden bench is nestled within this garden sanctuary, and I love to take my journal and sit out there… in the quiet. Well, it's not exactly quiet. Nature plays a

symphony in the mornings, which I love. I'm surrounded by the sound of jubilant birds announcing the start of a new day. The sun eagerly bids me a happy hello, while my plants shine with the polish of morning. I call it my retreat. My getaway. *My quiet place.* It's where I go to talk with my Lord and praise Him for the gift of a new day. To relish the quiet, gentle moments with Him before the demands of the day take over.

Do you have such a place?

Sometimes we have to get creative. For busy moms, a quiet place may consist of a bathroom break, an early morning closet appointment, a cup of tea at the table during nap time.

But here's something else I've learned. Even in the chaos of a busy day, I can retreat to my quiet place, my inner soul, where no one else goes but God and me. I can share a whispered moment of conversation with my Lord, no matter where I am at the time, and calm immediately drifts through my spirit like an inner tube on a lazy river.

Quiet moments are waiting in unexpected corners, rooms, and heart chambers. You need only to look for them, long for them, and go to them. Meet Him in the quiet places of your heart. It will make all the difference in your day. * DH

Scenic Overlook

Fools show their annoyance at once, but the prudent overlook an insult.
PROVERBS 12:16

If sixty is the new fifty and charcoal is the new black, is rude the new polite?

I watch HGTV when I'm in the kitchen. It helps to keep my mind off what sometimes takes on an air of drudgery—making a meal. I love to cook, especially the day after grocery shopping when the pantry and fridge are full of interesting possibilities. But I must admit, the responsibility doesn't always produce joy. Sometimes it screams, "Do I have to?"

I've seen several episodes of *House Hunters, House Hunters International, My First Place,* and other shows where prospective buyers view houses and condos before purchase. Watching is a geography lesson, an architectural lesson, a cultural lesson, and a lesson in "Whatever happened to common courtesy?"

The young couple from the East Coast looking to buy their first bungalow declares that their first place must have four bedrooms, three baths, a pool, a walk-in closet, granite countertops, and outdoor space. When they walk through the first showing, the young woman says, "I hate that color. Oh, this wallpaper is hideous!" The young man says, "They call this a garage?"

Contrast that with the British couple looking to purchase a vacation home in the south of France. Never losing their contented expressions, the couple picks their way through the rubble of a fixer-upper to the tenth power, making comments like, "This is a bit of a tight spot, isn't it?" "I should think a coat of paint would freshen this room a mite." "No indoor facilities? Well, that will take a moment of getting used to."

Yes, the British seem to have a natural grace about their approach to life, but the contrast makes me wonder how it became okay with many Americans to drop politeness in favor of brash annoyance.

We act as if a line of more than two in front of us is a personal insult. We fling names at those who irritate us by committing offenses as "large" as jamming the photocopier or taking the last cookie.

And our unspoken goal seems to be speed of annoyance. The faster we react, the more scathing our response, the stronger we are? Not according to God's Word. It's a fool who shows his annoyance at once. The smart ones, the strong of character, by God's standards, are those who choose to overlook an insult.

That probably means I should overlook the fact that my husband ate three bites of the pork chops I made last week and said, "Did you…did you do something different with the seasoning on these?"

"No. I used the same spice blend I used on the pork roast you liked so much last Sunday. Why?"

He scrunched his nose. "These taste weird."

When I said the meat seemed okay to me, he offered that maybe my taste buds were out of whack because of my head cold.

I think I'll overlook that. * *CR*

She Done Him Way Wrong

As for you, you meant evil against me; but God meant it for good.

GENESIS 50:20 NKJV

I can't imagine how Joseph felt when his jealous brothers sold him into slavery. Then his situation went from bad to worse when Potiphar's wife (Joseph's master's wife) tried to seduce him. Joseph refused, saying, "How then can I do this great wickedness, and sin against God?" (Genesis 39:9 NKJV). The woman was angered that she couldn't persuade him to sleep with her and, in spite, told her husband that Joseph attempted to rape her. Joseph was sent to prison (Genesis 39:10–20).

At the end of this biblical account, Joseph was reunited with his brothers, who begged his forgiveness. Joseph (a powerful man at that time) didn't order them to be publicly flogged, although he could have. Rather, Joseph forgave his brothers, saying, "You meant evil against me; but God meant it for good" (Genesis 50:20 NKJV).

Mind-blowing, isn't it? Divine forgiveness versus human nature's desire to retaliate? That's not to say that forgiveness always comes with a snap of two fingers. Many times forgiveness is a process, depending, of course, on the nature of the circumstance.

In her book *Counseling through Your Bible Handbook*, June Hunt writes that there are four stages to forgiveness:

1. Face the Offense: "You must face the truth of what actually happened…."

2. Feel the Offense: "Anger or even hatred toward an offender needs to be brought up out of the basement of our souls and dealt with."

3. Forgive the Offender: "You are called by God to forgive" (see Mark 11:25).

4. Find Oneness when Appropriate: "Relationships filled with resentment ultimately perish, while relationships filled with forgiveness ultimately prevail."

Did you ever ask, "How could she take him back?" or "How could he forgive her?" Well, forgiveness is an act of will powered by God's Word. It's how wives can forgive unfaithful husbands and vice versa. It's how adult children can forgive their abusive parents. This is how friends can forgive one another.

And with true forgiveness comes healing, followed by freedom, joy, peace, and most of all, the goodness of God!

* AB

Un-Ring That Bell

See then that you walk circumspectly, not as fools but as wise.

EPHESIANS 5:15 NKJV

A dear friend of mine recently received the final papers dissolving her twelve-year marriage.

I ordered Chinese takeout and took it over to her house that night so she wouldn't be alone. I didn't know what to say to comfort her, but her weepy disposition clearly declared that she needed comforting.

"The worst part," she told me later that same evening, "is that I can tell you the exact moment when my marriage ended. And it was my fault."

Dara and her husband, Eric, argued often. But on this one occasion, they let the momentum of their disagreement build instead of taking off to separate corners. Both of them said things they shouldn't have, and both of them behaved in ways unbecoming of a couple striving toward spending their lives together.

"We didn't speak to one another for three days after that," she said. "In my frustration, I rang the bell."

"The bell?" I asked.

"The one you can't un-ring. I said I wanted a divorce."

It was a snowball rolling down a hill. Dara and Eric both shifted into OVERDRIVE and began behaving according to emotion. Eric eventually moved out, and Dara was the first to visit an attorney. Now, a year later, here she sat in a small rental apartment, wondering why she'd let it all go so horribly wrong.

Emotions can be so dangerous, especially when we don't realize that we have a choice. We can follow them and let them guide the direction of our lives, or we can choose to set our feelings aside long enough to rule them rather than allowing them to rule us.

The better part of wisdom comes in understanding that our future will be decided by the choices we make. Stepping back, cooling off, and making an informed, intelligent decision, rather than ringing a bell that can never be un-rung, will make for a much more peaceful tomorrow.
* *SDB*

A Taste of Heaven

My soul shall be joyful in the LORD; it shall rejoice in His salvation.
PSALM 35:9 NKJV

I've had some of the most annoying frustrations lately. It would be easy to blame something or someone other than myself, but deep down, I know that my circumstances are no one else's fault. We just have to take that roller-coaster dip before we soar to the highest part of the track.

Some days, everything seems to go wrong. You forgot to set the alarm clock, so you're late for work. Then you get in the car and realize that you forgot to get gas on your way home the day before, so you have to stop, making you even later. When you get to the office, you discover that everyone's in the meeting room waiting for you because [gasp!] you're the one in charge of refreshments. And guess what? You're empty-handed.

If that's not enough to put a scowl on your face, I don't know what is. However, God calls us to be joyful, and He doesn't qualify it by saying "only when things are going well" or "only when you're in church." The deepest joy isn't something that circumstances can change; it only comes from knowing Christ.

I always got joy from my children—particularly when they were obedient…or sleeping. However, they were often determined to test my patience and faith that the Lord was always with me. At times I had to stop, turn my attention toward God, and ask for His guidance in how to handle a temper tantrum or for strength to say no to a heartfelt request, without losing my joy or making my children think I didn't find pleasure in having them with me all the time.

Sometimes we can't help but smile because everything is going so well. We feel happy when we have a wonderful meal of our favorite foods in front of us. It's delightful to have the means to take the family on a relaxing vacation. And we can be downright ecstatic when we drive off the car lot in a shiny new automobile. But that's not the joy God is talking about in this verse. He wants our joy to be deeper than anything the world can affect. He wants us to feel joy in knowing that He's our salvation. He wants what is best for our souls.

Have you ever met someone who puts on a happy face when they walk into church yet frown the second they leave the building? That person knows about the joy we only get from Christ, but she allows the world to zap it to misery because she reserves her "tastes of heaven" for that hour of Sunday morning worship.

Joy is always with us through the love of Christ and His promises of eternal life with Him. * *DM*

A Life of Abandon

*And there was a woman in the city who was a sinner; and when she learned that [Jesus]
was reclining at the table in the Pharisee's house, she brought an alabaster vial of perfume, and
standing behind Him at His feet, weeping, she began to wet His feet with her tears, and kept wiping them
with the hair of her head, and kissing His feet and anointing them with the perfume.*

LUKE 7:37–38 NASB

We don't even know the woman's name. Some commentators have suggested that she was Mary, the sister of Martha, or Mary Magdalene. She could have been a prostitute or some other outcast in Jewish society. Luke just tells us that she was a sinner.

Perhaps she first saw Jesus teaching on the steps of the temple. Maybe she hid and watched at a distance as He picked up children and held them on His lap. Or maybe she talked to the woman with the issue of blood who had touched the hem of His garment and was instantly made whole.

However the woman—this *sinner*—was associated with Jesus, one thing is clear. She didn't just know *about* Him. In fact, in the midst of this dinner party at a religious leader's house, it appears she was the only one who really knew Him—the one who understood Him best.

The Bible says that when Jesus entered Simon's house, no one washed His feet. No one kissed Him or anointed His head with oil. But this lady, who was not invited to the party, showed up and threw herself at Jesus's feet, kissing them and weeping her heart out. She poured expensive ointment—presumably all she had—and wiped His feet with her hair. It was an act of both honor and total trust.

This behavior was shocking to others at the table. *If only Jesus knew what a sinner she was, Simon thought to himself, He wouldn't let her carry on so. He certainly wouldn't let her touch Him. He must not be a prophet after all!*

Even as Simon was musing on these things, Jesus read his thoughts. He tells a story about a creditor who forgives two debts, one large and one small. "Which one do you think loved him the most, Simon?" Jesus asked him. And the answer was obvious: *the one who owed the most.* Jesus went on to compare the woman to that person who owed a lot of money. He said, "Her sins, which are many, have been forgiven, for she loved much" (Luke 7:47 NASB).

There are lots of important lessons in this story, but the thing that challenges me most is Jesus' description of the woman in that last sentence: *"She loved much."*

As I read the story of this woman who bathed Jesus's feet with her perfume and tears, wiping them off with her hair, I want that kind of reckless abandon. I want to be like her, to love Him like crazy and cling to His feet, regardless of what anyone else thinks. And to do that, I have to stay aware of my need.

The key to this woman's love for Jesus seems clear by her description. She was, indeed, a sinner. She was desperately in need of a Savior—and desperately aware of it. In her need she was not so different from me or you or even the Pharisees. But what about her awareness? This woman was so aware of what she was that she was willing to do anything to have His forgiveness, His love, His peace.

I'm afraid, in my pride, there are times I'm more like a Pharisee—blind to how needy I am. Once in a while, in severe mercy, the Lord pulls back the curtain and shows me just how ugly my heart can be. It's scary. In those moments, nothing else matters but Him. There's no other option but to fall at His feet, to throw myself on the altar of His love. I must honor His holiness, and I must trust Him not to turn me away.

I believe that's the message of this woman's life, and that's where I want to stay. * *GF*

Shalom to Your Nefesh!

The LORD replied, "My Presence will go with you, and I will give you rest."

EXODUS 33:14

I pulled another all-nighter last night and spent a few of those hours playing my favorite Bible game. It's where I close my eyes, open to any page, let my forefinger draw circles in the air, then come to rest on a random passage. I'm always astounded at how God uses this as a means to answer prayer or guide decisions. (Or keep me awake when I have deadlines to meet!)

So, last night, when verse after verse about the Sabbath presented itself, I was confused, because it wasn't Sunday. Was the Lord trying to tell me to pray for my dear Jewish friend, who celebrates every *Shabbat* as if it's Christmas or Easter?

Like her ancestors (and you and me), Shalva accepts as truth that we each have a *nefesh*, or soul. She also sees the world as a giant ticking clock that threatens to steal the calm and serenity required to draw close and commune with Him—not surprising for a woman whose very name means *tranquility*. Shalva is adamant in her belief that all God's children need to obey His command to spend the Shabbat seeking the peace and quiet required to rest our tired spirits and renew our bodies.

After a phone call assured me that all was well in Shalva's world, I explained the real reason for my call. "So," she said, laughing, "He used me well, then." I didn't get it and said so. "Please," came her good-natured retort, "with

the schedule you keep? I'm sure He's trying to make you understand that we *all* need to sleep. Why, even God Himself rested on the Sabbath!"

"But it isn't Sunday," I repeated.

Instead of the Old Testament references I expected to hear, she told me about a book she had read, written by her friend who'd recently returned from a church-sponsored trip to Africa. The missionaries hired natives to help carry supplies and made excellent time on the first leg of their journey. On the second morning, however, the men refused to move—a major disappointment to the eager-to-spread-the-word Christians. When asked why they insisted upon sitting and resting, their leader explained that because they'd moved too fast the day before, they needed to wait for their souls to catch up with their bodies.

"It's about balance," Shalva said in her quiet way. "It's important to allow ourselves to recover from life's too-fast pace…and it doesn't *always* have to happen on a Sunday."

Yes, even God Himself rested on the Sabbath. Not because creating the world had exhausted Him, but because, like a loving Father, He hoped to teach us by example the importance of nurturing ourselves—body, mind, and soul.

Tonight, when I lay down my head and close my eyes, I know I'll smile as I wish myself "Shalom!" I'll be praying that the grace of God will envelope *you* with peace too! * *LL*

Driving Lessons

As soon as Jesus heard the word that was spoken, He said to the ruler of the synagogue,
"Do not be afraid; only believe."

MARK 5:36 NKJV

Do you believe that God can keep you safe, even during life's scariest times?

I do. I taught my sons how to drive!

For parents, our children's driver's licenses are a benchmark in life that requires praying without ceasing as we're lying in bed at night, trying to fall asleep, while our young person is out driving the car. Time after time, the Lord had to remind me (and still does) that worrying is futile and faith is vital. During these times, I like to recite Philippians 4:6–7: "Be anxious for nothing, but in everything by prayer and supplication with thanksgiving let your requests be made known to God. And the peace of God, which surpasses all comprehension, will guard your hearts and your minds in Christ Jesus" (NASB). Then the Lord tells me, "Don't be afraid; only believe."

Believing and trusting are hard work because they involve a surrendering process—a giving-up of control. Like riding in the car with your teenager, who's sitting behind the steering wheel.

One of the most frightening experiences for me occurred when I rode in the backseat while my oldest son, Ben, drove. He had just earned his regular operator's license and wanted to drive home from church. He asked me to sit in the back so my middle son, Rick, could sit in the passenger seat—so they'd both look cool. I never knew such fear, sitting there in the backseat of my '88 black Ford Escort. But Ben and Rick sure did look cool.

"Slow down, Ben," I instructed with my heart pounding. "You're going too fast."

"Mom, the speed limit is 40, and I'm going 35."

"It feels like 75!" I gripped the side handle and my youngest son's arm.

"Mom, chill." My son wasn't being disrespectful, he was merely exasperated.

I tried to relax. It was then that I realized the most terrifying thing: I had no control. I'd given it up to my teenage son. What was I thinking? I was now at the mercy of my child who, at the age of eighteen, thought he was invincible.

We made it home safe and sound and my three sons survived their teenage years. So did I, for that matter, but the driving lessons taught me that none of us are in control of our world except God, and nothing happens to us or our loved ones that He doesn't know about.

How remarkable that my sons learned to drive and I learned to trust the Lord that much more. * AB

Gimme, Gimme

Now it came to pass, as He was praying in a certain place, when He ceased, that one of His disciples said to Him, "Lord, teach us to pray, as John also taught his disciples."

LUKE 11:1 NKJV

Gimme one of those cookies!"

My friend's head slowly swiveled until she stared deliberately at her six-year-old son, who stood on the other side of the counter. She seemed to be burning a hole right into him, and little Ethan began to melt around it.

"Ethan David, what did you say to me?"

The boy glanced at me, and a wave of crimson moved over his face and chest. Then he looked almost pitifully at his mother.

"I'm sorry, Mommy. May I have a cookie?"

"You may. Just one." And as he timidly took an oatmeal-raisin cookie from the plate between us, she added, "What do you say?"

"Thank you."

"And?"

"And excuse me."

Alison had taught her son well. He knew better than to barge into the kitchen, interrupt a conversation we were having, and demand a cookie—but Ethan's six-year-old enthusiasm had gotten the better of him. When he was reminded to step back and think about what he'd been taught, however, he was able to produce the desired results as well as please his mother.

We've been taught how to pray. We know that there is a certain etiquette to our prayers, but not a script. The Lord's Prayer guides us through.

First, there is gratitude and reverence for our God (*"hallowed be Thy name"*); then there is submission to His plan for our lives (*"Thy will be done"*); and we confess our sins, knowing that He is just and loving and willing to forgive (*"forgive us our trespasses"*); and so forth.

As in all things in life, there is a method to God's teachings and an inexplicable joy for the spirit when those teachings are engrained upon our hearts. Like Ethan, we may often burst into prayer with our frustrations and earthly desires, but there is a joy in entering first with praise for a loving and forgiving God who wants to hear about our hopes and dreams, even though He already knows every one of them intimately. * *SDB*

No Pain, No Gain

A happy heart makes the face cheerful, but heartache crushes the spirit.
PROVERBS 15:13

Have you ever walked through the valley of the shadow of death? Really been heartsick over what life has dealt? I've been there, and sometimes a Bible verse can be wielded at you like a weapon, not as one to give one hope. Oh, sure, people mean well, but we cannot go through our dark times next to people who tell us we deserve it. *Uh, I think you wanted Job's house next door, thanks.*

I was twenty-nine when I was diagnosed with multiple sclerosis. I'd gone blind one night; my eyes were jumping like the vertical hold on an old TV gone bad. Being an optimist, I was determined to fight this with everything I had. But to get my eyesight back, the "cure" was steroids via infusion followed by a long, tapering dose of more steroids.

These aren't the pretty steroids that make you bulky and muscular. No, these make you plump like a Ball Park hot dog, morph your face into a shade of violet blueberry, and, as an added bonus, give you acne like you've hit puberty. I still cannot stand to see pictures of myself during that time because I remember how sick I felt, how utterly lacking in energy I was.

During that time, I tried the MS "diet," exercise, and having my church anoint me with oil and pray for me. One day at church, a complete stranger came up to me and said, "You have MS because you have unconfessed sin in your life."

Honestly, my first thought was, "So do you. Why aren't you sick?"

Something about that statement, however, freed me to really trust that God was with me through all this. It gave me a cheerful heart because I laughed at the ridiculousness of walking up to a total stranger and saying something so negative. I wish now I'd said, "Hey, that's helpful. How about if you bring a meal over on Tuesday, O prophetic one?"

There are always things that will bring you down in this lifetime: sickness, death, breakups, losing your job. Some days you won't feel like laughing, and that's okay. King Solomon said, "Sorrow is better than laughter, because a sad face is good for the heart" (Ecclesiastes 7:3).

It's been fifteen years since I first went blind, and I haven't had that kind of attack since. I'm still walking—running, on a good day—still driving. I'm still working through the symptoms of MS, but I don't regret it for a moment. The sadness of being sick gave me more compassion. It taught me that sometimes we have to lean on others, and most importantly, it made me appreciate good health. * *KB*

Modeling Mercy

Be kind and merciful, and forgive others, just as God forgave you because of Christ.
EPHESIANS 4:32 CEV

Our world applauds the people we call role models. We have sports figures creating foundations for troubled youth, Hollywood celebs traveling the globe speaking out for the underprivileged, and everyday citizens doing their part to better their communities.

Would others consider you a role model and look up to you for the way you treat those around you? Sure, you've got your weaknesses, but overall do you reflect Jesus's kindness and mercy? Or when someone pushes your buttons, do you tend to respond with unkind words or simmer inside, even with vengeful thoughts? Maybe it's the coworker who makes you look incompetent or the fan who bashes your kids' sports team. Or perhaps it's your forgetful spouse, your disobedient children, or a thoughtless friend.

Spending time alone with Jesus is the best preparation to model His gentle and gracious character to the world around you. Getting to know God's temperament and reading how Jesus interacted with others will encourage you to extend compassion and forgiveness, especially to those with whom you'd rather even the score. Jesus's graceful words, "Father, forgive them," may well be the three most important words to guide you in upholding your reputation as a merciful God-follower. * *SGES*

Put Down That Remote

*I, even I, am he who blots out your transgressions for my own
sake and remembers your sins no more.*

ISAIAH 43:25

Hello, my name is Trish, and I'm a DVR addict.

Honestly, I don't know how I managed my ever-important television viewing before I had the amazing abilities of the Digital Video Recorder at my fingertips.

If a hot news story comes on while I'm taking a phone call, I can relax, knowing I can rewind to catch the news after I finish talking.

If I can't tell what a character just said because he's too cool to enunciate, I can not only rewind, but I can turn on captioning, letting my machine figure everything out for me and spoon-feed me my entertainment.

If I want to see how a particular special effect is accomplished, I can rewind and play it back frame by frame, until I thoroughly analyze the technique used to fool me into believing what the director would have me believe.

Best of all, if someone walks between me and the television right in the middle of something riveting, it doesn't matter. I remain calm, pick up my remote, rewind, and watch it again.

I wasn't always so attached to my DVR. The addiction crept up on me slowly. I learned how dependent I had become when I went to the theater with my son. It was a sci-fi film, and my mind wandered during an explanation that was important to the plot. So I started to ask my son to rewind for me before I caught myself. I realized that whatever I hadn't heard was lost forever. Or at least until I could rent the movie and watch it at home while clutching my DVR remote.

Aren't you relieved that God doesn't view our lives and behavior that way? I mean, clearly He has total control over the time-space continuum, so if He were inclined, He could glance back at any point in my life and review my bad choices, my appalling behavior, my sins. He could gel in His mind the times I completely disregarded or dishonored Him. He could easily compile a list of reasons why I shouldn't be of any concern to Him, not here on earth or forever in heaven.

But He chooses not to do that. He loves us that much.

And what I truly cherish is this: today's verse is from a book of the Bible written some seven hundred years before Christ's birth. Yet my sins—which break my heart and His—are "blotted out" today and every day, even though God has it within His infinite power to rewind and recollect them without a moment's effort. How?

Someone walks between God and me in order to block what God prefers to forget. Someone sacrificed everything so His Father would always see the best in me. * *TP*

Bridge Over Troubled Moving Vans

My yoke is easy and my burden is light.

MATTHEW 11:30

When word finally came back that everything was in order and approved and I was actually going to take ownership of the house I wanted, a whole new set of challenges arose for me. I realized I was going to have to actually *MOVE!*—even though I was in pretty precarious physical health.

I wasn't too worried at first because I'd put together a plan, and anyone who knows me knows how much I love a good plan! I have several local friends who would no doubt offer an hour here or there to help me pack, who would perhaps be willing to help me move things around to keep it orderly. After all, when Carrie Bradshaw moved, her friends made it a three-day group affair, right?

You know the dividend of assumptions, right? Not one of those friends offered to help at all. I was stunned. There were family commitments and tight schedules and basic life to take care of, and my struggles were left completely to my own devices to solve. Suddenly this massive blessing for which I was so grateful transformed into one of the biggest burdens of my life. I was completely overwhelmed. Wasn't the burden supposed to be *light*?

One evening, my childhood friend, Marian, called from Ohio. "I was thinking I might fly down around the time of the move," she said, "so I can be there to help you get settled." And of course I immediately burst into tears. I'm a crier. That's how I roll.

The rest of the work in preparation for the move seemed easier somehow, just by knowing that on the other end, Marian would be there. The night before the moving van was to arrive, I sat in my car at the airport as I waited for her flight to land and held back another flow of grateful tears.

Once we were back at the old house and surrounded by boxes, Marian and I chattered on about my hopes for the new place. And before we turned in for the night, my precious friend asked me, "What do you need me to do tomorrow before the movers come?"

There's an old saying about a burden shared no longer being an actual burden. Marian is the embodiment of that truth. By thinking with her heart and listening with her spirit, she unselfishly answered a need for me that eased my considerable load.

Before she left to go back to Ohio, I asked her if she knew she'd been the manifestation of answered prayer. She simply smiled. I don't think she'd really thought of it that way, which of course makes her all the more special as the answer to my prayers. * *SDB*

A Life of Resurrection

Very truly, I tell you, unless a grain of wheat falls into the earth and dies,
it remains just a single grain; but if it dies, it bears much fruit.

JOHN 12:24 NRSV

The theme of resurrection is the heart of Christianity. We stake everything on the fact that Jesus died for us and rose to live again. As a child, I grasped that truth and received salvation by faith. But it wasn't until later that I began to learn that the theme of Jesus's death and resurrection is played out in our daily lives over and over as we grow in a relationship with God.

The biggest death I've ever suffered professionally was the loss of a job I loved. After changing my major from biology to English, attending law school, and teaching, I believed I'd finally found my niche when I was hired as a writer for a Christian company. I spent a year being trained, investing in relationships, getting perfect evaluations, and reveling in the creative opportunities the position afforded. I thought I would work there forever. Then one day out of the clear blue sky, I was called into a meeting and told that my position had been eliminated; I had two weeks to clean out my desk. My boss seemed truly pained to relay the information, but there was nothing he could do. The company was downsizing.

I was crushed. Looking back now I can see that, among other things, I was very naive. Clueless as to how the corporate world operated. But I was also about to learn an important spiritual lesson that would serve me well for the rest of my life.

A friend and coworker met me outside after the meeting in which I was terminated. Our building was located near a field that bordered a wood, and there was a little path between the two. A fence separated the path from the wood.

We walked down the path in stony silence, both lost in a world of our own thoughts. Mine were a haze of pain and confusion, and I imagine that his were focused on how to help. We sat down together on a bale of hay at the edge of the meadow.

I do not remember anything that was said as we sat there, but I remember looking up through my tears and seeing a deer standing in the meadow. It was looking at me with eyes that burned like coals. As my friend and I stared at the deer, it suddenly started running toward us, gliding, really, across the field. It seemed it might run right over the top of us, but neither my friend nor I felt afraid. Just to the side of the hay bale, it turned and leapt—no, soared—over the fence and disappeared into the forest behind us. My friend and I sat gaping in awe.

After a time, he spoke first. "That deer is a sign to you, Gwen. I believe you are to view this experience of losing your job as that fence, with you as the deer. Soar past the death you feel today into the resurrection life God has for you, and do not look back."

It took awhile for me to see any fruit from the seed that was planted that day. It had to die and be hidden in a dark place. It had to be watered and sprout into a plant, and now that plant constantly has to be pruned. But the fact that you are reading this book today is proof of the resurrection that has taken place in my life.

God's way with us many times is through death, but He never intends to leave us there. Jesus came to lead us in resurrection life, onward and upward. * *GF*

It's All Relative

"Because he loves me," says the LORD, "I will rescue him;
I will protect him, for he acknowledges my name."

PSALM 91:14

Perspective has a lot to do with how we handle the victories and failures we encounter along the way. And I believe that perspective's greatest influence comes by grace— the kind of grace that changes our landscape.

Have you ever faced a mountain so big that you found yourself just sitting there and staring at it rather than figuring out a way to cross it? Perhaps you arrived at the base of that mountain by way of a bad medical report, the loss of a loved one, or an unfathomable betrayal. Whatever the source of your obstacle, at first blush, your initial reaction probably involved surrender. Most of us are programmed that way. Even if we don't stay in surrender mode, the inclination is most definitely there. But then something happens, doesn't it?

I like to think of that "something" as grace provided by a God who knew all about the mountain before we ever turned the corner to face it. In the middle of the night, an answer comes. Or after days of tears and anxiety, a new day dawns and there is a change of heart, a shift of perspective. It's supernatural, isn't it?

I love the story of young David. While everyone else was devastated at the thought of a giant, talking to one another about certain defeat and the possibility of surrender, David had a revelation that came by the very grace of God.

"I think I know the answer!" he may have exclaimed. "I know how to scale the mountain before us!"

Oh, how they must have laughed at him. This audacious little squirt with a sling and a stone was going to slay the giant? Was he joking, or simply insane? Talk about delusions of grandeur!

While everyone else had decided the giant was just too big to defeat, the Lord supplied David with a very different perspective. Yes, the giant was big. But the good news: he was too big to miss. And so that little upstart with the big vision picked up a stone, loaded his sling, and with one shot he took the mighty giant down. Can you imagine the noise of the impact when that giant hit the ground, beneath the thunder of celebration from all the naysayers?

The next time you're faced with an unanticipated mountain—or a really, really big giant—try to look at it from a different angle. What can you learn from this? What purpose does this giant serve in your life? The limitless grace of God is going to carry you through the battle. And the best part of it all is that every battle serves a purpose. Maybe, like David, you'll emerge on the other side to find that it has played some integral part in the overall plan God has for your life. * SDB

Zip It!

Therefore you are inexcusable, O man, whoever you are who judge,
for in whatever you judge another you condemn yourself; for you who judge practice
the same things. But we know that the judgment of God is according to truth
against those who practice such things. And do you think this, O man,
you who judge those practicing such things, and doing the same,
that you will escape the judgment of God?

ROMANS 2:1–3 NKJV

*D*id you hear about Connie Cubicle? I heard that she was written up because she spent all day surfing the Internet at the office."

"I heard that Mr. and Mrs. Rotten Neighbor were getting a divorce and she took off without the kids."

"Can you believe that Suzie Shortskirt came to work dressed like *that*?"

Or how about, "*My* kids would *never* do that"?

I can't even count the times I've looked at someone else and judged them when they (1) wore something too tight/too short/too gaudy, (2) let their kids throw temper tantrums in public, (3) did something unethical on the job, or (4) made a bad decision in a relationship. It's bad enough to judge these people in my own mind, but what makes it worse is when I tell someone what I'm thinking.

That's gossip.

No one wants to think of themselves as a gossip, but anytime we talk about someone else with an ounce of judgment, that's exactly what it is. Now, my question is, who is so perfect that they're above being judged?

Not me, that's for sure.

How about when someone tells you they know something no one else knows about the person on the other side of the office wall, and they're dying to share it with you? Whenever I hear this, I mentally rub my hands together, round my shoulders like a raccoon ready to dive into a Dumpster, and prepare myself for some juicy tidbits that'll make me feel superior.

That's gossip, too.

Even when we aren't the ones spreading the information, we're just as guilty of gossip when we listen to it because we're providing the opportunity for those who do the talking. It might make us feel good to be in-the-know for a little while, but that feeling doesn't last long. After a day or two, it plays on our minds and in our hearts, making us feel dirty and slimy—whether we're the ones spreading the gossip or the person on the receiving end.

It's just wrong, either way.

Every day, I need to focus on how I can help others rather than bring them down, no matter how much short-lived fun it is to talk about them. When someone says something judgmental about another person, I should try stopping the negativity and turning it around to see if there's something we can do to make things better. That's what God would want us to do. * *DM*

Gloriously Inefficient

The LORD will vindicate me; your love, LORD, endures forever—
do not abandon the works of your hands.

PSALM 138:8

I could have been an efficiency expert. I dislike grocery shopping because of the inefficiency of it. Pick an item off the shelf and put it into the grocery cart. Lift same item—and a hundred of its cousins—out of the cart and onto the checkout conveyor belt. Load them from the conveyor into bags and into the cart again. Already, the redundancy appalls me. Push the cart across the parking lot and unload those same groceries to the trunk of the car. Once home, haul those miserable bags of tonnage into the house, unpack each of the bags, and handle those grocery items yet again to find them spots in the cupboard, fridge, or freezer.

In what factory would that plan pass inspection? Any efficiency expert worth her clipboard would suggest that handling an item so many times is the height of *dummkopfness*.

That may be why my husband's idea of an ideal vacation gets check marks in the "You're Kidding, Right?" column on my clipboard. Oh, the inefficiency! Collect a bunch of fishing and canoeing equipment for weeks in the garage and a corner of my dining room (yes, ladies), cram it all into the truck, strap a canoe on top so you'll have a nice, high-pitched whistling sound to accompany the trip, drive forever past some perfectly good lakes and rivers until you get to the "right" one, pile the equipment into the canoe, paddle until just this side of the edge of the earth, unload the canoe, haul the equipment up Extreme Sports cliff faces to a relatively flat piece of granite, set up camp, sleep a minute, tear down camp, load it all into the canoe—and you see my point.

Even the grunts in a tennis match seem an energy drain my birthing coach would nix. I load the dishwasher while talking on the phone. I clean the top of the washing machine while filling it. I don't buy shirts that need ironing…or that might *potentially* need ironing if, say, left in the dryer too long. I don't like single-function kitchen tools. If it can't do more than one thing, it doesn't stay. Efficiency is the key.

Or is it?

It's hard to listen when efficiency is the goal. Compassion and efficiency don't mix well; compassion takes time. Grace sometimes requires excess movement—leaning in farther than halfway, stepping around piles of regret, dropping every other important responsibility to attend to the messy need of a human heart…

How many times have I missed a moment when the Lord's purpose for me was to make me gloriously inefficient? * *CR*

We Are Family

Ruth replied, "Don't urge me to leave you or to turn back from you.
Where you go I will go, and where you stay I will stay. Your people will be my people and your
God my God. Where you die I will die, and there I will be buried."

RUTH 1:16–17

My friend Jemelle is always the coolest person in the room. She's beautiful; she's straight-out-there, in-your-face direct; and she's a closet comedienne. I like to say she's a Hollywood A-Lister on the outside with the heart of a true Southern belle.

That's how I describe her *now*. When I met her on the first day of training for the only job I could find when I left California and moved to Florida, it was a completely different story.

I was out of my element, insecure about my new surroundings and feeling a little deflated about the turn my life had taken. I'm sure that had something to do with my perception that *Miss Thing* had judged me as *The Loser* in the room. I had no interest in getting to know her, but in that way God often has of moving us around like chess pieces so an opportunity can present itself, we just kept crossing paths. And it didn't take long for me to realize how wrong I'd been.

My mom's death closed the door on *family* for me, but Jemelle started including me in her holiday celebrations.

For Christmas Eve festivities, Easter dinners, the obligatory Southern tradition of black-eyed peas on New Year's Day, I'm at the Nelson-Tola family table. When I feel the most alone, confused, or frightened, Jemelle is one of the first people I call. When something wonderful happens, she's who I want to tell. She doesn't always say what I hope she will, but most of the time she is my soft place to fall when I need one the most. I adore her parents, Dot and Bud, and they've embraced me into the fold without hesitation.

Jemelle and her amazing husband adopted a little girl and named her Olivia. A year after that, they brought Nico home. Just as they opened their arms and offered family warmth to me when my blood ties had dissolved, Jemelle and Alberto wanted to give two more lost souls a soft place of their own. In the same way that the blood of Jesus grafts us all into His family, these children became grafted extensions of the family that means so much to me. And as Ruth said to Naomi, I say to Jemelle, "Don't urge me to leave you…. Your people will be my people." * *SDB*

Is That You, God?

Then He said, "Go out, and stand on the mountain before the LORD."
And behold, the LORD passed by, and a great and strong wind tore
into the mountains and broke the rocks in pieces before the LORD, but the LORD
was not in the wind; and after the wind an earthquake, but the LORD
was not in the earthquake; and after the earthquake a fire,
but the LORD was not in the fire; and after the fire a still small voice.

1 KINGS 19:11–12 NKJV

I used to think God looked and sounded like the Great Oz—you know, that round white face in the movie *The Wizard of Oz* who boomed out his replies and made Dorothy quake with fear in her sparkling ruby slippers. But as my relationship with God developed, I realized that my image of Him was far from accurate.

The Bible tells us in Genesis that God made man "in His own image" (Genesis 1:27 NKJV) and that He called for Adam and Eve as He was "walking in the garden in the cool of the day" (Genesis 3:8 NKJV). After studying that verse, I believed God actually walked around, enjoying His creation. Later in that same book, the Bible states, "But the Lord came down to see the city and the tower which the sons of men had built" (Genesis 11:5 NKJV). He actually left heaven to see what was happening on earth! So much for my "white round face" theory. The truth is, God walks and talks and seeks our fellowship. Amazing!

So many people have wacky assumptions about who the person of God is and what He is like. Some picture Him as an angry God, ready to consume anybody who steps out of line. Others see Him as an impersonal but powerful spirit. But that's not how the Bible describes God. He feels our pain, shares our frustrations, rejoices in our accomplishments, and cheers when we succeed. He calms our fears, and He has promised to protect us from all that is evil. He has promised to provide for our needs, and I have personally witnessed that fact. I have learned that the God of heaven is my beloved Savior and Friend.

Some months ago my husband and I had no income, as we were both self-employed. Our savings was spent and our checking accounts were empty. We didn't have that month's mortgage payment or the car payments, and the utility bills were due. I remember crying out to God, and I heard His "still small voice" speak to my heart, saying, "Even if you lose it all, I still have a plan for you."

The reply gave me such hope and peace. I didn't have to worry myself sick about our dilemma. It all belonged to God anyway. And I believed from that day forward that the Lord would provide for my husband and me. Suddenly I couldn't wait to see what He would do!

A few weeks later, an unexpected check arrived in the mail. Daniel and I were totally amazed and extremely grateful. The sum covered our mortgage and our bills and there was even some left over!

God is able!

Those three words sound so simple, so trite, and yet they ring so true. All we need to do is open our hearts and hear Him when He speaks to us and then believe.

Shhh…are you listening? * AKB

A Life of Submission

Father...not My will, but [always] Yours be done.

LUKE 22:42 AMP

I am the mother of a very gifted child who also fits the textbook definition of "strong willed." This will is something I celebrate most of the time. I enjoy her spunk, admire her passion, and delight in her fierce loyalty and determination. I recognize the value of her strength and know that if it is properly bent—not broken—it can be a beautiful thing. I dwell in these lovely possibilities most of the time. The rest of the time I am either praying or pulling out my hair. Or both.

Yesterday was a hair-pulling day. My daughter asked me for something she wanted. It was a simple request and, I'm sure, seemed to her a very good thing. To her it was not much to ask, and I could have easily said yes. But, as her mother, I could see that it wasn't the best thing, and the answer I gave her was *no*.

A fit ensued. There was kicking and screaming and much gnashing of teeth, which had to be dealt with accordingly. After peace was restored, there was opportunity for discussion.

In my great wisdom I explained that happy obedience takes a lot of trust. "You obeyed me," I said, "but only after I disciplined you. All of the crying and resisting caused you misery and wasted precious moments of our lives. Wouldn't it have been better to cheerfully accept the answer I gave you, even if it wasn't what you wanted to hear?"

"But I wanted you to say yes," she replied. "I really wanted that, and I didn't understand why you said *no*."

I told her, "You have to trust me that I know what is best, even when you don't understand. I am your mommy, and that is one of my jobs—to know what you need and to give it to you. When I say no it's because I can see that what you want is not what you need."

This was all hard for my young daughter to digest. She wanted her own way.

"Grace," I said, feeling the irony of her name for the millionth time, "do you know that I love you very, very much?"

"Yes."

"Can you trust me to do the thing I believe is best for you—the thing that will bring about the most good in your life—because of how much I love you?"

A pause. "Yes."

"You need to think about that when you ask me for something. Then, if I say *no*, you can be just as happy as if I said yes, because you know I will only do what I believe is good for you."

She eyed me warily. Then, finally, she accepted what I was saying as the truth.

I pray that the concept, as a tiny seed, takes root somewhere in her little heart. It's a lesson she'll refer to again and again, as I was reminded that night in my prayers—another strong-willed child presenting her requests.

"Father, I really want this and this and this and this to happen. Can I have those things, Lord? You, who have infinite wisdom, can surely see how wonderful it would be. And with inexhaustible resources, You can bring it to pass, can't You, Lord? Will You? Soon?"

"I certainly can, and I may. That's for Me to decide. But what if My answer is *no*? What then? Can you trust Me, as you advised your daughter? Do you really believe that I know best?" came the still, small voice.

Humbled, I had no alternative but to practice what I had preached. I had to lay down my will before *His* perfect will and trust His love.

An old hymn puts it this way: "Trust and obey, for there's no other way, to be happy in Jesus—but to trust and obey!"
* *GF*

Is Holiness for Today?

A highway will be there; it will be called the Way of Holiness.
The unclean will not journey on it; it will be for those who walk in that Way.

ISAIAH 35:8

Holiness—that sounds like such an antiquated concept. The very word conjures up images of late-nineteenth–century women in high-necked, long-sleeved, full-length dresses and men in stiff, starched white shirts under their funereal black suits—and not a smile to be found on the women or the men.

But God does call His people to a life of holiness. What do you make of that? How can that possibly resonate with people in the twenty-first century? It helps if you break down the word "holiness" into some of its essential components, such as prayer, devotion, obedience, and humility, which have nothing to do with dress codes or a grim countenance. Quite the opposite: true holiness produces freedom and joy.

At its core, holiness is a natural result of a right attitude toward God. Are you devoted to God? When you pray, do you approach Him in an attitude of obedience and humility, and do you live out those qualities in your everyday life? Then yours is very likely a life characterized by holiness—although you'd probably object to that, since your humility wouldn't allow you to claim that description for yourself. That's fine; God sees your holiness, and His opinion is the one that counts. * SGES

I Have the Pow—wer!

Behold, I give you the authority to trample on serpents and scorpions, and over all the power of the enemy, and nothing shall by any means hurt you. Nevertheless do not rejoice in this, that the spirits are subject to you, but rather rejoice because your names are written in heaven.

LUKE 10:19–20

When my sons were little, they enjoyed watching "Masters of the Universe." These cartoons starred He-Man, who would hold up his sword to the sky and proclaim, "I have the pow—wer...." Lightning flashed, thunder rumbled, and suddenly He-Man had the ability to take on the bad guys and win.

As Christians we really do have the "pow—wer." Jesus Christ has given it to us. No situation is insurmountable for believers in Him—not even evil spirits can stand against us. But the true battlefield is in the mind and the devil's desire is to disable each one of us, rendering us weak, fearful, and useless.

One of Satan's favorite tricks is to play back those proverbial "tapes" in our head. You know, the ones that go, "You'll never amount to anything" or "You're not pretty enough." Before long we're suffocating beneath a dark cloak of discouragement.

But we can lift our sword of the Spirit, which is the Word of God (see Ephesians 6:13–17), and suddenly we can be triumphant! * *AKB*

Give Thanks in All Circumstances

Be joyful always; pray continually; give thanks in all circumstances,
for this is God's will for you in Christ Jesus.

1 THESSALONIANS 5:16–18

There are many things I can deal with in this life, but a face without eyebrows? Can I be honest here? I'm *so* not thankful for that. A bald head? We can cover that with a turban or wig. No eyelashes? Use eyeliner. No eyebrows? "Houston, we've got a problem."

Chemotherapy has brought new meaning to the phrase "blank expression." On a side note, I walked into the kitchen the other day, forgetting that my eyebrows weren't penciled in yet, and my husband saw me for the first time, eyebrow-less. The surprise in his eyes provoked an immediate response. I lifted my hand in the Star Trek sign and said in a robotic voice, "Mmmm, I am from the Planet Votar."

Call me vain, but I want eyebrows. Yes, there are worse things in life than not having eyebrows, but in my fifty-four years, I've grown rather attached to them.

Still, I have to admit that it's a challenge to draw on eyebrows. Try it sometime. You'll see what I mean. My sweet husband tried to help when he bought me some eyebrow stencils, but they were thick—Groucho Marx thick. I would have needed a Magic Marker to fill them in. Not exactly the look I was going for. The worst part of drawing on my eyebrows is that I have a problem with keeping my hands off my face. I talk with my hands.

What? Lots of people do that, don't they?

Unfortunately, that means my hands are constantly touching my face. I never realized how much I did this until one day, over lunch, when I told a story and wiped out an entire eyebrow before I'd finished my salad.

Give thanks in all circumstances? It occurs to me that the important word in that phrase is not the "all," but rather the "in." I'm not giving thanks *for* my circumstances, but rather *in* them. While I am in the midst of these circumstances, I give Jesus thanks *for who He is.* I can be thankful "in" my life's circumstances, knowing that God is in control; He loves me. He is my joy and my constant companion.

And the truth is, I can actually give thanks for the eyebrow problem, because it has helped me to laugh along this journey. You may have a bad hair day, I may have a bad eyebrow day, but all in all, it's a downright good day. Because the way I see it, anything that makes me laugh with the joy of Jesus is a good day. A very good day. * *DH*

Don't Rush Me

The Lord is not slow in keeping his promise, as some understand slowness.
He is patient with you, not wanting anyone to perish, but everyone to come to repentance.

2 PETER 3:9

C'mon, Lauren, get the lead out," I remember telling my younger daughter, who had to do one more thing before leaving for school. "They're not gonna wait for you, ya know."

"I'm coming," she said. "Just don't rush me. I'll be on time." I stormed to my car and sat there tapping my fingertips on the steering wheel, fuming, and wondering why I always had to wait for her—or anyone for that matter. It seemed like I was the only person who ever looked at a clock and took my time commitments seriously.

Lauren finally came out to the car, carrying her books in one hand and her shoes in the other, with her bag slung over her shoulder. During the fifteen-minute drive to school, she put on her shoes, finished applying her makeup, and checked to make sure she had all her homework. We were halfway to the school when she let out a soft groan. "I left the most important thing on the dining room table," she said. "Can you bring it to me before second period?"

I made some noise but finally agreed to bring it to her. After all, she was in high school, and I didn't want this one homework assignment to keep her out of college. So I dropped her off, rushed home, grabbed her paper, and went back to the school, where I left her assignment with the administrative assistant at the front desk.

The rest of my day was just as frantic, so by the time everyone came back home, I was a mess. My husband gave me a sidelong glance. "You seem out of sorts. What happened?" That was all it took to get me started. I told him how I'd felt "behind the eight ball" all day. "Just because Lauren forgot her homework?" he asked, shaking his head.

Uh…yeah. "It threw me behind by at least a half hour."

"Do you think maybe you're doing too much?" He wasn't being sarcastic. He really wanted to know. I've been a freelance writer for a very long time, and most of my schedule was self-imposed. But still….

I guess by now it must be clear that I'm not the most patient person in the world. Second Peter 3:9 is a prime example of why I need to work on that. The Lord loves each and every one of us, and He's exercising patience before returning to save us for eternity. I definitely need to follow His lead. * DM

Purified and Sanctified

He will sit as a refiner and purifier of silver.

MALACHI 3:3

One afternoon, while chatting with a dear friend and catching up on one another's lives, I told her about a time-sensitive blessing I'd been praying about for months. As the deadline grew closer, I'd begun to lose faith, and I asked her for prayer coverage as I awaited an answer to my dilemma.

"Of course I'll pray for you," she promised. "But this is always the way God deals with you, Sandie. You're that person who makes it all the way to the scary cliff, teetering right on the edge, and that's when God snatches you to safety and provides just what you need. He never seems to show up for you any sooner than absolutely necessary."

That observation really stuck with me. Was that really how the Lord chose to deal with me? I went over the last few challenges I'd faced in my life, the really big ones where I'd prayed and prayed for an answer and—*what do you know!*—that's exactly what had happened.

In the book of Malachi, we're told that God presides over us as a refiner, in much the same way that silver is purified. That connection really makes me think about the way my life unfolds during those times that I find myself questioning whether or not God might have forgotten about me.

The silversmith heats a piece of silver over the hottest part of the fire for however long it takes for the impurities to melt away. If God "sits as a refiner," does this mean that He sits there with us when we're in the hot seat, watching over us to make sure we're not there any longer than we need to be? And what happens if we are?

If the silversmith holds the precious metal over the flames too long, the silver is destroyed. His full attention is required at all times to make sure that the purifying process is thorough but that the silver is removed from the heat when it needs to be.

The vision of my Father as the silversmith, refining and improving me, is a new joy in my life that I carry with me. I refer to that mental picture all the time: He tenderly holds me over the fire, cautious not to let me fall when the heat of the battle intensifies, paying close attention to the specific impurities that need to be eliminated. At that precise moment when I've taken all I can and the fire has done its work in me, He pulls me away from the flames and looks me over. If I'm pure and clean in that one area, shiny enough to reflect His image, there is (for the moment, at least) blessed relief. With each new purification by fire, I am another step closer to ultimate perfection in Christ Jesus.

How many times have you looked into the fire and forgotten that the silversmith had you well in hand? * *SDB*

A Life of Peace

My grace is sufficient for thee.

2 CORINTHIANS 12:9 KJV

As a young mother, Ally experienced the death of someone she loved very much. Although she was a Christian and sought the Lord in the months that followed the death, Ally sank into a depression and even had thoughts of taking her own life. Thankfully, she told her doctor about her struggle and the doctor prescribed an antidepressant that, along with prayer and support from family and friends, helped Ally get back on her feet.

Ally says that her faith was challenged on many levels through this difficult time. She believes one thing the Lord did in her life was to take her to a deeper level of trust in Him—a trust that gives her peace.

"I always wanted to control things," she admits. "I thought that if I did enough, prayed enough, and read my Bible enough, everything would work out. In the case of this loss, it had nothing to do with what I could control. It just happened."

As her world seemed to spin out of control, Ally held tight to the Lord. "It wasn't easy," she says, "and finally I had to face the anger I felt toward Him for what He allowed to happen." She says that the Lord showed her that His ways are not always our ways, and peace only comes when we trust that His way is best, even when it doesn't make sense. We have to relinquish the illusion of our control and accept His sovereignty, if we want to move forward in kingdom life.

Ally says she still has moments of wanting to protect everyone she loves from bad things. "I was in bed the other night and I started to panic that something bad was going to happen to my children. I felt the Lord speak to my heart, and He didn't say that nothing bad will ever happen. He said that no matter what, He is always with me."

Elisabeth Elliot writes, "God is enough. He may not be all we would ask for, if we are honest, but He is enough." This is a tough lesson to learn, but once it becomes real in our hearts that He is enough, then our peace can never be taken away. No matter what happens. * *GF*

Are We There Yet?

So you may walk in the way of goodness, and keep to the paths of righteousness.
PROVERBS 2:20 NKJV

Every person who has ever traveled with a child has heard, "Are we there yet?" And after the first dozen or so times, the answer is almost always preceded by a sigh and what feels like a recorded answer: "Not yet. Why don't you take a nap, so the time will go by faster?"

My children were always excited to go anywhere that involved packing their little purple "I love Grandma" suitcases and loading up the car with snacks and coloring books. They were generally pretty good for the first hour or so. However, it didn't take long before we started hearing noise from the backseat—little voices whining, "Are we there yet?" "How much longer?" "I'm tired," "Tell Daddy to drive faster," or "Why is it taking so long, Mommy? Are we lost?"

No, we weren't there; it would be another four, six, or eight hours. I often said, "Daddy can't drive faster because he's already going the speed limit" and "No, we're not lost."

Since most of our trips were to one of the grandparents' houses or our favorite beach in Florida, we knew the way. As long as we stayed on the familiar roads, there was no problem in getting there. We knew that if we took a detour, we might get lost, so we rarely did that.

Every destination has its own path—some extremely popular and others not so crowded. The times in my life that I've followed the enticements of the not-so-righteous target, I've quickly learned that the fun is short-lived. After the party was over and everyone was gone, a sad, often listless feeling overwhelmed me. The popular path may look shiny and pretty, but beneath the very thin surface, I've discovered slippery mud and quicksand.

Sometimes when things get rough, I wonder why I'm "not there yet." Then there are times when I'm offered little tidbits and signs that help to keep me focused on Him. Getting there is going to be amazing, but the journey is necessary and should be appreciated.

Fortunately for all sinners, God is ready to welcome us as the best earthly father should welcome his child. Are we there yet? Not yet, but I know that my journey down this solid path is much more rewarding than any created by my sinful nature. * DM

Kids! I'm Tellin' Ya!

I will heal their waywardness and love them freely, for my anger has turned away from them.

HOSEA 14:4

My adult daughter is a phenomenal person. She's smart, savvy, and a can-do girl. She's thoroughly reliable and straight-shooting.

But as a teenager? Not so much. She was such an obedient baby and child but, mercy, things sure changed after that.

I gave birth to her brother when she turned fourteen. So she hit her teen years with a new sibling, far less attention than Mom had ever given her before, a fairly new stepfather, a new hometown, a new school, and the task of making all new friends. She had a lot to tackle, and having her hormones kick in certainly didn't add stability to the equation.

So we had a few rough years there, during which I was constantly disciplining her. And no matter how badly she had behaved, no matter how often I caught her in a lie or skipping school or "partying," no matter how upset or angry I got with her, I hated having to punish her. It was the only part of parenting I remember with sadness. But not regret.

As an adult, my daughter often laughs about what a pain in the neck she was, how bad she was. I'm able to laugh about it too, now that it's all over and we're fabulous friends.

Now, my son was a different story. His first three years just about killed me. He was a powerful little cuss, and he quickly developed unshakable opinions about what he wanted. He was never one of those kids you could distract from the light socket with a jingly toy monkey. And

tantrums? He made the Tasmanian Devil look like a *puddy tat*. So we had our rough years early, and I had to do a major upgrade on my early-learning discipline practices.

It just so happened, if you haven't yet done the math, that both my kids had their "rough" patches at the very same time in my life. So Mom was taxed to the max.

Yet when my son hit four, he started to change. He had actually accepted the Lord at three—as well as a three-year-old can—and he became the sweetest kid ever. We soon learned he was extremely smart, he had a strong moral core, and he was absolutely loving and lovable. He's now in college, and he's remained that same terrific kid, even throughout his teenage years. I honestly don't think I've had to discipline him since he was three.

Those few years during which my teenaged daughter and toddler son seemed to have conspired to drive me insane brought out the worst in me. I was worn-out, short on patience, and often angry. But I was never out of love with my challenging kids. As most parents would say, I would have fought a grizzly bear for either one of them.

No doubt I've put God in this same position. He's probably been angry and had to discipline me, but I know He's always turned His anger away from me eventually. As a parent, I understand that. As His child, I am ever thankful for it. * *TP*

When Life Gets Squirrelly...

For every beast of the forest is mine, and the cattle upon a thousand hills.

PSALM 50:10 KJV

Others might scold the squirrel who raids my bird feeders and eats more seeds than a flock of chickadees, but I enjoy his antics!

First he's a four-footed circus performer, scampering across power lines to the telephone pole to the tree near my feeder.

Next he's the Man on the Flying Trapeze, sailing through the air, aiming for the feeder...and his next free meal of black sunflower seeds.

Then he's an acrobat, hanging upside down to reach even more of the delectable treats, which are stored in a feeder that was advertised as a brand-new design and guaranteed to be "completely squirrel-proof."

Now he's the peeping Tom who stands on my windowsill, with his paws to the glass...his way of saying, "Hey, the feeder is empty."

Like the postman, he arrives in good weather and in bad, braving rain and snow and summer's blistering heat—and I can't help but admire his perseverance. As Christians, we could all do with a little of that attitude, because unlike the nutty squirrel, our God and Father answers prayers even if we don't perform silly tricks to entertain Him.

But He might just get a chuckle out of seeing me staring into His window while I wait for Him to meet my needs...
* LL

Who Is Your Barnabas?

Barnabas took him and brought him to the apostles. He told them how Saul
on his journey had seen the Lord and that the Lord had spoken
to him, and how in Damascus he had preached fearlessly in the name of Jesus.

ACTS 9:27

Last year, I wrote a blog post based on the realization that we all have a Barnabas or two in our lives—someone who steps up for the sole purpose of our advancement rather than their own. I received more email about that one post than all the others from the previous month combined.

There's something that happens when we use our spiritual eyes to look into the distance rather than focus only on our own limited sphere. I like to call my sphere SandieLand. It's that place where everything revolves around ME, and anything else that affects ME is just secondary to—you guessed it!—ME. SandieLand can be a funny little place where perspective is skewed and wise decisions are seldom made. In SandieLand, I'm epic, a legend! In my own mind. But out there in the real world…not so much.

Paul started out as a pretty bad dude. Known as Saul of Tarsus, he devoted himself to the persecution of Christ's disciples. Then one day, walking along the road and minding his own business, probably lost in thought about how to make life miserable for those ignorant Christians, the Lord appeared to him in a flood of light. It was so profound that Paul was actually blinded for a few days from it, but when his sight came around again, he was a believer. A dramatic salvation experience is life-changing! I'm reminded of my own born-again experience and the stunned reaction of my Hollywood friends when I suddenly became a very different person.

I doubt anyone would have given Paul's Christian influence the time of day if not for Barnabas staking his reputation and standing up to tell people, "Look, this guy was just in Damascus boldly preaching about Jesus Christ. I'm telling you, he's for real!"

I've had a few people like Barnabas in my life, people who helped to pave the road intended for me. I know that every one of them was a gift of grace from God, and I'm convinced that Barnabas was anointed with that same kind of mission to set the stage for Paul's sharing the Good News throughout history in his preaching as well as his New Testament writings.

Would Paul have served God without Barnabas? Almost certainly. God's grace provides answers and avenues in places where they didn't previously exist, and He inspires others to take a stand and offer a leg up for those who can't do it for themselves.

Is there a Barnabas in your life that you haven't stopped to thank? I encourage you to do that—sooner rather than later. But more importantly…how can you deliver the grace of Barnabas into someone else's life? * *SDB*

Rocky Mountain College

Therefore shall ye lay up these my words in your heart and in your soul....Ye shall teach them to your children, speaking of them when thou sittest in thine house, and when thou walkest by the way, when thou liest down, and when thou risest up.

DEUTERONOMY 11:18–19 KJV

Cowboys and mountain men of yore weren't known for spouting philosophy or quoting Shakespeare, but a whole whoppin' bunch of 'em coulda been!

It took a long time, see, for the snow to melt and the rivers to thaw, confining them to cabins with little more to do than read. Scouring now-abandoned camps, lucky (if not nosy) tourists have stumbled upon yellowing editions of Keats, Scott, Wordsworth, James Fenimore Cooper, Jonathan Smith, and more.

Picture, if you will, a whiskered gent sipping thick black coffee by the light of an oil lantern. Shoulders cloaked by a bearskin blanket, he warms his fur-shod feet near the fire and teaches an illiterate bunkmate to read, using the Good Book as his how-to manual. They called this time, sealed away from civilization as they were, days at Rocky Mountain College.

Like those miners and buckskinners, I've survived many a bitter winter in much the same way, though admittedly my boots are faux fur and the blanket around my shoulders is microsuede. And though I'm usually free to hop into my trusty car and blaze the trails laid out by snowplows and salt trucks, the power lines have fallen enough times that I can readily identify with having to read by the light of a kerosene lamp, with the woodstove as my heat source.

Books are like friends, all with different looks and scents. But whether tall or fat, thin or squat, the pages bound between their covers promise to entertain, educate, enlighten, and inform. And the book that starts and ends every day—whether the snow barely covers the soles of my shoes or threatens to spill into my knee-high boots—is the Bible.

Thanks to a hearty concordance, I'm never far from solutions to my problems. Though the bowl of popcorn on my lap overflows, even the buttery-est kernels can't satisfy me in quite the same way as the stories in the gilt-edged pages of the Book.

The weather outside is snowing, but as winter gentles to spring, I hope I'll remember the verse from Jeremiah 15:16 that goes, "When your words came, I ate them; they were my joy and my heart's delight, for I bear your name, O Lord God Almighty," and take comfort from unrelenting rains and summer's drought and the hurricanes of autumn…

…so I'll show the world just what a Rocky Mountain College graduate is capable of! * *LL*

A Love Eternally There

In my distress I prayed to the LORD, and the Lord answered me and set me free.
PSALM 118:5 NLT

Anyone who has experienced the joy of taking wedding vows knows how it goes: "I, [your name], take you, [his name], to be my lawfully wedded husband, to have and to hold from this day forward, for better or worse, for richer or poorer, in sickness and in health, to love and to cherish, from this day forward, until death do us part. And if things don't work out, I will be out of there so fast, my dust will blind you, buddy boy."

Uh, no. I don't know a divorced Christian woman anywhere who married with the attitude that things might not work out. Love is awesome! And Christians commit to forever. But sometimes no matter how committed we are, marriage *doesn't* work out. If yours has, you know you're blessed. If yours hasn't, you're not alone. Sometimes spouses surprise us with alcoholism, abuse, or attraction to what just ain't right. Sometimes we come home to a terse note and an empty closet.

When I came home to such a situation, I went into a bit of shock. After sixteen years of marriage—every one of which was a struggle—I scrambled to figure out how life would ever be manageable again. I prayed. I called my best friend. I opened the local paper to find out just how unemployable I had become for having trusted that God wanted me to be a stay-at-home mom. But one thing I absolutely did not do? I did not turn against God.

God was my absolute rock all through my troubled marriage. I knew my heart was a huge part of the problem. I knew my husband's heart was the other huge part of the problem. But God? He was rooting for healing the entire time. He would have loved and rewarded complete surrender from the two of us. He didn't get it.

That's a scary place for a separated wife to be: feeling like her husband left out of extreme disappointment in her... and wondering if God was equally disappointed. How far away will *He* go?

In my fear, I cried out to Him. I was hurt; I was panicked; I was anxious about the future. And most of all, I thought He might just turn His back on *me*.

Perhaps you're in that place right now. Or maybe someone you know is in that place and she needs your support and prayers. Tell her—or tell yourself—that calling on Him is absolutely necessary and fruitful. He will uphold you. He will protect you. He will set you free. * *TP*

Chasing Dreams and Chasing Tails

He who pursues righteousness and love finds life, prosperity and honor.

PROVERBS 21:21

It's almost impossible to describe the drastic changes that took place in daily reality while living in the Silicon Valley during the tech boom. Companies were giving away BMWs to young engineers who signed on to work for them. Money appeared to be rolling in, hand over fist, for anyone who had an idea. The venture capitalists couldn't seem to give it away fast enough, and millions were made in a stock bubble that would eventually come to an end.

During this time, we had many friends who became filthy rich. As a family, we did well too, but we had friends moving into multimillion-dollar estates, buying luxury cars with cash, and sending their kids to elite private schools. If that isn't a perfect picture for how we, as God's children, become so entitled, I'm not sure what is.

It is such a natural thing to take that wealth and pursue something bigger and better (we ourselves got a fabulous built-in pool). If we take our eyes off the prize, it is so easy to pursue that which really doesn't make our lives any more fulfilled, our families any happier, or give our lives any great purpose. More stuff equals more earthly things to take care of and, ultimately, sucks the joy from one's life. After all, we're told not to build up our treasures on earth, where thieves can break in and steal them, but to build treasures in heaven.

We watched families self-destruct over the pursuit of money, over the love of work before family, over a complete lack of connection. Interestingly, the strongest couples some ten years later are those who gained nothing from the tech boom except a striking look at reality.

Having money is not a sin. The *love of money* is a sin, and I think it's so easy to get focused on what we don't have when others seem to have it all. But you can be happy right here, in the midst of whatever struggle God has given you today. You can pursue righteousness and love and live a life of prosperity and honor, no matter what your current situation.

As a witness to the testimony that money does not make you happy, ask yourself the serious question of what does make you happy. More connection? More family time? More nights out with the girls? More teaching? More serving?

God can quiet your heart. He can meet your needs, and He wants you to prosper where He has you planted. Look for your joys and your blessings, and pursue who God made you to be. * *KB*

A Life of Death

Then Jesus said to his disciples, "If anyone wants to follow in my footsteps he must give up all right to himself, take up his cross and follow me. For the man who wants to save his life will lose it; but the man who loses his life for my sake will find it."

MATTHEW 16:24–25 PHILLIPS

My dear friend and mentor, Roy Lessin, has a saying I like (one of many). I find myself using it daily as I'm learning what it means to live a beautiful life with the Lord. The saying is this: *Here's another thing to die to.*

The first time I heard Roy say this, I was sitting in his living room stewing about something that had gone wrong, someone who, I believed, had violated my rights. I can't even remember the particulars now. But I know myself and my tendency to take offense at a perceived slight, whether to myself or someone else, and I know I was mad. Hurt. Disappointed. Something hadn't gone the way I'd planned. Someone hadn't appreciated my contribution or ability. And instead of joining me in my rant about the injustice of it all, Roy simply chuckled. He shook his head. "Well, Gwen, here's another thing to die to."

The words pierced my heart. As I began to consider them, however, I felt a shift in my way of thinking. It was as if I was going down one road at full speed and suddenly Roy's words stopped me in my tracks. I could see where I was headed, and it really wasn't anywhere except frustration. In that moment I decided instead to turn another way—a better way.

How can death be a better way? The idea goes against everything in us; it is the antithesis of the human quest for survival. We think of standing up to our persecutors and fighting for our rights as the American way. We believe that not giving in—not accepting the death of our rights, our dreams, our plans—makes us more free. And there are cases when it does. There are cases when we should stand up and fight.

But I am learning that, at least in my life, there are many cases when I need to sit down and hush. To lay down my rights. To take up my cross instead and follow Jesus. I may have a right to my opinion, but that doesn't mean it's always right to share it. I may have the right to be angry with my coworker, but that doesn't mean it's always right to tell him off. I may have the right to storm out of the room or the right to treat someone the way they treat me or the right to do any number of things. But that doesn't mean it's *right* to assert my rights.

Jesus said that if I want to find my life, I have to lose it. Sometimes that means dying to a thousand little things a day—to my own preferences, my own timetable, my own sense of order and justice. It may be as simple as ironing my husband's shirt or as difficult as trusting God when I lose my job. It's amazing how often—and for how many situations—Roy's saying comes in handy!

It's a choice to die to ourselves and what we think we want. And it's not necessarily the easiest road to take. But it's a path to peace, and, in Jesus, dying leads us into resurrection life. * *GF*

LOL and ROTFL

Our mouths were filled with laughter, our tongues with songs of joy.
Then it was said among the nations, "The LORD has done great things for them."

PSALM 126:2

I'd feel lost without e-mail and IM. I love being able to stay in communication with friends and family all over the world. And how fun to be able to show when I'm laughing with a ☺ or an LOL. What did we ever do before the Internet?

More than twenty years ago, my family moved from Florida to Tennessee in the middle of January. The day before the movers arrived with all our worldly possessions, there was a snowstorm like one I'd never seen—and I've never liked cold weather. Within the first year of moving there, all of us got sick, my mother became an invalid, we realized our house was a money pit, and my husband lost his job due to a downturn in the economy. I felt like it couldn't get any worse. Fortunately, I was right.

Our lives are like roller coasters of joy, sorrow, and everything in between, and it's easy to get caught up in worry and frustration. Sometimes it seems like bad things come in multiples, making each day more miserable than the last. Our blinders often prevent us from seeing the fun and humor surrounding us.

As Christians, we look forward to eternal joy and freedom from suffering, God's promise. As we go through our days, we need to remember to LOL and ROTFL every chance we get. * *DM*

Justice Feels Good

When David heard that Nabal was dead, he said, "Praise be to the LORD, who has upheld my cause against Nabal for treating me with contempt. He has kept his servant from doing wrong and has brought Nabal's wrongdoing down on his own head."

1 SAMUEL 25:39

Let's face it, a just sentence feels good. If it didn't, the Lifetime Movie Network would be out of business. There would be no abyss-falling villains at the end of Disney movies, and there would certainly be no Court TV. When the unrighteous get theirs and we get to witness it, there's a certain satisfaction that comes over us as humans. As much as we'd like to be pious and beyond such pettiness, it secretly feels good to watch evil perish. Especially if we've seen the victims of its wrath suffer.

I admit it; this is why I love the story of Abigail in the Bible. She was married to an idiot. Nabal's name actually means "foolish," and worse than being a fool, he was a fool for no purpose—other than to be contrary and show his power. He might have sacrificed his entire family and all his servants for the opportunity to exert his rights over David and not give David and his men a few of his flock. Out of his foolishness came pure wickedness.

Fearing that her household and her children would perish over Nabal's decision, Abigail defied her husband and humbly appeared before David with supplies and an apology on behalf of Nabal's behavior. She asked David to remember her when he was able.

Abigail, being a smart wife, waited until morning after Nabal had slept off his drink to tell him of her actions. Rather than being grateful for being alive, Nabal was struck like a stone and died ten days later.

Now, I'm not wishing anyone dead. I'm only saying that, when the right man gets his, there's such a beauty in earthly justice. Abigail's fortitude and humility saved the lives of many. Not only that, but David returned for her later and asked her to be his wife. A vast improvement after Nabal, I'm certain.

I love this story of how a woman put her faith in God and defied evil. Naturally, we don't always get to see God's justice here on earth, but we can remember God's love for us when all feels lost. * KB

Praiseworthy Priorities

Because your greatest desire is to help your people, and you did not ask for wealth, riches, [or] fame...I will certainly give you the wisdom and knowledge you requested.

2 CHRONICLES 1:11–12

*I*f you discovered that you had a personal genie and could make one wish—anything you wanted—what would it be? A million bucks? A racy sports car? A trip around the world or a mansion? Most of us would be immediately consumed with possibilities for ourselves.

But what if, on the other hand, you discovered that there is a God in heaven who generously gives to those who make requests of Him concerning the healing of humanity, the mending of the world? What then?

Power in prayer is much more frequently experienced when we get beyond our own desires, our own interests, and our own needs. Not that those are unimportant, rather that those who see the bigger picture and seek the welfare of others tend to align themselves more objectively with God's motives and intentions.

Your heart begins to bend to the higher will of God when you earnestly pray for the welfare of other people. It changes you. It makes of you a person that God can entrust with vast wisdom and deep insight. Interestingly enough, such valuable commodities will answer most of your own concerns in life, but they will also equip you to faithfully handle wealth and power should it come your way. * SGES

Alternatives, Options, and Choices

Make me to go in the path of thy commandments;
for therein do I delight.
PSALM 119:35 KJV

Baseball great Yogi Berra earned more fame for his witty quotes than his expertise on the field, and the Berraism closest to my heart goes like this: "When you come to a fork in the road, take it."

I'm a great believer in motivational stuff, which explains why mottos like Yogi's surround my computer monitor. The rainbow of Post-it Notes that frame the screen make it possible—unconsciously, at least—for me to keep the good advice in mind as I work. I'll let you decide if their similarities are more funny than amazing, or if it's the other way around:

- "The turtle only makes progress when he chooses to stick his neck out" (James Bryant).
- "Excellence is not an accident; it's a choice" (Unknown).
- "Heaven on earth is a choice we make, not a place we find" (Wayne Dyer).
- "We are happy if we choose to be" (Alexander Solzhenitsyn).
- "The strongest principle of growth lies in human choice" (George Eliot).
- "Life is like a box of chocolates; you never know what you're gonna get" (Forrest Gump).

- "No one can tell us how much to give; the only safe rule is, give more than [you] can spare" (C. S. Lewis).
- "Tact is the art of choosing to make guests feel comfortable in your home when you really wish they were elsewhere" (George E. Bergman).
- "Before you choose to criticize someone, walk a mile in their shoes. That way, when you're finished, you're a mile away...and you have their shoes" (Frieda Norris).

Every day, a thousand times over, I'm forced to make choices: White bread or rye? Light or heavy starch? Take that call, or let the answering machine get it? Paper or plastic? Like ripples in a pond, everything I say and do (or decide not to say or do) has far-reaching effects not only on me but on everyone I come into contact with. No wonder Mom spent so much time trying to teach me that with each choice comes its own set of personal responsibilities!

So whether I choose to donate an old sofa to a home for battered women or bite my tongue when someone offends me, there are consequences...some that fill me with dread and others that leave me overjoyed.

How blessed I am to have a Lord who will help me make Christian choices, whether I call upon Him once or a thousand times! * *LL*

I'll Be a Fool for You

Fear of man will prove to be a snare,
but whoever trusts in the LORD is kept safe.

PROVERBS 29:25

Several years ago, a friend of mine heard from her sister-in-law, Kerry, who was absolutely floored about something. She had been running errands when she stopped at a convenience store for a soda. As she walked in, she felt the profound presence of God and was certain she heard Him instruct her to go to the back of the store and stand on her head.

I'm not making this up. But, honestly, what would *you* have done? I'm not sure I'm coordinated enough to even attempt a headstand, let alone worry about how foolish I'd look.

This dear sister in Christ, though, fought the fear of what others would think, and in total trust of God's will, did exactly as she felt she was divinely instructed. Within seconds, a female employee walked out of the store's back room, took one look at Kerry, screamed, and started babbling almost incoherently.

Kerry immediately righted herself and took the crying woman in hand. Apparently the employee, a borderline atheist, had given up on her lonely, difficult life. She'd been in the back room crying and contemplating the worst. In the midst of her depression, she called out to God. She had never been able to accept His existence or believe He loved her because the pain in her life seemed too bad to coexist with a loving God. Still, in her desperation she shared her anger with Him.

"I'll tell you what," she cried, "I'll believe You exist when I walk out of here and see someone standing on their head." Then she walked out of the back room and into the kingdom.

Now, if God put it into my head that there was someone contemplating suicide who would change her mind about Him and about life if I would only stand on my head in the middle of a convenience store, I'd surely put aside my fear of what others might think. I'd probably even recruit someone to help me get myself upside down. But to "hear" the instructions Kerry heard and obey without knowing why? I think I'd have to hear them like Charlton Heston heard the burning bush. I'd need to be *very* certain before I'd trust that what I "heard" was the Lord before setting aside the possible embarrassment of misunderstanding. That's the "fear of man" referred to in today's verse.

Joshua marched around Jericho. Gideon dismissed all but three hundred men before taking on the Midianite hordes. Jesus's adoptive father, Joseph, married a girl his contemporaries might have stoned. How loudly would you need to hear His voice before it would drown out the judgment of your fellow man? * *TP*

A Life of Quietness

In quietness and in confidence shall be your strength.
ISAIAH 30:15 KJV

There are many things I could say about Janie. She's my mother; I've known her all of my life. I told her once that she is hard for me to write about—not because there's nothing to say, but because there's so much to choose from. Our history together lends itself to thousands of stories of laughter, tears, and everything in between. Today I am thinking of her quietness.

Moma might say *quietness* is a strange word to associate with her. She was an elementary school teacher for thirty-three years. She played ball with the kids at recess, taught them silly songs as well as their lessons, and was no shrinking violet when it came to discipline.

My brother and I can vouch for that at home, as well. Moma brought us up with a good balance of firmness and fun, both of which involved a lot of communication. She wouldn't hesitate to explain things to us. We laughed a lot. But we also understood when things were serious. Moma never believed it was a sin for a woman to raise her voice if the situation was drastic.

The quietness I'm thinking of goes deeper than the tone of her voice (which most of the time is a nice, even mezzo-soprano). It's a quietness of spirit. I've seen my mother in several situations that try one's soul—and most of the time, no matter how loud and restless the world becomes, she keeps her heart at peace. This has been a great example to me.

One of the proudest moments I've ever had as her daughter was at a church business meeting. It was one of those disastrous times you hear about, when Christians go crazy and act like they're in a barroom brawl. It's painful to everyone when that happens. In truth, the drama of this night would have been much better suited to any venue other than the sanctuary of God's house.

I watched the arguments unfold in utter stupefaction. The cognitive dissonance between where I was and what was taking place was almost overwhelming. Decent Christian people yelled at each other and waved their arms in fury. I remember thinking, *Has everyone here lost their minds?*

My parents both sat in silence. I know they were as sad and bewildered as I was; many people were. But there seemed to be no helping it. I was crying out for God and needing Him to take control but could hear no voice of peace in the midst of the storm. However, when my mother slowly rose to her feet, His peace started to break through to my heart.

I don't remember everything she said. What I remember is that she was calm and purposeful—undeterred by the tensions flaring around her. She spoke words of truth in love that brought clarity to a roomful of hazy emotion. From there things got a little more reasonable, and the situation was finally brought to a resolution.

Others may have misunderstood or even disagreed with her for what my mother said that night. But, as her daughter, I learned something that transcended the moment. I learned how strong—and how beautiful—a quiet spirit can be. * *GF*

Love Me, Love My Baggage

You shall not only show me the kindness of the LORD while I still live, that I may not die;
but you shall not cut off your kindness from my house forever, no, not when
the LORD has cut off every one of the enemies of David from the face of the earth.

1 SAMUEL 20:14–15 NKJV

I grew up in a non-Christian home. Notice I didn't say "anti-Christian." My parents just didn't see the need for church, other than the occasional Easter and Christmas services. My mother claimed to believe in God, but she never spoke about her relationship with the Lord. My father didn't like to talk about faith issues at all. But at an early age, I knew that something was missing.

My father was a career air force man, which instantly made me a "military brat"—a term I now realize isn't the worst thing. Brats are spunky survivors, even if they are… well, brats. We moved often, which was both good and bad. I saw and did things most children never have the opportunity to experience. I also had to guard my heart when we picked up and moved away from friends I'd never see again. That was rough. Each time we relocated, my parents settled in with new jobs, but it was never that easy for me. I had to go through the entire process of learning about others and trying to fit in. However, I always knew in the back of my mind that I'd have to move again, so I never let anyone get too close; it would simply be too painful when I had to go somewhere else.

There were other issues that probably had a lot to do with the military. My father had temporary duty assignments that took him away from my mother and me for extended periods of time. I didn't see him for a couple of years when I was a toddler, so when he came back home, I was leery. Not long after I graduated from college, my parents divorced, which rattled my young adult life to the core.

Throughout my childhood, I met people who believed in the Lord—some of them military brats who attended services at the nondenominational base chapel. Others were locals who'd gone to the same church all their lives. I was fortunate enough to be invited, and it was there that I saw what was most important in this world. I learned that through faith in Christ, we have a home with God.

When my husband and I first met, there was an instant attraction, but we were both cautious. During one of our early conversations, he told me that he didn't want to pursue a relationship with me unless I was a believer. Fortunately, Christ had already become a vital part of my life, even without my parents' assistance. We had issues to overcome—our emotional baggage from the past—but our common faith in Christ led us to where we are today.

Everyone has baggage. However, God has promised us salvation through Christ, so that baggage is checked at the door when we enter His kingdom. * *DM*

Peer Pressure—Me?

When I said, "My foot is slipping," your love, O LORD, supported me.
When anxiety was great within me, your consolation brought joy to my soul.

PSALM 94:18–19

With a husband, two kids, and twenty-eight years to my credit, I decided to go back to college. An intense Maymester course seemed to provide the perfect way to get past the speech class I'd been dreading. After all, I'd only have to endure giving speeches for four weeks instead of an entire semester.

What I hadn't counted on was getting the head of the department for a professor. Nor had I counted on ten speeches as opposed to the usual two in a normal semester (many more students, thus fewer speeches—*go figure*). And I really hadn't planned on the class debate on pornography… out on the front lawn of Purdue University…with a bullhorn…and "heckling credits."

On the day of the debate, I prepared my arguments, prayed a lot, and headed to class, ready to join the others in the fight for morality.

My adrenaline skyrocketed as I immersed myself in the heat of debate. I enjoyed the heckling (and getting free points from the professor), spouting the evils of pornography, explaining it from the perspective of a wife and a mother and, obviously, a Christian.

Then came the bottom line.

The professor called a halt to the debate. He brought us all together and drew an imaginary line in the ground. "All who are for pornography, step over here," he said. "Those who are opposed, step over there."

Imagine my surprise when the only students opposed to pornography were two guys (and forgive me, but one wore his pants up to his neck and the other spoke a different language—I have to wonder if the latter even knew what we were debating) and yours truly. The peer pressure I felt at that moment surprised me.

Class dismissed. I kicked every rock and twig from my path on my way back to the car. "Here I was trying to do the right thing. Do you know how alone I felt, Lord?"

Even as I nursed my wounds, remorse set in. The absurdity of my question rang loud and clear. Of course Jesus knew exactly how I felt. Shame choked me. I cried all the way back to the parking garage. How could I ask such a question? If anyone knew what it felt like to be alone, Jesus did. He went to the cross for me, for you…alone.

By the time I settled in the car, I realized that whatever I face in this world, He goes before me. He understands, and His grace is sufficient to get me through.

This life lesson also gave me more patience and understanding with my own children when they faced the teenage years. His consolation truly did bring joy to my soul.
* DH

Who's That Lady?

*At least there is hope for a tree: If it is cut down, it will sprout again,
and its new shoots will not fail.*

JOB 14:7

After months of having my hair tugged and yanked by my firstborn, Alison, I decided to get it chopped off. I didn't have a babysitter who could watch her during the week, so I waited until the weekend when my husband, Wally, would be with us. We decided to take a family trip to the mall, where he agreed to window-shop with Alison while I went to the hair salon. It took about an hour, start to finish, and when I walked out of the salon, I was excited to show off my new 'do to my family.

I eagerly watched the main corridor of the mall until I spotted my husband and baby coming out of a store. My heart thudded as they got closer. I practically ran toward them until I was close enough to reach for my baby. The second I touched Alison, her eyes widened, a panicked look came over her chubby little face, and she let out an ear-piercing scream. It took a few seconds before I understood what had happened. *She didn't recognize me.* Some strange woman with short hair was grabbing at her, and she didn't like it a bit.

For the next couple of hours I talked to her, and Wally did his best to explain that I was still "Mommy," only with shorter hair. She stared at me dubiously, but she kept pulling back when I so much as touched her. It took time until, finally, she accepted the new "Mommy"—but I could tell by the way she looked at me, she didn't care for what she saw.

As Alison grew, so did my hair, and thankfully she'd gotten out of the habit of grabbing it. Although I enjoyed the shorter cut for a while, I'd always had longer hair, so I was glad to have it at least shoulder-length again.

Like my hair, after a tree is cut, it continues to grow unless it is pulled up by its roots—then it will die. After we pass away, we won't return to this earth in our current condition. I decide what happens with my hair—whether it is short or long. But our life after death is up to the Lord, and He has made it clear that through faith in Him, we will be with Him eternally. Trees need nourishment that they get from the soil, water, and sun. In order to keep my faith alive and healthy, I need to read my Bible and study His Word. * DM

Calling All Neglected Moms!

Then He said to the disciple, "Behold your mother!"
And from that hour that disciple took her to his own home.

JOHN 19:27

"Why don't you call me?"

"Mom, I'm busy."

"Listen, I'm busy, too, but how long does it take to pick up the phone, dial my number, and say, 'Hi, Mom, hope you're okay. Everything's good with me'? It would take all of thirty seconds."

My hardheaded son refuses to see my point. "I'm working two jobs and going to school."

I reply with an exasperated sigh. *No excuse*, I think to myself. After all, Jesus took time to remember His mother while dying on the cross!

Can you imagine being Mary and watching your son die an agonizing death? What a horror. Of course, Jesus's plan, even while dying on the cross, was to return three days later. Even so, it amazes me that our Lord made provisions for His mother even as He suffered, paying for the sins of all humanity.

But my adult son can't even give me a phone call once a week?

When I tell this to my son, his voice hardens. "Mom, Jesus is God. I'm just a normal person!"

"Oh, fine. I'll quit nagging. Just call me once in a while, okay?"

I hang up the phone and my conscience pricks. Maybe I was too hard on him. Are my expectations really too high? I mean, I'm asking my son for a lousy phone call, not a million bucks!

I fume as I go about my business around the house. After all I did for my sons, they can't even call me. Humph!

Later, my husband tells me that my mother called.

I wave a hand at him. "I'll call her later. I don't really feel like talking at the moment."

But then realization hits: I haven't been the most faithful in calling my mother. I mean, I call when I feel like it. She's always there for me. If she's busy, she calls me back. And she listens to me prattle on, sometimes for an hour or more.

Isn't that what moms are supposed to do? Be there for their kids, whenever they happen to call and want to chit-chat? Of course, circumstances may prevent moms from calling or receiving phone calls at the moment, but then the call's returned when there is time. Basic courtesies.

Hmm…

The decision made, I pick up the telephone. "Hi, Mom, I'm just returning your phone call." * *AKB*

Blind, But Now I See

I will lead the blind on unfamiliar roads. I will lead them on unfamiliar paths.
I will turn darkness into light in front of them. I will make rough places smooth.

ISAIAH 42:16 GWT

The exact illness is unknown, but many today conclude scarlet fever or meningitis robbed nineteen-month-old Helen Keller of her eyesight and hearing back in 1882. Fortunately, at the age of six Helen became a pupil of Anne Sullivan, a young woman visually impaired herself. Helen's breakthrough in communication came within a month as Anne was pouring cool water over Helen's hand and making motions for the word water in Helen's other hand.

In a literal sense, the almost-blind was leading the blind into an incredible adventure of language and knowledge. Through Miss Sullivan's continued guidance, Helen became the first deaf-blind person to earn a Bachelor of Arts degree.

Although we may not be physically blind, we sometimes stumble in the darkness of the unfamiliar. We sense God nudging us forward, but without a clue of the road ahead, we feel hesitant, awkwardly fumbling for sure footing.

The Bible encourages you to walk by faith, turning your eyes toward God and not depending solely on what you can see in this world. God promises to lead you through the unknown and shine light on the dark pathways. With Him as your faithful guide, your eyes will be opened to incredible adventures ahead. * SGES

A Life of the Spirit

Your beauty should come from within you—the beauty...
that will never be destroyed and is very precious to God.

1 PETER 3:4 NCV

As women, we are bombarded with many definitions of beauty. In popular culture as well as many Christian circles, it seems that beauty is sometimes defined by ideals we may either choose to reject outright or aspire to—but are never able to reach. Neither of these options is edifying for a real woman.

If we, as women, take seriously the directive offered in 1 Peter 3:4, which says, "Your beauty should come from within you," then it seems worth exploring just what real beauty is. Or what it can be.

First and foremost, a beautiful life is a life of the Spirit. The verse above is quoted from the New Century Version, which is easy to understand, but I also like how the King James puts it: "Let [your beauty] be the hidden man of the heart, in that which is not corruptible." That concept of the "hidden man of the heart" speaks to me. And what woman isn't looking for beauty that lasts—i.e., is "not corruptible"?

The hidden man of the heart—our hope for lasting beauty—is the Holy Spirit of God. It is by Him, through Him, and in Him that our hearts and therefore our lives can be transformed into something eternally, breathtakingly beautiful.

What exactly does that mean, though? And how do we find it? I believe Christian women can almost become as confused about the issue of beauty by sitting in some churches today—or by Christian media—as we do when we look at the world. Inner beauty, a beauty that lasts, a life lived in the Spirit—those things all sound good. But for some of us, these ideas seem just as unattainable as a size-four body or the perfect color of hair. We may decide to approach them like we do a job or a course of study—as something to work for, to achieve excellence in through personal ambition.

My friend Char tells a story about how she began to live a life of the Spirit. She was in Bible college, and at her school, you had to work to pay for your tuition. One day at her job the boss, who was also one of her professors, asked the group not to visit while they were working. He left the room, and they proceeded to talk.

That evening, Char felt convicted that she had been wrong to disobey her boss by talking while he was gone. She decided to find him and apologize. Expecting to be reprimanded for her misconduct, Char was very surprised when the professor looked at her and smiled. "I'm glad you've learned to listen to the voice of the Holy Spirit," he told her. And that was it.

In many ways, that *is* it. A life of the Spirit isn't some huge thing that happens to us all at once. We can't get a "spiritual makeover" or earn a Bible degree that suddenly makes us beautiful in the Spirit. It's an inner work of God that takes place when we say yes to His leading, moment by moment, one day at a time. * *GF*

When a DIL Goes AWOL

Hatred stirs up strife, but love covers all sins.

PROVERBS 10:12 NKJV

I have three sons. And when they got married I didn't think of myself as losing my precious "little boys," just gaining sweet, beautiful daughters.

Daughters. *At last* I wasn't outnumbered in a house full of males. I had someone to go shopping with while the Green Bay Packers played football on Sunday afternoons.

I felt particularly close to one DIL (daughter-in-law). I had led her to Christ before she and my son were married, and we had an amazing way of thinking along the same lines about various issues and situations. We could talk for hours. Once, when they stopped by to drop off something on their way to a dinner engagement, my son wouldn't even let my DIL get out of their SUV. He knew all too well that she and I would start gabbing and they'd never get to where they were going on time. I remember telling her that if I had ever had a daughter, it'd be her. She, in turn, sent me cards and bought me little treasures, many of which touted the joys of the mother/daughter relationship. She called me, sent emails, and made sure my son didn't forget Mother's Day.

So when I learned she'd filed for divorce, my heart broke.

For months I'd had inklings that something was amiss between my DIL and my son. I'd tried approaching him, asking questions, but he didn't appreciate what he perceived as my meddling. I conversed with my DIL and she revealed a few things; however, none seemed serious enough to end their five-year marriage. I backed off, not wanting to be that proverbial busybody MIL (mother-in-law).

Later I learned the truth; my DIL had met another guy and wanted to be with him.

"What about trust, honor, and commitment?" I wanted to shout at her. As she was in the military, I thought she reverenced those traits. Obviously she didn't. I had been wrong to assume otherwise. She didn't want to be my son's wife and part of our family anymore.

So much for having a daughter.

"You must hate her," a coworker remarked when I mentioned my son's pending divorce.

To my shame, I confessed that maybe I did hate her just a little bit—at first. But then God showed me that if you really love someone, you love that person forever, unconditionally…and I truly love my DIL.

Even now.

Months later, she and I met for lunch, facing each other for the first time since she'd filed for divorce. I greeted her with a hug—and before any words were spoken, my DIL sobbed and sobbed. I sensed the hurt that ran so deep within her. I wished she'd have let God heal her emotional wounds instead of turning to a new boyfriend who wouldn't ever meet that need.

When, at last, we finally talked, I was able to share my heart in a loving way. I said I didn't approve of her behavior, the adultery, but that I still loved her. She admitted that she thought I'd hate her. I assured her that I didn't. After all, what could hate accomplish when love conquers all?

* AKB

I'm the Mom, That's Why

*Honor your father and your mother, that your days may be long upon
the land which the LORD your God is giving you.*

EXODUS 20:12 NKJV

I had one of the most profound experiences of my life in early 2009. My firstborn, Alison, gave birth to my first grandchild. As her husband, Jason, and I stood beside her while she was in labor, I couldn't help but flash back to when she was born. What a life-changing experience!

Now that Alison, Jason, and Emma are home from the hospital, I see the impact that one tiny baby can have on so many. People from all over are flying and driving to see this newly expanded family. Diets have changed to accommodate the needs of a nursing child. The dog and cat have new positions in the family—still important and loved but no longer the primary focus of maternal and paternal energy. The once minimalist decor has changed to "early baby." Two loving parents are willing to sacrifice sleep, money, and everything else they once valued to ensure the safety and contentment of their precious child.

My favorite aspect of this whole experience is how I can see the fruits of my own sacrifices for my daughter. As she grew and developed, I sometimes wondered if I was doing the best for her. Now that she's a mother, I have no doubt that the best and most important thing my husband and I did was share the love of Christ. Alison and Jason are already discussing spiritual issues for Emma. They want to bring her up among other believers so she'll have every advantage possible in today's insane world.

Being a parent is difficult, even with the best and most well-behaved children. I have no doubt that Alison and Jason are up to the task as long as they keep Christ at the forefront of their lives. As Emma grows and develops, she'll test her parents—because that's what children do. With the guidance of biblical principles, they'll help her understand that the Lord's ways are greater than her own.

As I obnoxiously share photos of my first grandchild with anyone who'll stand still long enough to look, I have to remember that, first, she's a child of God. And every night before I go to sleep, I thank Him for blessing Alison and Jason with such a darling child. * *DM*

I Am Really Ticked Off!

For the wrath of man does not produce the righteousness of God.

JAMES 1:20 NKJV

I truly admire John the Baptist. I love his tenacity. I marvel at the way he pointed to Jesus instead of himself. He could have been proud. A multitude of people thought he was the Messiah. He could have given in to the temptation to proclaim himself a great man if nothing else, but he said he was just "the voice of one crying in the wilderness" (John 1:23).

Many times over the years, I have felt like a "voice of one crying in the wilderness," too, but in a very different way. "Clean your room." "Pick up your clothes." Was anybody listening? Hello–o?

That'd make me so angry. But I can honestly tell you now that my anger back then didn't change one single thing.

Even now that my sons are adults I feel like they don't hear me sometimes, and on occasion I feel insulted, angry.

"Listen, I'm important!" I feel like shouting. "I was the one who potty-trained you! Remember *that* the next time you use the men's room!"

Sheesh, the nerve of these kids!

It's at these tumultuous times in my life that God's still, small voice whispers, "Your anger doesn't produce My righteousness."

That's when reality sets in. You see, instead of getting angry, all I need to do is turn to God.

Pastor Joel Osteen, a prominent author and speaker, stated in one of his televised messages that when we get angry, we "give our power away." Anger taps us emotionally. Anger makes our stomachs hurt and gives us headaches. What's more, anger doesn't usually produce the change we desire, although things might change for the worst because of a temper fit. Friends and loved ones might not want to be around us if we're always ticked off about some situation or a negative response we've received along the way.

I guess I've learned that lesson the hard way.

But when we take our anger to the Lord, He can handle it. He's God. He's the One who is able to move mountains and part seas. He can heal the sick—and He can take away our anger and replace it with His perfect peace.

In her book *Praying God's Word Day by Day*, Beth Moore incorporates Matthew 5:34–35 when she writes, "Heaven is Your throne; earth is Your footstool. Therefore, anything over my head is under Your feet."

That includes those situations that really work our last nerve! * *AKB*

I Wanna Bend It Like Bailey

*But seek first his kingdom and his righteousness,
and all these things will be given to you as well.*

MATTHEW 6:33

I adore children, and my favorite age is right around three or four; they're just developing their communications skills but haven't quite perfected the transition from emotion to verbalization.

While babysitting for a friend's three-year-old, I encountered the challenge of keeping Bailey occupied so that she might forget that her beloved mommy had left the house without her. And it wasn't easy.

First, we played Safari. After strategically placing her most treasured stuffed animals around the house, Bailey put on a plastic pith helmet and climbed aboard her push-and-ride Jeep, and we toured the African plains of home to observe the animals in their natural habitat. When she spotted the giraffe leaning against the refrigerator, Bailey suddenly remembered who had given her that giraffe, and she started to cry for her mother.

Several games and a coloring book later, she accepted my invitation to a tea party in her bedroom. We donned straw hats, and Bailey tugged on little white crocheted gloves. Along with two of our very best doll friends, we sipped from empty teacups and munched imaginary scones with cream and strawberries. Bailey was enthralled!…*until the garage door went up*. Tossing the plastic teacup to the floor, she flew from the bedroom and down the hall. On her trail, I stepped over the hat and the gloves she'd shed on the way. I reached her just as the kitchen door opened and her mother walked in.

So excited to see her mom again at last, Bailey squealed with glee. When the words wouldn't come, she finally began hopping from one foot to the other, pumping her arms, clenching her fists, and contorting her little face. The return of her mother had trumped everything else, and thoughts of tea parties and safaris had fallen to the dust. I stood there watching as the child completely surrendered to the ecstatic happiness of seeing the one person who meant more to her than anything or anyone else.

On the drive home that afternoon, I tuned my radio to a local Christian station playing "I Can Only Imagine" by MercyMe, a song exploring the depths of our reaction when we finally see Christ face-to-face. As I sang along, Bailey's reaction to her mother's return home sprang to mind. How sweet would it be to the Lord if, at His presence, we just jumped up and down with the glee of little children! * *SDB*

The Gift of Trey

Ask and it will be given to you; seek and you will find;
knock and the door will be opened to you.

MATTHEW 7:7

Help! Please!"

I've heard it said that those are the only purely honest prayers. I don't know if that's true or not, but I know I've had my fair share of "Help!" and "Please" prayers when I felt too weak or too overwhelmed to pray, because the pain of not having that prayer answered seemed unfathomable to me.

When I was pregnant with my first child, something felt *wrong*. I went to the doctor, and at eleven weeks, the doctor coldly stated, "Nothing. No baby." My heart sank.

No, not my baby, God, please!

To make matters worse, a family member had impregnated his girlfriend and the baby was due the same day. I had to endure the baby showers, the wedding, and watching her blossom with child, all for someone who did it "wrong"—while not knowing if I would ever be a mother.

Sure, it was selfish. When we're hurting, we're not exactly beacons of sainthood. Sometimes we're more like spoiled children, stamping our feet for what we want *and want now!*

I had to work through those feelings and appreciate my relation's gift, while mourning my own loss and knowing that God's will is perfect, even if it felt unfair, irrational, and highlighted by someone else's good fortune. But God wants the best for us, and sometimes we have to trust that He knows what it is.

That doesn't stop us from desperate prayers, of course. We're only human. If I hadn't lost that first baby, I might not have had my Trey, who is the greatest firstborn any mother could dream of. Maybe his three fantastic siblings would be different; who knows? All I know is that painful experience brought me the greatest day of my life: *Trey's birth.*

Looking back, hindsight is 20/20, and God knew what He was doing. I try to remember that in present circumstances when His will seems to conflict with my own, but I don't always succeed. Let's face it. *I want what I want when I want it.* Don't we all, if we're honest? But we have to remember to ask, and if we're too weak to ask, that's when a glorious Friend can intervene for us.

Hebrews 11:1 tells us that faith is the substance of things hoped for, the evidence of things not seen (KJV). Sometimes I do wish it would be more obvious, but that's why I have to look back and remember. * KB

Chicken Little

*Therefore I say to you, do not worry about your life, what you will
eat or what you will drink; nor about your body, what you will put on.
Is not life more than food and the body more than clothing?*

MATTHEW 6:25 NKJV

The sky is falling."

"If anything can go wrong, it will."

"All good things must come to an end."

How has so much negativity crept into our lives? You'd think that with all the commercials about "Having it your way" and "You deserve the very best," we'd all be glowing with radiant joy.

My mother was a child of the Great Depression, so she constantly talked about having enough food to eat. Some of that rubbed off on me, and I still worry—even though I have a full refrigerator, enough clothes in my closet to not wear the same thing twice in a month, and possessions that can keep me occupied 24/7.

While grocery shopping, my mother was a woman on a mission—determined to provide for her family with the resolve that each meal might be our last if we didn't stock up and prepare for some unknown disaster.

"Why are you buying so much soup?" I once asked my mom, as she transferred two of each kind of Campbell's Soup from the store shelf to the basket.

"You never know when you'll run out," she replied as she turned the basket toward the household items to stock up on toilet paper.

With the innocence of a child, I tilted my head and studied the soup before turning back to her. "Can't we just buy some more?"

She tossed a multi-roll pack of toilet paper into the cart, quirked one corner of her mouth, frowned, shook her head, and pushed the basket toward the Spam, making me feel like my question didn't deserve an answer. I now understand that she didn't have an answer, and one thing she wasn't willing to say was that she didn't know something about the future—which brings me to my point: Does anyone know what the future brings?

I certainly don't. No matter how much I plan, anything can happen. The future is out of my control, which sometimes irks me because I seem to have turned into my mother. And yes, sometimes I feel like the sky is falling.

Now my firstborn has a child, and I see that the world is still intact. My daughter is doing some of the same things I did as a young mother—trying her best to create a perfect world to keep the sky from falling.

We need to stop worrying about the future and trust God with everything. * *DM*

A Life of Trust

Trust in the LORD with all your heart; do not depend on your own understanding.

PROVERBS 3:5 NLT

Carrie Oliver is one of my heroes. At age forty-six, she was a devoted wife and mother of three boys, a Christian counselor, a well-known speaker, and an author. By anyone's definition this blond-haired, green-eyed runner was living a beautiful life.

Then, on May 17, 2005, Carrie received the news that she had pancreatic cancer. This diagnosis alone is grim, but worse still was the fact that Carrie's tumor was inoperable and the cancer had already spread to a lymph node in her neck. Her response is recorded in her journal:

Trauma, tragedy, and crisis. Certainly in my experience of being a human I felt these things, but what I know to be true…is that there was a moment where I came face-to-face with my Lord Jesus Christ and we talked about my choices, and really there were only two. One choice would be to succumb to the trauma and tragedy of it all and sink into a deep, dark, angry, depressed state and perhaps give up and give in to the statistics of the cancer that was growing in my body. The other choice…was to "choose" to cling tightly to Jesus and to "live" desperately, needing Him twenty-four hours a day and trusting that He would be there for me just as His Scriptures have promised for thousands of years.

Against the odds, Carrie fought through two years of grueling chemo, radiation, and experimental treatments. Her life during those years seems to testify to what Paul wrote in 2 Corinthians 4:16: "Though outwardly we are wasting away, yet inwardly we are being renewed day by day".

Here is a sampling of how she documented her journey:

JUNE 14, 2005—*This was going to be a whole new faith walk. My sovereign Lord has allowed this, and He has also been at work manifesting Himself to me.… God is still using me. I have a purpose every day that I awaken for every moment that I am still on this earth.*

AUGUST 7, 2005—*The "what-ifs" start screaming at me. When I cry out to the Lord, He reminds me that I must not doubt His love and care and involvement in my life and He is healing me. Healing my sin, my fears, my doubts, my selfishness, my pride, and He is at work in my physical body, as well. Is this easy? Nope! Is it the best choice? Yes! We have choices every day. I choose my God and His promises.*

MAY 15, 2006—*I celebrate finding Jesus to be all that He says He is and trusting Him to strengthen me in my loneliest of moments and to believe that His love is really all I ever need.*

SEPTEMBER 22, 2006—*It takes courage to fight the battle… I am a woman that in her humanness is very afraid, is sick, is weak, and has no courage or strength. In my Lord Jesus Christ I am a woman whose name means "Strong," I have faith, a sense of what I am fighting for, and I have His arms to carry me.*

JUNE 13, 2007—*I feel very confined at times. There are very few things right now that I can do that I used to be able to do.… In confinement we can focus in on or feel the immobility, Sorge says, or we can experience the glorious intimacy of being held so firmly in the Lord's arms. I have to go with the arms of the Lord.… Jesus, I know that You love me, and… Jesus, I love You, for You still have not left me or forsaken me.*

That was her last entry; Carrie died a few days later.

Once again, it's not the outward things that define us, or defined Carrie Oliver, but the hidden person of the heart. She had the incorruptible beauty of a heart that trusts. Not even cancer could destroy it. It's the kind of beauty that lives on forever. * GF

Elvis Has Left the Building

Then he said to me, "This is the curse that goes out over the face of the whole earth:
'Every thief shall be expelled,' according to this side of the scroll; and,
'Every perjurer shall be expelled,' according to that side of it."

ZECHARIAH 5:3 NKJV

Yesterday I went to everyone's favorite big-box store in search of bargains. With the economy like it is today, who can afford to pay full price for anything? As I entered and walked past the greeter, an ominous feeling flooded me. The store was packed with moms pushing shopping carts, tired folks riding electric carts, and an assortment of harried men looking for socks/T-shirts/cookies/candy/whatever. I took a quick glance at my list to see if I could justify postponing my shopping or taking it elsewhere. Nope. There were too many things we needed, and by shopping at this particular store, the savings were substantial enough to plow forward.

I started in the book section, made my way over to the health-and-beauty aisle, and wound up in the electronics department, where I loaded my cart with paper and printer ink. As I turned the corner and headed toward the dairy aisle, I spotted a middle-aged woman dropping CDs from the sale bin into her tote as she nervously glanced around. The instant our gazes met, she knew I was on to her. She quickly turned and scurried off. My heart sank as I thought about my dilemma. The woman was clearly in the process of stealing merchandise, but I didn't have a lot of time because of an impending deadline. If I said something to management, I'd be detained, and there was no way I'd get out of the store in a timely manner. However, if I kept this little secret, I was pretty sure that would make me an accessory to the crime. As uncomfortable as it was, I knew what I needed to do. I'd ask the woman if she needed help buying her CDs. Maybe that would embarrass her enough to make her put them back. Okay, probably not, but it was worth a try.

Shoving my nearly empty cart in the direction the woman had gone, I had to dodge other shoppers. Then, suddenly, I saw the woman sobbing as she stood next to the store employee who'd apprehended her. I should have had more faith in the store security cameras. After I paid, loaded up my car with the bargains, and headed home, I let out a deep sigh as I thought about that woman who was willing to take the risk of stealing store merchandise—clearly not necessary items. Was she a kleptomaniac? Or did she have a thing for Elvis? Whatever the case, she felt entitled to help herself to stuff that didn't belong to her. Now what would happen to her? Probably not much for a few CDs, but still....

I was relieved that someone else had confronted this woman before I spoke to her, because I really didn't want to pay for her CDs. What should we do when we see someone in the act of doing something wrong? Is it up to us to confront that person or turn her in? Either decision is difficult, no matter what. I prayed for her when I got home, and I'll continue to pray for her—that the Lord will rescue her from this sin. At the same time, I need to remember that my own sin nature is no better—that when I covet something I have no business having, I'm as bad as a thief. Even if it is just an Elvis CD. *DM*

My Life as a Piñata

Hope deferred makes the heart sick, but a longing fulfilled is a tree of life.

PROVERBS 13:12

The Colleen Cobles and Jasmine Cresswells of the world have a gift for writing suspense. Oh, how I admire that ability. The Andrea Boeshaars and Nicholas Sparkses can grab hold of a reader's heartstrings, and they just don't let go. It seems like all of the great ones have a specific calling on their writing, a certain branding that defines them as writers.

When a new line of romantic comedy was announced, I excitedly approached the editor and gave her my pitch. She read the first couple of pages of what I had in mind and seemed almost enthusiastic when she asked me to put together a full proposal. I agonized over it for weeks before sending her a synopsis and three chapters. Then I waited. Instead of a form letter, I received a phone call from the editor several months later. Hope inflated my heart as I waited to hear the words I felt certain she planned to utter: "Congratulations! I'd like to offer you..." Talk about hope deferred! What I heard instead began with, "Look. I can see that you think you're really funny. But I'm here to tell you, Sandie, you are not."

The poor little corpse of my hope thudded to the pit of my stomach. I was heartbroken—and I felt physically ill as she went on for nearly fifteen minutes, telling me why I would likely never have a career as an author, most assuredly not writing romantic comedy, and certainly not for her publishing house.

It took me awhile to recover from that, but I somehow managed to dig through the rubble and find my calling again. For five years, I honed my craft and continued to write in spite of that editor's song playing in the back of my mind. You know how the Scriptures often say that God "suddenly" turns circumstances? Like in Acts 2:2, as the apostles awaited the return of the Lord and "suddenly a sound like the blowing of a violent wind came from heaven." One day the editor of a new line of inspirational romance contacted me about writing something for them. On that very day, a small bud emerged from the depths of my long-deferred hope. With the launch of *Love Finds You in Snowball, Arkansas*, I became known as an author of "*Laugh-Out-Loud*" romantic fiction. Six more comedies have followed, awards have been won, mail from readers has confirmed the call on my life, and my subsequent "tree of life" is flourishing beyond what I ever imagined.

Isn't that so like Him? Beauty for ashes, my friends; that's just how our God rolls. * SDB

Let My Mirror Reflect Joy

One dieth in his full strength, being wholly at ease and quiet...
and another dieth in the bitterness of his soul.

JOB 21:23, 25 KJV

I've struggled recently, trying to figure out how to deal with a person whose behavior makes it pretty clear that she resents me. Petty comments—made privately and in public—not only deeply hurt my feelings but cause discomfort for innocent bystanders who are subjected to her anger.

It doesn't matter, really, whether she's doing it on purpose. What matters is...it's starting to make me feel resentful. And therein, as Shakespeare so astutely said, lies the rub.

Because every time I think I've beat back my vexation with self-pep talks like "Get over yourself!" or "Focus on other things" or "Let it go," she fires another volley to remind me just how much she doesn't like me.

The problem has driven me to my knees a dozen times, where I tearfully pray to understand the why of it and beseech the Lord to fortify me with the strength of character to not succumb to resentment myself. But it's tough, letting go of the hurt, when I'm surrounded by reminders of her resentment. Just this morning, in an e-mail written to a list of recipients, came another snarky barb...and, behind it, the "grin" emoticon, to disguise its true meaning and intent.

Like children calling, "Tag, you're it!" her resentment sparked mine. Again. And because I hate that feeling (and the weakness that inspires it), I hit my knees. Again. And glory of glories, the Lord reminded me that the Good Book has plenty to say about resentment! It's a waste of time, for starters—time I could put to better use by serving Him. As Job 5:2 so aptly puts it, worrying over resentment is a foolish, useless emotion, since mirroring her resentment with more of my own only hurts me...and those the Lord has put me here to love and serve.

It came into my head that telling God how much her resentment hurts me isn't enough. I have to let down my guard and admit that, in my weakness, I'm tempted to resent her right back!

It also dawned on me that psychiatrists have a lot to say about resentment, too. Studies prove that, most times, it's deeply rooted in envy. I have absolutely no idea why she's jealous of me! But the idea that she might be struck a nerve, making me realize that if that's the explanation behind her mean-spirited behavior, she's suffering far more than I am! The very idea awakened protective feelings toward her, and my prayers instantly turned from "Help me, Lord!" to "Show me how I can help her!"

I believe in my heart that when her next carefully disguised emoticon punctuates a spiteful jab, it isn't going to hurt at all. * *LL*

Unfinished Business

The LORD will fulfill his purpose for me; your steadfast love,
O LORD, endures forever. Do not forsake the work of your hands.

PSALM 138:8 ESV

In my younger days as a stay-at-home mom, I had plenty to do but still looked for more to keep busy. After all, as my mother would say, "Idle hands are the Devil's workshop."

It was years before I realized that wasn't in the Bible. So with plenty of ambition, I learned how to do cross-stitch, make baskets and pinecone wreaths, sew, knit, crochet, and quilt. One would think that by the age of fifty-four I would have mastered at least a number of these ambitions, but instead all I have to show for it are boxes of incomplete projects. Yes, that's right. I said "incomplete projects." There's my nasty little secret laid bare before you.

It most likely shocks you to the core. It certainly did my husband. Always one to finish what he's started, I'm sure he had no idea when we were dating, sipping soda from the same cup and staring into each another's starry eyes, that he was falling in love with a woman who left partial cross-stitch quotes and buckets of aging pinecones lying around, untouched basket reeds still bunched together, faded fabrics lining the shelves, and colored yarns not yet rolled into balls.

Oh, the shame of it all.

To illustrate our differences further, my husband has a beautiful tenor voice. When in college, if the melodious strains of an aria had drifted through an open dorm window with all but the final note and my husband had been passing by, there is no doubt in my mind that he would have moved heaven and earth to search for a piano to play that last chord. He's a finisher, pure and simple.

When my husband drags me to the shed and points to the bowing shelves crowded with boxes of cottons, polyesters, basket reeds, handles, knitting needles, crochet needles, pinecones, cross-stitch threads, and quilting hoops, all worked in different stages of completion, I tell him I'm waiting for inspiration to strike. The look in his eye says he wouldn't mind giving me a whack of inspiration.

I don't know why he gets so worked up about it. I've no doubt I'll get back to them…one of these days. In the meantime, I have to admit, I'm encouraged to know that God doesn't abandon the works of His hands. He finishes what He starts. Of course, He's dealing with people and I'm dealing with man-made materials. Still, I suppose I should do something about my unfinished projects.

That settles it. Tomorrow I'll take the boxes to Goodwill. Besides, my daughter just called. She wants to teach me how to scrapbook…. * *DH*

Where's the Beef?

Better a meal of vegetables where there is love than a fattened calf with hatred.

PROVERBS 15:17

When I made the announcement to my husband that we were going to try for "meatless Mondays"—at least most of the time—to cut back on fatty foods and save a little money in the process, he didn't balk. In fact, he seemed to think it was a good idea. He knew I was doing it as an act of self-improvement rather than trying to deny him the rich taste of meat with every meal. I'm sure this wasn't what the Lord meant by this verse, but there is something to be said for cutting back, as long as it's done with love.

For a while, almost everyone I knew was grabbing everything within their reach—whether they could afford it or not. If there was room on their credit cards, they could buy the latest and greatest—shiny new cars, jewelry, clothes, houses.... When their kids wanted something, all they had to do was stick out their hands and suddenly a plastic card would appear. Why should parents deny their offspring whatever their hearts desired? Their human wants were temporarily satisfied, but when the next shiny thing came along…well…you know. Is that really love?

Hard times have since fallen on many families, and they've had to pull back and tighten up. When their children ask why they suddenly have to sacrifice anything, the once-indulgent parents are left trying to figure out how to explain true values. They may have been forced to sell their mini-mansions and move into smaller homes where they—*<gasp!>*—are forced to be in the same room with each other. This is something that would have been so much easier if they'd done that to begin with.

The Lord in His wisdom knew that a feast of everything we could possibly want would fill us temporarily, but later we'd be hungry again. No matter how much we have, there will always be an emptiness that can't ever be totally satisfied. However, a less-ostentatious meal of sharing His good news will last forever, leaving us satisfied and never hungering for more. After all, what more could anyone want besides living in His kingdom for eternity?

Joy fills me as I know His plan for me is richer and much more nourishing than anything I could ever satisfy myself with. When my husband and I sit down to a meal without meat, we're just as happy as we'd be if we had the thickest, juiciest steaks. It's not the food that brings us true joy but knowing that we have each other and the Lord is with us at every moment of our day. * DM

Quiet Time

Therefore, my beloved brethren, be ye steadfast, unmovable,
always abounding in the work of the Lord.

1 CORINTHIANS 15:58 KJV

The cowboys of the Old West were blessed with a wonderful gift for defining ordinary, everyday events in the most exciting and fascinating ways. Take, for example, "blazing star"—their description of a stampede of pack animals. If you ever see one, you'll instantly realize how accurate—and how poetic—their term is, as you watch the herd simultaneously burst in every direction, scattering like stardust.

I'm not proud to declare that I identify with those four-legged critters, because with very little distraction, my brain can blast off to who knows where, leaving whatever I might have been doing undone. At least until the Lord leads me back to my desk and reminds me of the assignment He's given.

Too many well-meaning friends and relatives who fancy themselves armchair shrinks have suggested that I might be afflicted with a touch of Attention Deficit Disorder...and when they spout their proclamation, it pleases me no end to announce, "I've been tested, and the pros say no to that!"

So if my problem isn't ADD, what explains my occasional inability to focus? To put it simply, I've forgotten to ask God to ground me with steadfastness, forgotten that He is immovable, that His Word is immovable, and that my faith needs to be immovable, too. "I am the Lord," says Malachi 3:6, "I change not" (KJV). (Y'think maybe if I read that verse enough times, the message will sink in deep enough to keep me on task, all through my days?)

It's doable if I remind myself, often, that the finale of 1 Corinthians 15:58 says, "forasmuch as ye know that your labour is not in vain in the Lord" (KJV).

Should be pretty simple, shouldn't it, when the answer to my question isn't some well-guarded secret but a black-and-white biblical truth: if I busy myself not with things of an earthly nature but with His work....

Good thing I have Him to lean on, isn't it, when my brain goes off like a blazing star! * LL

A Toddler for Life

Fear not, for I have redeemed you; I have called you by your name; you are Mine.
When you pass through the waters, I will be with you; and through the rivers, they shall not overflow you.
When you walk through the fire, you shall not be burned, nor shall the flame scorch you.

ISAIAH 43:1–2 NKJV

I went to the beach with Chloe and her daughter, a wide-eyed toddler named Emma. The two-year-old was quite an independent thinker and surprisingly swift on her feet considering how short a time she'd actually been on them. Slathered in sunscreen, donning a pink hat with a large yellow sunflower, and negotiating each flip-flopped step, the child was fearless.

Chloe, however, followed along behind her daughter, slightly bent into a sort of catcher's stance, ready for whatever surprise might pop up. As Emma came upon a large hole in the sand, Chloe lifted the little girl over it and then set her down on the other side, and the child toddled forward without missing a beat. When the foamy surf sped across the sand toward Emma, Chloe swept her up into her arms above it and then set her safely down again, her feet still going a mile a minute, once the waters retreated.

As I watched them, I realized that they were a beautiful, sunshiny picture-type of how the Lord must feel about us our whole lives long. His Word says that He has called us by name, the way Chloe and her husband decided that "Emma" was just the perfect name for their smiling blue-eyed baby.

"Did you notice Emma's hair?" Chloe asked me that afternoon.

"I'm sorry. What about her hair?"

"She's got at least one hundred more strands than the last time you saw her!"

In the same way that Chloe keeps count of Emma's hairs and how many steps she can take in a row, the Lord also knows the number of hairs on our heads and how fast we'll trot directly into trouble. He keeps each of our tears in a bottle, and His love for us is endless in that perfect parental way. I so love that! When we head for the deeper waters, the Lord is there just like a well-prepared and loving parent to sweep us up in His arms and to make sure we're not overtaken. When the flames reach out toward us, He tosses Himself over us like a cloak so we're supernaturally protected and safe until the danger has passed.

Even in the times when the danger isn't entirely averted and we scrape a knee or an elbow or worse, our loving Father is bent behind us in a catcher's stance, ready and willing to hold us tight in His glove and walk through it with us.

The realization that, in that way, I can live the carefree, fearless existence of a toddler for the rest of my life is somehow comforting. And looking back throughout history at the Jonahs and the Peters and the Pauls, I'm really happy that my God has a gazillion years of catching practice!

* *SDB*

I Wanna Be Like George

Pray without ceasing.
1 THESSALONIANS 5:17 KJV

I saw the neatest thing while surfing TV channels in the wee hours of the morning...a quote from George Washington's prayer journal. Scatterbrained me scribbled a note so that, later, I'd remember to investigate the journals of the father of our country.

Well, the sun rose—and thanks to my typically crazy-busy morning, the note was quickly buried beneath my shopping list, my to-do list, bills to be paid, and reminders of phone calls to return. When at last I sat down to begin my workday, I asked God to lead my tasks and the order in which I should perform them.

I'm sure you aren't surprised to learn that He reminded me about Washington's prayer journals. Obediently, I logged on to the Internet and found dozens of sites dedicated to the man's spiritual life. Fascinated, I read the heartfelt pleas made daily by this busy, important man and had to ask myself: If George the general, president, and husband and father found time to sit down and write meaningful, heartfelt words to the Lord God every day, why couldn't I?

Join me, won't you, in a prayer, quoted from George Washington's journal. "Direct my thoughts, words, and work. Wash away my sins in the immaculate blood of the Lamb, and purge my heart by Thy Holy Spirit...that I may with more freedom of mind and liberty of will, serve Thee, the everlasting God." * *LL*

Evidence of a Generous God

*If any of you needs wisdom, you should ask God for it. He is generous
to everyone and will give you wisdom without criticizing you.*

JAMES 1:5

When you think of God's generosity, what's the first thing that comes to your mind? Many consider it to be His material blessings—the nicer house than you ever thought you'd be living in, a car that runs smoothly, or maybe a totally unexpected raise. But God's generosity extends beyond the material world. The evidence of His generosity lies in the essence of who you are.

Through your relationship with God, you acquire unseen traits, character qualities, and values that become evident to others through your actions. Every wise decision you make in difficult circumstances reveals how generous God has been with His wisdom. Every time you forgive someone who in reality deserves your scorn and revenge, it shows how generous God has been in giving you the ability to extend forgiveness and mercy—undeserved kindness.

But those attributes don't come to you as if by magic. They become integrated into your character and your spirit as you spend intentional, purposeful time with God. You can get to know about God's attributes through personal study and the teaching of others, but to make them your own, you need to spend time alone with Him, allowing Him to lavish on you the qualities than come from Him alone. * SGES

A Life of Faith

*I am calling up memories of your sincere and unqualified faith (the leaning
of your entire personality on God in Christ in absolute trust and confidence
in His power, wisdom, and goodness), [a faith] that first lived permanently in
[the heart of] your grandmother Lois and your mother Eunice and now,
I am [fully] persuaded, [dwells] in you also.*

2 TIMOTHY 1:5 AMP

It is interesting to me how these two women made their mark on the world. We don't know anything about how they looked, what their natural talents were, or what they did for a living. This is the only verse in the Bible that even records their names. But in it, we are given a snapshot of beautiful lives—the lives they lived and the life they passed on to Timothy.

Notice that it is not Timothy's father Paul mentions in his letter. It's not Timothy's teacher, playmate, or his best friend. It is his mother and grandmother who are noted for their faithfulness, to Timothy and to God.

What does the snapshot look like? There's an old woman, Lois, and Eunice, who is probably middle-aged. A young man stands between them with a sack slung over his shoulder, as though ready to embark on a journey. He is smiling. He has been chosen to assist the most powerful missionary in the world.

The verse above also gives us a clue as to why Timothy was chosen. Paul says that a "sincere and unqualified faith"—"the leaning of [his] entire personality" on Jesus, with "absolute trust in [His] power, wisdom, and goodness"—dwells in Timothy. Wow. And it "first lived permanently" in the hearts of Lois and Eunice. How might that faith have been lived out in these women's daily lives? The Bible doesn't say, but I can imagine.

Maybe one day Eunice made a meal for someone who was sick and Timothy got to help even though he made a mess in the kitchen. Maybe she took him with her to deliver the meal. I'm sure there were times when Timothy tried their patience by bringing unwanted animals into the house or not picking up his things. Maybe Lois and Eunice were always loving. I doubt it, though. No human always is. Maybe they got angry and yelled at him sometimes but had the wisdom to apologize later. And maybe he learned humility from that.

I imagine that Lois and Eunice gave Timothy lots of hugs. I bet they taught him how to pray. I bet they sang to him and disciplined him and played with him. And I bet he learned a lot of things from them when they thought he wasn't looking.

We don't all have kids and grandkids, but all of us have a life. We have people around us who fall and hurt themselves and people who are sick. We have people who try our patience, people who need a hug, and people who watch us when we think they're not looking. We have people who need to hear us singing and people we need to stand up to. People we need to laugh with and people we can point to God when times are hard. I believe that's the legacy of Lois and Eunice and the way faith transfers from one life to another. One beautiful moment at a time. * *GF*

The Meeting from You-Know-Where

Therefore, brethren, having boldness to enter the Holiest by the blood of Jesus,
by a new and living way which He consecrated for us, through the veil, that is.

HEBREWS 10:19–20 NKJV

I sat in the waiting room for forty-five minutes before the receptionist finally called me over to her desk.

"I'm so sorry," she said, "but Mr. Devlin isn't going to be able to see you today after all."

I'd phoned ahead and waited for more than six weeks for this appointment. I was fully prepared with a marketing plan and references from other similar corporate types with whom we'd done business. I knew Devlin was in his office because everyone could hear him on the phone, shouting about some deal gone wrong, and he'd kept me waiting for forty-five minutes beyond our appointment time, during which he'd had his lunch delivered. Now he couldn't see me?

"I don't think so," I replied softly.

"Pardon me?"

"I said, I don't think so."

Recounting the bumps in the road leading up to that moment, I explained that I didn't need more than ten minutes of his time and respectfully told the receptionist that I would appreciate it if she would ask him again. She did, and I got the meeting I'd been waiting for. I was even able to strike a deal on behalf of my most important client within the first ten minutes in Devlin's office. When we parted, he told me he admired my tenacity.

I'd done everything right in setting up the meeting with this very elusive businessman, and now it was up to him to do the right thing. When it looked as if he wasn't going to follow through, I punched right through the outer veil with boldness (as well as courtesy), and it paid off.

Why is it that we are often so timid about taking our challenges and petitions to the throne of our Lord? He's done everything right to provide us the privilege of doing so, and yet we hesitate.

The cleansing blood of Jesus Christ has washed the pathway before us, making straight a road that was once very crooked, and a loving Savior awaits, hoping for the opportunity to bless us in some way. So may we consistently be reminded that the way has been consecrated for us.

Enter in, beyond the veil, with boldness and thanksgiving! * SDB

Hey, Baby, What's Your Sign?

*No one can lay any foundation other than
the one already laid, which is Jesus Christ.*

1 CORINTHIANS 3:11

Show me a woman who started dating in the sixties, seventies, or eighties, and I'll show you a woman who has heard, "Hey, baby, what's your sign?" at least once. And if she didn't marry the first guy she dated, I'm sure she heard it many more times. That question is good for a laugh and makes a good icebreaker though, right?

Not so much. When a guy asks for your sign, he's talking about your astrological sign. Where's the harm in that? Well, any time we look at something that even attempts to compete with our faith in Christ, we're playing in dangerous territory. It may seem innocent, but anything to do with astrology is based on false teachings, and God condemns it. In Jeremiah 10:2, the Lord says, "'Do not learn the ways of the nations or be terrified by signs in the sky, though the nations are terrified by them.'" I think this is pretty clear that we're not to look at the stars and planets for signs that predict our future.

I have to admit that I used to read my horoscope in the newspaper first thing in the morning. I never really took it seriously, and it seemed like a fun thing to do. It gave me something to talk about when I got to work, and everyone compared notes to see how our "stars lined up" with each other. If something went wrong during the day, we'd laugh, shrug it off, and blame our astrological sign. It was all done in good fun. Now that I know better, I look back and cringe. Astrology separates us from God by claiming that the stars and planets have more control over us than our Creator. That is just wrong. I strongly believe that only God knew my future when I was born—not some impersonal planet that doesn't have the ability to care or save me from my sin.

When we go through difficult times—which seem to be in abundance lately—it's tempting to reach out for the first thing that offers hope. But the hope isn't in our horoscope in the daily newspaper or someone claiming to know you based on your sun and moon sign. The only place where we can find solace and eternal peace is in God's Word. No matter how much fun it is or how many people around me bring it up, I've learned to just shake my head and say, "No, thank you. I already know my eternal future." * *DM*

Choices

This day I call heaven and earth as witnesses against you that I have set before you life and death, blessings and curses. Now choose life, so that you and your children may live and that you may love the Lord your God, listen to his voice, and hold fast to him. For the LORD is your life.

DEUTERONOMY 30:19–20

Most adult women—like me—can't remember any great stretch of time when they haven't been on some kind of diet. My teen years were diet-free, but, mercy, that was some other gal—that size-four wonder who hadn't a clue how fortunate she was, with her ignorance of consequences yet to come.

In my whippersnapper years, I ate whatever I wanted and suffered absolutely no effects. Today I *smell* a chocolate éclair and not only do I gain weight, but something somewhere gets squishier. So now I weigh the consequences of my culinary choices more than I did in my carefree youth.

As a matter of fact, today I weigh the consequences of *all* my choices more readily than I did when I was younger. The Lord surely did look after this fine young idiot. Each day He set before me life and death, blessings and curses, and left choices open to me. So often I chose poorly. He must have shaken His head and said, "Okay, let's try this again tomorrow. I'll give you another chance."

Perhaps years from now I'll look back on today and say the same thing: "Wow, I had no clue how poorly I chose

on a day-to-day basis. And I thought I was doing so well!" The Lord seems to accept that I'm doing the best I can, that I want very much to make decisions that will not only be good for me—for my health, my long-term goals, my children, my sphere of influence—but will also fit within His will for me. How can I do better?

We need to consider that even God's patience can be taxed. As He told Moses in Deuteronomy, He tells us: "*This day...I have set before you life and death, blessings and curses. Now choose life.*" He expects us to be active in how we live our lives and how we choose.

How do we know if we are truly "choosing life," as He advised Moses to do? We need look only a few words further in Deuteronomy to get a clue. "Now choose life, so that you and your children may live and that you may love the Lord your God, *listen to his voice, and hold fast to him. For the Lord is your life.*"

For the Lord is your life. That's what we're to choose, daily: the Lord. Listen. Hold fast. *He* is your life. * *TP*

A Life of Love

Jesus said to him, "'You shall love the LORD your God with all your heart,
with all your soul, and with all your mind.' This is the first
and great commandment. And the second
is like it: 'You shall love your neighbor as yourself.'"

MATTHEW 22:37–39 NKJV

Lots and lots of people have a special grandma. In fact, the myriad of names that our society has produced for the word *grandmother* reflects the very special and unique relationship some of us have been privileged to have: We don't just have a "grandmother," we have a nanny, a memaw, a mamaw, or a granny. And I was in no way an exception to this unwritten law: I had a GaGa. When my toddler lips could not fully form the word "Grandma," what eeked out instead was this two-syllable infantile word that stuck like molasses taffy: GaGa. My grandmother fell hopelessly in love with her new name, and that was that!

GaGa had only one son and two granddaughters. Sadly, her husband had abandoned her w–a–a–y before I was even born. So it doesn't require great leaps to imagine how readily and easily her granddaughters became central to her life. She spoiled us in every way she possibly could with her meager income, and I never took her love and devotion for granted. She was equally as special and central to my world, as well.

GaGa didn't have much wealth or worldly treats to share with us. She hadn't had an inheritance from her poor parents to build upon. She didn't have a dozen pair of shoes, a fancy coat, or a nice car. She never had central heat and air or a dishwasher. Yet I never once thought of her as poor. She had more friends than anyone I have ever heard of! It was rare to be at her home without one of them "dropping by." Her phone produced a steady ring of friendly callers.

GaGa had a way of making everyone in her life feel special. Whenever you'd call her, she would generally say, "I was just thinkin' about you!"—and she undoubtedly was. You see, GaGa wasn't all about herself; she was about *the people* in her life. It was never about *her* selfish interests or ambitions, it was about everybody else's. It is this quality that endeared her not just to me and my family but to our entire community.

It was with great anticipation that I prepared to interview my grandmother on a borrowed video camera. She was in her seventies and, as far as I could tell, a monument in our town and in my life. I was thrilled at the prospect of capturing her witty charm and abundant love on film. At the end of the interview, I asked one last pointed question: "GaGa, do you have any advice for future generations?"

I fully anticipated her to say, "Love God with all your body, mind, and strength," for she surely did, and I was sure she would want her grandchildren and great-grandchildren to do the same. If she didn't say that, I was certain her answer would be: "Be the best person you can be, all the time and every time," for she had certainly led a life of endurance and perseverance. You see, I thought I knew what she would say to capture her life's essence. While what she did say was not in opposition to these ideas, it touched me deeply.

"Just love everybody. Help everybody all you can." * *GF*

A Friend Is a Friend Is a Friend... Then Again, Maybe Not!

Blessed are those who are persecuted for righteousness' sake, for theirs is the kingdom of heaven.
MATTHEW 5:10 NKJV

My husband, Daniel, was an alcoholic. He's not anymore. He's not even a "recovering alcoholic." Rather, he's a forgiven alcoholic, and he's been sober for some sixteen years. But it wasn't like God waved a magic wand and suddenly things were wonderful. Daniel and I were met with a succession of trials, but the Lord saw us through.

One Sunday night a special speaker came to our church and delivered an impromptu message on the sin of alcoholism. This speaker had planned to talk about something else that night; however, our local newspaper had run a story in its Sunday edition about how Wisconsin is in the top ranks for being home to the most alcoholics in the United States. After all, we are basically the beer capital of the world.

The speaker's message really touched my husband; he realized he didn't have to rehash all the ugliness of his past or go through years of counseling in order to quit drinking. He just had to repent and turn from it, embrace God's goodness, and accept God's healing.

That's the first step. Next came telling our friends and family members that we had both quit drinking.

Now you'd think people would be happy when an alcoholic says, "I'm done drinking and hurting my family. I'm starting a whole new life." But, incredibly, the opposite is often true. Some of our family members actually tried to sabotage Daniel's resolution. Our close friends stopped inviting us to their homes and to parties. It broke my heart to realize that my friends weren't true friends; they'd merely been drinking buddies. However, we found support at our local church. We made new friends—good friends. We still had fun. In fact, we've had more fun because we're not sick and hungover the next day! We might have lost a lot at first, but God replaced everything we lost and added more.

Stepping out into the Light takes a lot of courage. Be prepared for the backlash. Steady yourself with God's Word—and then enjoy the insurmountable blessings that follow! * AKB

God Always Plans Ahead

"So there is hope for your descendants," declares the Lord.

JEREMIAH 31:17

I didn't even know we had armadillos in Florida! They were all over the place in Texas, but the humid, hurricane-ridden peninsula of Florida just never struck me as a habitat for animals that have to wear armor 24/7. But just like God, whether you believe or not, they're here!

There are many qualities about these creatures that I have come to despise.

They are obnoxious. Even when caught in the act of digging a hole in one's yard, they ignore shouts, threats, even soda cans hurled in frustration that just bounce right off their backs.

They come out at two or three in the morning, to the great torment and frustration of dogs living inside. Consequently, home owners are ripped from a sound sleep almost every night by their furious, barking dog.

They're completely indiscriminate adversaries. They dig holes everywhere. Like near the side of the driveway by the car so you lose your footing; next to the garage, until they reach the foundation—then they keep right on digging!; under the fence so that the dog thinks she stands a chance of fitting beneath it…and ultimately gets stuck.

One recent afternoon, my dog Sophie started barking and snarling at the sliding door to the backyard, and I immediately began searching for the culprit. Instead of an armadillo, my eyes landed on a baby bird and its mother chirping wildly from atop the fence, cheering on her baby as it hopped and flapped in an effort to take flight. Closer examination revealed a nest in the tree branches above the bird, and I realized Baby had fallen from it, unable to fly beyond the confines of my backyard.

To my absolute horror, a huge black crow swooped in out of nowhere and went after the little bird. Mama and I both sprang into action to shoo the crow away. It took several attempts to deter the big bully, and while I shook my fist at it, Mama did something completely unexpected by nudging her baby toward the fence until it fell into a shallow hole left by…an armadillo!

While Baby stayed in that hole, Mama flew up to the nest, presumably to look after her other little ones. Once the coast was definitely clear and the black crow had flown off in pursuit of easier prey, the mother bird hopped down to encourage her offspring to come out from its hiding place and try once again to fly over the fence.

I couldn't help marveling over the fact that the damages done by my greatest nemesis in recent memory had actually provided much-needed shelter in time of crisis. If not for that messy hole under my fence, that baby bird might not have escaped.

Isn't that just like God? He so often casts the net beneath our high-wire act long before we ever realize we're going to fall. Those things which are meant for our harm, God has already fully understood, and He has set our escape into place ahead of time. * SDB

The Hands (and Feet) of Time

*To every thing there is a season, and a time
to every purpose under the heaven.*

ECCLESIASTES 3:1 KJV

I'm a bit of a history buff, so whenever it seems I'm letting the clocks in my house rule me, I try to dwell on the words of Winston Churchill. Uttered during a World War II meeting with Franklin D. Roosevelt and Joseph Stalin, he said, "What are we? Just specks of dust that have settled in the night on the map of the world."

I'm a neatnik by nature, so the idea that every human being inhabiting the earth can be viewed as a speck of dust instantly transports my mind from a fixation on time to wondering how many cans of Pledge it'll take to clean up *that* mess!

Good old Plautus understood, as early as 200 BC, what a serious conundrum it is—this importance we humans put on the passage of time. "When I was a boy," he wrote, "my belly was my sundial—one more sure, truer, and more exact than any of them. This dial told me when 'twas proper time to go to dinner, when I had ought to eat. But nowadays, why even when I have, I can't fall to unless the sun gives me leave. The town's so full of these confounded dials, the greatest part of its inhabitants shrunk up with hunger, creep along the streets."

Imagine how flustered the poor fella would be if he lived in our time, with clocks in every room and on TV channel selectors, caller IDs, and cell phones! What amazing prose might he pen if he heard what we so often say to one another: "If only I had more time..." "Oh, please just give me a minute!" "Goodness but the time flies!" "I haven't a moment to spare." "Um, do you have a second?" Father Time, it seems, rules the world along with everything and every*one* in it!

I often joke about what I consider a serious lack of time by saying, "If only there were forty-eight hours in every day!" But that implies our God has erred, by doling out too few hours. And really, who can know the mind of God?

We're reminded over and over in Scripture that God knew *precisely* what He was doing, meting out the days, weeks, and years of His creation. Psalm 90:1–2 tells us He embraces eternity and that He's the Master and Creator of time. Science backs this up in the first and second laws of thermodynamics: Energy and matter cannot be created or destroyed by man, and whatever decays can never all be replaced.

We're stuck, it seems, between the proverbial rock and hard place...the meat in a "deal with it" sandwich. Since only God knows the number of days He intends for us to spend on planet Earth, the best we can do is pray we'll make the best use of our time here. * *LL*

What If?

To me, who am less than the least of all the saints, this grace was given,
that I should preach among the Gentiles the unsearchable riches of Christ.

EPHESIANS 3:8 NKJV

I hate to admit this, but I sometimes lie awake at night and wonder "what if."

What if I'd been more obedient to my parents? What if I'd apologized to that friend in high school—the one I turned my back on when she needed someone to talk to? What if I'd actually majored in something more substantial in college? What if I'd been nicer in the grocery store and let the exhausted mother of tots go ahead of me at the deli? What if I'd stopped to pick up that scared, lost puppy on the side of the road? What if I'd turned off my favorite TV show to listen to my daughter tell about her day?

Yeah, I have regrets. I have the desire to do what God calls me to do, but I slip up every single day. I need to do better, but no matter how much nicer and more compassionate I become, it's still not good enough. Does this mean I should hang my head and worry some more? Should I run through my laundry list of what-ifs and wring my hands?

No.

Regrets are burdensome. They weigh on our minds and hearts and give us plenty of reasons to stay in bed all day.

Fortunately, God gave us Christ to wipe away any sins that we might regret. Knowing that the Lord has forgiven us should bring us a peace that's impossible without Him. We're rich with God's grace and mercy.

Knowing that I'm a sinner from birth can be frustrating. However, I have no doubt that I'll be with the Lord for eternity, without an ounce of help from me. He did it all.

The only thing I can do is use my agonizing memories to remind me of how lost I'd be without Him. I don't deserve this wonderful blessing, but because I'm a child of God, I have His love and the promise of eternal life with Him. What a beautiful gift!

I think I'll resolve to focus more on God's grace than all the what-ifs that bog me down. * DM

Shelter

The name of the LORD is a fortified tower;
the righteous run to it and are safe.

PROVERBS 18:10

I wonder if the cops would find my fingerprints on the remote control. Not that there'd be any reason for law enforcement to dust it for fingerprints. My prints are all over the washing machine knobs, the dryer controls, the dishwasher handle, the broom handle, the vacuum cleaner, the phone, the computer keyboard...

The television remote?

As in many households, the remote is more my husband's area of expertise.

We don't agree on much when it comes to television viewing. The incessant blare of a basketball game between two teams I've never heard of can send me into an emotional seizure. The droning monotone of the History Channel puts me into a temporary coma. For some reason, reruns—of almost anything—feel like chewing yesterday's gum. Maybe it's a phase I'm going through.

But my husband and I do agree on one type of show—survival shows, especially the non-Hollywood kind. We're fascinated by people who find ingenious ways of surviving being stranded in the Alaskan wilderness or on a remote Indonesian island or in a desert, on a glacier, in an untamed jungle...

From our overstuffed chairs, we coach the survivors.

"See those cattails? You can use the fluff inside to start a fire. You need fire."

"Don't drink that pond scum. I don't care how thirsty you are, you'll be sorry if you— Oh, man!"

"If you don't lash that bamboo raft tighter, when you hit the rapids it'll— Told you so."

"What do you mean, you have nothing to eat? Can't anyone figure out how to catch fish?" (That, from my husband, the fisherman.)

We're in awe of those who face their fears and rappel down the cliff face, who endure one miserable night after another, who pull something meaningful out of the debris washed up by a storm or out of the depths of their character.

As we look around at our neighbors and church family, we feel the same sense of awe. The couple facing their medical fears, lowering themselves over the cliff face anyway. The caregiver enduring one miserable night after another. The young man picking through the driftwood of his life, finding a little something he can use.

On the televised survival shows, the inexperienced, uneducated, or unwilling-to-learn leave shelter-building for last, after they've tanned or napped or looked for pretty seashells. The same is true in life, I guess.

Two palm fronds and a stick? You call that a shelter? Let me show you the Fortress I run to for shelter, the impenetrable Refuge, the strong and unbreachable Tower the team (Father, Son, and Holy Spirit) provides for me. It won't collapse in the middle of the night. Hurricane winds can't topple it. Earthquakes can't rattle it. Impeccable design. And it's portable. It goes where I go. * *CR*

Rooks, Pawns, and Faithful Moves

Trust in him at all times, you people; pour out your hearts to him; for God is our refuge.
PSALM 62:8

My widowed cousin put her faith in a dating service, and her daughter met the love of her life on Myspace. A couple at our church relied on a Korean-based agency to match them with a beautiful daughter, and a friend believed his Russian bride would be everything the brochure promised.

Me? I don't even trust the *word* "trust"! And why would I, when one minute it's a verb ("Trust me, I'll pay back every penny of that loan!"); in the next, it's a noun ("Free toaster for opening an account!"). Translated from ancient Norse, *traust* equals comfort. Really? I should feel comfortable relying on this thing that can't decide what it is?

I needn't be a chess champion to understand that I need to look four to six moves ahead or prepare to hear "Checkmate!" When the weatherman predicts a blizzard, I stock up on milk and toilet paper. Uncle Joe's coming? Better hide the beer. I'm "insurance poor," thanks to auto/house/health/life policies, and I print MapQuest directions before leaving on a car trip.

Lack of trust in things and people is what makes me plan for every eventuality. So it always surprises unbelievers to hear that my heart overflows with hope. They don't understand that trust and faith are very different entities—or that my faith stems from belief in a merciful Father who promises that if I put my trust in *Him*, He will be my protection, my refuge, my strength.

When unbelievers ask how I can accept on faith that God will deliver on His promises, I say faith in God is easy! It doesn't require plans. Or maps. Or thinking four to six moves ahead. Putting my trust in the people and things of the world isn't anywhere near as easy as putting my faith in the Lord!

Speaking of easy, my church friends are finding it easy to love their raven-haired daughter. My cousin's easy-to-love beau is a "keeper." Sadly, things aren't easy for the guy whose mail-order bride emptied his bank account and disappeared. And my cousin's daughter didn't have an easy time reading about her dreamboat's new girlfriend...on his Myspace page.

In the park last week, I saw two elderly gents hunched over a chessboard. "If you learn well the meaning of trust," said one as he nabbed the black knight, "others will give you the earth."

His friend toppled the white queen and snorted, "But betray them, and they'll hunt you to the ends of the earth."

What a blessing that, as Christians, we only need to look *one* move ahead and place our trust in the Almighty! * *LL*

From Rock 'n' Roll to the Solid Rock

He has put a new song in my mouth.

PSALM 40:3 NKJV

About nineteen years ago, I was a rock 'n' roll junkie. I knew the names of performers and singer-songwriters, the history of their careers and their rock bands. I'd wake up to my music, and if I heard my song, that meant I'd have a good day. The lyrics influenced my decisions, which, in turn, affected my abilities as a mother and a wife. I'd listen to my music at work, to and from work, and blare it from my speakers at home. This music was my driving force, the essence of my very being.

But then God saved me. I didn't think much of my music at first. I added God to it. I suppose I figured God was cool and changed with the times. Then I learned God is "the same yesterday, today, and forever" (Hebrews 13:8 NKJV). Soon after that, the Lord showed me that the lyrics of the tunes I so enjoyed contradicted His Word. The music itself was an idol in my life, and it became apparent to me that I needed to give it up.

I made the choice to obey the Holy Spirit.

One night our church had an Acts 19:19 party, at which we burned our "curious art," as the King James Version refers to it. We piled up all our books and record albums, CDs, videos—anything belonging to us that we felt had hindered our walk with Christ. The pile was huge, and if someone had estimated its worth, I'm sure it would have been thousands of dollars. Sure, we could have sold the items and given the cash to the church; however, burning the items seemed so symbolic for many of us. These possessions had us under a kind of spell that kept us separated from the love of Christ.

For me, the Lord put a new song in my mouth.

My hope is built on nothing less
Than Jesus' blood and righteousness.
I dare not trust the sweetest frame
But wholly lean on Jesus' name.
On Christ the solid Rock, I stand—
All other ground is sinking sand.

EDWARD MOTE, 1797–1874

* AKB

It's a Dog's Life

God is not a God of disorder but of peace.

1 CORINTHIANS 14:33

I adopted my sheepdog Caleb when he was barely a year old, and he died at sixteen from bone cancer. I knew I stood no chance of forging a connection like that with an animal again. After all, Caleb had taken me through my own cancer before I accompanied him on his battle, and we'd been best buddies, constant companions.

When I met Sophie at Rescue Day in the parking lot of the pet supply store, the first thing I noticed in her eyes (behind unmistakable fear) was a strange sort of recognition. She looked at me as if she'd spotted an old friend. I heard stories about her past that broke my heart, and the skittish little red-haired collie struck me as a very different dog than my Caleb. Still, I wanted to give her a home.

On our first night together, she slept in the hallway outside my bedroom, watching me from a distance. When the time came for lights-out, our eyes met for a long moment, and I patted the bed, inviting her to join me—but she crossed her paws and laid her head on them. About two hours later, however, I opened my eyes and found her standing next to the bed, her ears cocked as she stared at me.

"What's wrong?" I asked. She took a step backward then surprised me as she jumped up on the bed beside me. I set my hand on her head and stroked her pointed ears as I said a prayer over her. She looked up at me gratefully when I was through, staring into my eyes with such profound emotion.

"I can promise you this," I told her in a whisper. "I'll never hurt you, and I'll take very good care of you. I know how much discord there's been in your life up to now, but this is a house of peace. You'll be safe here. If we learn to love one another along the way, all the better."

There hasn't been a single night since then that Sophie hasn't curled up beside me. Often she waits for the very instant that I sit down on the bed, and she'll hop up and toss herself into my lap with complete, trusting abandon. Sophie and I have indeed learned to love one another, and I think we provide reciprocal peace that we both value beyond measure. It wasn't until recently, several years into our relationship, that I realized I'd heard those same words spoken to me once upon a time. The Lord had invited me to rest with Him and promised me I would find peace in His arms, just as Sophie had found peace in mine. * *SDB*

A Life of Obedience

Do not seek what you should eat or what you should drink, nor have an anxious mind.
For all these things the nations of the world seek after, and your Father knows that you
need these things. But seek the kingdom of God, and all these things shall be added to you.

LUKE 12:29–31 NKJV

Carly knew she needed to make a cake for a dear friend who had lost her husband not long ago. She got out all the ingredients for her famous homemade chocolate cake and icing and started mixing, spooning, and baking. In the middle of all of this, however, Carly felt the Lord say, "Make another chocolate cake."

"What? Lord, I feel like You are telling me to make another chocolate cake…." Carly could not audibly hear the Lord speak, but she knew that He was speaking nonetheless. Not only was she supposed to make another chocolate cake, it was supposed to be put into a disposable pan. So Carly went to work on another cake and baked it in a disposable pan. She felt a little crazy but obeyed anyway.

She started to make her famous chocolate icing when the voice stopped her and said, "No nuts."

"No nuts! I always put nuts in my icing. Are You sure I am supposed to leave them out?"

"No nuts."

Though it pained her to do so, Carly made the icing without nuts. Before long, she had two beautiful chocolate cakes on her counter. She knew where one was going. And she believed that before the day was through, the other one would find a home, too. So she waited.

In just a little while, her doorbell rang. She had been expecting someone from church to come over to help her with her computer. When she opened the door, her jaw dropped. Her friend Ted did not look like himself at all. In fact, he closely resembled a chipmunk hoarding nuts for the winter.

"Ted, what happened to you?" Carly asked.

He explained as best he could through the gauze in his cheeks that he had all of his wisdom teeth taken out, his wife was out of town, and he was sick of slurping soup. He went on to ask, "Is that chocolate cake I smell?"

Carly smiled and asked, "Could you eat chocolate cake if it didn't have any nuts in it?"

Ted, with a look of fierce excitement in his eyes, said, "Yes, Mrs. Carly, I sure could."

"Well then, Ted, I made you a cake today."

Isn't it amazing that the God of the universe cares so much for us that He wants us to have chocolate cake? Ted did not have to have chocolate cake to live. He could have made it just fine without it, but it was important to the Lord that he had not just a piece of cake but the whole thing.

The Lord cared so much about Ted that He prompted Carly to bake an extra cake that morning. And because she listened and obeyed, Carly got to participate in an extra-sweet blessing. The Lord was in her kitchen just like He is with you right now—in your favorite chair, in the car as you're riding along, anywhere you are—He is there. And He is watching you, speaking to you, loving you, and meeting all of your needs right down to the finest details. What a beautiful example of obedience, the story of Carly and her cake. But more importantly, what an awesome God! * *GF*

The Influential Woman

So Esther answered, "If it pleases the king, let the king and Haman
come today to the banquet that I have prepared for him."... So the king and Haman went
to the banquet.... The king said to Esther, "What is your petition? It shall be granted
you. What is your request, up to half the kingdom? It shall be done!"

ESTHER 5:4 NKJV

Believe it or not, women have a lot of power in their homes. My sons used to laugh and jokingly say, "If Mama ain't happy, nobody's happy." This phrase was usually thrown around on cleaning day when my poor sons were tortured into picking up their bedrooms (I say that facetiously). However, there's some truth to the cliché. The Bible says, "The wise woman builds her house, but the foolish pulls it down with her hands" (Proverbs 14:1 NKJV).

Amazingly, we women have some mysterious ability to destroy our husbands, sons, and daughters with abusive words and thoughtless actions. We have some inexplicable influence over our husbands, too, like Queen Esther, who saved the entire Jewish nation by persuading her husband to defeat the man seeking Israel's destruction. Yeah, I guess you could say she "buttered up" the king with the banquet before springing her request on him. But you know what they say: Attitude is everything. Esther had to make sure that God prepared the king's heart, and we all know that the way to a man's heart is through his stomach.

Seriously, I think today's biblical passage goes to show that if we wives approach our husbands correctly, we can have a mighty hand in effectively running our homes. I don't mean to diminish a single mom's power in the home, but let's face it: It tends to be more difficult to work ideas around a hardheaded man who happens to live under the same roof. And if we're stubborn, determined, and overly ambitious, we can influence our husbands into making unwise decisions. Consequently, we may suffer for it. I think many times women have that much power in their homes, but they just don't realize it.

I also believe there's real-live spiritual warfare going on, and Satan knows that if he is able to destroy a marriage, the institution of family, he can destroy a nation. But a godly woman, like the stuff Queen Esther was made of, can build up or restore her home and her family through faith and prayer. * *AKB*

A Life of Courage

Then I will go to the king, even though it is against the law, and if I die, I die.

ESTHER 4:16 NCV

I like Esther. In a Bible full of books named after men, she's one of only two women that made the list. That's pretty remarkable. More significant than that, however, is her courage.

Esther's story begins when King Xerxes gets angry because his wife, Queen Vashti, won't parade herself in front of his friends at a party. He banishes her and then, out of all the maidens in the kingdom, picks Esther to take her place.

Meanwhile, the king's henchman, Haman, had cooked up a plan to destroy all of Esther's people, the Jews. It was up to her to try to save them. But there was one problem: The law said that anyone who appeared before the king uninvited would be put to death. Esther knew she faced the reality of death if she went to the king. In Esther 4:9–11, we see that she tried to hedge around it, essentially saying, "I'll be killed…. Everybody knows that the law says the king has to summon me, and he hasn't done that in thirty days." But her cousin, Mordecai, convinces her to risk everything. He says, "Perhaps you're here for such a time as this," and Esther takes those words to heart.

As she plans what to do, Esther seems so brave, so visionary. She tells Mordecai to get all the Jews to fast and pray for her. When they do, God gives her an ingenious strategy that will not only deliver Israel but trap Haman and bring judgment upon him. Esther rises up in courage, counting the cost, and obeys God—even to the point of death. And we all know what happens. God comes through.

There's no question that Esther is a hero. Something I like about her story, however, is that she is also very human.

Very flawed. Esther obviously is not sure what will happen if she goes to see the king. In fact, she's so scared of being killed that she really doesn't want to go at all. She wavers. She has to be talked into doing the right thing. This is a woman I can relate to.

As humans, don't we do this, too? I don't always respond to a crisis with immediate courage. I wish I did, but sometimes it takes some urging to get me to trust God. And how many times have I asked for prayer or prayed about something myself and then been surprised when God actually came through? I'm ashamed to admit it. Like Esther, I think that sometimes I expect Him to let me down, and it's a surprise when He doesn't.

Something important I learn from Esther is that it's not about her, like it's not about me. She could no more control the king's response than I can control the weather. All she could do was be obedient. Courage for her meant putting herself completely in God's hands and trusting Him with the outcome—even if it meant death.

Esther has the impulse—the dream to do something great—but in herself, that's all it is. A dream. Fueled by God's power at work within her, however, Esther presents her request to the king, and her courage saves her people.

The book of Esther is the story of a powerful queen who lives a beautiful life. But part of her beauty, for me, lies in her limitations. Esther's weakness becomes the perfect medium for a display of heaven's splendor—a supernatural courage. It's not really Esther that does the great thing, after all. It's God. He can do great things in our weaknesses, too. * *GF*

I Know Your Name

*The LORD said to Moses, "I will do the very thing you have asked, because
I am pleased with you and I know you by name."*
EXODUS 33:17

I can't remember names. It's as though I've missed out on some kind of memory gene or something. I've gone to church with people for years whose names, when push comes to shove, just don't come to mind.

At one book signing, a woman I knew came up and bought a book of mine. She was from my church, but her name was buried deep within a dust-covered file at the back of my brain, and it refused to open. I could have gotten by, exchanging a few pleasantries, but when she bought my book and asked me to sign it, I knew I was in trouble.

I used the standard line I use when I forget a name. With a smile, I looked at her and said, "Since people spell their names differently, I'd better ask how you spell yours." Perspiration popped out on my forehead as the clock ticked in her silence.

"Jan," she said in a voice void of emotion. "J-A-N." She left a long pause between each letter.

Okay, so I'm slow, but I'm not that slow.

"Kind of hard to misspell that one," I said with a nervous laugh.

I have no idea what happened after that. I can't remember.

However, you can rest easy about one thing. I'll never forget her name again. At least, I don't think I will.

Believe me, I work on this problem. I've tried using the method where you remember something on a person's face with the idea that it will give you a clue to their name. But when I look at them, I think, *Was it that mole on her cheek that was supposed to tell me something? Her green eyes? The unibrow?* I get so off track, the name gets dumped in an empty corner and white noise fills my head.

These scenarios happen far too often—to the point where I run down store aisles and hide behind huge toilet-paper displays just to avoid a familiar face whose name I can't recall.

The good news is that our Father knows us by name. *By name!* No matter where life takes us, if we settle on the far side of the sea, His hand will guide us. If we hide out in some podunk town, He is there. And get this. He has the hairs on our head numbered—whether we're going through chemo or not! We never have to worry that He will forget us. He knows every intimate detail about us. We are His! * *DH*

When Did He Get So Smart?

When You said, "Seek My face," my heart said to You,
"Your face, LORD, I will seek."
PSALM 27:8 NKJV

I was a "daddy's girl" when I was growing up. My six-foot-three-inch tough-guy Marine Corps–officer father was often putty in my hands. I knew just how to get around him.

So imagine my surprise when, at the age of sixteen, I helped my mom with dinner, washed the dishes afterward, and then presented my father's favorite (banana cream pie) for dessert...but I couldn't get him to agree to allow me to join my boyfriend's band on a national tour!

"You should have asked me before you went to all this trouble," he told me. "The answer would have been the same."

In that universal sixteen-year-old way, I was aghast! All his fatherly reasons why I wasn't going to be allowed to spend my summer touring the country with my boyfriend were pretty much lost on me. I wanted to go, and my mind was racing with ideas on how I could make that happen.

"You know," my dad said to me later that night, "some-day you're going to ask me something and, after I answer, you're going to wonder to yourself, 'When did my old man get so smart?'"

"Well, this isn't that day," I replied dryly.

I know. I was a haughty teenager.

"So this is probably like spitting into the wind," he said from the doorway of my bedroom, "but I'm going to say it to you anyway. There is no price tag hanging on your well-being. There aren't enough chores you can do or pies you can make to buy an answer you want to hear when it's something that I feel is going to interfere with your safety."

It wasn't until years later that I realized how my dad had quickly discerned the motives behind my actions that day—and so many other days, too. He loved it when I helped around the house and made sure to be at the table with the family for dinner, and he was so appreciative when I went out of my way to do something I knew would please him. But the fact that I knew that and, typical of a teenager, used it to try to get something in return took all the flavor out of it for him.

My father didn't want anything from me except my love and respect. He wanted me to spend time with the family because they were important to me. He wanted me to "seek his face," not what he might be holding in his hand.

Honestly, I can't help wondering as I look back: When did he get so smart? * *SDB*

Never-Ending Discovery

Every day I will praise you and extol your name for ever and ever. Great is the LORD and most worthy of praise; his greatness no one can fathom.

PSALM 145:2–3

The more time you spend with God, the more aware you become that you will never reach the end of your discovery of Him. He exceeds the limits of human understanding.

Why? Because God is infinitely great and we are finite creatures. Just as is true with numbers, an infinite Being does not have limits where finite creatures do. There simply is no end to the wonders of God.

Take, for instance, His wisdom. No matter how many times you read His Word, you'll find that you will never plumb the depths of its meaning, you'll never reach the end of His understanding. God's wisdom is beyond fathoming because His mind is more vast than the universe.

Or consider His infinite power. Have you ever seen evidence that God's power has been overreached? Neither men nor angels have ever thwarted His ability to accomplish His will.

And how about His love? Have you ever reached the limits of God's love? If you search throughout Scripture, you'll find that no one has ever done so. There are those who reject His love and refuse to receive it. But there is never a case in which God's love has ever been exhausted. It endures forever. How thrilling to realize that the discovery will outlast you. * SGES

Honesty and Honor

Honor your father.
EXODUS 20:12 NLT

God gives fathers the sacred task of preparing their children to be fathered by God Himself. That's a tall order! Most dads try their best but understand their own limitations. Most dads look back at their fathering years with a mixture of satisfaction and regret.

Your own experience with the one you called "dad" can run the gamut. Some of us had fathers who were wise and wonderful. Some of us had fathers who were abusive. For some of us, dad was absent altogether. Your response to the fathering you received (or missed) might be gratitude or anger, laughter or sorrow, or a mixture of all this and more.

This provides us with a great opportunity to process with God an important part of our lives. As you take time with your heavenly Father, your relationship with your earthly father is an important topic to discuss. What are your real feelings toward your dad? Share them with God. Let Him inside that protected place in your heart. Share with Him your fond memories and your disappointments. Ask Him for His perspective. As you do, you will gain new insights into your relationship with your dad and forge a deeper relationship with God. * SGES

Husband for Sale—Cheap!

Wives, submit to your own husbands, as to the Lord. For the husband is head of the wife, as also Christ is head of the church; and He is the Savior of the body. Therefore, just as the church is subject to Christ, so let the wives be to their own husbands in everything.

EPHESIANS 5:22–24 NKJV

I love my husband. He's a great guy. He tries very hard to make me happy—and he's usually successful. I'm basically a joyful woman.

But there are times when I'd like to sell off my beloved to the highest bidder. Make that *any* bidder! It's those frustrating times when he won't share his thoughts with me and decisions have to be made; I need to know what he's thinking! It's those aggravating moments when I try to tell him about a personal crisis and he rolls his eyes like I've just uttered the stupidest thing in the world.

Okay, sure, he's put up with a lot from me. I like to shop. But he likes to watch football, basketball, and baseball on TV (throw NASCAR into that mix, too). Yeah, I suppose my habit is more expensive. However, I do have a job outside the home and contribute to our family's income. But it's also true that I write books, short stories, and devotions (an all-consuming ministry) when I could be spending time with him—but if he doesn't talk anyhow, what's the point? Oh, and I can't forget that for the first twenty-five years of our marriage, my husband suffered through my PMS (that's "post" and "pre"). But I gave him three wonderful, healthy sons—and he didn't have to do anything but stand there and watch me push and strain as our boys entered the world. What's more, he snored right through the 2 a.m. feedings—

make that the 2, 4, and 6 a.m. feedings!

But over the years, he's proved himself faithful. There have been no other women in his life. (I think I'm all he can handle.) He doesn't do drugs, drink, smoke, or chew. He makes my lunch for me before I leave for work. He habitually checks my minivan's oil and the air pressure in its tires. He makes sure my vehicle is washed. He does the laundry (I can't remember the last time I used the washing machine), and he loads and unloads the dishwasher. He loves me and would do anything for me if he thought it would make me happy. Most of all, he loves the Lord Jesus Christ.

Can a woman really ask for anything more? Sure she can!

We're never truly satisfied, are we? That's human nature. The flesh. And the flesh wars against the Spirit of God, tugging, pulling, and causing us to see all the negative things in our spouses instead of focusing on the positive.

It's a constant battle, but our Lord is a forgiving God (1 John 1:9). He's also a God who has His hands firmly gripping the steering wheel of life. All we have to do is plant ourselves in the passenger seat and let Him take us where He will.

As for my husband—all bids are off, girls. I guess I'll keep him. * AKB

When Friendship Hurts

Say to wisdom, "You are my sister," and to insight, "You are my relative."
PROVERBS 7:4

When someone says, "Hey, Loree, I'd like you to meet So-and-so," what am I to do, hand out an "Are you trustworthy?" questionnaire and keep my distance until she fills it out? I prefer to give her my hand and leave the "Is she trustworthy?" part to God.

The trouble is, I don't always remember to ask for His guidance. And even when I do, I'm not always good at reading His answers.

Take, for example, a woman I met years ago, when she and her husband were newcomers to our church. Married and a stay-at-home mom, she also hoped someday to see her words in print. With all we had in common, this budding friendship seemed too good to be true. As we swapped recipes and sipped herbal tea while our children romped in her backyard or mine, it never crossed my mind to ask what *God* thought of the relationship.

In the coming year, He blessed me with articles and short stories that appeared in newspapers and magazines. I took a one-night-a-week job, teaching "Writing and Marketing Freelance Articles" at the community college…step one in realizing my dream of having a novel published.

Meanwhile, my friend self-published her own novel, and I was proud to agree when she asked for my help in marketing it. Then, she came to me for a recommendation and guidance so that she, too, could teach at the college, and I gave it…all without first asking for the *Father's* guidance.

Not long afterward, as I recovered from a serious illness, my friend came to visit with a box of candies in one hand and a stack of papers in the other. If I hadn't read her ad in the local paper the following week, I might never have known that, while borrowing my copy machine, she'd also "borrowed" class and workshop notes, lesson plans, and my business proposal for an in-house writers' studio.

Deeply hurt and disappointed, I took the heartache—finally—to the Lord, and He provided still more evidence that it's never too late to bring my problems, however big or small, to His throne.

If I'd gone to Him sooner, might I have spared myself this sadness? Absolutely!

But just as my earthly father ran alongside me, holding the seat as I learned to ride my two-wheeler, my heavenly Father knew that the only way I'd figure out the delicate balance between trust and true friendship was if He let go and let me fall.

In the following months, my friend quietly faded from my life. Too busy running her writers' studio to find time to call or visit? Perhaps. I prefer to think that *she* gained something from the experience too. * *LL*

From Dust Bunny to Dust

As a father has compassion on his children, so the LORD has compassion on those who fear him.
PSALM 103:13

Not everyone dusts the house the way I do. Many people dust more often than once a presidential term. I always mean to do better, but the truth is, if I didn't host my book club meetings a few times a year, we'd be talking scenes from *Tales from the Crypt* around here. The house is clean, but it does get dusty.

Part of the problem is that, no matter how hard I try, that doggone dust comes right back again. Despite the sweat of my brow, there is simply no way to ban the dust long-term. So I kind of gave up awhile ago.

I'm thankful God isn't like me. No matter how often I come back—feeble, sinful, selfish, and disobedient—He doesn't give up on me. He doesn't give up on any of us. The next verse provides a hint as to why God is so patient with us. "As a father has compassion on his children, so the Lord has compassion on those who fear him; *for he knows how we are formed, he remembers that we are dust*" (Psalm 103:13–14, emphasis added).

Even I couldn't gather up enough dust to form an entire human. But the Lord has the wherewithal and the power to do exactly that. When we fail, God never forgets the fact that—although He loves us unconditionally—we are but dust. I ask you, fellow dust bunny: how do we merit that kind of love?

Sometimes we don't even *try* to deserve His love. Sometimes we get all puffed up about ourselves and our rights, our pride, our expectations of respect and consideration. God doesn't forget our origins, but sometimes we do.

And how about when we *do* try to deserve His love? No matter how hard we might try, there is no way for us to get it right. No way to become innocent children of God. No way to achieve the right to call ourselves His. No way except *One.*

God knew when He formed us from the dust that we'd fall short. Jesus knew it too. And the Holy Spirit has always been ready, just waiting for us to receive God's gift, to ask Jesus to forgive and save us, and to accept the filling of the Holy Spirit.

One of the kindest considerations our Father gives us is His constant compassion. Yes, we are to "fear" our Father by respecting Him, but we need never fear He will brush "the dust" off His sandals and reject us, even though we keep coming back dirty and imperfect.

God isn't like I am with dust, disgusted when it shows up again. He *loves* that we keep coming back. * *TP*

I Wanna Hold Your Hand

Trust in the LORD with all your heart and lean not on your own understanding.

PROVERBS 3:5

For the past several days, I've been pondering this verse. I thought about how many worldly things we trust—family, friends, jobs, money, homes, cars, newspapers, magazines, and even hobbies. As Christians, we want to live our lives close to people and things we can trust. But no matter how wonderful that sounds, all those things will let us down—even family and friends. The only thing we can count on is the Lord. Yesterday, that point was driven home…or should I say *pounded* home?

My husband wanted to play golf, so I decided to go visit my dad and step-mom. Her birthday was coming up soon, so it seemed like a good time to bring her a gift and spend a little time with them, not having seen them in a while. I'd been there a couple of hours when my cell phone rang. The caller ID said HOME, so I knew it was my husband. I assumed he was asking where I was, when I planned to return home, and what was for dinner.

Instead, he said something that made my heart drop. "I was injured on the golf course," he stated, his voice all gravelly. "As I turned the corner in the golf cart, my foot hit a curb, and something in my ankle snapped. What should I do?"

After asking if he thought it was broken and getting his I-don't-know reply, I paused for a moment to think about how long it would take me to get home and bring him to the emergency room. An hour—too long. So I asked him if he could drive himself to the hospital. I felt terrible, like I was letting him down. If I'd been home, he could have leaned on me and we would have immediately been on our way to get medical attention.

He assured me he could drive, so I hung up, said my good-byes to my dad and step-mom, then hurried home. An hour later, Wally hobbled into the house, leaning on crutches. "These things are hard to maneuver," he said. Once he placed them against the wall, he didn't pick them up again. Instead, he hopped around.

Proverbs 3:5 popped into my head. Although the verse isn't talking about physical crutches, it's easy to compare them to our understanding and how different that is from the Lord's strength. Crutches are annoying and cumbersome, while the Lord's strong shoulders are always there for us to rely on. * DM

Always Appreciated

Come and see what God has done, his awesome deeds for mankind!
PSALM 66:5

My Mr.-Magoo-like eyesight has been one of my more notorious physical characteristics throughout life.

Two years before the 1966 rubella vaccine was discovered, I was struck during the pandemic that swept Europe and the US. There were other children and infants who fared worse than me, losing their hearing, sight, mental faculties, even their lives. I returned to school unaware that my eyes had been affected. I was a good reader before I got sick, but suddenly I couldn't grasp the words on the board. My teacher could tell—I was squinting—and off to the clinic she sent me.

All these years I've worn goofy glasses and hard contact lenses (which I chased across windy school yards or frantically hunted on disco dance floors). I've fallen asleep wearing my lenses and awoken with scratched corneas and eye infections. At forty-something, I started wearing reading glasses on top of the contacts—and there's just something wrong with that picture.

I've always craved LASIK surgery, but it seemed right up there, luxury-wise, with designer purses, Brazilian blowouts, and annual jaunts to the Caribbean. Still, the lure of fuss-free vision prompted a saving frenzy. Once I felt flush enough to pay for the surgery, I took the plunge. I finally had it done last year, and I love the results.

Still, I've already become so used to seeing without glasses that sometimes I take it for granted. I got out of the shower the other day and was reminded of how fantastic it was to see everything around me clearly and comfortably.

As I've done ever since the surgery, I stopped to thank God for the gift of my corrected vision.

I know what terrible vision is like, so I have a greater appreciation for my new clarity. Similarly, people who live with physical challenges—the inability to hear, walk, go through a day without pain—know by contrast how much better their lives could be. Nevertheless, we're *all* blessed by "what God has done."

Sometimes I catch myself subtly moping about the disappointments of my day. I get out of bed dreading some task I have to do that day, or I go to bed aware of something that didn't pan out the way I had hoped. *Why not, Lord? Why me, God?* I can even stretch that dissatisfaction to cover the responsibilities and results of the past week. Or month. Or year.

How much better my days would seem if I started and ended them by considering how my body—even this imperfect one—is blessed. How much brighter my outlook would be if I considered how He protects my loved ones and my friends. How much more content I'd be if each night I took the time to appreciate my comfortable bed…food in the pantry…freedom to worship…the vast, beautiful skies…the smallest hummingbird…the warm sun…the cool breeze. The many gorgeous vistas here and abroad. Music. Laughter. Breath. My heartbeat.

Salvation.

Oh, come and see what our God has done! There is so much to appreciate. * *TP*

A Life of Faithfulness

Because of the LORD's great love we are not consumed, for his compassions never fail.
They are new every morning; great is your faithfulness.

LAMENTATIONS 3:22–23

One morning during the worst season of my marriage, I woke up to find this verse in bold letters hanging on our refrigerator. My husband had put it there as a reminder to me and, I'm sure, to himself that God had not forgotten us.

We'd sung all the verses to "Great Is Thy Faithfulness" at our fairy-tale wedding, where we were described as a "power couple" by various friends from college. Successful socially as well as in academics (and he in sports), we started our marriage on the crest of a wave that, it seemed, we'd be able to ride forever. Six years later, however, we were without jobs, broke, and searching for God's direction.

We'd taken a leap of faith, thinking we were embarking on a great spiritual adventure. Only, as sometimes happens in such adventures, we fell flat on our faces. After several months with seemingly no answers in sight, we ended up in my hometown running a café/bed and breakfast. We lived in one bedroom on the premises. Stone went from head coach to head waiter. And I used all of my education and expertise to chop salad ingredients in a sweltering kitchen.

Three months into this experience, I found out I was pregnant. These were not exactly the ideal circumstances we'd envisioned for starting a family.

I learned many, many lessons in that season—enough to fill another book. But the most important one is that God is faithful. The Bible says that even "if we are faithless, he remains faithful" (2 Timothy 2:13 NRSV). Even when we miscalculate and falter in our faith, even when we mess up. In time He provided the way of escape—a new job and a ministry for Stone, writing assignments for me, and a whole house where we could live and raise our baby.

At times the Lord seems silent, but He is always there, blessing and keeping us in His eternal love. Looking back now I can see how He was at work—even in that dark time—to bring things together for our good. Deuteronomy 33:27 reads, "The eternal God is thy refuge, and underneath are the everlasting arms" (KJV). Whether you're soaring like an eagle or falling toward rock bottom, Jesus is there to catch you. His faithfulness will never fail. * *GF*

The Character of True Love

Love suffers long and is kind; love does not envy; love does not parade itself, is not puffed up; does not behave rudely, does not seek its own, is not provoked, thinks no evil; does not rejoice in iniquity, but rejoices in the truth; bears all things, believes all things, hopes all things, endures all things. Love never fails.

1 CORINTHIANS 13:4–8 NKJV

Karen and I became best friends very soon after our first meeting. We made each other laugh, even in the awful times, and we trusted each other with our deepest concerns and fears. We were prayer partners, girlfriends, sisters.

When I was diagnosed with uterine cancer, Karen was the first person I turned to. She confessed right away that she wasn't sure she could face the battle ahead, but despite this fact, I had faith in the strength I'd always drawn from her friendship, and I reminded her that this was what we were given to battle. I was confident that we could face it together.

One of the things that often occurs with cancer patients between diagnosis and treatment is that their filters shut down. The way they talk to their family and friends, the way they behave in general, is colored by the anger and fear and roller-coaster emotions that they haven't had the time or ability to process. I was terrified, and I just couldn't get a handle on how to face what was littering the road ahead of me. This is no excuse for harsh words or touchy reactions; it's just an explanation.

To say that I was less than soft-spoken and kind would be a gross understatement, and Karen took the brunt of it in those first days. Still, I've never been more shocked than when I received a curt two-line e-mail from her saying that I should find someone else to take me to the hospital for my surgery; she wouldn't be picking me up. I called her, I e-mailed her, I reached out to her in every way I could think of, believing that an apology was warranted and, afterward, there would be forgiveness and understanding. And restoration.

Almost five years have passed since that e-mail from Karen. Despite my best efforts, I've never heard another word from her. She never knew that the first surgery for the uterine cancer revealed stage III ovarian cancer, as well. She never knew how I struggled through two more surgeries and five weeks of daily radiation, or how alone I felt without her. For nearly three years afterward, I fought bitterness and disappointment, anger and the intense pain that comes with that sort of abandonment. It took three solid years before I could think of her without crying or begin the walk down the road toward forgiving her.

I am happy to report that, with the ability to forgive Karen at last, the Lord has also brought me this revelation knowledge: forgiving Karen is a blessing to my heart, not hers; and people are going to fail you every day of the week, but true love, which is the very character of God Himself, never will. * *SDB*

A Thorny Situation

I am the rose of Sharon, and the lily of the valleys.
SONG OF SOLOMON 2:1 KJV

It was a small prayer, one that some might call insignificant. "Don't waste God's precious time on a plea that your silly roses will flourish!" said one of my husband's relatives.

But I asked anyway.

Why?

Because I'm convinced it's the very reason I gather more than beautiful blooms from the thorny bushes and why I'm able to take such joy in every velvety petal!

When powdery mildew threatened to overtake the plantings in my garden, I performed every trick in the "How to Grow Roses" handbook.

Once I got that situation under control, aphids invaded—but stubborn determination (and a book called *Roses for Dummies*) solved that problem, too.

Summer's drought continued. Then spider mites set up housekeeping among the prickly stalks. My poor flowers budded but they didn't have the strength to bloom. And, oh, how I missed the delectable scent of my ruby-red Mr. Lincolns!

Still I refused to cry "uncle"! On my knees, pruning the brown-spotted yellow lower leaves of my White Ladies, I prayed that the Lord would tell me what to do to save these, His oh-so-lovely creations. And no sooner had I uttered "Amen" than a ladybug zoomed in and then settled on a snowy bud. Soon I realized that she'd brought a couple hundred of her closest friends and relatives along for the flight, for I began noticing black-dotted red beetles on the blooms and leaves of every plant...and dozens more marching toward the hearts of my prized roses.

But it was as a praying mantis clung to one spiky stalk that I knew

God didn't consider my prayer insignificant at all, for He'd sent a mini army of six-legged soldiers to protect His delightful roses.

How humbled I was, how blessed I felt, knowing that He wants to attends to our every need and desire—even those that others see as a waste of His time! * *LL*

Morning Wake-Up Call

The Sovereign LORD has given me well-instructed tongue, to know the word that sustains the weary.
He wakens me morning by morning, wakens my ear to listen like one being instructed.

ISAIAH 50:4

Morning people amaze me. You know the type. They wake up with smiles on their faces. Then they bounce their way to the kitchen, where they prepare a healthy concoction of fruits, juices, wheat germ, and maybe something that came from the backyard garden.

When I was a kid, I thought those people drove themselves to get up in the morning, and certainly there are those who do (but they are not "morning people" in the truest sense of the word). Imagine my horror when I discovered that there were people who actually—wait for it— love to get up with the rising of the morning sun!

This is just wrong on so many levels.

I wish I could tell you that when the alarm goes off, I automatically spring into action. But honestly, nary a muscle moves on my body until the alarm screams at least three times, and then only the slightest twitch of a nerve gives a faint indication of life inside this physical shell. If not for the scent of coffee luring my pajama-clad, fluffy-slippered self into the kitchen, I'd probably stay in bed till noon.

Now, make no mistake, I do not get up with the rising of the sun. I've heard it's a beautiful sight, but I witness sunrise enough on the front of my Raisin Bran box. I want to sleep as late as possible. It's truly better for everyone in my world.

Still, we all know that duty calls. There is work to be done, calls to be made, lists to be accomplished. So I drag myself out of bed and reluctantly give in to the start of a new day.

Before I dive into my workday, however, I open God's Word and see what He wants to tell me, and then we "discuss" it. It's during my morning prayer that He will bring to mind those for whom I need to pray, call, visit, or send a card. I love when He plans my day. How rewarding it is when someone says they received the card or phone call just when they needed it. Of course, it was because God knew their need and prompted me to help His work.

I don't look forward to mornings, but I do look forward to my time with Him. It's in my quiet place that I find His perspective, guidance, grace, mercy, joy, and strength for another day.

We are His hands and feet. He wants to use us in our world to make a difference for the kingdom—whether it's morning, noon, or evening. Are you listening? * *DH*

Gold Rush

Gold there is, and rubies in abundance, but lips that speak knowledge are a rare jewel.

PROVERBS 20:15

Jesus never said anything dumb.

Can you imagine never having to apologize for something you said? Never suffering embarrassment over calling your insurance agent's wife by another name? No string of unsightly "ums" in a job interview or speaking gig? Imagine a relationship with no "Sorry, that's not what I meant." How much more sleep might I have enjoyed if my mind hadn't replayed the missteps my mouth made earlier that day? Can you imagine the relief of knowing that every word spoken was golden?

My husband was enamored with the televised real-life drama of a team of rookie gold miners who left their homes and families with one purpose—to strike it rich with Alaskan gold. The team had aging, cobbled equipment and just enough knowledge to be dangerous. Propelled by a series of calamities a fiction editor would have declared too numerous to be believed, the men scraped and pitted and pockmarked the Alaskan wilderness in search of golden treasure.

They panned by hand and processed rocks and soil with nerve-rattling giant machinery. Nothing. They collected buckets of black sand that held the promise of gold flakes. Nothing. They stayed up all night pumping water out of caverns they'd created, looking for a long-buried and long-silent waterfall with an elusive pot of gold at its base.

The men spent all they had and kept spending, ignoring their overdue mortgages and the bill collectors at their doors back home because of the lure of gold.

A mountain of discarded dirt and gold-less rocks, injuries, illness, and broken relationships stood as testaments to the draw of a precious metal so valuable a medicine bottle full could buy a car.

The men burned through tankers full of fuel and truckloads of food and all their reserves of patience. The summer they thought would net them a fortune turned into snow and bone-chilling temperatures that threatened their chances to recover even the cost of the Ben-Gay they'd used on screaming muscles.

Then, finally, there it was. A nugget. And another. Not enough to get them out of financial trouble, but enough to feed their frenzy for more.

Months of work and sacrifice. Monumental expenditures of everything worth spending in pursuit of something they deemed worth saving.

And God says, by comparison, that gold is plentiful. What He considers rare are lips that speak true knowledge.

What if I looked at my opinions as if they were pyrite—fool's gold—and at genuine knowledge as genuine gold? How many words could I pan out of my day? How many conversations would I discard, dross not worth saving? What if I spoke, Tweeted, Facebooked, and wrote only words that mattered?

What if I moved so closely in tune with the Spirit of God that I could have the same confidence Jesus did—with no dumb words?

Imagine. * *CR*

Control Freak

Our God is a God who saves; from the Sovereign LORD comes escape from death.
PSALM 68:20

I used to be afraid to fly. I'm convinced that it was about the lack of control. Handing my safety over to a complete stranger behind the door is as irrational to me as giving my power to the Wizard of Oz—the man behind the curtain, if you will. So if I did travel, it was done with clutched fingers around the armrests and lots of prayer.

Then, one day after 9/11, I got a call to go on a television show in New York to talk about my book. The only thing I'd rather do *less* than talk publicly about my book is to do so on the other side of the country in New York City with only a day's notice.

It was the day of my son's eighth birthday party, and everything went wrong that day. I didn't have time to get a new outfit for TV; I didn't have time to stop for cash; and I wasn't that great at traveling, so I didn't know that taxis in NYC don't take credit cards. Once on the ground, I also got word that the publicist changed hotels on me and my directions were no longer valid.

In other words, everything that could go wrong—did.

But you know what? God had all of it covered. For instance, the hotel was high-end, and the bellman paid my cab fare until I could get cash.

That trip changed my life. No, I didn't do all that well on TV, and I did miss my son's birthday party, and I was also the coldest I have ever been in my life because of my inability to understand what real winter feels like. But I learned something that day.

I learned that God is truly in control and that if I believe it, I have nothing to fear. If it's my day to go, He's got that covered too because all I have to do is believe on the Lord Jesus Christ, confess that belief with my mouth, and I will be saved from eternal death.

When we spend our time worrying, we are spending our time saying that God isn't there, that He can't handle this one thing…and that's just not true. My will may not be His, but His is better.

Now I fly at least once a month. Travel is no longer a fear, and I enjoy every moment of my trips. That was worth everything not going my way, right? * *KB*

Just Do It

We live by faith, not by sight.
2 CORINTHIANS 5:7

I was twenty-five years old when I turned a corner and suddenly the life I'd come to know was gone. No more marriage, home, job, or familiarity with anyone or anything. With nothing more than what I could fit into the back of a Ford Fiesta, I drove for two days to start my life over. And for a girl who'd grown up in Cincinnati, Ohio, I felt like a dot on the map in a city as vast as Los Angeles.

I moved in with the family of someone I'd met when I was a teenager; we'd been little more than pen pals over the years in between. But for some reason I never fully understood, she and her mother opened their home to this wayward mess of a person and gave me a roof over my head until I could figure it all out.

The job search turned very bleak very fast, and one afternoon just two weeks after my arrival in Southern California, reality took a nosedive with my spirits strapped onboard. "The only experience I have is office work," I told my friend. "And the thought of being a secretary for the rest of my life is almost unbearable."

Roanne sighed in reply. "Well," she said, "what would be your dream job? If you could do anything you wanted to do, what would it be?" I laughed. "I would be a writer." "What kind of writer?" "Any kind. Ideally, a screenwriter or a novelist. But since that's not likely to happen…"

After a moment's thought, Roanne left the room. When she returned a few minutes later, she dragged a huge manual typewriter to the counter, piled a stack of blank white paper next to it, and pulled out the bar stool.

"You want to write?" she asked me. Before I could reply, she pointed at the counter. "Forget what you can't do and think about what you can. Write something."

Even now as I retell the story, it sounds ridiculous. But over the next couple of months, in between interviews and temporary office assignments, I tapped out the worst book that's ever been written, and Roanne had the audacity to send it to several publishers. The rejections poured in, and I eventually threw away the typed pages. I wrote three more terrible novels while going to film school at night… and four screenplays after that before one of my scripts was finally optioned.

In that one ridiculous moment, floundering around in the most hopeless and terrifying season of my life, someone looked me in the eyes and told me that my dreams might actually be attainable. And the profound exhilaration that followed rolled out a vision that pushed me forward toward the writer that I am today. * *SDB*

Fifty is the New Thirty

Do not cast me away when I am old; do not forsake me when my strength is gone.
PSALM 71:9

Hot young chicks are in high demand in this world; shriveled-up old prunes are not. The question is, who gets to decide at what point the hot chick is all dried-up and ready to be cast aside? Our kids? Our grandkids? Um…I don't think so. At least not now…maybe never.

I remember thinking in my late teens and early twenties that anyone over thirty was old. Back in the day (never mind the year), once a woman reached the big three-oh, she either started wearing double-knits and orthotics or she lied about her age.

Fortunately, things have changed and the old-age line has shifted. Cosmetic companies began producing beauty products to smooth out our wrinkles and erase age spots, making fifty the new thirty. Our kids grew up with hip moms who looked like they could be older sisters— much to the kids' dismay. We started working out and staying in shape. We have cool haircuts that cost more than dinner out for a family of four. Our hair color is whatever we want it to be, and we don't mind changing it to the hue du jour. There's no need to get old, even when we're ready for the retirement home. From what I hear, there's some serious partying going on in those places these days.

I have two daughters who are both in their twenties. One is a single, educated, career woman, and the other is a married, educated mommy. Yeah, that makes me a grandmother, but, hey, we haven't determined where that old-age line is yet—although my children might look at it differently. When my daughters were little, they thought I was smart. At some point in the preteen years, I became a feebleminded meddler and invisible when it was convenient. Then as they blossomed into adults, the most amazing thing happened: I suddenly got smart again. Now I'm grateful that my daughters and I have a warm, loving relationship based on mutual respect. I can't imagine them or my husband turning me away as I grow old and wrinkled.

As I think about this verse, "Do not cast me away when I am old…," I also consider myself fortunate that as a believer, I never have to worry about God getting tired of me or seeing me as less worthy of His love at any point in my life, no matter how old I get. Old age may steal my taut, firm skin and replace it with a saggy, baggy hide, but I know the Lord sees beauty in His creation. * DM

A Life of Service

For you have been called to live in freedom, my brothers and sisters....
Use your freedom to serve one another in love.

GALATIANS 5:13 NLT

I don't know Camilla all that well; I wish I knew her better. We live in the same community and she has kids around my age, but her kids and I went to different schools so we didn't really know each other. Though our families are acquainted like most families in small towns, our lives might never have intersected had it not been for her husband. He built our house.

I remember the night Stone and I drove over to Guy Richard and Camilla's place. We had set up a meeting to show him our house plans, to see what he thought about building it and how much it would cost. I guess it was an interview, but in my mind he was hired if he wanted the job. I knew I wanted him as builder because he had such a great reputation.

While Stone and Guy Richard discussed numbers at the dining room table, my eyes wandered to the walls. There were pictures of kids and family paraphernalia covering every square inch of space. Camilla, who had already served us ice water, was bringing in groceries through the back door. I remember she had several gallons of milk, and I thought vaguely, *Isn't it just the two of them living here? They must like milk.*

At some point, I left Stone at the table and moved to the bar that faced where Camilla was rummaging around in the kitchen. It was a Saturday night, close to bedtime, and yet she appeared to be assembling a feast. There were baking dishes all over the counters—some full of barbecue chicken,

others with beef and several different vegetables.

"Are we in your way?" I asked her, wondering what huge party she must be catering.

"Oh, no!" Her eyes were warm and kind as she wiped her brow with a free hand. "I'm just getting ready for tomorrow."

All of Camilla's kids were coming over the next day for lunch—all seven of them—and their families. When I asked her how many people that was, she showed me a framed picture that resembled a small army. I turned to her in surprise, and she just grinned. She seemed as happy as a child on Christmas morning. Furthermore, she told me she does it every Sunday.

"The preacher down at the church came to visit me one time and asked why I never come to Sunday school." Camilla smiled at me. "I told him I can make it to the service, but I've got to cook all morning before that. I believe God wants me to make lunch for my family, and as long as I'm able to do it, I'll be in the kitchen during Sunday school." She chuckled. "I guess when I get too old to cook, I might start going."

This bit of homespun theology might seem outrageous to some people, but it resonated with me. While I love to worship God at Sunday school, I felt just as near to Him in Camilla's kitchen. I'll bet her kids and their kids do, too.
* GF

My Way

Now a leper came to Him, imploring Him, kneeling down to Him and saying to Him,
"If You are willing, You can make me clean." Then Jesus, moved with compassion,
stretched out His hand and touched him, and said to him, "I am willing; be cleansed."
As soon as He had spoken, immediately the leprosy left him, and he was cleansed.

MARK 1:40–42 NKJV

Between working hard all my life at various jobs and being the best wife and mother I can be, I feel like it's time to have things my way. What's wrong with that? Isn't getting what we deserve the ultimate goal?

Fortunately for all of us, it's not.

Stay with me on this. Yeah, I've been a good wife and mother. My husband is happy and well-fed. My children have grown up to be productive Christian adults. As an employee, I showed up on time, completed all my tasks in the best way I knew how, and showed loyalty toward whatever company I worked for.

So why shouldn't I get what I deserve?

Well, for starters, I'm not Jesus. He's the only perfect person who ever walked the earth. Behind my "good woman" facade is a dirty rotten sinner. I don't set out to do bad things, but terrible thoughts creep into my head. Sometimes what I want is more important to me than the needs of others. I get angry, and I feel left out. When someone who doesn't seem as deserving as me gets something I want, I harbor harsh feelings. I get sick and tired of stuff that is insignificant in the big scheme of things.

In other words, I lose sight of my purpose in this life, which is to glorify Jesus.

This attitude should be in everything I do—from how I talk to people to the way I pray to God. Do I ask for a list of things I think I deserve? Or do I lay my heart on the line and ask that His will be done?

Even though I think I know what's good for me, the only One who truly knows is God. When we pray, we need to remember that what we want is often shiny on the outside but dirty on the inside. Our way isn't necessarily His way. The Lord's will is all-knowing and all good. Like a parent who forces a child to eat her vegetables, He knows what will make us strong in our walk with Him. * *DM*

Supply and Demand

As far as the east is from the west, so far has he removed our transgressions from us.
PSALM 103:12

Have you ever tried to explain the grace of God to someone? It's one of the most beautiful and humbling blessings in our lives—that amazing promise that nothing can separate us from the love and forgiveness of our God—and yet the concept is so hard for some people to wrap their brains around. It's not even a case of supply and demand, is it? How do we tell them there's not only enough but also an abundance available, *beyond* what we need?

I have one particular friend who just can't get past this one issue in her spiritual journey.

"You mean to tell me," she recapped after a particularly long conversation about my beliefs, "some guy can go out and torture and murder someone and live a completely worthless life, but on his deathbed, he can just say, 'Oops, sorry!' and he's forgiven everything? That guy should be punished, not find some touchy-feely forgiveness."

"Well," I replied thoughtfully, praying to find the right words, "it's not exactly that simple. He can't just *say it*. Forgiveness is about far more than a couple of words; it's about the thoughts and intents of the heart. He has to really *mean it*, have true remorse."

"Well, how are you going to know if he means it or not?"

"It doesn't matter if I think he does. God knows whether he's sincere, and He's the one who ultimately judges us all."

We went back and forth like that for an hour, looking at hypothetical murderers and rapists and con men, every one of whom my friend used as an effective barrier between herself and God. It kind of broke my heart, really, because she's one of the sweetest people I've ever met, and I want so much to hang out with her in eternity.

I've often looked back at the conversation, wondering if there was something else I could have said, some genius way I might have explained the loving grace of God so that she might have looked past the murderer in her imagination who clearly didn't deserve a place in heaven. Another criminal comes to mind when I remember that exchange, the one who turned to the Man hanging on the cross beside him to ask that he be remembered when Jesus reached His kingdom. And so every time I pray for my treasured friend now, I ask the Lord to lead her to that kind of grace. Even if she rebels until the very last minute of her life, I pray that she will turn to Him in search of salvation so we can share the joy that comes after this life. * *SDB*

The Prayer Wars

Give thanks in all circumstances, for this is the will of God in Christ Jesus for you.
1 THESSALONIANS 5:18

*M*y grandkids love to say grace.

Not the rote "God Is Great, God Is Good" poem we're all familiar with, but something pure and simple and straight from the heart, because that's how they've been taught to pray. Suffice it to say, Sunday dinners at my house are interesting. And the food is usually cold by the time the blessing ends, because the word "simple" to my grandkids has no connection to the word "brief"!

Last week, for example, my granddaughter decided we should all take turns saying a blessing.

"But it isn't even Thanksgiving," said her twin, Steven.

"Just because it isn't Thanksgiving doesn't mean we can't say thanks," Samantha shot back.

"Well, all right," he agreed, "but you have to start." He pointed to his grandfather, who sat on Sam's left. "And go *that way* around the table."

Her head bobbed as she did a mental head count, and she whispered, "Twelve whole prayers! God is gonna *love* this!" Smiling, she bowed her head, folded her hands, and opened with, "Dear Lord, we thank You for all this food and for making the seeds, and for the men and women who grew them into plants and the truck drivers who delivered the plants to the Super-Fresh." She opened one eye and whispered, "Granddad, your turn."

"We thank You for our good health and our homes, and—"

"—and Grandmom," Steven chimed in, "who cooked all of this *and* set the table *and* made chocolate cake."

"Hey, it wasn't your turn," pretty Payton said, before adding, "Thank You, dear God, that I got five gold stars last week. And that Emily's pinkeye is all better. *And* that Mr. Arnold's puppy didn't get runned over when it runned into the street."

"And that baby Warner's poopy diaper didn't leak on his crib," Steven said.

"Steven!" Samantha said with a gasp. "You can't say 'poopy' in a prayer!"

He faced Samantha. "Why not? God made people, and people poop!"

Shoulders slumped, she groaned and shook her head as baby Warner said, "Poop!"

"Boys," Samantha groaned. Then, "Please God, let the soldiers all stay safe, and don't let their children miss them too much until they get home. And send lots of food and clean water to the hurricane people."

"Yes, yes!" Payton squealed. "And clothes and blankets for the children, and flashlights so they won't be a-scared when it gets dark out."

Meeting with God in this way recharges my batteries; what He does through each of us, by faith as we receive His grace, has eternity stamped on it.

Since my own childhood, I've held fast to Jesus's words: "I [have] come that they might have life, and that they might have it more abundantly" (John 10:10 KJV). I searched the faces of loved ones seated around the table— the adults stifling chuckles as the children continued to pray— and wondered, could life get any more grace-filled than this? * LL

Too Successful for Your Own Good

I praise you, Father, Lord of heaven and earth, because you have hidden these things from the wise and learned, and revealed them to little children.

LUKE 10:2

Here's a pop quiz for you. What do these people have in common?

- Industrialist/businessman/philanthropist Andrew Carnegie (of Carnegie Hall fame).
- Physiologist/psychologist/physician Ivan Pavlov (of Pavlovian dog fame).
- Actress Katharine Hepburn (winner of four Academy Awards).
- American investor/philanthropist Warren Buffett (one of the richest men in the world).
- Chinese martial artist Bruce Lee (undisputed king of martial arts).
- Rock-and-roll legend Mick Jagger (ancient—but still kicking—rocker).
- Facebook developer Mark Zuckerberg (one of *Time* magazine's Most Influential People when he was just twenty-six).

Yes, they all are (or were) famous. All successful in their fields. All brilliant in their own areas of expertise.

And all self-professed atheists.

Now, there's not a dummy in the bunch. They were each blessed with some extraordinary talent. But, apparently, none of them recognized (or recognizes) his or her blessings as *blessings*. Surely they recognized that they were gifted, but they credited themselves or past mentors or hard knocks with getting them where they got to be.

That's beyond sad. These people weren't pygmies in some remote jungle. No doubt every one of them went around the block often enough to have heard the gospel message at least once. Each of them emphatically responded, "Thanks, but no thanks."

Jesus spoke today's verse when some of His disciples came back to Him after telling others the same thing John the Baptist did: "Prepare the way for the Lord" (Mark 1:3). "'The kingdom of God has come near to you'" (Luke 10:9). (And was He ever!) While many people repented of their sins and turned to God, many others didn't. Jesus thanked His Father for withholding the truth from those who considered themselves far too "wise and learned" to submit to God. And He thanked God for those so willing to humble themselves to God that they were like children.

Anyone who has that deep, abiding relationship with Christ knows what Jesus was talking about. Every one of us was told, at some point in our lives, that God lives, that we were created in His image but were separated from His perfect holiness because of sin. We were each told that Christ died in our place—He took on the punishment we had coming for our sins. And we were told that we simply needed to recognize ourselves as sinners who needed that sacrifice on His part, to accept that fact and to accept His amazing, loving gesture for what it was. Unconditional love. Salvation. Redemption. The only way.

One needn't really know or understand *anything* else to be considered blameless in God's eyes. You don't need to get a degree in apologetics or become a biblical scholar (or any kind of scholar, for that matter).

Christ's gracious choice to make that humble sacrifice and our choice to come to Him like children both boil down to the same condition of the heart. And it's not wisdom. It's not accomplishment. It's not learning. It's acceptance. * *TP*

Empowered by Forgiving Others

Peter came and said to Him, "Lord, how
often shall my brother sin against
me and I forgive him? Up to seven times?"

MATTHEW 18:21 NASB

It's easy to think that forgiving someone else benefits the culprit but taxes the victim. In reality, it works quite differently than that. Forgiving another person's violation empowers the offended.

What is forgiveness? It's simply turning over our unresolved anger to God. We were wronged. We probably had a right to be angry. But anger is like ice cream on a hot day. If we let it go too long, we have a mess on our hands. It may be okay to get angry, but it's not okay to stay angry. Unresolved anger turns into bitterness that rots us from the inside. That's why we need to turn the anger, the offense, the perpetrator over to God.

Forgiving someone does not require us to contact the offender or renew any kind of relationship with him. The level of friendship we have with someone is based on that person's track record of trustworthiness, not on whether we have forgiven him.

But forgiving someone does require us to process a transaction in the presence of God. We hand the offense, the anger, the wrongdoer over to Jesus. We can be sure that whatever we place in His hands will be well taken care of. * SGES

Only Believe

"The LORD your God in your midst, the Mighty One, will save;
He will rejoice over you with gladness, He will quiet
you with His love, He will rejoice over you with singing."

ZEPHANIAH 3:17 NKJV

It's totally amazing to me that our almighty God, the One who created the heavens and the earth, the moon and the stars, is always nearby—there whenever I need Him. When I'm afraid or anxious, He calms me down. He loves me, and He's actually jazzed that I'm part of His family.

What about you?

I realize this biblical truth is hard to fathom if you're a person who has emerged from a less than perfect past. To think that a heavenly Father would "rejoice over you" with gladness and singing doesn't quite compute when an earthly dad has been abusive. The simple act of believing is often complicated by negative outside influences.

In her best-selling book entitled *Battlefield of the Mind Devotional*, Joyce Meyer wrote: "You may have had a miserable past; you may even be in current circumstances that are very negative and depressing. You may be facing situations that are so bad it seems you have no real reason to hope. But I say to you boldly: Your future is not determined by your past or your present!" She goes on to urge readers to "start believing God's Word is true."

I made that very decision to believe God years ago. I had come from a Wednesday night church service in which I heard the gospel. I felt confused about what the Bible teaches regarding salvation, but then, as I stood in front of my kitchen sink washing dishes, I realized my need for God. I prayed, feeling like I wasn't worthy of such a gift, and asked Jesus Christ into my life, my heart. Then and there I felt a peace flow over me and I knew my prayer had been heard—and answered. I knew biblical truth was the right and only truth. I believed God. After that day an entire universe of hope and blessing opened up to me.

It can happen for you, too! Only believe. * *AKB*

Bossy Bosserson

*Confess your trespasses to one another, and pray
for one another, that you may be healed. The effective,
fervent prayer of a righteous man avails much.*

JAMES 5:16 NKJV

Carole had been a project manager for something like ten years, so most of the editors in my department had worked with her at one time or another. I had what I considered to be the misfortune of being assigned to a half dozen different projects with Carole at the helm. She was often the butt of private jokes about the "criminally organized," and team members would sometimes salute her as she passed. She'd gained the nickname of Bossy Bosserson, but it was only used quietly in certain circles.

One afternoon following an extremely long conference call, I went downstairs to the cafe for a cappuccino—and I noticed Carole sitting alone in the corner, nursing a cup of tea. After I grabbed my coffee and headed for the door, I glanced back at her and saw that she was crying.

Every instinct I had told me to keep on going, but for some reason I just couldn't do it. I approached her cautiously and then slipped into the chair across from her.

"Carole, is there something I can do for you? Can I get you some more tea?"

At first, she glared at me. And then her face just seemed to melt like hot wax, into the saddest grimace I'd ever seen, and tears cascaded down her face in streams.

"I'm sorry. Please just leave me alone," she said.

I finally agreed, and I left her there despite my reluctance to do so. That day, I started praying for Carole. Every now and then at first, but then each time she came to mind. I prayed for her broken heart and for her tendency to steamroll over her coworkers. I asked the Lord to touch her in some way, in whatever way she needed so badly, and to reveal Himself to her.

"Oh, Lord, just help her to be...nice. She's so miserable that she makes everyone around her miserable, too. Bossy needs a huge dose of Your kindness."

Less than a month later, I found myself sitting in that same spot where I'd seen Carole sipping her tea. This time she took the chair across from me, and she smiled.

"You're far away," she observed.

"I'm just thinking about our meeting this afternoon."

"Well, I want you to know that I think you're doing a wonderful job," she said. "I don't think I tell you that often enough."

I've seldom come face-to-face with such profound answered prayer, but to this day, Bossy Bosserson is a living memorial to me, proving that fervent prayer does indeed avail much.* SDB

Slower Now

The LORD is gracious and compassionate, slow to anger and rich in love.
PSALM 145:8

My daughter Amy called to say she was sorry. Again. In true déjà-vu style, her kindergartner unintentionally reenacted a scene at school so reminiscent of something Amy did thirty years ago that little Hannah could have served detention for copycatting as well as for disregarding the playground rules.

Detention. Kindergarten. What's wrong with this picture?

Fresh from her own daughter's remorse, my firstborn apologized for an offense thirty years old because she saw it reenacted in her child. Her apology made me laugh. What goes around comes around, as they say.

I'd always resisted the threat some parents hurl at their kids: "I hope you have a child just like you!" I wish I could spare my daughter from parental angst, from embarrassment and concern and frustration. But you have to admit it's kind of funny when detention history repeats itself.

Wisdom and love tell me to pray for my grandkids and for the amazing people who parent them. Detention's no laughing matter if it doesn't lead to a change in behavior.

Where have I heard that before?

I'm slower than I used to be. When Amy and her two brothers put snow down a schoolmate's neck or pulled a zero on their homework because they forgot to turn it in <*sigh*>, I reacted with one of several instant Mom Responses as if the message were already written and all I had to do was hit SEND.

"…living up to potential…" "…responsibility…" "…respect authority…" "Be ye kind one to another…or else!"

The fine line between frustration and anger wavered like the horizontal hold on a 1950s television screen. (I saw one once at the Smithsonian. And, okay, in my family's living room.)

Today, when my grandchildren misbehave, I have to concentrate to keep from chuckling. When one of them tried to flush a handful of golf balls, a manila folder, and a paintbrush, I—the person who didn't have to tear into the plumbing project—thought it was creative. When another, at little more than a year old, stacked pillows to form a staircase to help him reach something he found intriguing, I snatched him to safety, restarted my heart, and said, "The boy's going to make a fine engineer." When his brother played stylist and gave them both inventive haircuts, my first response was to take pictures.

Another grandson perfected melodrama before he turned two, dropping his chin to his chest and slumping his shoulders to register life-altering heartbreak. Anything could trigger the toddler version of a broken heart.

"No, you can't have another snack right now." "Sorry, but you have to wear socks with those shoes." "Honey, it's raining."

Adorable, right?

The Lord doesn't find my misbehavior cute—that unkind word, impatience with my husband, avoidance of what I know He wants me to do. He doesn't chuckle at my melodrama or comment that my attempt to manufacture an answer to prayer shows my engineering skills.

But where would I be if He weren't slow to anger and rich in love? * *CR*

A Life of Stillness

Stand in awe...commune with your own heart...and be still.

PSALM 4:4 KJV

*I*t was one of those moments—like being poised on the edge of a star just before it falls. It's yours to savor, just for that moment. A moment packed with meaning. A moment ripe with truth. A moment that will sustain you in other moments, other days.

Blink and you will miss it. Speak and it is gone. Max Lucado calls these times "eternal moments." And he says you better cherish them when they come to you. I am happy to say that this time, we did.

We had just heard the news of a family tragedy. My husband's cousin Eric, age thirty-three, died in his home of some unknown (until that time) anomaly in one of his lungs. He had just dressed his four-year-old daughter, Emily, for preschool, walked into the living room, and fell down dead, taking his last breath in his wife's arms.

The information sent us into shock. We had just seen him on a recent trip to the town where most of Stone's relatives live.

Eric was a jolly "good old boy," who shared with us how proud he was of his daughter and his plans for the future with his job and his wife Tina's beauty shop. Our little family—there were only four of us at that time—sat around our deck talking about the news. We were all so sad. He was the second son Aunt Sue and Uncle Wilford have lost. Such an overwhelming sorrow to be borne, now twice. It was unbelievable.

Grace was thinking and talking about Emily. Stone was thinking about Eric. And I was thinking about Tina, Eric's sweet wife. Such was the scene on our deck, the four of us, with Harper driving his new car up and down and the river serene and beautiful, flowing on as before, far below us. Occasionally a boat or train went by without noticing us. Leaves rustled. We could feel the gentle breath of the soft, cool wind.

Somehow we quickly and quietly ended up in the hammock. All of us. Stone spread his arms wide, holding me, Harper, and Grace, keeping us from falling out of our somewhat precarious positions. The hammock, though threatening to throw us, also enfolded us like a cocoon and tightly pressed us together. We didn't talk much. Words weren't needed. I believe we all, at some level, felt it. It was one of those moments. We were together, we were alive and healthy and safe, and we let the moment be. We cherished it.

After the moment passed, the heaviness of death and its accompanying grief returned. Stone began to make plans to drive across the state to go to the services. Grace began drawing pictures to send to Emily—"cards." I cooked food and ironed clothes for Stone to take with him. Soon we saw him out the door with kisses.

Many lessons can be learned from such situations, I'm sure. Teachers, preachers, musicians, and other thinkers and artists strive to somehow get at the meaning of it all and help us understand. I'm grateful when these insights are shared. For me, however, the greatest lesson this time was found in the hammock. "Be still. 'Be still, and know that I am God.' I will come and minister to you."

Some of the things He ministered to my heart were these: Love with all of your heart. Hold on to the ones you love while you have them. You never know when life, like the hammock, may throw you out against something hard and it will be painful. But when it enfolds you like a warm cocoon, don't miss the wonder of it. Beauty—like such moments in the hammock—is ours for the taking, if we have eyes to see it and hearts to grasp it. There is splendor in stillness. * *GF*

Yes, Virginia, There Is Grace in Silly Putty!

A gossip betrays a confidence, but a trustworthy person keeps a secret.
PROVERBS 11:13

Whether we realize it or not, every mother is blessed with *acting talent*. As proof, let me tell you about one sunny Saturday afternoon from my past:

"Oh, Timmy was no trouble, no trouble at all!" the birthday boy's mom said, smiling like a pageant winner when the little monster's dad came to fetch him. (I'd worn that all-teeth, no-truth smile enough times to recognize artificial sweetener when I saw it.)

When my own all-in-pink cutie-pie asked if I could make the six helium balloons tied to her wrist fit into the backseat with her little sister, the dog, the baby's car seat, *and* the diaper bag, I said, "Are you kidding? Mommies can do *anything*!" Experience taught me that the bobbing inflatables would render the rearview mirror useless, but I'd survived many a white-knuckled drive home from clown-and-cake shindigs....

Arriving home, my li'l darling scattered the contents of her goodie bag across the kitchen table, and a colorful plastic egg rolled out. I nearly ground my molars to dust, hiding my disdain; what kind of fiend subjects another mother to the evils of Silly Putty? While immersing the party dress into a tub of clean-and-soak, I hid another scowl. Who serves grape juice at a kids' party?

The kind who leaves her husband for an old high-school sweetheart—if the rumors in the carpool lane were true.

My best friend's daughter had attended the party too; commiseration was sure to keep my well-acted "I'm okay, you're okay" grin in place until sweetie pie's sugar high wore off. I reached for the phone...but something stopped me.

Ancient Chinese proverbs and childlike slurs echoed in my head (things like, "If you control your tongue, you will master your life" and "What you say bounces off me and sticks to you"). Gossip, I'd learned, can turn an innocent lump of Silly Putty into the ominous ball of tar that costarred with Steve McQueen in *The Blob*.

I remembered, too, a Bible study where my pastor criticized the church for being the only army that kills its wounded; he'd counseled troubled sisters in faith who, instead of receiving the love and encouragement of fellow Christians, had felt the slice of sharp tongues.

I grabbed the Good Book, and God led me to Proverbs 26:22. Red-faced with shame, I opened the plastic egg, pressed the blob briefly to that gilded page, then carefully rolled it up and stored it in its colorful container.

Now, whenever I'm tempted to participate in gossip, I *un*roll it and read, "The words of a gossip are like choice morsels; they go down to the inmost parts."

...all while "acting" as though I'd only hidden the egg to protect my carpets and upholstery from the destructive powers of Silly Putty. * LL

Why Me, Lord?

He chose David his servant and took him from the sheep pens; from tending the sheep he brought him to be the shepherd of his people Jacob, of Israel his inheritance.

PSALM 78:70–71

What's my *purpose*?

We all wonder that at some point, right? Entire mega enterprises have been built around our innate desire to understand why, specifically, God put each of us here on earth. As Christians eager to show our appreciation for Christ's gift of salvation, we're particularly keen to know how we can live our lives according to His plan. We all wonder, *Why am I here?*

Some people have clearly been chosen to be Christian leaders—pastors, worship leaders, Bible study leaders, Sunday school teachers…. They usually know they've been chosen because they *enjoy* what they're doing. Yes, some people perform these tasks out of a sense of obligation, but others experience God-given peace and pleasure in their roles, which is a surefire indication they're doing what He meant them to do.

If God saw kingly potential in a small, lowly shepherd like our boy David, there's no reason to think He doesn't have some equally crucial purpose for each of us. Maybe we won't rule kingdoms, but we can each further the only kingdom that counts.

I gain peace and pleasure from writing, so I like to think that my novels serve His kingdom, and occasional reader feedback tells me how they do. He hasn't called me home yet, so I imagine He has more work for me, whether it's through writing or personal interaction or just being in the right place at the right time.

For people who have great suffering in their lives, the question is a tough one. Does their suffering serve some eternal purpose? I don't think any of us can fully grasp that idea. I do know that my own sister's suffering and her death at a young age directly led me to Christ. Who knows how many others followed that path because of her?

Maybe my purpose is found in a role the world finds mundane. Parenting can be thankless and edifying at the same time. Even if one's relationship with her child is strained, she may be the one model of Christ's unconditional love that child will ever know. A pretty heavy purpose, that.

Still more intriguing is the fact that I may have been chosen for one specific moment of service for the kingdom, one word or brief action that will lead a lost soul to Him. I once learned after the fact that something I said off-the-cuff caused another person to turn to Christ. In case I've been chosen for many such moments, it's my job to keep my mind and heart open to those opportunities. Because if *that* ain't purpose, I don't know what is. * *TP*

From the Mouths of Babes

But by the grace of God I am what I am, and his grace to me was not without effect.

1 CORINTHIANS 15:10

I lived in a Los Angeles suburb at the time, working as the director of the children's ministry at my home church while studying my writing craft. I had a very happy life… and then a big shoe dropped on me out of nowhere. I'd been deeply betrayed by someone I never could have imagined capable of such a thing. I was devastated.

While on nursery duty with a close friend one Sunday morning, I rocked a sleeping baby in my arms as she changed the diaper of another while we chatted. "I'm absolutely destroyed," I confided. "I can't even think clearly about where to go from here. The situation is overwhelming, and it's just too big out there in front of me."

"What's too big, Miss Sandie?"

One of my special, favorite five-year-olds had wandered in from the classroom next door.

"Oh, I'm just working through some grown-up problems," I told him. "And until I figure things out, they just look really big to me. Does that make sense?"

His little brow furrowed, and he thought it over with deep intensity before he finally nodded. "I guess so," he replied. "Can I help?"

"Nope," I said as I smiled at him. "You go on over and finish craft time now, okay?"

He nodded and obediently opened the door to his classroom and stepped inside.

About an hour later, after the last baby had been picked up from the nursery, I stood at the sink washing pacifiers, and that same little boy walked up behind me and tapped my arm. "Hey, Miss Sandie, look through my spyglass," he said softly, and he held up a small plastic telescope. But he lifted it toward my face by the wrong end.

"I think it goes the other way," I instructed. But when I tried to turn it around, he resisted.

"No," he cried. "If you look through this end, everything in front of you looks smaller. Remember when you said it was too big in front of you? Through this end, it won't seem so big."

When the depth of what that little five-year-old boy told me began to sink in, I tried to hold back the tears, but they spilled out anyway.

"You know what," I said to him. "You just reminded me of something I already should have known. Your spyglass shows me how I see things from one end and how God sees the same things from the other one. I think you might be some kind of boy genius!"

He burst into laughter at that, and it sounded a lot like music to me. Before I knew it, my heart was lighter and I laughed with him.

Many times over the years that have followed that Sunday morning, I've calmed myself by remembering to "turn the telescope around" for a fresh look at my life from a different perspective. * *SDB*

Still Waiting!

*The Lord is not slow in keeping his promise, as some
understand slowness. Instead he is patient with you, not wanting
anyone to perish but everyone to come to repentance.*

2 PETER 3:9

I remember the day my son-in-law got baptized in church, broke into a huge grin, and publicly proclaimed, "Jesus is Lord." Of course, I cried; as much as I loved him, I had worried because he never seemed all that interested in knowing about Christ and what He offered. Hearing him happily give his life to the Lord was a dream come true.

And then my next thought was, "Okay, Lord, I'm ready now. All my kids are saved. Come on back!"

That was about a decade ago. I think we all know how that plan worked out. But I do catch myself thinking like the person who frantically runs to catch a bus before it's actually time for departure and then gets impatient about how long it's taking to get going. *I'm on it now, so let's get going already!* Or I think that way about my loved ones. Once me and mine are onboard, isn't it time to go?

Uh, no, apparently not.

I'm thrilled to have come to Christ before He comes back for us, aren't you? We see in today's verse that the Lord wants everyone to wise up and come to repentance. Of course, history has shown that that isn't going to happen, thanks to a little thing we call free will. And God knows full well who is and isn't going to make that decision within the lifetime allotted here on earth.

I find it fascinating to think about that one last person yet to make the decision, prompting Christ's return. I sometimes picture the occurrence like a hugely amplified one-millionth-customer celebration, where that one person walks through the turnstile and sets off a marching band, cheerleaders jumping all over the place, and confetti raining down everywhere. Sometimes I wonder if that person has been born yet. Wouldn't it be a blast to play a role in that last person's coming to Christ?

Which brings us to some interesting wording in today's verse. "He is patient with you." Certainly the Lord is patient with His children as He waits for us to accept His free gift of salvation. But might He also be showing patience with us with regard to our efforts at sharing Him with others? Our efforts at demonstrating His grace by our actions?

I think so. Just a few verses further down, Peter says, "You ought to live holy and godly lives as you look forward to the day of God and speed its coming."

Speed His coming? Well, all right! I thoroughly love my life here on earth, but I'm so eager to meet Him in person! And I want everyone I know to meet Him, too. * *TP*

I Just Got Comfortable

Yet the LORD longs to be gracious to you; therefore he will rise up to show you compassion.
ISAIAH 30:18

The blogger asked, "What's the most romantic thing your husband did for you?"

Asked me to marry him at the foot of the cellar stairs? Volunteered to gut the fish we caught on our honeymoon? Bought me a luggage scale? (Apparently he was moved with compassion at the memory of me on my knees while curbside at the airport, jettisoning underwear and stuffing blue jeans in my purse to prevent an overage charge.)

There was that time he handed me the remote and said, "Watch whatever you want to watch."

"Really?"

"Yeah. I'm going out to the garage."

It was romantic when he washed my hair after a bulging disc flattened me. He draped a garbage bag over the end of the couch to which I was glued and puddled one end of the garbage bag in a five-gallon bucket. As I watched his strong, flannel-clad arms as he poured warm water over my hair, his kindness seemed so Jesus-like. So tender.

The *most* romantic moment of our life together?

When he brought me coffee on the balcony of our rental villa in Tuscany. When he wrote my name in the raked gravel of a Japanese garden. When he bought space on the JumboTron at a Packers game to tell the Monday Night Football viewing audience—pretty much everybody—that he loved me.

Oh, wait. Those things happened to someone else.

I did have a list of romantic gestures from which to choose to answer the blogger. Sweet moments when my husband's expressions of love made me say, "How romantic!"

Like the other day. He got out of his recliner.

We'd nestled into our quiet-evening-alone-together routine—he in his recliner and me in my chair that daily reminds me why I should have purchased a rocker. There's something "off" about that chair. Looks nice but sits funny, like a salad dressing with too much vinegar or stuffing with half a teaspoon too much sage.

I'd found the perfect angle, though. Throw pillows just so. Feet propped up on the ottoman. Book in hand. And my cup of tea?

In the microwave, two rooms away.

"Let me get it for you." My husband, the most romantic guy in the world at that moment, rose out of his chair. Left his own comfort. To serve me.

He rose to show me compassion. Just like Jesus does. "Let Me get that for you," He says.

"I'm worried about my kids, Lord."

"Let Me get that for you."

"I can't think of a response to the woman at work who wants to drag me into her cauldron of gossip."

"Let Me get that for you."

"I'm having a hard time with _____ [fill in the blank]."

He rises to show me compassion and says, "Let Me get that for you." He doesn't just resign Himself to be gracious or reluctantly agree to cut me some slack. He longs to be gracious to me. He's *looking* for ways to bless me.

How divinely romantic! * CR

A Life of Worship

A certain woman named Lydia, a seller of purple, of the city of Thyatira, which worshipped God, heard us: whose heart the Lord opened, that she attended unto the things which were spoken of Paul.

ACTS 16:14 KJV

Lydia's story is one that seems particularly relevant for women today who want to live a beautiful life before God. Unlike traditional images we sometimes see of women in the Bible who lived outwardly quiet lives, often in the shadows of their husbands, Lydia is introduced distinctively as a businesswoman who worshiped God.

Now, don't get me wrong. I'm not knocking an outwardly quiet life. After all, that's the sort of life I live. I'm a stay-at-home mom who cooks, cleans, does laundry, irons, and taxis my kids back and forth to school. My husband is the breadwinner of our family. I like to make soup for people who are sick, play the piano for church, and babysit my nieces. Other than teaching a couple of literature classes and writing, I live in total obscurity, way out in the country in a small town in Arkansas. I am certainly not a businesswoman, though I know many godly women who are.

The Bible says to "make it your ambition to lead a quiet life" (1 Thessalonians 4:11 NASB). In our culture, ambition and quietness seem diametrically opposed to one another. Many women may feel that to be ambitious, they must draw attention to their accomplishments, to "live loud," and, in a sense, make their voices heard. Still others, like some Christian women I've known, seem almost afraid to express their individual gifts if those gifts fall outside the realm of service, hospitality, or mercy. There's a myth that circulates among Christian women in some places that *quietness* means silence and a woman's place is always behind the scenes.

Neither view is healthy or accurate. *The Bible Knowledge Commentary* translates *quiet* in the verse above as "a sense of restfulness." It does not mean *silent*, but on the contrary, "undisturbed, settled, not noisy." The writer of the commentary goes on to explain that "Paul was telling the Thessalonians to be less frantic, not less exuberant." While much of the world, including many Christians, seems to judge quietness—or the lack thereof—by what they see women doing, I believe quietness is something more than what's apparent on the outside. I can say from experience that quietness doesn't come naturally just because a woman stays home. And I believe Lydia's example demonstrates that quietness is not in any way lessened—or hindered—by having a career. The heart of the matter is worship.

To worship, we have to rest in our spirits. No matter what our calling or gifts, all of us have to be deliberate about it. I do, at home with my kids and the many chores and sometimes chaos that ensues; a businesswoman like Lydia would deliberately have to quiet her heart and meditate on the Lord in order to worship Him. That's what she's doing when Paul finds her on the riverbank praying with other women. And the Bible says her heart was opened by the Lord to receive the truth Paul was teaching.

Whether we as women are called to work outside the home or inside, to be rich or to be poor, married or single, mothers or not—is really not the point, any more than the shape of our noses. Nothing outward makes us ugly or beautiful. What makes us beautiful is when we worship God, wherever we are, whatever we're doing. Quietness in spirit is the gateway to worship—and worship invites Him to open our hearts and fill us with His truth. * *GF*

Weary to the Bone

Come to Me, all you who labor and are heavy laden, and I will give you rest.
MATTHEW 11:28 NKJV

You're just too Christian for us."

"Wow," I replied dryly. "I didn't know there was such a thing. And is it even legal for you to say that to me?"

It felt like everything I did as an editorial supervisor for two straight years had been scrutinized, judged, or corrected on a personal level. And now having Scripture taped on my computer screen to encourage myself as I fought through a health problem had been reported to the main office as inappropriate. It was just about all I could take.

I left that meeting feeling more tired than I ever knew a person could feel. Weary to the bone and beyond; weary all the way to my soul. I packed up a box of my personal things, offered my resignation, and numbly meandered to the parking lot. My limits had been met and crossed months prior, and I'd been hanging on and enduring for as long as I possibly could. I was finally finished.

When I got home, I dropped the cardboard box with my coffee mug and framed photos and sat down in front of the computer. I went directly to a job site and submitted my resume to the first available editorial job I could find. Once I hit the SEND button, I started to cry.

Deep within me, I felt the sweet and gentle whisper of my Father: *"Bring me your burdens. I will give you rest."*

I got up from the computer, went into my bedroom, and stretched out facedown across the bed. I cried before the Lord for a solid hour, recounting what He already knew about the challenges and obstacles and strength-zapping battles I'd been waging at my job.

When I'd dried my last tear, I took a deep breath and fell into a fast, hard sleep. It was already dark outside when the ringing of the phone awakened me, and I answered without looking at the caller identification (which I almost never do).

It was the hiring supervisor for the company to which I had applied a few hours earlier. "Your resume is very impressive," she said. "You seem like a perfect fit for the editorial position we've been trying to fill."

That call was the catalyst for one of the best and most fulfilling jobs I've ever had, and it's so comforting to know that the net had been cast beneath me long before I even knew I would need it. While I was still struggling against the current of a job that was taxing everything I had inside me, the Lord had prepared the ground to bless me when the time came to move on. * *SDB*

What's Your Hurry?

Wait on the LORD; be of good courage, and he shall strengthen thine heart: wait, I say, on the LORD.

PSALM 27:14 KJV

Did you ever wonder how Oklahomans earned the nickname "Sooners"? Some historians believe that the term's origin dates back to the days when settlers "jumped the gun" and claimed land in the Cherokee Strip before it was legal to do so.

And in the days of the open range, it was common practice for cattlemen to schedule specific dates for the round-ups in each area. Rustlers and hustlers who "worked the cows" to get mavericks and slicks (unbranded cows) for themselves—ahead of the roundup—were branded "sooners" by honest cowboys.

It's no surprise, then, to learn that such "haste makes waste" behaviors have roots in the pages of the Good Book. "He that believeth shall not make haste," says Isaiah 28:16. Job's plea in chapter 30, verse 13 was, "They break up my road; they succeed in destroying me—without anyone's helping them." John describes how Jewish leaders didn't much like watching victims suffer on the Sabbath, so they asked Pilate to break their legs to hasten their deaths.

So it appears that being in a perpetual hurry hasn't been good for man since, well, the dawn of mankind!

I'm guilty of "making haste" and "hurrying," and though I try to convince others—and myself—that every rush-rush activity is for a very good reason, the fact is, most things simply aren't all that urgent, no matter how convincing my explanations are to the contrary!

What I'm working on in my Quest for a Better Loree is to balance my good intentions and great plans for improving charitable programs, my preferred fund-raising organizations, my own work, and the place I call home alongside my relationship with Christ. I need to heed the safety lessons I stalwartly taught my children: Stop, look, and listen, then ask myself if the good deeds I'm doing are to bring glory to myself…or to my Lord and Savior.

I want to follow where He leads, but how can I know *where* He wants me to go if my brain's all a-twitter with to-do list instructions and I'm exhausted from trying to cram three days of work into one twenty-four-hour period?

When I'm stressed out, tired, and feeling "put upon," it's almost always because I've forgotten the wisdom found in Psalm 27:14: "Wait, I say, on the Lord" (KJV).

And if I'm smart, I'll do it "sooner" rather than later!

* LL

Be on Guard

Above all else, guard your heart, for it is the wellspring of life.

PROVERBS 4:23

A conservative politician recently resigned after admitting to an affair with a staff member. His confession appeared genuine and broken. My heart goes out to him as he works to mend his tattered family.

Now, don't get me wrong. I was very disappointed and upset about the matter, to say the least. We expect more from godly people who are telling others to abstain and take the moral high road and yet fail to do so themselves. It's easy to point fingers and say, "They should have known better." And, of course, they should have.

Still, it happens.

I'm not excusing his behavior. It's wrong, pure and simple. Yet, all week long I've been thinking about what could happen in a person's life to bring them to that place of deceit and self-destruction. After much thought and reflection, I've come to the conclusion that we get so busy with the demands in our lives that sometimes we shut God out. It's easy to do. We skip our quiet time because we're late for work. Then the next day, it happens again. By the end of the week, we don't even miss Him. The next thing we know, it's time for church and we have no idea where we've placed our Bible.

The truth is, we try to face life's struggles and temptations in our own strength, and it just doesn't work. There are some things we just cannot battle on our own. We must connect to our life source, the Vine, our Lord, on a daily basis, for much-needed spiritual nourishment.

The sad confession by Mr. Politician made me take stock of my own life. I dare not take a step into my day without spending time with my Lord to refuel. Not because of legalistic reasons, but because I'm very much aware of my own human inadequacy to face the challenges of life. I desperately need His power within me to do His work in a hurting world. "I can do everything *through him* who gives me strength" (Philippians 4:13, emphasis added). That's the only way I can do anything.

How about you? Is God the top priority in your life? Do you ask for His leading before you begin your day, or do you dare to walk the dusty, uncertain path of life on your own? The only true way to guard your heart is to spend time with Him. Confess your need for Him today, and ask Him to strengthen you as you minister to a dark, broken world. Then go out and make a difference. * DM

What Are You Doing Here, Elijah?

Have no fear of sudden disaster or of the ruin that overtakes the wicked,
for the LORD will be at your side and will keep your foot from being snared.

PROVERBS 3:25–26

In 1 Kings, Elijah called out to God to show Baal's followers who really ruled the roost, and the Lord answered his prayer with a very dramatic show. "Then the fire of the Lord fell," it says in chapter 18, verse 38, "and burned up the sacrifice, the wood, the stones and the soil, and also licked up the water in the trench." How cool was that? Don't we just love it when God's hand rests upon us for the world to see that we're *His*? He saves us from a bad situation and we're reminded that He's in charge, that He is able, that He is faithful.

It's worth noting here that, not long after God's fire display, Elijah drew the wrath of a vengeful woman named Jezebel. And what was the first thing he did? He ran for his life, first to Judah, then into the wilderness, and later into a mountain cave to hide out.

We're so much like Elijah, aren't we? Why can't we ever seem to remember that God's love and grace aren't given for just one situation, that He doesn't just answer one prayer and move on?

Many years ago, I found myself miserable in a day job that seemed to take everything out of me. At the end of the day, there never seemed to be enough creativity in me to put ten words on a page. My dreams of a writing career had begun to evaporate, and the stress of working a day job only added to the spiral. I'd built up my savings to where I had enough money to cover me for a year. I decided to take a chance on myself, and I quit my day job and settled into the writer life.

But that first book didn't sell, and before I knew it, I was out of time—and money. Deflated, I started my search for another day job. But finding another job proved to be next to impossible. The straits grew quite dire, and just about the time I ran out of options, a couple of miracles (including a job offer) snatched me back from the edge of losing everything.

Over the years, I've never forgotten that season. And recently, when my company was purchased by another one and my peers began talking of severance packages and job searches, it wasn't the last-minute save or God's promised grace and care that I remembered. It was the fear and anxiety of the decline.

When Elijah told the story of God's arrival outside of the cave, he spoke of an earthquake, heavy winds, and fire. But God wasn't in any of those things. No, instead, God was found in the soft, gentle whisper.

And so as I wait for the future to unfold, that's what I hang onto. I remind myself that God sustains throughout the trials, and His answer always comes. Even if it does come at the last possible moment. * *SDB*

Hey! Watch Where You're Going!

Direct my footsteps according to your word; let no sin rule over me.

PSALM 119:133

One of my favorite ways of exercising is to walk on my treadmill. The logistics in my home dictate its placement. I can't have it facing a window, so I'm not able to pretend I'm walking outdoors like a normal person. Neither am I able to have face it toward the TV (unless I get rid of my couch, which could be a problem when friends come to visit—there's something less than cozy about sipping a cup of tea while sitting on a treadmill). I seldom listen to music while I walk, but I usually read for a mile or two.

And now I've confessed how *slowly* I walk on said treadmill. Others could never hold a book steady while exercising. I probably *could* sip tea during my activity. Hey, don't judge me. It's better than nothing, right?

One of the best things about reading novels while "working out" is that I get distracted by someone else's story, and before I know it, I've done the entire walk without once wishing it would hurry up and be over.

Sometimes, though, the distraction is too intense. More than once, I've learned a mini-lesson in Newton's laws of motion, when my forward-moving self has accidentally stepped just slightly off the moving track and met with rigid resistance. All kinds of acrobatics take place before I finally go down. One time this happened when I had a rocking chair a little too close too the back of the treadmill, so I was unable to actually shoot off the conveyor belt. The chair kept me momentarily trapped there, bouncing around like a big bag of volleyballs, before I managed to roll myself off.

These are the moments when one is relieved to be alone and off camera.

It's so easy to get distracted from the path the Lord establishes for each one of us. Sometimes I focus too intently on what someone else is doing or has accomplished, and I fall out of step with what's important on my walk. So, too, many have taken just a few steps here, a few steps there, in directions they know can't possibly be meant for them—into a bar, when they know alcohol is a weakness; into an environment fraught with sexual temptation; into a conversation virtually guaranteed to lead to gossip; into a financial endeavor that hasn't for a moment been prayed over.

The writer of today's verse clearly knew the power of sin and how easily it can pull any one of us away from the blessings God has set out for our future. Occasionally, sin is like a dramatic fall from a cliff. Or a fast-moving treadmill. But more often than not, sin redirects our path one subtle step at a time. Before we know it, we're bouncing around like a big old bag of volleyballs, getting bruised, battered, and trying to crawl away from the consequences of our missteps. Divine guidance never looked so good! * *TP*

There's Always Room for Cheesecake

Rejoice always, pray continually.
1 THESSALONIANS 5:16–17

In the face of TV and newspaper reports of famines, floods, fires, earthquakes, tsunamis, and tornadoes, it's easy to understand the "pray continually" element of this Bible verse. Stories of war, foreclosures, and crime, though, make the "rejoice always" part not so easy. After all, according to Webster, the very word *rejoice* means "celebrate, exult, be glad." So how's a believer to feel joy when confronted with all the horrible things going on in our world?

A very similar discussion took place just last week while dining with friends when, for every negative item our friend Pete quoted from the evening news, Dan offered a positive:

Pete: "Gas prices are up. *Again!*"

Dan: "Did you hear about the kids who set up a car wash at the gas station and then donated the money to help a family displaced by a house fire?"

Pete: "That crazy governor of ours is talking about raising taxes. Again!"

Dan: "And did you hear that he launched a program to protect nursing-home residents from neglect and abuse?"

On and on it continued, through the soup-and-salad course, as the bowl of braised potatoes went back and forth, all but drowning out my carefully selected dinner music and dragging our formerly upbeat moods down, down, down, like the waxy white drips on the centerpiece candles.

While my guests halfheartedly sipped decaf coffee and poked at the very-berry cheesecake I'd spent hours baking and decorating, I turned off the stereo and grabbed my guitar. They pretty much ignored my strumming. Pretty much ignored those first few songs too. But when I launched into the old standby, "How Great Thou Art," they joined in crooning lyrics committed to heart as children. Back then we might have been old enough to memorize the words, but we were a long, long way from the maturity and wisdom required to grasp the true meaning behind stanzas that spoke of the awesome wonder found in every forest glade and birdsong, from every mountain and babbling brook, and, yes, even in the rolling thunder: *"He is there."*

For a while there, Pessimist Pete sang solo, tears shimmering in his eyes as the rhythmical praise of composer Carl Boberg passed his lips. "...That on the cross, my burden gladly bearing, He bled and died to take away my sin..."

Once the amen was sung, he sat back, a serene smile lighting his formerly gloomy face. "Well," he said, breaking the companionable silence, *"there's* a clear reminder that there has always been suffering and strife in this ol' world"—he took a sip of his decaf—"and that Jesus, by His supreme sacrifice, erased any excuse we frail humans can think up to rationalize our fears."

While we nodded our agreement, Pete requested a second helping of cheesecake. "And this time," he said, laughing, "I'm gonna enjoy every delectable calorie!" * *LL*

Oops! Wrong Building!

You will show me the path of life; in Your presence is fullness of joy;
at Your right hand are pleasures forevermore.

PSALM 16:11 NKJV

My mom was the youngest of eight children, and each of her siblings was very different from the others, but my special favorite was Aunt Mary. She was a perfect combination of Mrs. C. from *Happy Days* and Edith Bunker from *All in the Family*—a pure mixture of heart and truth. Just when you thought she might actually be off her rocker, Aunt Mary would come up with something that was pure gold.

I spent time with her over the summer whenever I could. She lived in a tiny town called Barberton where the most exciting thing we ever did was meet a couple of my aunts for lunch and shop for yarn at the Five-and-Dime afterward or take a drive into the country to buy produce for dinner from a roadside stand. I would never admit it to anyone at the time, but I loved those vacations in Barberton.

One particularly hot summer, I visited Aunt Mary for a week, when I was absolutely heartbroken over a boy back home. He'd asked one of my best friends to the autumn dance instead of me, and I felt as if my teenage life was over.

"I did everything I could to make him like me," I declared. "I wore my hair the way he liked it; I had him over for swimming dates and barbecues. I even let him beat me at Monopoly! I just can't understand what I did wrong."

I'll never forget that moment.

Aunt Mary was drying dishes, and she turned around, leaned against the sink, and sighed.

"You just leaned your ladder against the wrong building," she said.

That was the kind of thing she would often say. No hint about what it meant, but it was delivered with such an expression of assurance that you just knew something was there. Somewhere.

"I was at the market," she explained, "and I saw a magazine at the checkout with a big headline on it reading, 'So busy climbing the corporate ladder that you haven't realized your ladder is up against the wrong building?'"

Hmm…I'm sorry. What?

"That's you," she stated. "You were so busy trying to get a boyfriend, you didn't stop to think that you might be chasing after the wrong boy."

And there it was. Pure gold.

More than four decades have passed since that summer with Aunt Mary, but I can remember the moment like it was yesterday. I've leaned my ladder against a lot of wrong buildings in my life, but her words often act as the ringing bell that causes me to step back and re-evaluate. * *SDB*

Try It—You'll Like It

For in that He Himself has suffered, being tempted,
He is able to aid those who are tempted.

HEBREWS 2:18 NKJV

If it feels good, why not do it? Who's it going to hurt?"

The temptations of today are greater than ever! As if we didn't have enough desires on our own, TV and radio commercials flaunt one product after another, with the false claim that we "deserve" it all.

Ha! What I think I deserve is some quiet time, away from false desire that will only break me down and distance me from the God I love—the God who saved me through Christ.

Some temptations are more powerful than others. Mine are too much chocolate, too much bread, too much sushi, and too much queso dip with my chips. Put a plate of any of those in front of me, regardless of how much is on that plate, and chances are it'll be gone before I even realize it was there. Of course, this results in extra weight around the waist and hips.

One of my friends was married to a philanderer whose temptation of having extramarital relationships destroyed his marriage, a much more difficult problem to overcome. A lot of people suffered—my friend, her ex-husband, and their children. He tried it and liked it. Her life was turned upside down because of it.

Some people use drugs to feel better. Why not? After all, if it's not hurting anyone else and it makes you feel good, what's the problem? Right?

Well, for one thing, unless it's prescribed by a physician to make you healthier, it's wrong.

Another temptation I've personally witnessed is gossip at the office. Who doesn't want to listen in on a conversation with juicy tidbits about a coworker or the boss? It's easy to justify, too, because it's "work-related." What would happen if at least one person in each group took the high road and spoke up whenever someone had something derogatory to say about another person? The likely scenario is that those who want to gossip will take their "trash talk" somewhere else.

This will put those who choose not to participate at a disadvantage, right?

Not really. If we resist the temptation to do what we know is wrong—whether it's overeat, have an extramarital affair, do something illegal and unethical, or participate in gossip in any way—the Lord will honor our desire to be right with Him. * *DM*

Freedom for the Soul

If we confess our sins, He is faithful and just
to forgive us our sins and to cleanse us from all unrighteousness.

1 JOHN 1:9 NKJV

Years ago, I felt justified in calling out a sister in Christ. I told her off; she'd deserved it—or so I thought. Later, to my horror, that woman's husband and another man from church came over to set me straight. The woman's husband was a deacon, and she'd informed him of what had transpired between us. He brought another deacon with him.

Sitting in my living room, the two men were actually very kind in their reprimand. It wasn't long before I realized they were right: I'd let my temper get the best of me. While I didn't use bad language or raise my voice, the way I handled the situation, and my reaction, was wrong.

Faced with the truth, I was humbled. I felt awful. I apologized to my sister-in-Christ, who said she was sorry, too. Then I begged God's forgiveness. In fact, I repented every fifteen minutes for the next two days. I decided I was a terrible person, a horrible Christian. You see, no one beats me up like I beat me up!

My oldest son, who'd been studying for the ministry, noticed I was sad and discouraged. I guess what gave it away was that I'd crawled into bed with the covers pulled up to my chin—at four o'clock in the afternoon.

"I thought that situation was over and done with, Mom," Ben said, leaning against the door frame.

"Not for me. I can't believe I let that happen. Why did I react so badly?"

Ben disappeared for a few minutes then returned with his Bible. "Mom, Proverbs 24:16 says that a righteous man can fall seven times and still get up again. By 'men' God means *mankind*. It means women, too."

"Thanks for the clarification," I quipped. I sat up and pulled the Bible onto my lap. I read the verse.

"Everybody makes mistakes. You tripped, Mom. You fell. But now you have to pick yourself up again." Reaching over, he flipped through the delicate pages of God's Word and found another verse. "Look at this one. It says that if we confess our sins, God is faithful and just to forgive us and cleanse us from all unrighteousness. Did you ask God's forgiveness?"

"Yes. Numerous times."

"Once is enough." He paused. "Don't you believe God?"

"Well, yes, but…" I drew in a deep breath. "Oh, you're right. I'm my own worst enemy."

I slunked out of bed. It occurred to me that if God was faithful and just to forgive me, then I should forgive myself. I needed to pick myself up and go on with my life. To learn from the mistake but not wallow in the guilt.

Years later, the tendency is still there to wallow in guilt whenever I stumble, trip, or fall—like we all do. We all will. We're human and imperfect. But I've learned that forgiveness is key to bypassing guilt and moving forward with life. Forgiveness is, in a word, freeing. * *AKB*

A Life of Belief

For we walk by faith, not by sight.

2 CORINTHIANS 5:7 KJV

For me, life on earth is full of the abundance Jesus speaks of in John 10:10, when He says He came that we might have life and "have it more abundantly" (KJV). I live in a beautiful country setting, in a peaceful hamlet called Ozark on the Arkansas River. I have a wonderful husband, precious children, my extended family all around me, and I love my job. At times, the kingdom of heaven is so near that I can almost see it, touch it, feel it. And yet, this is not one of those times.

This week, the small town where I live has been touched by two major tragedies. The suicide of a school leader and the reported rape of a former "Miss OHS" in her new home in Mississippi has left everyone reeling. People are asking "Why?" Families are grieving. Churches are praying. I am lying awake at night pondering the mystery of suffering.

Both times this week I was informed of the news by a phone call. A strange thing happened as I listened to the people who told me each heartbreaking story. Of course I felt sad and also shocked. But the more I listened, the more I also felt anger rising up—at the enemy. His breath seemed so near that I could almost smell it, taste it, feel it. He was glad to hear the bad news. His is the kingdom of this earth.

As evil has once more surfaced in my personal version of Eden, I have been reminded that no matter how good life is at times here, this world is not our home. And I have been challenged to walk according to the laws of a different country. We can believe our circumstances or the climate of our surroundings, which can quickly change as mine did this week. Or we can believe God, choosing, instead of the natural reality we can see, the spiritual reality that is in Jesus. We can cling to eternal truths no matter what wind is blowing through the kingdom of this world.

"Peace always—in all things," advises Amy Carmichael. I must lift up my eyes above the kingdom of this world and find my help in the Lord. Peace is possible in all things for those who walk in faith. * *GF*

"Hoover" You Waiting For?

For the eyes of the LORD range throughout the earth to strengthen those whose hearts are fully committed to him.

2 CHRONICLES 16:9

This morning, in the middle of a cleaning frenzy, the telephone rang. I really, *really* hate it when that happens, especially when Hoover and I are workin' some serious moves to Hall & Oates' "Private Eyes." In my rush to quiet the incessant ringing, I tripped over Hoover's cord and nearly landed face-first in a pile of Pledge-soaked rags. "Go soak your head in a bucket of Pine-Sol!" is what I wanted to bark into the receiver. Fortunately for my friend, who'd called in search of a sympathetic shoulder, I merely growled, "Hello?"

Turns out Tina's daughter—long embroiled in a turbulent relationship—almost left her husband.

It was the "almost" that had upset Tina. "I hate to see any marriage end," she cried, "but I can't stand knowing that my bipolar son-in-law, Joseph, could snap and turn the kids into domestic violence statistics." On the heels of a shaky sigh, she added, "Where is *God* in all of this?"

My heart ached for her. As a mom and grandmom myself, I identified with her fear and helplessness.

I took a breath and summoned divine guidance, because this sure didn't seem like the right time to say "Look to Jesus in your time of need" or "God is your refuge and your strength." As she recited Joseph's non-Christian flaws, I was reminded of the biblical king Asa and his battle with Israel's Baasha. Instead of turning to God for help, Asa purchased protection by way of a treaty with yet another king... and it cost him. Big-time.

Tina was listing Joseph-the-unbeliever's latest wrongdoings when the story of pianist Andor Földes came to my mind. He was barely sixteen and embroiled in the most tumultuous year of his life when Franz Liszt's last surviving student asked him to play. Though it was the last thing he felt like doing, Földes chose the most difficult sonatas in his repertoire—Schumann, Bach, Beethoven—and when he finished, renowned Emil von Sauer kissed his forehead. "After *my* first lesson with Liszt," said von Sauer, "he kissed my forehead. 'Take good care of that kiss,' he said, 'for it is from Beethoven himself.' I have been waiting for years to find a student worthy to pass it on to." Quite a hefty responsibility, one I'm sure young Földes, like his talented predecessors, took quite seriously when it was his turn to hand down the esteemed tradition.

By contrast, God's grace requires nothing of us but belief in Him and acceptance of the generous gift of His love. I'll keep right on praying for Tina, for her daughter and her grandchildren, and for Joe too, that he might one day bask in the joy that goes hand in hand with knowing the amazing comfort of God's grace. * *LL*

Can't Get No Satisfaction

*Surely, LORD, you bless the righteous; you surround
them with your favor as with a shield.*

PSALM 5:12

I had a laundry list of things I wanted when I finally purchased my first home. It had to have a fenced back-yard with lots of green grass for Sophie to roll around in; I needed a third bedroom for an office, a second bathroom so I never had to share, a connected garage and laundry room, and a lot of light filtering through a ton of windows. Oh, and I wanted my mortgage payment to stay within two hundred dollars of the monthly rent I already paid.

"Enough already," a good friend cautioned me. "You can't have everything, Sandie. You'll learn soon enough that you're going to have to compromise."

But why?

I'd waited a very long time to purchase my first home all on my own. I had prayed and hoped and dreamed; I'd cut out pictures from magazines and catalogs and glued them into a "dream book." I priced a new sofa for the home I hadn't yet purchased, and I chose paint colors for the master bedroom and the office I hadn't even seen.

For some reason, God created me with the ability to see things from a hopeful perspective. People have often remarked about what a "big dreamer" I am. "Sandie's not easily satisfied," an ex-boyfriend once declared to one of my closest friends. "I just don't think anyone can ever live up to her expectations."

I wasn't particularly sad about the fact that we broke up soon after that, but I do sometimes wish I'd had the opportunity to tell him he'd never have had to live up to my hopes and dreams for my life because they didn't really have anything to do with him. Instead, they had everything to do with God.

"I guess I'm just a 'glass half empty' kind of guy," he'd told me early on, in a tone that let me know I'd been warned. "I just don't believe in getting my hopes too high; I expect the worst and hope for the best, and that way I'm almost never disappointed."

I remember thinking, *Wow. What a sad way to live!* I suppose I'm the exact opposite of him. I like to expect the best and hope it won't be the worst, and my glass is mostly full. I tend to revel in the grace and favor promised to me in the Scriptures, and I often make plans based on that favor. I mean, I'm not saying I've never been deflated or had my hopes dashed, but when I read that God's favor surrounds me like a shield, I consciously wear that shield out into the world. Sometimes it gets knocked around a bit, and in a few cases it's let me down, but I still don't leave home without it! Does that mean I'm never satisfied, or does it mean that I just know how big my God is? * *SDB*

The Right Words at the Right Time

A man finds joy in giving an apt reply—and how good is a timely word!
PROVERBS 15:23

Years ago, at a family gathering, we had so many people attending the meal that many of us sat away from the table with our plates in our laps. My older brother, dressed in his finest, sat on the rug cross-legged, cradling his plate with his legs. Without warning, his plate flipped like a Tiddlywink, and his entire meal—roast beef, gravy, potatoes, gravy, peas, *did I say gravy?*—poured swiftly into his lap.

Everyone around him grabbed their plates and moved out of the way as if his food were explosive. He sat in shock, staring at his lap.

My mother, however, said, "Boy, are *you* lucky."

Now, I'm sure what my mother meant was something like, "Boy, are you lucky your food had cooled somewhat; otherwise, you would have burned yourself something fierce." Or, "Boy, are you lucky your food didn't spill all over the Persian rug. It will cost far less to dry-clean your suit than to clean or replace that rug." Or, "Boy, are you lucky you're not on a date, because you look pretty ridiculous right now."

But the timing and wording of Mom's comment prompted my brother to laugh incredulously and point to the mess in his lap. "You call *this* lucky?"

We've all had times when we meant well but chose the wrong words or spoke in an untimely manner: a compliment to one person insulted another; an offhanded attempt at humor turned out to be grossly inappropriate; a comment to make a point shouldn't have been made at that particular moment.

And then there are those wonderful experiences when the Lord uses our words to give comfort, to bring joy, to verify one of His truths, or to draw someone closer to Him. Sometimes we don't even realize it's happening. Once I made an off-the-cuff comment to a seeker and later learned it was instrumental in her coming to Christ. I definitely "[found] joy in giving an apt reply."

We needn't be poets, either. Years ago, a Christian friend spoke to me about Jesus. All I remember today is how she inhaled as if smelling a beautiful aroma before saying, "He's just so…*wonderful*."

As Christians we represent Jesus, so it makes sense to pray that He'll bless us with the right words at the right time, especially if what we say might open someone's heart to Him. * TP

Be Nice (Especially When It's Tough)!

Add to your faith...patience; and to patience godliness; and to godliness brotherly kindness.
2 PETER 1:5–7 KJV

*Y*esterday, as I stood in the grocery store checkout line, I grew a little flustered while rummaging in my purse for money and my "reduce the price" card. (Maybe you have one of those bottomless pit satchels that allows you to carry everything but the kitchen sink, too...) In my overzealousness to dig for my wallet, my address book fell out and slid under the magazine rack.

Well, imagine my surprise when the gentleman behind me got onto his hands and knees on my behalf! He got up, dusted off his trousers and the mini phone book, and winked. "There you go, little lady," he said, smiling. My heartfelt "Thank you" hardly seemed sufficient, but what more could I do...or say?

The nice man and I chatted as my purchases rolled by on the black conveyor belt: The weatherman predicted rain tonight; weren't those tabloid headlines hilarious; he hoped the tickle in his throat wouldn't become the full-blown flu that had laid his wife low all week....

Something inching down the conveyor belt—a two-for-one package of an effervescent product that promised to nip germs in the bud—caught my eye. While he distractedly searched his pocket for a credit card, I paid for it, separated the two products, and handed one to him.

The poor guy looked as shocked as I'd felt when he hit the floor to retrieve my address book. Isn't it a shame that small acts of kindness like that aren't a routine part of everyone's days!

Driving home, I remembered the story of the little girl who walked along the seashore after high tide and found a dozen starfish on the sand. Bending down, she picked one up as a man passing by said, "You realize, don't you, that it's impossible to save them all." The little girl tossed the starfish into the water. "Maybe," she replied, "but at least I saved *that* one."

As I put away my groceries, I turned on the small black-and-white TV in my kitchen and saw what has become my all-time favorite commercial: A man picks up an empty soda bottle on the ground at a county fair and tosses it into a trash can; a woman on the Ferris wheel, who'd witnessed this good citizen's behavior, later helps an elderly gentleman climb the stairs; a mom sees her act of kindness and returns photos forgotten by a young couple on a carnival ride...and on and on. These seemingly insignificant displays of good citizenship, of human compassion, of *Christianity*, make us all feel a little better about ourselves, our lives, and the world at large. And isn't it wonderful that those feelings are contagious!

We needn't be "out and about" to participate in such behavior. We could, instead, call a relative who's trying to survive the anniversary of a loved one's passing. Or e-mail a friend to say happy birthday. Rake leaves or shovel snow for an elderly neighbor. Don't ask permission or make an announcement—just do it! So go ahead...infect someone in *your* world with kindness today! * *LL*

Broken Hearts Restored!

A man's spirit sustains him in sickness, but a crushed spirit who can bear?
PROVERBS 18:14

This is such a profound verse because the human body can endure so much. Once, I interviewed an incredible Christian woman who had been shot more than twenty-six times. A victim of terrorism, she was the only survivor in a car of five missionaries. Her husband, who had battled to get her safely to the hospital, died from the attack.

What I remember most vividly about the interview—which was less than a year after this tragedy happened—was not her body's wounds, which included a gouge the size of a tennis ball in her knee. I remember her heart. It was broken. She trusted God's plan. She knew the Lord had spared her for a reason, but she woke up across the world in a Texas hospital with her life completely changed. Her husband was with Jesus; her hand was permanently disfigured; and her own hopes of having a child with her husband were forever dashed.

The human body is amazing. God has created it to have restorative, healing powers…but our hearts are different. If you've ever been in a place where hope is absent, where God's reasons are unfathomable, where His voice is silent,

you understand. When the body is weak, we can hope for a different future. We might even see peace in the quiet time to pray. But where hope is absent, the heart truly suffers. In these moments, a Bible verse from a well-meaning friend can seem like a weapon wielded (remember Job's buddies?).

Life may never be the same, but it will be worth living again. It was for Carrie, in the wake of such horrors. I've been in a place where I didn't see light at the end of the tunnel—and the tunnel had a train bearing down upon me. God was speaking to me, but His answer was different from my friend's. He gave me the strength to move out of that place, but it was not easy and it was not quick. His answer included an outcome I didn't foresee or desire.

Suffering is part of the human experience, and we grow in compassion and understanding through the pain. If you are stuck in that tunnel, if you don't know which way to turn—rest in Him. Give yourself time to heal and restore, because while the body may restore itself in minimal time, the heart takes much longer. Be still and know that He is God. * *KB*

What's a Friend For?

Greater love has no one than this,
that he lay down his life for his friends.

JOHN 15:13

I need your help. An attorney will be here in about fifteen minutes, and he says we have to have witnesses."

This call came from a tearful neighbor after she found out that her husband had a terminal illness. Although they are in their seventies, they didn't have a will until they felt they needed one, and then suddenly it was urgent. So I went next door to witness the signing of the will. My heart ached as I sat across the table from a man whose health is so bad he probably won't be with us much longer. My hand shook as I wrote my name beneath his, and it took every bit of my self-control to keep from crying. I *so* didn't want to be there, but they needed me.

I've called friends to help me with various things—from asking for advice on an outfit for a special event to moving my furniture when I couldn't afford to hire professionals. Most of those times, my friends were right there, ready and willing to do whatever was needed. And I appreciated every bit of assistance they gave.

My friends were willing to take risks for me by coming when I called. When I asked if an outfit made me look like a wide load from the rear, I expected honesty— but there was no guarantee my feelings wouldn't be hurt. A true friend would tell me and gently steer me to something more flattering, at the risk of upsetting me. One friend offered to come over and watch my children so my husband and I could have a date night. When I asked for help with moving furniture, I was asking my friends to take a day out of their busy lives, sweat in intense Florida heat, and risk injury to themselves when they picked up my triple dresser and king-size bed.

I'm grateful for my friends because they're almost always willing to come through for me. I want to be a friend to others, even when it involves taking risks. But when I think about what God did by sending His Son to die for us…*whoa*! That's way more than we can request from any friend on earth. I can't even imagine asking anyone to give up his or her life for me. The beauty of God's sacrifice is even more amazing since we never had to ask for it. He did it because He knew we needed salvation—something we could never handle on our own. Talk about a true, everlasting friend! He's the friend we should open our hearts to above all others. * DM

The View from Here

The LORD upholds all those who fall and lifts up all who are bowed down.

PSALM 145:14

What a view!

It's a phrase that pulses through the dialogue between prospective home owners and their bright-eyed, smooth-talking realty agents.

"So, are you ready to make an offer?" an agent asks, with cell phone in one hand and pen in the other.

"The kitchen's outdated. The bathrooms need upgrades. The bedrooms are cramped, and there's one too few of them for our family's needs."

"But will you look at that view!"

"Sold."

It may not happen that simply, but a great view is often on the list of must-haves for home buyers. When I dream about the ideal home, the first frame in my mental slide show isn't the slick countertops or the walk-in closets or the jetted tub. It's the view. A wide expanse of water, a smooth stretch of sand, mountains, woodlands, a manicured lawn, and an Eden-like garden. Yes, I know a real-estate agent would have a rough time matching a property to my wish list...and an even harder time reconciling to our family budget. That's why it's a dream rather than a plan. My dream has a view.

As longevity and arthritis curled her spine like a shepherd's hook, an elderly woman from my home church found her view reduced to the patch of carpet, the sidewalk, the floor tiles right in front of her feet. She leaned heavily on a cane, which I first assumed was because of her bad hip. But I now wonder if it wasn't to keep her from tipping over onto her forehead.

Cowlick to bunion, she probably rounded up to five feet on her driver's license when she could still see over the steering wheel. Those of us who cared about her learned to bend down and look up in order to carry on a conversation with the bent woman.

I can't imagine having such a restricted view of life—carpet fibers and thresholds. The scuffed toes of people's shoes. Crawling things and cracks in the asphalt.

Wouldn't you think her spirit would be bowed down too?

Far from it. Though her physical gaze was fixed on the ground beneath her, her spiritual gaze was locked on Jesus. Her attitude wasn't grounded; it soared.

Unable to make eye contact with people, she maintained constant eye contact with the Lord. No wonder her life remained one of irrepressible joy. That's the secret, isn't it? It's all about the view. When I focus on the potholes at my feet, the toenail fungus and muddy footprints of life, I live bent. But even when circumstances force my attention downward, I have viewpoint options. Despite concerns that threaten to curl my spine, I can have a clear, unrestricted line of sight to the Author of grace. When my heart locks gazes with Him, He straightens my internal posture and changes my outlook so I see life from His perspective. Will you look at that amazing view! * CR

Oh Happy Day!

*Do not be anxious about anything, but in
everything, by prayer and petition, with thanksgiving,
present your requests to God.*

PHILIPPIANS 4:6–7 NIV

At the start of every year, I unwrap my new calendar and immediately flip to the August page. And though the weather outside my window is bitterly cold and blustery winds send the snow into drifts, I pray for warmth as the thermometer refuses to budge above zero and ask the Father to allow me a few memories of "heat and humidity" as my gaze locks on a photo of a shorts-and-T-shirts-clad family, who are happily picnicking under an azure sky. I can almost feel the warmth of the sticky breeze, and I thank God for the momentary respite from winter.

Considering the sweltering heat that's commonplace in August, it's no surprise that the month was named for Augustus Caesar, one of history's most hotheaded rulers. I pity my oldest daughter and little sister, both born in August (and stuck with that sickly peridot birthstone), and I cringe, because the flower of their month is the gladiolus... which is so often favored in funeral bouquets.

On a brighter note, though, Ecuador, Korea, India, Indonesia, and Uruguay are among the countries that won their independence during August. In Scotland, people attend the Edinburgh Festival, while in other European countries, citizens and tourists celebrate "workers' day," all in August. Here in the States, August is Picnic Month, Inventors' Month, Back to School Month, and, believe it or not, Catfish Month.

Presidents Benjamin Harrison, Herbert Hoover, Lyndon Johnson, and Bill Clinton were born in August, while on the other side of "life," historical August newspapers reported that Wild Bill Hickok was shot dead in a Deadwood saloon, Gertrude Ederle became the first woman to swim the English Channel, and Liz Taylor divorced Richard Burton (for the second time) in August. Elvis died and Hurricane Katrina struck...in August.

My parents, in-laws, and my husband and I share an August anniversary. So as I stare at the cloud-dotted sky and the sea of emerald lawn that flows on the August page of a calendar so new that it still wafts the scent of ink, I'm reminded of the plaque above my desk that reads, GOD LOVES AUGUST! * *LL*

Eagle's Wings

But those who hope in the Lord will renew their strength.
They will soar on wings like eagles; they will run and not grow weary,
they will walk and not be faint.

ISAIAH 40:31

One of my favorite parts in *Lord of the Rings* is when Gandalf the wizard is rescued from atop evil Saruman's tower by Gwaihir, a massive eagle. (Note: I had to look up most of those names—I'm not a total nerd.) The scene is exhilarating and provides Gandalf (and the viewer) great relief. Before the eagle arrives, the poor man—er, wizard—is completely exhausted after a long, bitter battle; he's stuck in a spot where no one can help him; and goodness knows the last time he had a shower or a decent meal.

Some days I can totally identify. I'll bet you can too. Maybe you have a house to keep, a family to raise, a husband to please, a job to finish, and far too little time in your day. Maybe your situation isn't even *that* good. You can't afford a house, you have strife in your family (or *no* family), you can't *find* a job, and the days slip past you at an alarming rate.

On those days, I wish a massive eagle would swoop down and fly me somewhere far away from my responsibilities and worries. But I'd settle for a cleaning crew, a secretary, a chauffeur, a beauty entourage, and a yacht full of cash. I mean, the chances of my getting all that are as good as the chance that I'm going to be soaring on wings of eagles anytime soon, right?

But God promises that soaring to us, if we hope in Him. Other translations of today's verse address those who *wait* on the Lord and those who *trust* in Him. So God wants us to hope, wait, and trust. That, I think I can do.

When you think about it, that's what our faith is all about. When we give our lives to Jesus and tell Him we believe He's done it all for us—saved us from a horrible spot where no one else could have helped us—we're placing all our hopes in Him. We're agreeing to wait, as long as He dictates, for blissful, perfect eternity (and even for every blessing He has planned for us here on earth). We're saying we trust everything He's said and done, no matter what happens while we live on earth.

Regardless of what you experience in life—soaring happiness or wearying adversity—knowing you've placed it all on His shoulders does renew your strength, don't you think? Each time we renew our hope, He'll renew our strength. * *TP*

Friends in High Places

Before they call I will answer; while they are still speaking I will hear.

ISAIAH 65:24

I love me some Diann Hunt! The woman is extraordinary. She's funny, talented, insightful, and such a good friend. In addition to all of that, of course, we share a very unique thread in that we've both battled ovarian cancer and won. When she delivered the news to me recently that her battle was on again, I hung up the phone, doubled over, and sobbed for I don't know how long. Before the day was out, I'd posted a message on Facebook telling people I wanted to start a prayer loop on behalf of my friend; anyone interested could e-mail me privately.

A dozen of us took up the flag and let it fly. Before the end of the day, we were praying fervently for Diann. One by one, other people's needs came to light as well, and we began praying about those too. Around two or three in the morning on the second day, I found myself doubled over again—this time in excruciating pain. I was alone. I started vomiting and writhing from the intensity of the pain, and I finally picked up the phone and called an ambulance.

In the emergency room, waiting for the pain medication in my IV to take effect, my thoughts went to Diann and then to the prayer loop. Ten minutes later, I'd sent a message through my best friend to ask them all to pray for me.

There were X-rays and ultrasounds and blood work, all in order to detect kidney stones and a very bad infection that had spread from my bladder to my left kidney. At around ten o'clock that morning, they sent me home. By the time I got there and was settled, even before I took the quiet time to pray on my own, my BlackBerry had filled up with message after message from the loop. All those beautiful prayer warriors had been crying out to the Lord on my behalf for hours.

In the days that followed, there were some complications. I needed more tests, had to see my own doctor, and continued to struggle with feeling better. All the while, the faithful prayers flowed, and I felt their vigor; the grace of it all just engulfed me as I regained my strength during the next week.

I find it so ironic that I'd been the one to spearhead this group of people into a prayer group, and I was the one who benefited from the fruits of their willing spirits. My God had secured and spread out a net beneath me before I ever found myself on the unexpected high wire. And He'd used a phenomenal group of people to do it. What started for the benefit of Diann, and even me, developed into so much more. It's an ongoing support system that reaches far beyond a dozen women who just serve the same loving God.
*SDB

Out with the Old, In with the New

The LORD bless and keep you; the LORD make His face shine on you and be gracious to you; the LORD turn his face toward you and give you peace.

NUMBERS 6:24–26

Don't you just love those ads that come tucked into your Sunday paper? You know, the ones that promise that you can walk into a store and leave with just about anything, from a wide-screen television to a top-of-the-line computer…and not pay a penny *for two whole years*! What we don't love is the way that big fat payment due sneaks up and bites us once the twenty-four months are up.

This past Christmas, my husband and I made a pact: we'd trade our clunky old television set for one of those jazzy new wide-screen versions, and because it wasn't inexpensive, the TV would serve as birthday, anniversary, Mother's, and Fathers' Day gifts throughout the year. And we'd make regular payments, y'know, to spare ourselves the whole ugly "outrun the payment monster" scene.

We've enjoyed the dickens out of the TV. Writing those checks every month? Not so much. But the whole buy-now, pay-later process got me to thinking about how many other old things we've traded for new. Hundreds, I'd guess, over the course of our decades-long marriage. And *that* got me to thinking about how God gave us the Old Testament after the New one.

I made the mistake of bringing this up at Bible study. I say "mistake" because oh, what a noise it started! "The Old Testament is 'all law,'" said one guy, "and the New Testament is 'all grace!'" His wife agreed—*loudly*. "The Old Testament God was harsh and unforgiving. But He softened up when He became a Father."

"Do you realize," I asked, "that there are at least twenty references to grace in the Old Testament?"

Husband: "But it didn't mean the same thing."

Wife: "Right! It meant *favor*."

Semantics? I didn't think so then. I don't think so now. But <shrug> to each his own Bible, right?

Wrong! Noah found grace at the Bible's start (Genesis 6:8), and Esther got some too (Esther 2:17). Grace and glory are found in Psalm 84:11, and the Messianic king was filled with grace and kindness in Psalm 45:2. And if the Twenty-third Psalm isn't 100 percent grace, I don't know what is!

I'm sure our heavenly Father saw this mini-debate eons before that Bible study meeting had even been scheduled, and because it's a microscopic example of how Christians would convince themselves that they could walk out of life by paying for their sins with good deeds and prayers, He rewrote the old laws…and replaced them with one brand-new, easy-to-understand rule: thanks to the sacrifice of God's only Son, we can walk out of life and into paradise because *Jesus* paid for our sins…

…and we'll never experience that scary, "The bill is due; pay up!" feeling again. * *LL*

Skinny Fingers

For the law was given through Moses;
grace and truth came through Jesus Christ.

JOHN 1:17

I have to celebrate my hands."

Far from a narcissistic declaration, when those words came out of my daughter's mouth, we both knew we were witnesses to a profound insight.

We know what it means to "struggle with our weight," which sounds like wrestling a sweaty sumo guy for permission to breathe. Okay, that's a better analogy than I thought it was going to be.

Carbs like us too much. They stalk us, crave a little time with us, beg until we let them rent space on our hips. But we've both set our minds to eat healthier and no longer grab food unthinkingly (as often) or for all the wrong reasons—emotional ache, paper cut, first day of spring…. I've decided to let vegetables dominate my dinner plate. Daughter Amy has shown remarkable discipline in cutting calories. We're far from where we want to be. But we recognize the importance of acknowledging small victories.

We still don't like our chins. Any of them. But Amy's thrilled that her hands look different. Her fingers are slim. Noticeable progress. Slim isn't a word that works its way into daily conversation in our family. I had to look it up to make sure I spelled it correctly. Amy's fingers are slim.

Mine look trimmer too. My wedding rings slop around freely as opposed to lodging in that fleshy ditch where they've lived so long.

We still have enough excess to make us good candidates for being marooned on a desert island for a good chunk of time without any danger of our bikinis falling off (yeah, like we'd wear bikinis), but we're celebrating small victories on our way to the larger ones. Dropping a size. Buttoning a jacket. Having to belt a once-tight pair of slacks.

What does that observation have to do with John 1:17?

Freedom.

The closer we come to our health goals, the more we recognize the difference between where we were and where we want to be.

The law God gave through Moses showed us where we ought to be and how utterly impossible it was to get there without the promised Messiah. The grace and truth that came through Christ brought us the freedom of possibility, the joy of progress, and the hope of growing to reflect Him rather than our former selves.

When I'm tempted to mourn the fact that, spiritually, I still have more than enough chins, I'm going to take a closer look at what's different in me because of Jesus. What's gone, conquered, reined in, trimmer because of Him?

At one time, I would have shared a tidbit of gossip. I would have stormed off if someone offended me. I used to skirt the truth when filling in the "weight" question on my driver's license renewal. Even before vegetables, God and I conquered that temptation. I remember when I'd say I would pray but never follow through. Small victories.

My fingers are slimmer. I have to celebrate my hands.

* CR

Don't Forget the Here and Now

"For I know the plans I have for you," declares the LORD, "plans to prosper you and not to harm you, plans to give you hope and a future."

JEREMIAH 29:11

I've often recounted this verse as the one that carried me through to the other side of ovarian cancer. I was on the treatment table in the hospital when the Lord brought this verse to my heart, promising me a future and a hope, and I clung to that Scripture with steel talons from that moment forward. No one needed to hear that there was a future ahead more than I did.

Something happens to you when you've fought against "the C beast" and emerged to hear those two beautiful words you've been dreaming about: CANCER FREE. I think my friend and coauthor Diann Hunt would probably agree. It changes a person. Your outlook on life shifts, and you stop putting things off so readily. The bigger picture is still important, but your focus becomes much more here-and-now.

I'm a true believer in affirmations. Since Scripture tells us that life and death are in the power of our own tongues, I try to speak life as often as I can. Part of that effort comes in a list of affirmations that I've written down, and I say them aloud after my daily prayers.

"I can do all things through Christ which strengtheneth me" (Philippians 4:13 KJV).

The Lord goes before me, making crooked places straight.

I am thinner, stronger, and healthier today than I was yester-day. (I like to think positively.)

Before any of the others, the first affirmation of the day is always the same: *This is the day the Lord has made. I will rejoice and be glad in it.* It's based on Psalm 118:24. I've said it out loud nearly every day of my life for the past several years; I've read it in the Bible a couple of dozen times or more. And yet I didn't make the connection with the verse that followed until recently. Verse 25 (KJV) adds: "O Lord, I beseech thee, send now prosperity."

David didn't pray that the Lord prosper him eventually or someday. He boldly asked Him to send it *now*, without delay, the sooner the better.

I love that about David. He was a very emotional guy. Despite the fact that he frequently looked into the future for what God would do, he also spent a good bit of the Psalms communing with God about the here and now.

How much better does it get than to serve a God with everything in hand? He promises us a future, but He also concerns Himself with providing hope for today. * *SDB*

A Life of Meekness

Then when you realize your worthlessness before the Lord,
He will lift you up, encourage and help you.

JAMES 4:10 TLB

For the full year before it happened, I dreaded my class reunion. A person hopes, if she is going to attend such a gathering, to be skinny, beautiful, happy, and successful at the appointed time. If this is not possible, she can always not go and face everyone. This applies, of course, as long as she is not the president of the class and expected to plan the whole thing.

I could never have ignored that duty. It was one of my campaign slogans back in twelfth grade. I honestly believe it was one of the main reasons I was elected—back then I was thought of as a "very responsible young lady." So, with the generous help of a large number of class members, I set about planning, and the date was set.

When the time came, I was in the midst of moving and up to my ears in boxes. Stone and I were moving out of our restaurant business, as it had closed the same week, and at the time we had one part-time job between us. This sort of state was not conducive to our marital bliss.

I could not find anything, like pictures or other mementos, nor could I find cute clothes to wear, as I was eight months pregnant and the size of a small elephant. I had one pair of Birkenstocks that fit on my feet, they were so grossly swollen, and those had to go with everything from the picnic to the semi-formal banquet.

In short, I had to will myself to go. Somewhere deep inside, I felt that old sense of responsibility to my class and my friends. These were the people I had preached to about Jesus and the importance of a relationship with Him, how that's what makes your life complete. I had listed a Bible verse as my motto in our senior yearbook: "You have everything when you have Christ…." I had tried to live my life with them as a good friend and a good example, and for as long as I could remember they had supported me by voting me president, along with "Most Courteous," "Friendliest," "Class Favorite," "Most Likely to Succeed…."

Most Likely to Succeed. Cheerleader Co-captain. The former Miss Ozark High School. Homecoming Maid. For all they knew, I should have graduated from medical school by now and be filling Mother Teresa's place as head missionary to India (this was my senior's prediction at the prom). But, instead, I showed up at an all-time low to my ten-year reunion.

It's hard to explain exactly what happened once I got there. I don't know what I expected—shock, maybe? Pity? Worse, a smugness that Miss Smarty Pants wasn't quite so smart and together after all? I don't think I consciously expected anything, but knowing the reality of human pride and fear, these thoughts had to be there somewhere in my subconscious. Why else would I not want to go?

When I got there, swallowing my pride as I stepped out of the car, a miracle occurred. I found none of what I feared; all I found was love. Laughter. Acceptance. Even appreciation and understanding. With each hug, each kind word spoken to me or about me to my husband, I began to retrieve pieces of myself that for the past year had been buried. A lot of those people, old friends who knew me pretty well, reminded me of who I was. Not necessarily the most successful, and definitely not the reigning beauty queen, but a daughter of the King who had made a difference in some of their lives.

It was beautiful. It was needed. It was a gift from God to help and encourage me and lift me up. * *GF*

Eat and Be Merry

Blessed are you who hunger now, for you will be satisfied.
Blessed are you who weep now, for you will laugh.

LUKE 6:23

Have you ever been in a place where you thought you'd never laugh again? Sometimes the burdens of life can be so daunting, it's hard to see the way out, much less have a giggle during the valley. And hunger? I know people who have been on a diet for their entire lives, and they don't ever seem satisfied. So when I see God's promises written out the way they are in today's verse, seeming so elusive and miraculous, I often question my own sanity and ponder the question, "Does God mean in this lifetime?"

When my kids were young, I used to scrapbook. Now that they're older, I'm so busy driving them around, I never have time to document the occasions—but the finished books have reminded me that what was once so painful is now a great source of laughter. Maybe that's what God means: that we'll view life differently from another vantage point.

When I had four children under six years of age, I did not live in the present much—I *survived*. I barked orders and expected compliance, though sometimes more explanation was actually necessary. One Easter, my church had an outdoor Good Friday service, complete with communion. I'd been raised Catholic, where children didn't get to take communion until they'd gone through a series of classes and understood the depth of the encounter. Why I thought my boys (aged two, four, and five) would understand this, I'm not sure. They were all whining for dinner, but my husband and I said to the boys, "We're going to take communion and come back to the car, and we'll go eat."

They all nodded. We hurried to the front of the line so that we could leave and get the kids fed—it was late for them. We ripped off our pieces of communion bread and headed to the minivan. When I finally turned around to help them into the van and tell my boys about communion, instead of the great teachable moment I imagined, they stood next to the vehicle with an entire loaf of French bread, and their chipmunk cheeks were round and in motion.

"Did you take the communion bread?" I asked in horror.

"We're not hungry anymore," my oldest said with a happy smile.

My husband arrived, and I pointed out our latest family faux pas. "Should I take it back?"

"Do you think they want it back?" he asked.

I supposed not.

God will bring us joy from the ashes. He will satisfy our hungers and cries even if we're too weak to know what to ask Him for. He understands. * *KB*

A Stinky Situation

The Lord is good to all; he has compassion on all he has made.

PSALM 145:9

Baltimore is under attack!

The assailants? Pentatomidae, the largest family of insects in the superfamily Pentatomoidea of the Hemiptera order. In plain English, we've been invaded by stinkbugs.

Protected by a hideous shell, these nightmare-inducing creepy-crawlies don't bite (like mosquitoes) or sting (like wasps)…though they *could*, if they had a mind to poke their probosces into human flesh. Fortunately, they're too busy devouring apples and peaches in the neighboring orchards or feasting on the beefeater tomatoes in my garden. Just knowing that they were outside and multiplying by the millions (literally!) was bad enough. But then the disgusting li'l critters rode indoors on our shoulders and got to work at draining the green from my houseplants!

Like creatures from a science-fiction movie, they made their way from Asia to Baltimore by way of Pittsburgh. (So I think it's only fair that Steel Town citizens send their "Terrible Towels" to Charm City; as we use them to render stinkbugs unconscious, we might also diminish the rivalry that exists between Ravens and Steelers fans.)

During those first weeks of the buggy assault, I read every stinkbug article I could get my hands on. Spiders can't eat them (the shells are too hard), and the gag-a-maggot odor protects them from birds. Unlike worms, they don't enrich the earth; unlike bees, they can't pollinate plants. Despite years of tedious experiments, scientists haven't found anything that will kill the arrogant pests that have an uncanny ability to stand on two hind legs, waving pronged forefeet as if to say, "We're stayin', and there ain't a thing you can do about it. Neener, neener!"

One day, I spied a stinkbug on the kitchen floor, unafraid and in no particular hurry to reach its destination. But then, why would it feel rushed or frightened when God blessed it with a hardy constitution and no known enemies?

To that point, I'd called them ugly. Unsettling. Useless. But as I watched it waddle toward the dining room, I got an inkling of what the Almighty might have had in mind when He fashioned the little tomato demolishers.

"The LORD is good to all," says Psalm 145:9, "and he has compassion on all he has made." *Perhaps,* I thought, gently gathering the little bug into a nest of facial tissue, *God put stinkbugs on the earth not to pollinate flowers or mulch soil, not even to terrorize humans…but to remind us that if He could love and protect stinkbugs, of all things, how much more must He want to love and care for us…the beings He made in His own image and likeness!*

Like the stinkbug, I moved toward the powder room, unafraid and in no particular hurry. "You're going into the sewer," I said, "and there isn't a thing you can do about it. Neener neener!" * *LL*

Tongue Twister

A gossip betrays a confidence, but a trustworthy man keeps a secret.

PROVERBS 11:13

In my younger years, I knew a woman whose favorite pastime seemed to be gossiping. She gossiped about anything and everything. I'd see her talking to friends, cupping her hand around her mouth and whispering news that appeared to be a "secret," and I'd bristle.

With a background as a legal secretary, I knew the meaning of keeping a confidence. My job depended on it. I couldn't go around yammering about cases brought into our office. In later years, I became a court reporter with plenty of "juicy tales" to tell, but again, extreme confidence was crucial to our business.

This woman hurt people with news that should have been kept private and seemed to delight when others hadn't been privy to stories on which she had the inside scoop. I'd seen the damage her loose tongue had left behind, and I didn't like it one bit.

Still, my gossiping friend taught me a very important lesson.

One day, the Lord seemed to impress upon my heart to pray for her. Oh, I was only too happy to comply. I rolled up my sleeves and went to work on my knees, praying that God would show her just how wrong she was for speaking when she should have been silent—and asking Him to give her what she deserved for her unkind remarks. Soon I realized I wasn't truly praying for her, but rather complaining about her.

The Lord seemed to whisper that I should pray blessings on her, her family, and her job, as though praying for a special friend and wanting God's best for her.

Needless to say, I was less than thrilled with the idea. (And I had the nerve to judge *her*?) Yet if God said to do it, I would do it.

So I began to pray for her, as I felt I was being led. I imagine you know what happened. *I* changed. I truly began to see her through different eyes. Her family needs concerned me. I wanted God's best for all of them. Before long, I counted it a privilege to pray for her and her family.

I have no idea if she ever stopped her gossiping ways. It's been many years since I've seen her or her family. But I still have a soft place in my heart for them.

There is a reason God admonishes us not to gossip. It betrays friends and hurts people. The next time you're tempted to do it, don't! And if you know someone who does, pray for them. Pray for them as a true friend; in the end, I believe God will bless you both. * *DH*

Heritage Rights

"No weapon forged against you will prevail, and you will refute every tongue that accuses you. This is the heritage of the servants of the LORD, and this is their vindication from me," declares the LORD.

ISAIAH 54:17

During more than ten years of friendship, Carol became a sort of spiritual mother to me. She taught me so much, not just by sharing her profound knowledge of God's Word and His principles, but also by modeling behavior as my mentor and example.

Carol and her husband were very wealthy, and she told me many times what a mixed blessing that could be. I came to understand the meaning well after her husband passed away and people with dollar signs in their eyes crept out of the woodwork. My friend found herself immersed in turmoil, anxiety, and lawsuits, all while she dealt with her own devastating loss. Javelins of accusation flew at her, lies swirled around her—and much like the labor pains of a pregnant woman, the intensity of each attack increased in severity.

We would sneak away sometimes in the afternoon to one of Carol's favorite spots and order large cups of hazelnut coffee and one warm berry tart with a scoop of ice cream on top, which we split. We cried together and prayed together, and often the afternoon came to a close with the two of us giggling about what the Lord was sure to do in order to bring about vindication.

The war waged against Carol came in sporadic, heated battles. But each time, my friend held fast to the spirit of the same Scripture, claiming the promise of God that it is our very heritage as His children: accusing tongues will be refuted, and weapons formed against us will not prosper.

"I don't know how you do it," I told her one afternoon. "How do you keep going?"

"I have a very sharp sword," she told me, referring to the sword of the Spirit, which is the Word of God. "I have the promise that, at the end of this road, I'll be vindicated."

My friend eventually found that vindication, and those attackers insinuating themselves into every fold of her life disappeared. Years passed, and we often spoke of the wonderful final victory.

Carol passed away a couple of years ago, and I've never quite recovered from the loss. I cling vehemently to those things I learned from my dear friend, to the secret conversations and all the giggles we shared. Recently, however, those same enemies that disappeared so long ago have resurfaced, staking a claim to everything they lost the first time around. And every time I pray about my fresh anger and resentment toward them, I am armed with just the right Scripture, the one that fits perfectly in my hand in the form of a sword. * *SDB*

Indiana Jones Syndrome

Whoever digs a pit may fall into it; whoever breaks through a wall may be bitten by a snake.
ECCLESIASTES 10:8

Wow! Ecclesiastes 10:8 packs some powerful and graphic words, but it carries so much meaning on a lot of different levels.

As I ponder the visual, I think about one of the ways it can be interpreted, and it's related to being a good neighbor versus a bad one. I live in a planned suburban neighborhood with houses that are fairly close together. We have an active homeowners' association, so it's hard not to know other people's business.

Most of the people on our street behave…usually, anyway. We're a friendly bunch. When people get sick, we bring them fruit or muffins. We stand out in the yard together and stare at the sky, looking for rain clouds during a drought. And we commiserate when it rains so much that the lawn mowers get bogged down in the mud beneath knee-high grass. My husband and I own an extension ladder and a power washer that we swap out with a neighbor who has a fertilizer spreader and an edger. About a dozen houses on our side of the street have the same lawn service, so we get a group discount. This whole neighborhood thing is a nice arrangement when things go well.

Occasionally—and fortunately very rarely—someone stirs up trouble. A rumor starts when a teenager takes advantage of his parents going out of town and throws a party—or someone's spouse suddenly isn't there anymore. Is the child on drugs? Is the couple getting a divorce and breaking up the family? These start out as questions that eventually turn into statements. Whoever starts the rumor is guilty of digging dirt in the neighbor's yard, and if that person isn't careful, it's a deep hole to fall into. And the snakes in the bottom of that hole are all the repercussions of spreading malicious rumors. While it temporarily may be fun to talk about someone, later on, that fun can make matters worse—not only for the subject of the gossip but for the people spreading it.

I love a good story as much as the next person, and I've listened to way more gossip than I should have. As titillating as it may be, it feels dirty and disgusting later on. I know it's not pleasing to God for us to be involved in malicious talk at any level. He makes it very clear how He feels in this verse. I want to wake up each morning feeling refreshed and able to face my day without having to mess with the slimy snakes that come from any pit I have dug in a neighbor's yard. * DM

The Blessings Jar

Brothers and sisters, pray for us that the message of the Lord
may spread rapidly and be honored.

2 THESSALONIANS 3:1

I'm the first to admit that my life is like a big jar overflowing with blessings.

Like most Christians, when there's a leak in the jar, I pray. The bigger the leak, the harder I pray, and if it's a really big crack, I ask fellow believers to pray *with* me. Not long ago, when tragedy struck my family, I started the prayer chain with a favorite relative.

Several years earlier, Aunt Kate had been diagnosed with an incurable cancer. Though three rounds of chemo, two more of radiation, all while swallowing experimental drugs, did little more than make her bald and skinny, we lifted her in prayer. After months of suffering, Kate went in for a routine blood test...and the lab found no cancer. Shocked, her oncologist ordered more tests. "There's no sign of cancer," he admitted, "and I have no medical or scientific explanation for the cure."

Who better to ask to join me in prayer than the woman who was the living, breathing, *healthy* recipient of a grace-filled, God-made miracle!

Imagine my surprise when she refused, citing 1 Timothy 2:5–6. "He is *God*," she scolded, "and already knows about your petty problems...*and* will resolve them as He sees fit." By the time we hung up, I could barely read the verse through my tears: "There is one God and one mediator between God and mankind, the man Jesus Christ, who gave himself as a ransom for all people."

I'd read the passage many times, but *my* interpretation led me to believe that the Old Testament practice of sacrificing animals to earn an audience with God ended when Jesus died on the cross. His sacrifice allowed us to stand unashamed before the Father in praise and in prayer, for ourselves and on behalf of others. Had I misconstrued the meaning of that verse?

In a word, *no*!

All through the Bible, we find reference after reference, encouraging believers to pray in agreement about individual and community concerns. Asking others to join us in prayer is an act of humility that allows God to accomplish things we could never achieve as individuals. The apostle Paul understood this only too well and repeatedly asked people to pray for him.

The Almighty tells us to serve one another, and one of the best ways we can do that is to pray for them *and with them*.

By the grace of God, Aunt Kate is still cancer-free. And the petty problem I brought to her that day, years ago? I'm happy to report that it's solved and (almost) forgotten!

"How wide and long and high and deep is the love of Christ"! * *LL*

Badge of Dishonor

Bear with each other and forgive one another if any of you has a grievance
against someone. Forgive as the Lord forgave you.
COLOSSIANS 3:13

Elaine had endured a tumultuous adolescence that left her with battle scars she made no effort to cover up. She was very young when her mother had been killed by a drunk driver—and she'd once been held up at gunpoint, which ingrained another traumatic experience for her. It didn't take long in our acquaintance for me to recognize the drunk driver and the gunman as badges pinned to her identity, and she frequently vowed to never forgive either of them. "My anger toward them is part of who I am. I'll never let it go."

Really? I found that so sad. I often spoke about the concept of the supernatural forgiveness I'd found through my faith, and I made promises to Elaine about the joy she could experience if she made a conscious choice to forgive those two strangers who'd played pivotal (albeit devastating) roles in her life. I sent her Scripture verses and chatted with her for hours on end, but it always came down to the same refusal to let go. Not only had these two men become an integral part of her, but they also provided a flag that she could plant on any hilltop at any time as an excuse for bad behavior. It became clear that she had no intention of ever setting aside those flags, and the more I tried to reason with her, the more her anger turned on me along with those

men. Finally, one day when I found myself holding my own bitterness and unforgiveness—toward Elaine—I took it to the throne, found myself washed clean of it, and turned and walked away. The only times I've ever looked back have been those times when I've prayed for my former friend, which I've done a lot over the years.

There have been seasons in my life where I've displayed my own flags of unforgiving bitterness, so I understood Elaine's penchant for hanging on to them. But one thing I've learned from my journey with Jesus is that a tremendous sacrifice was made so that I might be forgiven, so that I might be pure and clean enough to sit at the feet of a Father who adores me. How could I possibly hold on to anger, bitterness, and resentment while peering into the crystal-clear eyes of that loving Father?

The great philosopher and anti-apartheid activist Nelson Mandela once said, "Resentment is like drinking poison and waiting for it to kill your enemy." Truer words outside of Scripture have never been spoken. Is there someone you haven't forgiven? Has that bitterness been around so long that it's become a part of your identity? Make a choice today. Replace it with a badge of humility, and become a reflection of the unending grace extended to you. * *SDB*

This Itty-Bitty Light of Mine

When I consider your heavens, the work of your fingers,
the moon and the stars, which you have set in place, what is man that you are
mindful of him, the son of man that you care for him?

PSALM 8:3–4

One of my favorite memories entails a family trip to Cape Hatteras, North Carolina. Our first night there, I joined my kids, nieces, and nephews out on the deck of the house we rented. The house sat right on the beach, so we were able to turn out all the lights and lie there in total darkness, staring up at the vast sky.

Only a few stars twinkled at first, but as our eyes slowly grew accustomed to the dark, more and more stars became evident. In time, the sky was awash in stars. I couldn't help but become mesmerized.

I also couldn't help but feel *really* small.

I'm no science whiz, but even I know that each of those stars, including the ones we couldn't see at first, is like our sun in general size and intensity. Our sun is actually an average-to-small star. But the universe is so huge and those stars are so far away, they only twinkle for us. And that's just our galaxy.

Okay, I have to stop there. That's all I remember from *Bill Nye the Science Guy*. But you get the picture. We can understand why David asked what he did in today's verses: Why us, Lord? Why do we rate Your consideration and care? Your love?

No doubt, as a shepherd David occasionally lay out in the fields and did exactly what I did with the kids that evening in Hatteras. It's difficult to ignore God's majesty when you look at the heavens and understand that He set everything in its place out there. After doing all that, why would He be mindful of little man?

There is amazing honor in the fact that He loves us like that. Regardless of how puny we are in comparison with the rest of creation, He considers us so important He gave His only Child to redeem us.

Ironically, the more we understand that honor, the easier it should be to embrace humility. There's a point to Christian humility. As John the Baptist said of our relationship with Christ, "He must become greater; [we] must become less" (John 3:30). We do a better job of reflecting God's love—Christ's love—when we behave humbly, rather than lording our privileged status over someone. Like the stars at night reflect the light of the sun, we should strive to reflect Christ's light twenty-four hours a day. * *TP*

A Thrill a Minute

What good is it for someone to gain the whole world, yet forfeit their soul?
MARK 8:36

When I was a little girl, few things excited me more than when my parents said, "Put on your sneakers and grab your jackets, kids; we're going to the amusement park!" Back then, I was an adventure junkie; the bigger and scarier the ride, the better I liked it. I'm not sure when—or why—it happened, but one day the thrill of hurtling through space turned into white-hot fear, and these days, I can't hang curtains unless the chair I'm standing on is guaranteed not to reel and rock, not even a smidge!

My dream about becoming an author reminds me of one of those roller-coaster rides. The "big idea"? That was me, standing in the "this-author-wants-to-be-published" line, waiting to belt myself into the car. Each *tick-tick-tick* as it climbed to the top of the first hill? *Stage One, Story Development.* Those next ticks? Setting, then character development, point of view, conflict, and dialogue. Those ups and downs earned titles such as *Edits* and *Rewrites* and *Second-Guessing Myself.* That last hill—the steepest and most terrifying of all: Typing "The End." And then, the final stomach-churning plummet that made me hold my breath and doubled my heartbeat as I hit the SEND key.

And after exhaling that big gulp of air? Why, I got right back into line, of course, and waited as the editors and agents I'd sent my story to sifted through the people-tall stacks of mail piled on their desks to get to mine. I stared at the phone and watched the mailbox. I read e-mail, but

"We'd like to offer a contract!" wasn't among any of the messages.

So I got back into line. Again. And I buckled myself in. Again…despite what my published author friends told me about the types of novels that didn't sell, despite the arduous years they'd poured into writing them. They complained about small publishing houses that were being gobbled up by bigger ones and midsized companies that had gone belly-up. They groaned when editors took extended maternity leave after telling them how much they believed in their stories. They whimpered as bookstore chains folded, whined when distributors stopped distributing. Then agents culled their client lists, and the editors not on maternity leave began pulling double-duty, making that long and painful wait between SEND and REPLY take twice as much time as it had before.

I couldn't help but ask: "Is my dream worth all this agony?"

I said a loud and resounding "Yes!"

And whatever *your* dream is, "Yes" should be your answer too. Because whether part or all of your dream comes true, you will have yet another reason to glorify God your Father, who used every up-and-down moment you endured to prove His love…

…and thrill you with the exhilarating gift of His grace.
* LL

A Life of Endurance

I have fought the good fight, I have finished the race, I have kept the faith.

2 TIMOTHY 4:7

It was mid-August, time for school to start. Being a teacher's kid, a teacher's wife, and a teacher myself, I order my days by the school calendar. On this day, I sat down with my children to discuss our goals for the coming year.

"What are some things you'd like to learn?" I asked Harper, who was then two. "Want to learn to write your name? Count to one hundred?"

"I want to learn to not be scared of granddaddy longlegs," he said simply.

Turning my attention to Grace, who was five—technically school-age—I had loftier academic visions. "What about you?"

"I want to learn to ride my bike by myself, with no training wheels."

My brows began to crease. "What about reading, writing, and piano?"

"I don't care as much about that as I do my bike," she declared. "Will you teach me?"

There was nothing to do but say yes, so we set the calendar aside and geared up for a biking lesson.

We dragged her little bike to the flattest part of the yard. Grace gathered her courage and started pedaling as I steadied her. As soon as I let go, she fell over. Whimpering, she got up, dusted off, and went for it again. For what seemed like hours, we repeated the process.

On the second day, she quit falling as soon as I let go, stopping herself instead with her feet. That was good, I told her, but she needed to keep pedaling so she wouldn't stop.

She wanted me to run along as she pedaled, acting as a human training wheel. It was backbreaking work, and I finally had to stop.

I explained it was time for the next step, to keep pedaling when I let go. I would give her a good push, and then it would be up to her to keep going. She was terrified, and with good reason—she'd had some tough falls, and her legs were covered with bruises. Pedaling, keeping her balance, and turning—it all seemed like too much.

At one point she was ready to quit, so I gave her a pep talk. "You're almost there! Keep going! It will be worth it!" I jumped up and down like a cheerleader.

She got back on the bike—sweaty, dirt-filled blond hair stringing out from her pink helmet. And that day she did it. Grace circled on her bike with a smoothness to match her name. We both laughed with the triumph, and Harper cheered like she'd won the Tour de France. It was not yet September, and she had achieved her goal for the year.

Grace's bicycle-riding experience taught me a lesson in falling and getting up. What stood between Grace and her goal was the sheer willingness to try one more time. And just when it was the hardest to try again, she succeeded. How true are Paul's words of encouragement: "Fight the good fight, holding on to faith" (1 Timothy 1:18–19); "We are more than conquerors through him who loved us" (Romans 8:37); and "I can do everything through him who gives me strength" (Philippians 4:13). * *GF*

No Good Deed Goes Unpunished

Thus says the LORD to you: "Do not be afraid nor dismayed because of this great multitude, for the battle is not yours, but God's."

2 CHRONICLES 20:15 NKJV

The public defender assigned to my case laughed at his own wit after telling me, "No good deed goes unpunished in this world." I didn't find it amusing at all.

I'd worked hard to put together a silent auction to raise funds for a children's charity; but when the charity wanted to take over the running of the auction, I first talked it over with my celebrity client who'd been sponsoring the event. We both agreed that, since it was his name and reputation overseeing the details, we wanted to keep it under our wing. He instructed me to collect the auction items we'd been storing in their offices but to assure them that the funds raised would still be turned over to them when all was said and done. We'd done it a dozen times before, and that seemed like the sensible response.

A few hours later, however, the police arrived at my door, and I was faced with the accusation of Grand Theft.

For a Goody Two-Shoes like myself, a brush with law enforcement was a staggering first. Over the course of several weeks, the drama seemed to escalate daily...all because of what had originated as a simple act of kindness on the part of myself and my client.

As I wrestled with what to say to a judge and how best to keep the story concise and factual, I began sleeping less and worrying more. My imagination got the better of me, and the worst *Law and Order* scenarios played out in my mind—most of them ending with me cowering behind bars, holding a tin cup, and wondering how my life had turned out

that way. I tried to remind myself that this was not the plan God had for me, that I'd done nothing wrong, and that the outcome would surely be to my benefit.

On the morning of the hearing, I clung to a strip of wrinkled paper shoved deep into my pocket, a note that a friend had sent to remind me that the battle was not mine.

"That battle belongs to God," she wrote. "You're protected and loved."

However, when the hearing started off with a statement being read from my client where he relinquished any responsibility for the ordeal and claimed that I had acted on my own, all my comfort dried up and withered away, and that piece of paper in my pocket offered no further reassurances. I was terrified. And so hurt.

The hearing lasted an excruciating fifty minutes (but it seemed like the whole day), at the end of which all charges against me were dropped. I limped out of the courtroom that day, wrung out and exhausted. It didn't have to be that way, of course, because my friend's note said it all.

That battle waged against me had little, if anything, to do with me. It was about pride and suspicion and mistrust—and probably greed. It was about all the things the Lord has been battling on our behalf since the dawn of time. In truth, that battle belonged to God the whole time, like most of the big ones do.

The little ones, too, come to think of it. * *SDB*

I Am Not Ashamed

As the Scripture says, "Anyone who trusts in him
will never be put to shame."

ROMANS 10:11

I wasn't a Christian in college. We had a few kids on our dorm floor who were Christians. We called them the "God Squad," and we made fun of them pretty regularly behind their backs. Nice, huh?

However, there was this gorgeous blond guy at the end of my dorm. I knew he wanted to date me, but he didn't ask, and I used to wonder why. *No ego problems here*, I guess. His door was always open, and he invited anyone in to talk when life was rough.

I had a particularly busy college schedule. I worked two jobs, and I went to school at night and two days during the week. I was dubbed the "Floor Ghost" because I was never in the dorm, and only my roommate knew me well. We were both late-nighters known to run out for Big Gulps in the middle of the night—even with a recent murder one block from our dorm.

Can I just say here that God cares for the least of these? Even when they're ignorant?

Anyway, one dateless Friday night, I wandered by this guy's room on my way home from work, and his door was open. He was listening to music and reading his Bible. When he turned around to face me, I felt *stuck!*...

not wanting a sermon but with nowhere to go. I suddenly became like a deer caught in headlights.

"Hi," he said gently, and he invited me in—keeping the door open the entire time I was there. I don't know how long we talked. I can't even remember anything that was said, but I do remember that the conversation had a profound impact on me.

He had a godly peace and warmth about him. Our discussion was very intimate without crossing any boundaries, and I felt unsure about what had transpired. I will not say I fell down and committed my life to the Lord. At least another year passed before that happened.

Whenever I read Romans 1:16—"I am not ashamed of the gospel, because it is the power of God for the salvation of everyone who believes: first for the Jew, then for the Gentile"—this conversation comes back to me. I remember that if I am embarrassed, God is behind me providing the supernatural *oomph* I need to see beyond myself.

To this day, those events in college make no sense to me. Why have they stuck with me? There is only One explanation that I can think of. * *KB*

Dignity, Really?

She is clothed with strength and dignity; she can laugh at the days to come.

PROVERBS 31:25

After I was diagnosed with ovarian cancer, the Lord seemed to impress today's Scripture upon my mind. I couldn't imagine why that verse, of all verses, would come to my mind time and again. Later, God seemed to confirm through two other people that it would be *my verse* for the road I was traveling.

I'm writing this four months after my diagnosis, and the verse has served me well—all except for the dignity thing. Maybe it's just me, but I don't feel very dignified without hair. I mean, if I try to imagine myself bald in front of, oh, my favorite singer (Wayne Watson) or my favorite Bible teacher (Beth Moore), I will tell you right here and right now, that "dignity" thing won't be working for me—to say nothing of the no eyebrows/eyelashes thing.

However, to be honest, not having hair has its rewards. I never have to shave my legs. Facial hair is no longer a concern. And it only takes me five minutes to get "my" hair ready for public viewing.

God has given me His strength, for which I am grateful. His joy fills my days, so I have no trouble laughing at the days to come, for which I'm also grateful.

Still, there's that "dignity" word. And please don't get me started about all the prodding, poking, and invasion of privacy I have going on when I'm in the presence of medical personnel. Where is the dignity in that?

Such a little word, but how it had haunted me at night when I stretched on my turban. It followed me into the doctor's office when I draped on a paper-thin gown with more openings than a Broadway play.

So with great frustration, I decided to look up the word in the dictionary. Listen to this; it's so cool. One of the definitions simply said "Worthiness."

Worthiness? I never in a million years would have put those words together—dignity...worthiness? Wow. As I pondered that explanation, the reality of what God's Word was saying to me began to seep into my understanding. Just as I am clothed in His strength, I am clothed in His dignity. In other words, I am wrapped in *His* worthiness, not mine! I can laugh at the days to come because *He* is worthy!

Woo-hooo!

No one wants to be sick, least of all have cancer—but knowing that He is with us every step of our earthly journey, come what may (illness, divorce, financial distress...), and knowing that He clothes us with His strength and His dignity (worthiness), we truly can laugh at the days to come! * DH

Hair Today, Gone...Today

Who of you by worrying can add a single hour to his life?
MATTHEW 6:27

My ex-husband and I managed to become comfortable around each other shortly after we parted. A hairdresser, he still cut and colored my hair for me—it was an adventure for both of us. The short time during which we were married and for years afterward, we had fun with my hair, changing its cut and color every few months.

The last time he laid a finger on my locks, though, it merely needed trimming. At the time, I was a bleached blond and wore it in a deliberately tousled 'do nearly down to my shoulders. I loved it. He was just about finished with the trim and had even blown it dry when he stood behind me, studied the results in the mirror, suddenly grabbed the entire right side of my hair, and cut off the handful in one fell swoop. Apparently he had decided an asymmetrical look might be fun.

I couldn't have broken into tears any faster if he had hit me with a brick. We all know how long it takes to grow out hair, and now I hardly had any hair where I'd had quite a lot only moments before. I'm a pale gal, so on the bleached-out, buzz-cut side, I actually looked...bald. Once I got hold of my emotions and all sharp objects had been moved out of my reach, my ex cut the other side—really, what else could I do but let him? And I had him color my hair dark so I'd at least look like I actually had hair.

It was a horrid look for me. I was scary. I looked like a puffy, punky Cruella de Vil without the trademark white streak. I didn't make that observation to him—believe me, I wasn't about to give him any other ideas.

I stressed about being seen in public—for months. I had to learn to let it go. For someone as vain as I was then, that took effort. But what if I had worried every day of that awful growing-out period? Would my hair have grown back any faster? No.

So it is with worrying about adversities (or potential adversities) in life—about whether matters will work out as we think they should. Whether our fears come to fruition or don't, whether we get what we want or we don't, will worrying have any effect on the outcome of anything? Worrying didn't add a single centimeter to my hair. Will it add a single hour to your life?

God knows what's going on. Trust Him! * *TP*

Crisis Intervention

The Lord has heard my cry for mercy; the Lord accepts my prayer.
PSALM 6:9

Divorce used to be a topic that good Christians didn't talk about or even sometimes admit to. However, on the landscape of today's America, divorce is everywhere. And so are the hurting people who have survived it.

I hadn't yet turned my life over to God when I impulsively married the wrong man, so I didn't quite know where to turn when the relationship became abusive. Alcohol, violence, name-calling, threats, and bullying became a regular part of my life. At its best, my marriage seemed more like two children playing house; at its worst, I became isolated hundreds of miles from my family and friends. I allowed a lifelong battle with my weight and a dysfunctional relationship with food to overwhelm me; I became fearful, unhealthy, even severely agoraphobic. When one of my husband's coworkers, someone I hardly knew, suggested that I stage an intervention about his abuse of alcohol (and his wife), I remember thinking, "An intervention for him? I'm the one who needs an intervention!"

My conversation with that virtual stranger proved to be life-changing for me. As my alcoholic husband drifted off into a drunken coma that Saturday night, I sat on the sofa in the dark, praying to a God I wasn't even sure was there.

My husband had found my spiral notebooks of story ideas and destroyed them, along with precious mementos of my past and the addresses and phone numbers of anyone to whom I might have reached out for help. "What happened to that girl I used to be?" I asked the ceiling, realizing only much later that this was the form prayer had taken. "Remember her? I knew how to love and be loved; I had dreams of writing big Hollywood movies and living near the beach." It was at that moment that I realized how accurate I'd been in assessing my need for a drastic and immediate intervention, and I vowed to the ceiling to perform my own! Intervention, that is.

Three months later, I had mastered many of my fears, at least enough to function outside the door of our apartment. Soon I packed my little car with only what it would hold and escaped to Los Angeles, where I eventually went to film school and learned to write screenplays. I couldn't afford to live at the beach, but I certainly did visit often. Still carrying those visions of the girl I once was and the woman I one day hoped to be in my back pocket as a reminder, I one day met the Savior who had designed them (and me). He made it very clear that He had heard my prayers and answered them, and He miraculously extended something to me I didn't quite understand—but I jumped at it! He offered me the grace to move forward. * SDB

Show Me the Money

The Lord sends poverty and wealth; he humbles and he exalts.

1 SAMUEL 2:7

My husband has been in the financial-services industry for many years. We've seen both ends of the poverty/wealth spectrum in many of his clients. There isn't a big difference in people's expectations between those with the highest and the lowest net worths. The most significant distinguishing factor seems to be their faith that ties in with their view of life, regardless of how much money is in their account.

I know from our personal experiences of struggling while my husband built his business that not having money is frustrating, but our faith kept us together as a family; we never doubted God's love because He never abandoned us at any time. He made sure we had a roof over our heads, something to wear, and food on the table. After my husband's business matured, we knew God still had our backs and loved us the same as always. That never changed, even when our circumstances did. We actually became comfortable, and we were able to do a few things we'd always wanted to do.

Then a couple of years ago, the economy tanked and there was no longer quite as much money coming in because my husband, kindhearted man that he is, spent countless hours working for his clients to salvage as much as he could of their hard-earned money without regard for his own income. Fortunately, our daughters were already grown and self-supporting, so our current income needs aren't as great as they once were.

The Lord's will in our lives is based on what He knows we need at the time. He uses both poverty and wealth to teach us, love us, and discipline us in ways we may not understand. As difficult as it has been at times, accepting the fluctuations in income has become almost second nature to my husband and me. Occasionally He needs to bring us to our knees, and He does it so effectively.

Money is mentioned in the Bible hundreds of times, so God obviously considers it relevant to our lives. His perspective is quite different from ours, though, and I think we need to pay closer attention to what He says. He's not so much against having wealth, but He warns us about our attitude toward it. I've found that when I looked at money to define anything about myself as a person, I've been miserable, regardless of how much I had or didn't have. On the flip side, when my focus is on Him, I see money as something that comes when needed and goes when it becomes too consuming, and I find joy in His promise of eternal life. * *DM*

When We Forget Who's Listening

Those who look to him are radiant; their faces are never covered with shame.

PSALM 14:5

Years ago, when my son was in grade school, he and a couple of his friends from church were playing just below my open bedroom window—so I happened to hear when the two friends decided to teach my son how to spell a vulgar word in sign language. They actually said each of the letters as they formed them, so the irony of their getting busted while using sign language was not lost on me. They were sweet, well-behaved kids; their play had simply degenerated gradually without their noticing it.

To his credit, my son didn't join in the high jinks, but I calmly went downstairs and called him in along with the other boys. The other boys' moms were (and are) dear friends of mine, and I knew they would prefer I didn't ignore this "teaching moment."

I brought the boys back to my room and could tell they were completely unaware that I had heard them. But the window was still open. I had them stand near the window, and I simply said, "What can you hear from here?" Birds tweeted clearly. Katydids sang in the trees. The sprinkler ticked back and forth.

It didn't take long for their guilty consciences to fill in the blanks. The melodrama was swift. One of the boys groaned and sank against the wall until he crumpled to the floor and covered his face with his hands. The other burst into tears of shame and fear. My guess is that my son was thanking heaven he had kept his mouth shut.

I still remember being disgraced horribly when, as a child, I behaved in a vulgar manner and got caught by my mother…so I made a point of talking kindly with the boys. I told them they just had to remember that even if another person couldn't hear them, they still needed to try to honor God with their words. I told them adults needed to do that too. But I think they were just relieved I wasn't going to put them in shackles and cart them home to their parents.

Shame is a horrible feeling, and I know I've never done or said anything to merit it without having momentarily forgotten about God first. When I'm in church, wholly focused on worship music, a good sermon, and the Lord's love and guidance, that's probably the closest I'll ever get to radiance, because I'm looking to Him. There's certainly something to be said for surrounding yourself with godly people, godly pleasures, godly teaching, and just…God.
* TP

Come Blow Your Horn

Let someone else praise you, and not your own mouth;
an outsider, and not your own lips.

PROVERBS 27:2

I wasn't one of those kids who performed with the high-school orchestra, and I didn't join the marching band either. Mostly that's because the only instrument available was the trumpet, and even back then, I wasn't any good at tooting my own horn.

Oh, I have no trouble at all, boasting about my husband, my kids, and my grandkids. They're as perfect as feet-on-the-ground humans can be. They're gorgeous. And smart. Successful, loving, and kind. They're linked directly to me, either by marriage or by blood, and because of that, I automatically get bragging rights. (Just ask anyone whose bangs have been mussed as I whip out the accordion-like photo holder in my wallet!) But praising the attributes and accomplishments of people I love isn't the same as singing my *own* praises. Not by a long shot!

I'm the first to admit that patting myself on the back is physically impossible (what if I dislocate a shoulder?) and emotionally uncomfortable. A dangerous thing to admit, considering what I do for a living. In the days of Hemingway, publishers could afford to promote authors and their books. These days, PR and marketing is a do-it-yourself—or a do-it-or-die—proposition. I have a fear of heights, so walking the tightrope as I try to find a healthy balance of what to say about myself and what to leave out is downright nerve-racking.

Family, friends, even fellow authors cite the "Don't hide your light under a bushel" verse to coax me out into the open. So why does this former sang-for-my-supper entertainer have such a hard time standing in the limelight, when my gifts are God-given and, for the most part, used to glorify Him? (As soon as I find the answer to that one, you'll be the first to know.)

In the meantime, I thank the good Lord for blessing me with readers—men, women, and kids—who write to tell me what they did (and sometimes, what they didn't!) like about my stories. Their words confirm my decision to write faith-based fiction rather than "the other stuff." I'm honored that, of all the books they could choose, they so often choose mine. I'm proud that, over the years, so many readers have become treasured friends.

I'm reminded of the rhyme my gal pals and I recited while skipping rope on the playground: "First comes love, then comes marriage…"

In this case, first came grace, then came faith, and I can no more take credit for my so-called talents or gifts than I could play "Lady of Spain" on that bugle without making the audience cringe and cover their ears. What I am and what I accomplish in this life is solely by the grace of God.

And that's the triumph I'm happy to trumpet about!
* LL

Divine Purpose for Dummies

The teaching of the wise is a fountain of life, turning a person from the snares of death.

PROVERBS 13:14

My brother and his wife are botanists. Terry built a greenhouse for Laurie, and I remember watching her tend her flowers and plants one time while visiting them in Louisiana. Without saying a word, Laurie fully *communicated* with them as she tended to their needs. It was almost a spiritual experience, and I went home to California *inspired*! I planted some seeds, bought a couple of plants…and killed them all within a month.

Send an unruly dog with no manners or self-control to live with me for a month and I'll teach that dog to save Timmy from the well! But plants? Not my gift. So imagine my horror when I opened the door recently to find an enormous plant there to greet me. Sweet sentiment from the sender, but they obviously hadn't received the memo about me.

I quickly moved the massive thing to the backyard patio, and two days later, it had that look that tulips get. No matter what you do for them, tulips tend to wilt quickly, bending to their death—much like the big plant on my patio, sloped down to the ground, dejected and unhappy.

I dumped a bunch of water on it, and the next morning it appeared less unhappy. I moved it out of the direct Florida sunshine, and it thrived a little more. The problem with this scenario is that I am now faced with a daily race to the patio to see what I've done to Luther. (This is what I call it.

Luther. I don't know why.)

For many years, I've nursed a bit of a grudge about the fact that God chose to make it impossible for me to bear children. The maternal instinct in me is, and always has been, enormous. Kids often follow me around like I'm the Pied Piper; babies always reach for me first; and I've become The Awesome (visiting) Aunt to the children of my closest friends. But still, never one of my own.

The truth is…sometimes I forget to feed my dog. Although Sophie is pretty great at gently reminding me and she's very forgiving once her bowl is full…Luther? Not so much, with his constant moody displays and guilty chastisement when I forget the water. And to compound the matter, people remark when they see him. "What have you *done* to that plant?"

So I now have adopted a daily plan because of Luther: every morning, water the plant (and the dog). Check for direct sunlight (and a full bowl). Now and then, plant food (and doggie treats) is definitely in order. Try not to kill the plant (or the dog).

It came late in life, but I think I'm on to something here. Perhaps God's grace includes an individual plan for each of us. Maybe some of us are meant to be moms and greenhouse owners; others of us, doting family friends who go home to our dogs and silk plants. * *SDB*

So Very Righteous!

Gray hair is a crown of splendor; it is attained by a righteous life.
PROVERBS 16:31

Let's face it, gray hair doesn't feel all that glorious. In fact, "restoring" our natural color from gray is a billion-dollar industry. How many natural blonds do you think actually exist? We are inundated daily with a shallow image of the perfect woman. She has a Pilates figure. She has long, lustrous hair without extensions, and her wrinkles have been erased by a toxic filler.

In a world obsessed with beauty, we can lose sight of the fact that God tells us beauty is fleeting; as the outside is crumbling, the inside is becoming more beautiful. What's so wonderful about this verse is that it reminds us that although we as humans may focus on the exterior, God is concerned with renewing our souls each day, and life should cost us something. If we remain untouched by living, have we actually experienced life?

One of my magazines arrived with two separate stories. One was about a "real housewife" who, at forty-seven, looks like she's twenty-seven. Her skin is dewy and taut. Her complexion shows no visible signs of aging. Her blond hair appears bouncy and brilliant. On the very next page was the story of a woman who looks about sixty-five but is also forty-seven. She wears long, straggly gray hair. Her clothes are ill-fitting, and her hands are wrinkled and covered with age spots. She has lived her entire life in a coal miner's realm and recently lost her husband in an underground explosion.

The irony of these two women, these two stories just one page apart, was not lost on me. One of them was being held up as a model of beauty for her age; the other, as a victim of a rough life. Like a stretched wineskin, the latter had used herself to the point of strain, while the first probably had a full-time staff helping her to look so good.

In heaven, we won't have a staff. We won't need one. God will not judge us by how long we let our roots grow out. He will not ask us about that extra ten pounds of baby fat we carry.

Should we give up vanity altogether? Probably not. Our spouses/children/friends might object, since we do live in society. Do we really want the church to be a standout section of Quasimodos? Maybe not. However, wouldn't it be great if our soul "grew out" and we noticed that first?

"God, I need a touch-up! Come and fill me up!" * KB

Talk a Lot, Talk a Little More

*Perfume and incense bring joy to the heart, and the pleasantness
of one's friend springs from his earnest counsel.*

PROVERBS 27:9

Some of my friends are single women. A few are dating again; a few aren't. But the evolution of the dating relationships has been fascinating, and some of our comments could only be comfortably made between friends who trust each other.

"I've decided I like my life the way it is. I love dating Ben, but I like to get home to my own place too."

"I just really want to be married again. I miss taking care of a man."

"I think you're looking for a reason to stop seeing Ed, but he's too nice to break up with."

"I don't really want romance. I'd just like to have a male friend to go out with once in a while."

"I want that last piece of cheesecake."

Obviously, dating isn't our only topic of conversation. We deliberate decisions about our children, our jobs, our health, our plans. We discuss our faith and how the Lord has touched us. We get together and enjoy the occasional meal or movie, but the main point of our gatherings is to talk out life. Women need that. That's how God designed us.

John Gray's *Men Are from Mars, Women Are from Venus* was released in 1992, yet so much of what he wrote still rings true over two decades later. I think he hit quite a few nails on the head.

I was married for years before I managed to get occasional time away with girlfriends. I still remember how I came home after the first time, absolutely light-headed with pleasure. Although I enjoyed my family time, I had forgotten how important my friends were. I hadn't talked and laughed so much in ages. It's just different with women than it is with men or kids. And when a woman needs advice, she's glad to have strong friendships with other godly women.

Men appreciate the "earnest counsel" of their friends, as the verse states, but first they tend to do much of their pondering alone. By the time a man goes to his friend for advice, he's usually got a bottom line in mind and is just seeking a nod of assurance.

Women, on the other hand, tend to ponder out loud, with the earnest counsel of friends coming back to them in the same way—out loud. If a man had to hear all that thinking, he'd likely go nuts.

If you're married or dating and consider it selfish to spend time developing godly female friendships, think again. You need it. Your man needs it. And God likens such friendships to pleasant perfume and incense. * *TP*

I Quit!

My sheep hear My voice, and I know them, and they follow Me. And I give them eternal life, and they shall never perish; neither shall anyone snatch them out of My hand.

JOHN 10:27–28 NKJV

Oh, it's no use. Just forget it. Why do I bother? Nobody cares… Discouragement: The state of being deprived of confidence and courage. Like an ugly weed in a beautiful flower garden, discouragement can creep into our lives and choke our happiness. I've been there. I'm sure you have, too.

So how does one kill this wicked vine called discouragement? As a life coach, I teach three basic principles to begin the process:

1. Take your eyes off yourself and your situation.

In his best-selling book *The Purpose-Driven Life*, Rick Warren writes, "It's not about you. The purpose of your life is far greater than your own personal fulfillment, your peace of mind, or even your happiness. It's far greater than your family, your career, or even your wildest dreams and ambitions. If you want to know why you were placed on this planet, you must begin with God. You were born by His purpose and for His purpose."

Jesus Christ gave us eternal life, and no one can ever take that away from us. That truth alone ought to make us smile all day long. Even more incredible is to think that God created us to fulfill His divine plan. Focusing on Him will make the problems of the day seem like pebbles, not giant boulders that cannot be moved.

2. Read the Bible.

God's Word is very applicable for today's world and life's issues. Return to the Word Ministries states the following on its Web site, www.returntotheword.org: "The truths of God's Word [have] effectively shown the way for believers for thousands of years. More than ever, this generation needs to turn again to God Almighty for the answers to life's questions."

In essence, God's Word sets believers straight in their day-to-day attitudes and thought patterns. Without God's guidance, via His Word, believers are vulnerable to humanistic worldviews—after all, we are all human. But we need the divine!

3. Be a blessing to others.

Helping others can vaporize discouragement. Try assisting a stressed coworker even if it's not your job to do so, or help the elderly woman next door carry in her groceries.

Jesus, the Good Shepherd, said that His sheep (Christians) hear His voice and follow Him. A tall order, since our Savior led a selfless life. But with the Holy Spirit's help, we can accomplish His will. And while there may be no monetary reward in going out of our way for others, there is a spiritual one…it's called joy. * *AKB*

Shaking in My Boots

The fear of the Lord is the beginning of wisdom, and knowledge of the Holy One is understanding.
PROVERBS 9:10

When my older daughter, Alison, was not quite three years old, we took a chance and brought her into the church sanctuary. Rather than put her in the nursery or sit in the back, we sat in the second pew from the front. She was well-behaved, and it was the only pew with enough room for us to spread out with my "mommy bag," my husband, Alison, and my nearly-nine-months-pregnant body. That turned out to be one of the most interesting and educational church services we ever attended—one I'll never forget.

Our church was designed with the pews set in a semi-circle around the pulpit, where our larger-than-life pastor, with his full beard, piercing eyes, and booming voice, could pace yet stay close to his congregation. He made eye contact with everyone in front of him, so it seemed as though he spoke to each person individually. I noticed that each time he came toward us, Alison would suddenly stiffen. Her mouth would open, and her eyes would widen. I didn't understand what was going on with her until she finally whispered, "Mommy, here comes God." Then she gripped my hand and held on tight until the pastor paced back to the other side of the pulpit.

It took every ounce of self-restraint not to laugh or even smile. I leaned over and whispered back, "Honey, he's not God. He's our pastor who preaches God's Word."

Alison's forehead crinkled as she glanced at Pastor Robinson. She tilted her head and looked at me. "How do you know He's not God?"

It's difficult to explain this to a toddler, but after church, my husband and I did the best we could by explaining that the pastor was a man who was passionate about his faith and was called by God to tell the congregation about His Word. After she was satisfied with our answers, she went to her room to play. Wally and I looked at each other and sighed. Finally he said, "At least she knows the importance of reverence when it comes to the Lord."

We still tease Alison about that day, but my husband had a valid point. Our daughter was in awe of God. Although her image of Him had been placed on a mortal man, she had the innate sense that He wasn't one of us. He's much bigger and greater than we'll ever be, and that is the beginning of the understanding we have through total admiration and awe of our Creator. Whenever I start to get full of myself, I remind myself of our talk with Alison. * *DH*

A Life of Devotion

Do everything in love.

1 CORINTHIANS 16:14

I witnessed splendor in anguish. I was there during the last days of a beautiful life.

It was an honor and a privilege to know Thelma. Though I did not get the opportunity to know her very long, I caught a glimpse of her wonderful spirit and lovely heart. She was a mother, a social worker, a grandmother, a great cook, and a fun person to be around.

I married her grandson and soon discovered that he was crazy about his granny. Whenever we would visit his parents in our early years of marriage, we'd always stop by granny's so he could give her a hug and a kiss.

My husband's mother, Janie, had the good fortune to have Thelma for a mother. Janie and Thelma were very close. They had a very special and sacred bond.

Thelma had cancer, and not long after she recovered from surgery and chemotherapy, she began to have strokes. It was unimaginable. She had always been such a healthy person. Why was this happening to her? There were so many unanswered questions and things we did not understand during the weeks and months that followed. We did not understand why she had to suffer for such a long time. It was heartbreaking to watch her once-healthy body decay and die.

Even though this was a difficult time for our family, there was something gloriously beautiful that shone through the aches and the pain and the tears.

It was a wonder to watch Janie take care of her mother.

If you had been there, you would have seen her honor her mother when she needed it the most. You would have witnessed Janie cook for her, clean for her, and wash her face every day. She wheeled her mother around to go shopping, to the doctor, and to a world-renowned clinic, hoping for a miracle. She wiped her tears, brushed her hair, and read her the paper. Janie did everything she could for her mother.

She did it all in love.

For most of her illness, Thelma lived with Janie. Toward the end of Thelma's battle with cancer, she moved to a nearby nursing home. I remember Janie going to see her, bringing her cheerful presents, sitting by her bed, holding her hand, and listening to her. Near the end of the battle, Thelma moved back to her own home for just a little while. That was the place for her to say good-bye. That was the place where she watched Janie grow up. It was where she cooked popcorn and squeezed her grandchildren. It was where we all watched her beautiful life on earth come to an end.

And even then, I watched Janie. I watched her eyes whisper to her mother all of the love she had in her heart for her. She made her as comfortable and safe as she possibly could. She took care of her mother better than any caregiver I have ever seen.

It was nothing short of amazing to see the light shine through my mother-in-law. She would be the first to tell you that it was not her light, though. It was the light of Jesus that helped her stay together when everything seemed to be falling apart. It was Jesus holding Janie's hand and comforting her. He was her strength. He was her support.

Our family got to see two women love each other to the end. We watched a daughter care for her mother. And we watched her let her go. The miracle of it all is the same miracle we all can have—and that comes from knowing Jesus.

There is nothing in this world that can separate us from His love. He is always here for us, in happiness and in sadness. We do not have to wait until we get to heaven to experience His love for us. It is right here, right now, for everyone who receives Him. I thank Him for loving us so well and for teaching me, through Janie, how to do everything in love. * *GF*

The Wealth of Wisdom

Happy are those who find wisdom, and those who get understanding,
for her income is better than silver, and her revenue better than gold.
PROVERBS 3:13–14 NRSV

Did you know that spending time alone with God is the secret to obtaining great wealth? That is, unless wealth is only to be measured in monetary and material terms.

Wealth, in any culture, is measured by what is most highly valued. Where chronic drought and famine occur, the wealthy are those who have plenty of food to eat. Where knowledge is considered the greatest commodity, those who accumulate multiple academic degrees are viewed as prosperous. In the world of racing, the owner of the fastest car is the one to be envied.

But in the kingdom of God, one of the most valuable assets is the wisdom that only comes from spending time with Him. Wisdom is the enlightened perspective developed through spiritual training and experience of God. It is born of revelation, sustained by insight, and applied with understanding. Only God can disseminate true wisdom, and He does so generously for those who ask.

Wisdom is the inevitable outcome of an authentic encounter with God in prayer and in worship. In worship, you experience the humbling awareness of God's otherness; while in prayer, you bend your will to His sovereignty and power. The combination of humility and submission makes the perfect ground for wisdom to take root and grow.
* SGES

I Could Have Been Someone

I am like an olive tree flourishing in the house of God;
I trust in God's unfailing love for ever and ever.

PSALM 52:8

I could have really been somebody. If I'd gotten that job I applied for right out of college, my life would be totally different. It would have been the perfect position for me to climb the corporate ladder and really make a name for myself.

After getting my degree in Recreational Administration, I assumed I'd be able to march into my favorite theme park corporate office, knock on the human resources door, and be welcomed with open arms. Instead, the expressionless receptionist handed me a paper application, told me to fill it out, and asked which character I wanted to try out for.

Character? Me? I chuckled. No, she didn't understand. I wanted to be in *charge* of the characters. I wanted to plan recreational activities for the guests. After she listened to my explanation, her lips turned upward into a smirk. "Do you want a job at the park or not?" she asked.

Sheepishly, I accepted the application, walked over to one of the tables, and started filling it out. Okay, so I'd start out as a character—probably Grumpy, based on the way I was feeling at the time. But I'd be the best Grumpy they ever had, and they'd see my brilliance. It wouldn't be long before I'd get promoted to the job of my dreams.

After I finished filling out the application, I got up and walked over to the long line that had formed in front of the reception desk. The guy at the head of the line asked if they promoted from within—and if so, what his chances were of getting a better job in a year or so. The receptionist told him it was a possibility but highly unlikely because they used headhunters for permanent positions. My future was beginning to dim, but being the positive person I am, I handed her my application with a forced smile. She took it and said they'd get back to me if they were interested. At that moment, I knew my future wasn't at that theme park.

On my way home, I prayed that the Lord would direct me to a career path that was right for me. I had no idea what else I wanted to do, because after reading about a guy who was an activities director for a major theme park, that was all I ever thought I wanted. No other career appealed to me at the time. But as the years passed, God took control and directed me in the path of His choosing. And I have no doubt that His wisdom put me into the place that is best for me. * DM

Hairless Wonder

*You have searched me, L*ORD*, and you know me. You know when I sit and when
I rise; you perceive my thoughts from afar. You discern
my going out and my lying down; you are familiar with all my ways.*

PSALM 139:1–3

Once I learned that I needed chemo, I decided to take action and get my head shaved ahead of time. If I was going to look like Bruce Willis, *I* would make it happen, not the chemo. I was determined to wear stylish turbans and wigs of all colors and lengths, which would, no doubt, cast suspicion upon my sweet, faithful husband who would be seen with a "different" woman every night.

So while I was at the Cancer Treatment Center of America, I made arrangements to go to the salon and have my hair cut. The stylist had done this many times for patients, so I felt secure in her capable hands.

In the back room, away from prying eyes, she talked to me about what she would do before she set to work. I was fine—until the buzz of the clippers jarred my raw nerves. I saw a strand of long hair fall to the floor. The air suddenly turned thick, and it was hard to breathe. My chest grew tight. I wanted to scream at the injustice of it all, to say the cancer, the appointment, everything was a mistake. This couldn't be happening to me.

Oh, God, where are You? I can't do this!

Then, amazingly, God's Word flooded my heart: "O Lord, you have searched me and you know me." *Falling hair. So much hair.* "You know when I sit and when I rise." *Do You see what she's doing to me? Make her stop!* "You perceive my thoughts from afar." *I'm so scared.* "You discern my going out and my lying down; you are familiar with all my ways."

Naked. Exposed. Vulnerable. Frail.

"Lean on Me. We'll get through this…together."

That day, I sensed His tears mingle with mine and fall to the floor with my hair. His words melted over me and calmed my spirit in a way my words can never adequately explain. From that moment on, I knew I would get through this, one step at a time, come what may, because He would never leave me.

I don't know what you're facing, but if He can calm me in the midst of my storm, He can do it for you—and He will do it for you, if you ask Him. Our Father who knows us better than anyone and loves us infinitely more than we could ever imagine is here for You. Will you go to Him with your need? He's waiting. * DH

Karaoke Isn't All Bad

My people are destroyed for lack of knowledge.

HOSEA 4:6 NKJV

I saw a news story recently about a four-year-old who was home alone with his mother. She was performing daily chores like laundry and dinner, doing all the things she did every day at that time. But she had the misfortune of taking one little misstep, and she fell all the way down a flight of stairs. The little boy knelt at her side, calling out to her, but she was unconscious. And Daddy wasn't due home for hours yet.

The headlines reporting this news story could have been horrific: "Young Boy Watches as Mom Dies" or "Child Traumatized by Mother's Household Accident."

Instead, one innocent little educational game the boy's mom had played with him the week prior changed the whole outcome of a terrible situation. She'd taught her young son his address...in a song.

Because Mom knew the value of her son having his personal information available, she'd made up a song about what to do in an emergency and how to tell authorities where he lived. The little boy knew to pick up her cell phone and dial 911, and then he sang the song again and again until the operator on the other end of the line was able to dispatch emergency technicians to the home.

When she'd taught the little boy his address, Mom had done it with the thought in mind that if anyone ever snatched him away from her, he could tell someone where he lived. Never once did she imagine he would be using that information to save her own life.

As I watched the news program, I thought about how there really aren't any coincidences in a life that follows after God. One little song taught to a four-year-old, for whatever reason, was the catalyst to save a life. The Word of God provides an instructional life for the reader. Seemingly insignificant tidbits and golden nuggets of information are imparted upon the Christian believer in verse after verse.

And then one day something occurs. A loved one is sick; a parent dies; a job is lost; or a home is foreclosed upon. At those times, reaching into our pocket and producing one of those golden nuggets to hang onto is going to make all the difference, just the way that address song changed the course of a young mother's life.

I'm reminded of a Sunday school song I used to sing with my students: "Greater is He that is in me; greater is He that is in me; greater is He that is in me than he that is in the world."

I'm humming that song more often these days...just in case I need a sudden reminder. * *SDB*

Quiet on the Set!

As cold waters to a thirsty soul, so is good news from a far country.
PROVERBS 25:25 KJV

Hollywood never disappoints, does it? No wonder we're inundated with nicknames for the city, like "La-La Land" and "Tinseltown"! Those who live and work near that big white sign on the hill provide us with hours of mystifying entertainment.

And how about DC? Most of us view politicians as wannabe actors in a race to see who's made the morning news. Not a day goes by that some elected official doesn't open his door to accept a subpoena for not paying his taxes, for embezzling money from his campaign fund, for cheating on his spouse. Sometimes there's a news crew on his porch, waiting like hungry hyenas to catch his shocked reaction.

But the media could save its time, because stuff like that is so routine and ordinary that it doesn't even shock me anymore. Is it any wonder Americans are thirsty for *good* news?

I praise Him for blessing me with a loving family, devoted friends, helpful neighbors, and wonderful coworkers, because when the headlines deliver bad tidings, I need only look to them and their everyday achievements for my good news "fix." I'm surrounded by loved ones whose simple, godly lives are a constant source of peaceful inspiration. And if this quiet life ever grows boring, we can count on actors and politicians to spice it up…without ever having to leave the house! * *LL*

Do You Want Fries with That?

*For after all these things the Gentiles seek. For your heavenly Father knows that
you need all these things. But seek first the kingdom of God
and His righteousness, and all these things shall be added to you.*

MATTHEW 6:32–33 NKJV

Honey, while you're up, would you mind getting me a glass of water?"

I glared at my husband and wondered why he always waited until I got up to suddenly want something. I begrudgingly headed to the cupboard, pulled out a glass, then trudged over to the refrigerator to get him some ice water. I'd already forgotten why I got up in the first place.

As I handed my husband his glass of ice water, he took it while his focus never once left the TV screen. Just as I was about to offer up a sarcastic comment, one of my daughters popped in. "Mom, I need a new cell phone. This one doesn't have a camera."

Now I couldn't resist. With sarcasm dripping from my voice, I asked,

"Do you want fries with that?"

Suddenly I had my husband's attention. "Huh?"

I smirked at my husband, who sat there and stared at me, his jaw slack and his eyes wide. He clearly thought I'd lost my mind.

"That's just an expression," I explained.

"Oh." He looked at me with concern. "Are you okay?"

Another cutting comment hovered on the tip of my tongue, but I bit it back. With a sigh, I flopped down on the sofa. "I don't know. No matter how much we do, it's never enough." I folded my arms and snorted. "And I feel like a servant around here."

"What's wrong with being a servant?"

I couldn't think of a kind response to that, so I just shrugged.

"Do you think I ask too much of you?" he asked gently.

With a lump in my throat, I slowly nodded. "Yes, sometimes."

I watched as his chin jutted, a look of fierce determination washing over his face. "Girls, you need to come in here. Now."

"But, Daddy…"

"Now," he repeated. "We need to have a family prayer."

One of my girls moaned. "We just prayed at dinner."

Rather than argue, he reached out and took my daughter's hand. As soon as the other one joined us, we bowed our heads and prayed that the Lord would give us all a servant attitude. When we opened our eyes, he looked at me and grinned. "Now is there anything I can do for you?" * *DM*

At Least Something in Common

All the believers were together and had everything in common.

ACTS 2:44

I'm a selfish gal. I'm not proud of the fact, but I recognize it. I'm so bad that, when I had a houseful of people living with me, I had a secret chocolate drawer near my computer. I kept chocolate out in the open for others too—but I hoarded my special stash in case the general supply ran out.

You may wonder what selfishness has to do with today's verse. At first glance, the verse sounds as if it refers to the joy of gathering with like-minded Christians. And that's what we all seek when we choose the church we'll attend on Sundays, right? We want to be sure the pastor's teaching fits with our perception of God's Word or makes a mighty strong argument for why our perception needs tweaking. If we find that, won't the congregation of believers eventually have "everything in common"?

Yet within the context of the rest of the chapter, the verse is actually about sharing our wealth with others. The next verse talks about believers "selling their possessions and goods" and giving "to anyone as he had need." I've even read a commentary that says this was the basic idea old Karl Marx was shooting for—but his followers enforced the concept through violence and imprisonment. I can imagine how much time in the gulag I'd be saddled with if they got a load of my chocolate drawer.

Now, I'm not *heartless*. Like most people, when I stop and consider those truly less fortunate than me, my heart opens wider. An ad airs about the International Fellowship of Christians and Jews and I give with little hesitation. I see an adorable, impoverished Honduran child via World Vision and gladly sign up as his monthly sponsor. I walk down a city street, see the growing number of homeless people, and start passing out dollar bills I would have easily spent on chocolate, lattes, or any other number of frivolous indulgences.

I need to do that more often. I give at church, just like your typical attendee. That's easy enough—I write out a check as part of my church preparation, just like putting on mascara and making sure my Bible is in the car. Certainly that kind of giving is enough. We're only instructed to tithe, after all. Most churches delegate a good portion of congregants' donations to charitable causes, so it's not as if our tithes are only used for administrating the church's business.

Still, there's something about hands-on giving that brings out the real warm fuzzies *and* keeps me appreciative of how blessed my own circumstances are. I admit, I won't sell *all* my possessions and goods in order to give to everyone as he has need. I'm simply not that generous, I'm afraid. But if I refrain from buying a possession here or a designer coffee there, I can more readily give according to my neighbor's needs in a way that will bless us both. * *TP*

Entertaining the Angels Among Us

*Do not forget to entertain strangers, for by so doing some people
have entertained angels without knowing it.*

HEBREWS 13:2

I grew up with a mentally retarded brother—or "developmentally disabled," as they call it today. In one way, this was a complete gift to me because I got to discover the true insides of a person by how they treated my brother. I've seen educated, wealthy people treat him as though he were something on the bottom of their shoe. And I've seen scary, chain-wearing, leather-clad bikers treat him with their full attention, as if nothing was more important than to hear what he had to say.

When I was in college, I worked in an upscale hotel, and I saw wealthy, spoiled-rotten people treat hotel workers like vermin. There was no gratitude in them. To this day, it breaks my heart that people can treat others this way because of worldly attributes like money, position, or appearance. It's the polar opposite of the way God would want it. His teachings tell us that those qualifiers have nothing to do with His love for us or the love He directs us to have toward others.

Sometimes our ministries and duties at church seem to go unnoticed, and we may wonder if we're not squandering God's time or if we're supposed to do something "more important." Maybe we're not really sure of our purpose—but I know without a doubt that God has a plan for our works. How we treat *the least of these* has a huge impact on hearts all around us. I know this because of my brother and a brief encounter with a stranger. I know this because one day, more than twenty-five years ago, a biker dude was nice to my brother in a Round Table Pizza restaurant. I learned a great deal about entertaining angels that day…and about the way God expects us to behave toward the people in the world around us.

So if someone has ever treated you as if you didn't matter, if you're having a day where you don't feel all that important in terms of God's kingdom and His plans, remember that God views you as the apple of His eye, the object of His affections. He clings to your every word, and He looks you in the eyes as if there's not another place He'd rather be. You matter to Him. * *KB*

A Life of Letting Go

Love goes on forever.

1 CORINTHIANS 13:8 TLB

I've just had one of the worst weeks I can remember, and though I can point to several different factors that contributed to my emotional demise (my house was a mess, I had a fender-bender, I failed again at my attempt to eat right and exercise, and I didn't get any writing done), the central glaring cause of my horrible week was that my son, Harper, started kindergarten. I wasn't ready, to say the least.

Now, I know some of you are thinking, *What's the big deal?* For many people it's not a life change when their kids go to school; they've been going to preschool for years. Some moms, even stay-at-home moms, are glad when their children go to school. They celebrate the new opportunities and exciting experiences their children—and they—will have. It's considered a healthy, natural part of life, and I respect that. They're probably the sane ones. Only I'm not one of those moms. It feels so *unnatural* to me.

While I enjoy my work and have plenty of goals I want to accomplish that aren't directly related to child-rearing, there's this strong attachment I feel to home and having my kids there. It goes beyond visceral. It's animal. I'm a mother hen, and I like all of my chicks under my wings, even if they get in the way when I'm trying to type a manuscript.

Monday morning was a morning I'll never forget. I'd carefully ironed Harper's clothes the night before, and we'd checked his backpack for the fifteenth time. When he got dressed that morning, he bounded into my room. "Do you think my teacher will like me?" he asked as I combed his wheat-colored hair. His eyes shone like big blue diamonds. I hugged him to me tight and said, "I know she will!" And I was hoping she'd *love* him. We both desperately needed her to.

When my husband and I walked him to his room at County Line Elementary School, there was a bulletin board outside that said WELCOME. Mrs. Vernon, the teacher, greeted him with a hug. Her eyes were warm and genuine, and her smile seemed to wrap Harper in a blanket of safety. I saw his confidence rising, the fun beginning, and I knew it was time for me to bow out.

Stone and I said little on the drive home. Before he left for work, we offered a prayer for our daughter Grace and Harper asking God's blessings on their new year at school. I held back the dam when Stone hugged me good-bye...but when the door closed behind him, I sat down in my quiet house and cried.

Adelaide, my baby, was at my sister-in-law's house, and I had planned to work that day on this book. But every word I typed seemed to lead me back to Harper and Grace and what was once a beautiful life but was gone. I heard their footsteps on the floor behind me and saw their shadows playing in the yard.

A black veil fell over my day. Instead of writing, I mourned. I mourned the changes that had happened and the changes yet to come. Had I cherished them enough? Loved them enough? Showed it enough? Prepared them enough? I hoped so, because those days of being home—all those hours that are strung together like pearls of a beautiful necklace—they're gone. That necklace is complete. That story ended.

It's taking me awhile to adjust to the next story, the one that's just beginning. I know there's so much to look forward to. At the Spirit's coaxing, I peeked out from behind the veil this week. The Lord is doing a new thing, and it's my job to embrace it.

One thing I'll take away from this experience is the reminder that life is a vapor. Nothing here on earth lasts forever. Nothing, that is, except the love we put into those days, those hours that get strung together like pearls of a necklace. I want mine to be full of it. * *GF*

Change Is Good

Jesus Christ is the same yesterday and today and forever.

HEBREWS 13:8

You know, I've been thinking," my sister said one day. "When I was in my twenties, I knew I had behaved like an idiot in my teens."

I had to agree with her there. We both had.

"And then, in my thirties, I looked back on my twenties. I made some horrible decisions in my twenties. Horrible! So I was pretty much an idiot in my twenties too." She laughed and shook her head about her naiveté.

I wasn't sure I liked where this conversation was going.

"I thought I had it all going on by the time I was thirty," she said. "But now, in my forties, I can see that I didn't know what I was doing in my thirties either. So I was kind of an idiot then, no matter what I thought at the time."

She shrugged and pushed her lips out, a world-weary heaviness to her eyelids. "It's taken me all this time to figure it out. Maybe I'm just an idiot."

Of course, she exaggerated. She had done plenty of growing and learning, just as we all do. But I understood her point. We usually don't go through life thinking we're clueless or deliberately making bad decisions—turning left when we really should be turning right or saying yes when, in hindsight, a big fat *no* was so obviously the wiser answer. But part of changing and growing is recognizing your mistakes of the past, determining to do better in the present, and taking for granted you'll look back in the future and adjust for where you went right or wrong.

For us, change is good.

But what utter chaos life would be if Jesus were like we are. If His life goals in His thirties changed as a result of what He experienced at the hands of man…if He retracted His promise to be with us always, "to the very end of the age," when it was clear how much of our lives we would squander while doing stupid or sinful things.

Of course, His eternal stability doesn't mean He's a cardboard cutout. He's not devoid of humor, appreciation, sorrow, or care over how we live our lives. But we can't surprise Him with our behavior. He knew about every facet of our behavior before He chose to die for us. So He'll never desert us. He'll always love us. His requirement of us will always be the same: to accept His love and the sacrifice He made for us. That has never changed, and it never will. * *TP*

Mercy's Law

He saved us, not because of righteous things we had done but because of his mercy.

TITUS 3:5

For a woman who can count good hair days on one hand...in a mitten...it was a glorious moment. I hadn't made it from the church entrance to the inner doors of the sanctuary before three people stopped me to say, "Hey! I like your hair!"

I looked over my shoulder, but what do you know? They were talking to me.

"Thank you."

"I like the highlights."

Me too. A little adventuresome, maybe. But the carefully placed triangle of ripened-wheat highlights against the burnt caramel underlayers made me feel perky. Besides, the technique camouflaged the encroaching gray.

When the fourth person stopped me to comment on the new 'do, my husband rolled his eyes. He what? That's right. He rolled his eyes. The person who'd complimented my hair said to him, "You don't like it?"

No doubt suffering from some undiscovered medical condition that made him lose all sense of propriety and both of the fragile romantic cells he'd retained throughout our marriage, my husband looked at the wheat triangle and then at the commenter and said, "I keep expecting to see 101 dalmatians coming around the corner."

If I could have captured the looks on the faces of the bystanders...

Cruella de Vil? He thought my hair looked like an evil villainess's?

"Aw, honey. You say the sweetest things!"

That wasn't my reaction. If I remember correctly, I asked our pastor if that morning's sermon happened to be on marriage.

Days earlier, I'd spoken to a MOPS (Mothers of Preschoolers) group. My topic? "Mercy's Laws of Marriage." If Murphy's Law says anything that can go wrong will go wrong, Murphy's Laws of Marriage are similar. The only shirt your husband wants to wear on Sunday is the one that isn't ironed. Only if company is minutes away will your husband want to tackle the plumbing project that's been on his to-do list since the Reagan administration. The potential for forgetfulness is in direct proportion to the event's importance.

My point that day was that as certain as I was of Murphy's Laws of Marriage, I wish I'd known earlier about Mercy's Laws of Marriage—that in God's way of looking at things (including me), mercy gets the last word.

So, as I sat in church beside the man who'd just compared my new hairdo to the coiffure of one of the most disliked women in the world of animation, a woman who hated puppies, I considered my options.

Find a metaphor to describe his cactus-needle beard.

Refuse to talk to my husband for the rest of the day.

Forget he said anything. Show him the kind of mercy the Lord shows me when I do or say something incredibly insensitive and not even a little bit funny.

As the worship music faded and Pastor adjusted his headset microphone, I made my decision. I'd forgive my husband before he asked me to.

Almost as startling as that swipe of wheat across my burnt caramel hair. * *CR*

Don't Get Wise, Bubble Eyes

Do not be wise in your own eyes; fear the LORD and shun evil.

PROVERBS 3:7

I'll never forget my college semester exams. Every time they rolled around, I invested in a jar of instant coffee, pulled out all my notes from the class lectures, and locked myself in my dorm room, resisting the temptation to go hang out with friends who didn't intend to return the next semester. I needed to study so I could make good enough grades to come back and do it all over again until I graduated. I spent hours going through my notes, trying to figure out what might be on the exams. As I memorized facts, I gained knowledge—some that would slip away after the exam and some that might stick in my head. After the exams were over, I awaited (sometimes eagerly, but often with dread) my final grade in each class. I took classes year-round, so I managed to graduate in a little more than three years. How smart was that?

After successfully completing the requirements of my degree, it didn't take long to discover the difference between knowledge and wisdom. In job after job, I found that the courses I took were abstract and not always applicable in the real world. And I also learned that college hadn't prepared me for everything life threw at me. What a blow to my self-inflated ego. I had the knowledge from years of studies but not the wisdom to apply it. Fortunately, I'd gone to church off and on throughout college. During my last semester and my internship, I met a retired pastor and started attending church with his family. Through them, I learned the difference between God's wisdom and my own. How humbling!

I don't know where the saying "Don't get wise, bubble eyes" came from, but I remember hearing it—and, yes, I'll admit saying it a few times—quite a bit during the seventies. I don't think the biblical implications of it crossed our minds back then, but think about it. When we rely on our own limited wisdom without filtering it through our Christian worldview, we're generally wrong. Trusting in our own wisdom is like trying to swim across an ocean without a lifeboat. There are so many things we don't know and can't possibly ever know.

Most people equate wisdom with knowledge…and in our human perspective, that's accurate. However, I can research and study for days, months, or years to gain knowledge, yet I may still not have much more wisdom. God's wisdom is all-encompassing; ours is limited as it is sifted through our wants, needs, and personal experiences. * *DM*

Silence Really Can Be Golden

A fool gives full vent to his anger, but a wise man keeps himself under control.

PROVERBS 29:11

My father used to say that I was a child born in mid-conversation. I always had something to say, no matter what the subject; and in an argument, I simply had to have the final word. It drove my military-officer father straight out of his mind.

"You know," my mother said to me one afternoon following a particularly poorly chosen battle with my father, "there are some people in the world who choose not to express every emotion they have at the very moment they have it. They hold a little something back."

I'm sorry. Foreign-language alert. English, please?

I was around fourteen when we had that conversation. It was a solid couple of decades before I caught up to her thinking, and there was a very long string of repercussions along the way before I got there. As I matured and grew older, however, I learned that words hold a lot of power and sometimes their utterance can set things into motion that can't be stopped.

"I was furious with him," a close friend told me as she paced from the kitchen to the dining room and back again. "I literally saw red. I just remember turning and screaming at him, telling him I couldn't believe what a disappointment he'd become, how I'd never trust him again."

And then she'd uttered the words that she wouldn't be able to take back. "I told him to get out of the house, and the sooner the better."

"Christine, he's your son," I reminded her. "You really tossed him out of the house?"

Within ten minutes of her saying the words, things were rolling along behind them and she had no time to snatch them back. Her seventeen-year old son had packed a duffel bag and two boxes, loaded them into his car, and pulled out of the driveway. Christine spent every day of the next three years wishing she could take back the anger she'd unleashed on her son and lamenting the fact that she hadn't thought to control her tirade.

I've been praying with Christine since then that her son would come home. Her faith has wobbled now and again, and some days it was just harder to believe that Justin would eventually return. But today I got the call from my friend. Justin walked through the door while Christine and her husband were having their morning coffee.

"He looks like a stranger. I've lost three years because of one moment of uncontrolled anger," she cried. "What a terrible way to learn a lesson!" * *SDB*

Fine by Me

A person may think their own ways are right, but the LORD weighs the heart.

PROVERBS 21:2

I love to be right. In a gleeful, in-your-face kind of way. I'm not proud of it, but I have to admit this dark part of my personality. Worse yet, I'm a trivia buff, so I'm right a good part of the time.

Do you despise me yet?

I picked up this little habit (one might say *sin nature*) from my father. He loves to be right as well. The problem is, we never agree on anything, and while our arguments have led us to many an Internet check as we search for the facts, ultimately neither of us is inclined to change our opinions. We generally stick to our own belief system and walk away satisfied. The rest of the dinner table may be left fighting indigestion, but my father and I are fulfilled, each feeling a sense of rightness.

The thing about this kind of "rightness" is that, by its very nature, it stirs up dissension, which God hates. Then, if you add the whole "honor thy father and mother" idea, I'm on very shaky ground. Still, I know these arguments stir my father's heart in a good-for-his-digestion kind of way. It keeps us both developing more brain cells.

This is why I love Proverbs 21:2. *God looks at the heart.* He knows my motives. He knows how much I love my earthly father and want to see him in the kingdom with me and his grandchildren. God also knows that my father,

being Italian and all, loves a good argument.

To me, today's Scripture is a daily-check verse. Is my heart in the right place? Am I doing this in love or because "God says so"? Am I beating someone over the head with my views sans love?

The story of Mary and Martha is the perfect biblical showcase of how God looks at the heart (see Luke 10:38–41). Martha is distracted by the preparations, while Mary sits at Jesus's feet and listens. Martha tattles, "Lord, don't You care that my sister has left me to do all the work by myself?"

Jesus replies, "Martha, Martha, you are worried and upset about many things, but only one thing is needed. Mary has chosen what is better, and it will not be taken away from her."

Oh, snap! Martha's motives were not from a place of love. They focused on duty. How easy it can be to assume that someone is acting in love when they are, in fact, wanting to be noticed for their efforts. Sometimes the love comes after an event, like when we volunteer for our church nursery and grow to love the children. The point is that we must constantly search our hearts and check our motives.

Being right isn't always what it appears to be on the surface. * KB

Ears to Hear

How gracious he will be when you cry for help! As soon as he hears, he will answer you.

ISAIAH 30:19

A ten-year-old boy with intense ear pain needs immediate attention. Every mom knows that. The clinic was closed for the night, so we took our son to the emergency room for what turned into hours of waiting and a "we'll never forget this" memory.

Not one to complain (he still isn't), Matt had apparently endured the pain in his right ear for quite a while before he told me about it. No doubt Matt had an ear infection, one that couldn't wait until morning, judging by the distress on our son's face.

The emergency-room doctor checked Matt's medical records, examined Matt's left ear, then examined his right, and said, "I see he's had tubes inserted."

"No, that's our other son. Luke's the one with all the ear infections. Matt hasn't had much trouble since he had his tonsils out at four." *Which*, I wanted to add, *should be right there on his medical records.*

The doctor pulled away from peering into Matt's ear to look at me. "Well, he has a tube in this ear. The left one must have fallen out."

I would have remembered if Matt had had ear-drainage tubes inserted. I distinctly remembered the procedure with his younger brother. No mama easily takes to the idea of her child going under anesthesia…or forgets how hard it can be on the child when he comes out of it. Luke screamed in the recovery room. He wasn't a happy boy after that procedure. This much I knew. Luke had ear tubes. Matt did not.

"It's green. Right there," Doctor Well-oh-yeah said, gesturing with some kind of needle-nosed instrument he aimed at Matt's ear canal.

A minute later, we all stared at the tiny green tube the doctor had extracted from my son's ear and laid on the stainless-steel tray.

Using two sets of needle-nosed something or others, the doctor poked at a loose edge on the tube. It uncurled.

A gum wrapper.

How did a gum wrapper get rolled that tightly? How did it get embedded into Matt's eardrum? The obvious answers involved a ten-year-old boy, one who shrugged his shoulders and said, "I dunno."

One would think he could hear better with a gum wrapper removed from his ear. I don't remember noticing an improvement. He was still a ten-year-old boy.

As embarrassing as it was for all of us to chalk up an ER visit to a stick of Doublemint, it made a memory. As I thought about that incident today, it made me all the more appreciative of a God who hears. Clearly. No encumbrance. Nothing in the way. Nothing to distract Him from loving us and wanting to bless us.

I appreciate a God whose mighty hand hovers over the SEND button, eager to set answers in motion the moment He hears our cry for help. Our God hears everything. And in yet one more expression of His grace, He acts as soon as He hears. Sometimes sooner. * CR

True Refreshment

A generous man will prosper; he who refreshes others will himself be refreshed.

PROVERBS 11:25

I have a friend who has discovered the secret of today's Scripture. I've never met anyone who thinks of others the way this friend does (well, other than Mother Teresa, whom, incidentally, I have *not* met—though I will meet her in heaven one day). When there is a need, my friend is there. No matter who it is, she will do whatever it takes to help someone. It's in her nature. She has the nature of Jesus.

It amazes me how some people, like my friend, are automatically geared that way. The first thing that seems to pop into their heads is how they can help someone, while others tend to focus on their own problems and never once seem to consider how they might reach out to someone else.

Maybe it's something learned over time by watching parents or friends put others first. Maybe it's strength of character. Or maybe it's Jesus working (though some of us may not be listening).

Sometimes my circumstances scream loudly for attention and it's hard to focus on anything else. I want to wallow in self-pity, down a two-pound bag of M&Ms while watching *Sleepless in Seattle*, and slip into a chocolate-induced coma. During those times, I have to remind myself that there's always someone who has more need than I do. Perhaps that person not only has had a bad day, but they have no M&Ms to get them through it.

Now, lest you think I turn to chocolate instead of the Lord during times of crisis, I want you to know that M&Ms, for me, are much more than chocolate. I belong to a group consisting of ladies who call ourselves the M&Ms, which is short for *Monday Mentors*. We started as a Bible study group and have morphed into a once-a-month meeting where we share our life's struggles, joys, and, well, M&Ms (the chocolate ones). We pray together, keep in touch through e-mail, and, in short, put each other's needs above our own. There is nothing I wouldn't do for them.

There is something refreshing about refreshing others. Who can *you* encourage today? Who needs to be reminded that someone cares—that Jesus is reaching out to them in their loneliness, in their need? Maybe you are their hope for better days ahead.

Go on. Forget about yourself. Go out and help someone else. And be sure to take your M&Ms. * *DH*

A Cut Above

*I am the true vine, and my Father is the husbandman. Every branch
in me that beareth not fruit he taketh away: and every branch that beareth
fruit, he purgeth it, that it may bring forth more fruit.*

JOHN 15:1–2 KJV

I'm the first to admit I know diddly about growing grapes—or any other kind of fruit, for that matter. But trial and error has taught me a thing or three about caring for roses. I have a dozen lovely rosebushes out back, each a different color, variety, and temperament. Some produce gorgeous flowers with little more than sunshine and rainfall, while others require supreme effort and patience to bloom.

The toughest part of my job as a "cultivator" is knowing *when* to go at the shrubs with sharp pruning shears and *which* branches to lop off. Some make it easy for me, by displaying spindly growth or disease. Others make me look closer while trying to remember just how many blooms each produced.

Snipping off the dead stuff is a no-brainer. They're ugly. They drain the plant of energy as it tries to revive what's "gone bad." And let's face it: If they can't pump out pretty petals, what good are they?

SNIP!

After a heavy rain, some branches can grow long and scraggly. They'll spit out a flower here and there, but those blooms won't be robust, and they won't last long, either.

SNIP!

Still other branches please the eye and nose with dozens of beautiful buds…but after a few weeks of that, they'll wear themselves out.

SNIP!

The Lord works miracles with His children in much the same way. We rarely like seeing the flash of His pruning shears, and we like being the recipient of His snippers even less. But He knows what He's doing, and if we're honest with ourselves, we recognize how much we needed a little pruning.

I'm notorious for working long, grueling days to "grow" my writing career. But God's pruning has taught me that if I don't take time to care for my soul, myself, and my family, He's more than willing to lop at my so-called growth. Illness—nothing truly serious but enough to force me into quiet R & R—has been His method for reminding me of what's truly important. It's while I rest and recuperate that I slow down enough to count my blessings…and afterward, I'm more fruitful and productive than before!

Why is it, I wonder, that when times are tough, we eagerly fall to our knees—yet when things are going great, we think it's safe to stray…a little, anyway…from Him?

Maybe it's because we fear He'll see it's time to whip out those shears… * LL

A Reason to Sing

The Lord has chastened me severely, but he has not given me over to death.

PSALM 118:18

When I consider how my life has played out so far, I'm amazed at how little hardship I've suffered. I mean, I've experienced plenty of loss, heartbreak, and problems in the financial and health areas, but relative to many of my friends and acquaintances? A cakewalk. Maybe it's because the Lord knows what a powder puff I am; I don't know.

And I always hesitate to look at anything adverse that's happening in my life or anyone else's as the Lord's "chastening," as the term is used in today's verse. One only has to read Job to figure out that we can't ever expect to understand why bad things happen to good people, other than those consequences obviously tied to bad decisions we've made—and I've experienced a few of *those chastenings.*

Still, I do find myself trying to ferret out why certain bad things have come my way—the bad things that don't seem to be the result of stupid or sinful choices on my part. Are they just part of living in a sinful world, or is the Lord trying to tell me something? If I'm going through a bad time because He wants me to figure something out, I want to figure it out *tout de suite.*

I can't say I've been highly successful in that.

It's interesting to note that Psalm 118 and the few psalms before it are always read (sung, actually) at Passover.

It makes sense that the Jews would celebrate deliverance from death when commemorating the original Passover, right? And Psalm 118 contains a few other nuggets of joy, including, "Give thanks to the LORD, for he is good; his love endures forever" (verse 29). Wonderful stuff that sets off familiar worship songs in my mind.

But consider it a step further. If verses like these are typically sung during the Passover meal, chances are good that they were sung at the Last Supper. Matthew even tells us that, after Jesus broke the bread and drank the wine and proclaimed the sacrifice He was about to make for all mankind, "they" sang (Matthew 26:30).

Do you think He sang too? Do you think He sang the Passover psalms? Can you imagine Him singing about how wonderful the day was, how there was reason for rejoicing, how God's love endures forever, right before He was to be taken to the cross? And can you imagine His rejoicing that God had not given Him over to death?

Kind of puts a *real* eternal perspective on things, doesn't it? If Jesus wasn't being given over to death, certainly none of us are, if we've given our hearts to Him.

Kind of makes me want to sing. * *TP*

Here Comes the Judge

Do not judge, or you too will be judged.

MATTHEW 7:1

He tells us not to judge, or we'll be judged. Oops! Well, it's sort of too late for me. I've done way more than my share of judging, and it started a long time ago. Like before I had kids, when I saw an unruly toddler throwing a temper-tantrum in a restaurant. "My kid would never do that." *<snort>* Right! Just like my kid would never tell a lie, talk back, or say words that are on our family's "bad words" list. *<snicker>* Those thoughts of having the perfect, well-behaved child faded as soon as my daughters started walking and talking. *And why is that woman scowling at me like that?* Okay, so I admit that my kids could scream along with the best of them. *Sourpuss* must not have kids of her own.

How about the time I saw the guy in the next cubicle cleaning out his desk? What did he do to get the axe? Must've been something terrible for the company not to give him any notice. That judgment lasted for about two days—until everyone in my department was called into a meeting and informed that the company needed to cut back. They were sad to lose one of their most valuable employees, but when he found out there were going to be cutbacks, he volunteered to leave because he was so close to retirement anyway. He didn't want anyone else to lose their jobs. I felt like a rat for judging him when he was willing to give up something for the good of others.

We've been ordered not to judge, but how many people can honestly say they've followed His order? Very few, I bet. Think about it and reflect on how, when we judge, we assume something that is (a) none of our business and (b) downright wrong. See, that's the thing. Judging others based on assumptions is asking for trouble. We risk our credibility with others when we assume something based on how things look, and God knows the impurity in our hearts when we make assumptions. How dare we judge others when we're just as bad as—or worse than—the people being judged.

One important thing to remember about judging, though, is that we are still to exercise discernment. There is a difference between right and wrong, and we've been given people in positions of authority who may judge based on the laws of the land.

I'm working on looking at others without judging them. It isn't easy for me, but unless I want people to judge me based on incorrect assumptions, I need to do that. * *DM*

Bottles (and Bottles!) of Tears

Record my misery; list my tears on your scroll—are they not in your record?
PSALM 56:8

I love this Scripture! It's one of the first verses that really grabbed me and stuck with me when I started studying the Word. The translation I read at the time said, "You number my wanderings; put my tears into Your bottle" (NKJV). Oh, how I love that picture!

A college friend once told me she thought I wasted a lot of energy by "allowing myself" to be such an emotional person. "All the tears and inner turmoil could be energy so much better spent!" she exclaimed. I remember laughing instead of responding, wondering how one simply *decides* not to cry when their feelings have been hurt or they've been disappointed. For me, it's never been a matter of turning the waterworks on or off; it's more of an involuntary response, like sneezing.

I cry at a Hallmark commercial or a movie trailer, so you can imagine how many tears fall at a personal injustice or a misunderstanding with a friend. The idea that Jesus pays such close attention to what's going on with me that He collects them, keeps an audit, or saves them up in a bottle on His office shelf is one that paints the picture that I am *cherished*. I am so *valuable* to Him that He keeps track of my tears!

I think we Christians spend a lot of time talking and thinking and praying about how wondrous God is. We praise Him for His greatness, His omnipotence, His overwhelming glory. He's huge and powerful, and nothing is impossible for Him. As the great Rich Mullins taught us, "Our God is an awesome God! He reigns from heaven above!"

Shew! It's staggering, isn't it?

But what of the sweet, intimate love He has for us? That's a little more difficult to comprehend at times, right? After all, we're so unworthy, so faithless.

When my marriage was falling apart, I went to stay with my parents for a couple of weeks while I decided what to do. One night, my husband called the house to speak to me, and I heard my mother say, "No, I don't hate you. But you have to understand that my daughter has cried herself to sleep over you six out of eight nights in a row, so that's going to impact me."

Although my relationship with her was somewhat strained during that time, I remember taking a step back from what stood between us when I heard that phone conversation. My mom had kept track of the tears I'd shed, and on a much smaller scale than the great God of all keeping an account of my heartaches!

Grace allows us to share intimacy with our Father in the shadow of His greatness. And today's Scripture reminds us of that glorious dichotomy. It tells us that He cares so deeply about us that He keeps track of our misery and pain. Every tear shed is counted, like the hairs on our head are numbered. How cool is that? * *SDB*

My Big Fat American Dream

Better to be a nobody and yet have a servant than pretend to be somebody and have no food.
A righteous man cares for the needs of his animal, but the kindest acts of the wicked are cruel.
He who works his land will have abundant food, but he who chases fantasies lacks judgment.

PROVERBS 12:9–11

My big fat American dream has consumed me! I have a great house. We have more room than we need, the latest appliances, a yard filled with high-maintenance landscaping, and a welcoming porch that gives the impression that a hospitable family lives here—even though we don't even know some of our neighbors.

We have other great junk, too, like cars, TVs, and computers! Our kitchen is filled with all the coolest gadgets shown on the Food Network because "You never know when you might need a citrus zester."

So why am I so frazzled?

As I look at my life, I realize that the things my hard work has paid for have put me in bondage and won't let go unless I understand basic biblical principles. Taking a step back and looking at the big picture—what really matters most in our lives—I have to ask myself this obvious question: Will having the latest and greatest worldly things take us to our ultimate goal? If it's to die rich in the world's eyes, yes. But if it's to die in this world and reawaken with the Lord, absolutely not! And then I hear those words from Proverbs chapter 12.

Better to be a nobody and yet have a servant than pretend to be somebody and have no food.

Should I work hard? Of course.

He who works his land will have abundant food...

We work to live and enjoy His blessings, which are not of this world.

...but he who chases fantasies lacks judgment.

Say what? All those things I've worked so hard to attain are merely fantasies that show a lack of judgment? In a nutshell...yes.

So do I have to sell my house and all its contents and live a life of poverty in order to be godlier? Not unless I can't afford to maintain what I've already been blessed with. However, it is time for my husband and me to take stock of what we have and vow to appreciate everything the Lord has allowed us to bring into our lives. Then we need to focus on moving forward in a more faithful way and pray before we acquire anything new. Our children don't need most of what they have, but they do need to learn good stewardship—as do my husband and I.

Rather than spending time poring over catalogs and drooling over TV commercials, the time has come to begin each day with prayer, to be thankful, and to ask for guidance in every decision we make. We don't need to focus so much on what our money will buy but instead on working to the glory of the Lord.

I will be satisfied with my blessings and pray for Him to use me to do His will rather than my own. * *DM*

unHappy Anniversary

You will forget the shame of your youth and remember no more
the reproach of your widowhood. For your Maker is your husband—
the Lord Almighty is his name.

ISAIAH 54:4–5

Coop and Lynette had been married for thirty years. Despite their silver hair and matching crow's feet, one might have suspected they'd just met after five minutes in their presence. Coop pulled out her chair and brought her roses at least once each month, and he lit up the whole place the instant Lynette floated through any doorway toward him.

They didn't have a lot of money, but they managed to put a little away all year toward the standing anniversary tradition they'd developed. Dressed to the tens in their ballroom-best, after an elegant dinner at one of the city's finest restaurants, Coop took Lynette dancing. She said that waltzing with her husband never failed to bring visions of fairy tales and happily-ever-afters.

Coop had been called to Phoenix just before their thirty-first anniversary, but he called Lynette from the road and said he would be home in plenty of time to shower and change so that they could make their seven p.m. dinner reservation. By six o'clock, Lynette put the finishing touches on her hair, sprayed it into place, and sat down in the chair by the window. She dropped a few items into her evening bag while she watched for Coop's arrival.

At seven, she called Coop's friend in Phoenix; at 7:30, her heart began to race; by 8:30, she twisted the ribbon on her elegant green dress as she dialed the state police. By eleven o'clock that night, Lynette recounted later, she realized that her life was over. Coop had been killed in a head-on collision while his wife waited for him to take her dancing.

A year passed before the realization set in and two years until her first thought every morning didn't flash to Coop. After four years, we happened across each other's paths at the dry cleaner and went to a nearby café for tea. I asked the vibrant, smiling woman across from me how she'd managed.

"Coop did everything for me," she said before glancing up at me with an intent smile. "I was completely out of my element without him; I was terrified. But what I came to realize is that Coop was only on loan to me. My true Husband, the One with me when I came into this world and the One with me when I eventually leave it, never departs from me. Jesus is my True Companion."

Lynette's assurance and solid faith pricked me in that moment with the reminder that no matter how connected we are to the people around us, those people are only on loan to us. Our Maker, Savior, Husband, Provider, and Healer come in one consistent, dependable, divorce-free partner. * *SDB*

Nothin' Like a Little Frettin' with Your Coffee

Fear not, for I am with you; be not dismayed, for I am your God.
I will strengthen you, yes, I will help you, I will uphold you with My righteous right hand.

ISAIAH 41:10 NKJV

I'm worried. There's a situation going on at work where it's my manager's word against mine. My employer's human resources department has gotten involved. What a mess!

I sip my coffee and stare at my Bible, which lies on the kitchen table.

They'll never believe me. They'll take her side over mine.

I run a finger along the edge of God's Word.

Lord, what am I going to do? How much of an issue should I make of this? Why didn't I see this trouble brewing?

I take another drink of coffee, wondering what I should eat for breakfast. After a few moments of deliberation, I get up from my chair at the table and prepare two boiled eggs and a piece of toast.

Thank You for this food, Lord.

As I eat, I think about the situation going on at work. I worry about the outcome. I sip my coffee and fret some more.

Lord, why can't I hear Your voice? I'm sitting here talking to You, and You're so quiet.

As if God tapped me on the shoulder, my attention is drawn to my Bible. I am prompted to open it up. As I flip through the delicate pages, I come to today's verse in the book of Isaiah, chapter 40. Suddenly I realized I'd been having a monologue and not dialogue! No wonder I couldn't hear God.

"Fear not…I am with you… Be not dismayed, for I am your God… I will strengthen you…. I will help you….

My vision blurs with tears after reading my Savior's love letter to me. His Word is true; God cannot lie (Titus 1:2).

"I will uphold you with My righteous right hand." Thank You, Jesus.

Hours later, I walk into my manager's office and sit down. Nervous flutters fill my insides, but I hang on to what God promised.

"I talked with Human Resources." My manager squares her shoulders and folds her hands on her desk. "We found a discrepancy in your file. A correction will be made."

"So I was right?"

My manager hesitates before nodding in admission.

Relief washes over me. Minutes later, I leave her office, breathing a sigh of relief. *Wow, that was easy, Lord.*

His gentle rebuke fills my soul. *I told you not to fret. I've got you covered.*

Okay, no more frettin' with my coffee. From now on, I only fret to God. * *AKB*

A Fresh Slate

Because of the LORD's great love we are not consumed, for his compassions never fail.
They are new every morning; great is your faithfulness.

LAMENTATIONS 3:22–23

My husband is an elementary school teacher. When September rolls around each year, he is as excited as his students. We go shopping for clothes and school supplies, and he gets his room ready for the kids. The smell of sharpened pencils, fresh chalk, and cleaning supplies fills the room. New wall hangings, posters, clean blackboards, and a tidy desk all mark the beginning of a school year.

Each year, he learns something from the year before—which tools strike interest in the hearts of the students, what presentations worked and which ones flopped. He considers new ways to motivate the daydreamers and challenge the restless. He takes his newfound knowledge into the next year in hopes of doing a better job than before.

Some days he comes home and feels as though he didn't accomplish a thing. Other days he wonders how he could ever do any other job. Every class offers new challenges of its own, and my husband faces each one head-on, with renewed encouragement and excitement for another year.

In short, he gets a fresh slate.

When my kids were little, I wanted to be just like Caroline Ingalls. You know, kindness lifting from my lips like a soft minuet and wisdom rolling into every word. Unfortunately, it didn't work like that for me.

There were days when the kids were rowdy and I had a headache—I don't think Caroline ever had those. My patience was short and the tone of my voice carried around the block like a marine corps sergeant. Unfortunately, I resembled Mrs. Oleson more than I did Mrs. Ingalls.

I prayed for wisdom, gentleness, and, yes, even patience. So many nights I wondered what kind of memories I had created for my children that day. I'd fall on my knees and pray, "Lord, help them to forget everything I did wrong and remember if I did anything right." It must have worked. They speak fondly of their childhood.

Some days are hard. The challenges seem too great to bear. Sometimes we can't seem to work beyond our past. We feel that God is silent and we're all alone. But then His Word reminds us that His compassions never fail. They are new every morning! Great is His faithfulness!

Forget about yesterday. *This* is the day that the Lord has made. You have the opportunity to start all over. Trust God with it. Go into a hurting world and make brand-new memories—memories that matter. You have a fresh slate. Go with His blessings. * DH

A Life of Freedom

The Spirit of the Lord GOD is upon Me, because the LORD has anointed
Me to preach good tidings to the poor; He has sent Me to heal the brokenhearted,
to proclaim liberty to the captives, and the opening of the prison to those who are bound.

ISAIAH 61:1 NKJV

Growing up in the same town, I knew who Dena was. Our families went way back, and her younger sister, Beth, was a friend of mine in high school.

Beth idolized Dena. Through her I heard how successful Dena was in everything, how smart, how wildly popular.

Beth didn't talk much about the wreck that happened several years before, when Dena was in high school and we were mere grade-schoolers. I knew about it, of course; everyone in town did. But the details were sketchy in my mind. I was too young to understand.

When I graduated from high school, Beth was a junior. Dena was in another state, on her way to becoming a successful lawyer. I didn't see either one of them again until I moved back to my hometown and opened a café. By this time Dena had moved home, too. She came into my café with a group of attorneys who provided free legal services to low-income families.

Dena's easy manner, quick wit, and relaxed leadership style were all things that impressed me as I served the lawyers' cheese soup and chicken salads. For all of her intelligence, she seemed to exude a generosity of spirit that was guileless. I thought she was a person I'd like to get to know.

When I later became a stay-at-home mom in search of some interesting friends, I called her up out of the blue, and we decided to get together for a play date since she was a stay-at-home mom, too. It didn't take many meetings to bring us to the point of sharing the deep things of our hearts.

One day as we played with our girls, I asked Dena to tell me about the accident. Her big eyes instantly welled up with tears. "Some friends and I were out partying, and I was driving. I lost control of the car, and one of my best friends was killed."

The pain on her face showed me the magnitude of the wound, and a part of me felt sorry for opening it up. But another part knew—and knows from experience—that this opening up of ourselves can be a part of our healing.

She went on to tell me how the experience had changed her life forever. How kind the parents of her dead friend had been. "They never treated me badly or like they blamed me, but I have often blamed myself."

In the years that followed the tragedy, Dena tried to hide her free spirit under a cloak of grief that she pulled tight around her, searching for ways to become a better Christian. In her guilt and confusion, she began to define herself—and others—by rules of behavior. She thought she could make herself good and acceptable to God by refraining from certain activities. And she admits that she began to judge others by that same harsh standard.

"One evening," Dena said, "my eyes were opened to the futility of judgment. Judgment is bondage, whether we're judging ourselves or others. I set up those standards to try to atone for myself. But, I realized that spiritual freedom is not something we attain by reaching standards we have set for ourselves. I also realized that I cannot place my standards upon others. Being delivered from judgment freed my heart to know something of God's true, inner beauty."

The burden of judgment Dena had carried since the accident fell from her shoulders that day, and she is vigilant in her efforts to avoid picking it back up. Though she will always regret what happened in that horrible wreck, she believes that the Lord has released her from judgment. And from the bondage of judging others. * *GF*

A "Work" in Progress

In all thy ways, acknowledge him, and he shall direct thy paths.
PROVERBS 3:6 KJV

A few weeks ago, I applied for the position of assistant editor for a local newspaper. But every time I prayed about this job, I was left with a feeling that I should just wait.

A few days after my interview, I ran into a former student who's a secretary at the publication. I understood why I'd been so unsettled when the woman went on to tell me about problems at her newspaper. Crazy things were going on over there, she admitted, with editors being axed, reporters quitting right and left, and morale at an all-time low. She had no idea what had caused all the unrest, but she concluded with a warning to expect a call from her boss about "my" job.

Then in today's mail was a fat envelope from one of the companies that publishes my novels, filled with letters from my readers. "I love your stories!" said one. "Please don't ever stop writing!" said another. I heard God's voice telling me that He speaks to my readers through the stories I write. "This is the gift I have given to you," He seemed to be saying, "to touch My children's hearts and stir their souls."

I went straight to the phone, withdrew my job application, and headed to my desk to work on my latest idea. He has made me a missionary with the books I write, delivering His Word to those in need. * LL

Strength Training

LORD, be gracious to us; we long for you.
Be our strength every morning, our salvation in time of distress.

ISAIAH 33:2

I wonder if the Lord chuckles at us like we do when watching a toddler boy take a professional bodybuilder stance, flexing his muscles and growling, as if that makes him stronger.

Two sons and three grandsons into this adventure of life, I've watched at least five versions of "Show me how strong you are." The two-foot-nothing child would push up his shirtsleeves to his shoulders, make tiny fists with his tiny hands, lean forward as he fluffs his biceps and forearms, and shake with the extreme effort. *Grrrrrr!*

How could we do anything but laugh? Thirty pounds of mini muscles pretending to be strong. A ball of fury run on a single AAA battery.

And…that's me. Not the thirty pounds part, unless you use one of those "to the sixth power" symbols. But I act like a delusional toddler when I think I'm strong enough to endure difficulty without Him, strong enough to resist temptation without Him, strong enough to get myself out of trouble—*thank You very much*—without Him. Like a toddler growling at an invisible foe. How cute!

And how utterly hysterical that picture must seem to Almighty God.

"Aren't those humans adorable when they flex their muscles?"

"See how strong I am" is a statement that often immediately precedes a nasty fall. "Watch me juggle these forty things" foretells that something's about to drop. "Look how far I can jump" comes right before "Ow! Call 911!"

And still the Lord stands poised to give all of Himself for all of my need, despite my delusions of strength, my miscalculations about the difference between the size of my muscles and the scope of the giants I face.

One would think that someone like me, who thrives on efficiency and organizes her errands so every parking lot is a right-hand turn, would have learned the lesson long ago. My strength is puny in light of His. So what does He do? He offers to loan me His—the unfailing, bigger-than-any-problem, never-runs-out-of-batteries, perpetual, instant, overcoming Conqueror kind of strength. He says, "Ask Me. I'll be your strength."

Help me out here, Lord.

"Done."

Well, let me have a chance to tell You why it is I need a little more strength.

"A *little* more?"

Okay, a lot more.

"Doesn't matter the reason. You need it. You'll have it."

What an incredible gift!

I'm asked to handle a difficult task. Oh, you too? Sounds doable until I get a few minutes into it and realize it's far beyond my natural abilities. I'm unqualified. Unprepared. Not knowledgeable enough to even explain how inadequate I am. And He loans me His strength to get the job done. Again.

The difference between us is profound. I'm a baby acting like a superhero. He's…a Superhero. But He doesn't mock me for it. He loves me. How did I get so blessed?

How did we get so blessed? * CR

Enemies? Who, Me?

As for me, far be it from me that I should sin against the LORD by failing to pray for you. And I will teach you the way that is good and right.

1 SAMUEL 12:23

Do you have any enemies? I mean, hard-core enemies? I don't think I do, when I really consider it. Certainly I have the same big-time enemies as the rest of the civilized world—the ones who terrorize for a living. But personally? When I hear Matthew's admonishment to love my enemies, no one in particular comes to mind.

Still, if I ratchet it down a notch to people who put a crimp in my life, who rather passively work against me for one reason or another…there, I suppose, I could come up with a few names. Can you?

I think that was what Samuel addressed in today's verse. He had been asked by his "employers," essentially, to replace himself: to find someone to become king of Israel, to step down as judge, and to not let the door hit him on the backside on his way out. He admonished the Israelites for desiring a king (when they already had *the* King). But then he said he'd be sinning against the Lord if he failed to pray for them.

So these weren't people plotting Samuel's demise. They didn't hate him, as enemies hate. But they demeaned him, rejected him, and treated him unfairly.

Now we're talking. I can *certainly* identify there. How about you? But I can't say I've ever thought, *I need to be sure to pray for {him/her/them}. I'd be sinning against God if I didn't.* But that's what Samuel (and God) says we're to do. Frankly, I'd just as soon I didn't come across this verse.

But I did, and now you did too. If you've been paying attention, you've already identified who that person is (or those people are) in your life. And consider this: you may be the only person in the world praying for that person. Not only is that sad for them, but that's an honor for you. And it also could be why the person is such a pill.

While we're at it, let's broaden the criteria: include the man who'll cut you off in traffic this week; the woman with thirty items in the express aisle; the surly kid with his boxers hanging over his sagging jeans; the girl with the pierced tongue and foul mouth; the next person who makes you frown… * *TP*

....

....

....

....

....

....

....

....

Practice Makes Perfect

Therefore submit to God. Resist the devil and he will flee from you.
JAMES 4:7 NKJV

At one time in my life, I was going for long walks about five days a week. However, after a foot injury, I realized one day that it had been almost two months since I'd gone for a walk. Just hoofing it from the parking garage into my office set my heart to pounding and the rest of me to huffing and puffing. This was my body's way of telling me that it was time to lace up the walking shoes and get my fanny into gear!

So on Monday night, when the weather was cool and a soft breeze was blowing, I did just that. I was tired after only a fraction of the distance I could formerly walk, but I pressed on. At least I was moving again.

On Wednesday night, I went again. I couldn't rack up much more distance than the previous time, but I felt pretty good about following through with my Monday-Wednesday-Friday plan.

On Friday, though, my head was turned by an invitation to join a girlfriend at our favorite Mexican restaurant. And by the end of the weekend, my Monday-Wednesday-Friday plan had slipped from my mind and out the door without so much as a creak on the floorboards.

"So how's your walking schedule going?" I was asked a couple of weeks later.

"Oh, well, umm, not so great lately."

The truth was, I'd forgotten all about that schedule. With new resolve at the reminder, I hit the REFRESH button on my brain and decided to start anew. But after a week or so, the distractions won out.

"I don't know what my problem is," I heard someone say on a morning talk show. "I mean to get fit and stay active, but I just don't have the time."

The guest was a fitness trainer, and he explained the importance of keeping a routine for at least one full month. He purported that, after a certain amount of time of doing the same thing again and again, something clicks inside the brain and it becomes a habit—and for most people that span of time is a month.

I remembered when my neighbor quit smoking; she'd been told the same thing by her pastor. "Resist and keep resisting until the devil flees," the pastor had said. I supposed the same premise would hold true for forming good habits as well as destroying old ones.

Recently, when a girlfriend called on a Wednesday night to invite me to the movies, I sang, "Resisting you, devil! I'm going for a walk." Later, we laughed at the idea that by joining me for my walk rather than crunching buttered popcorn at the movies, she was doing a little resisting of her own. * *SDB*

A Tough Pill to Swallow

Come and hear, all you who fear God; let me tell you what he has done for me.

PSALM 66:16

"Would you rather be right, or would you rather be happy?"

It's a question that has plagued mankind since, well, the beginning of mankind. From the cradle, it seems, the main goal in life is to "be" happy:

Fresh diaper? Happy baby!

Shiny new trike? Happy toddler!

Driver's license? Happy teen!

Clean room? Happy mom!

Full college scholarship? Happy dad!

We tell ourselves it doesn't take much to make us happy, but woe to the traffic light that turns red when we're late or the thoughtless driver whose fast-food wrapper ends up in our front yard. Someone in the fifteen-or-less line put seventeen items on the belt? Unacceptable! And I'm every bit as guilty as anyone else of the back-and-forth between happy and not happy, as evidenced by my last sinus infection:

One call to my doctor and, voilà, I had an appointment. Color me happy!

But on the way there, I got stuck in traffic. Not so happy.

Found a parking space right in front of the door. Hap–hap–happy!

But I found standing-room-only in the waiting room. *<sigh>*

Nurse invited me into the exam room on time. Yay!

But it took nearly an hour before the doctor came in. *<groan>*

Got to the drugstore in record time. Ta-da!

But a computer crash had deleted me from the system. *<grrr>*

"Oh, well," said I, hoping my smile would erase the pharmacy tech's frown. It did not. I fanned Blue Cross cards across the counter, wondering why *she* was in such a snit. Wasn't me who crashed the system. I had truth (i.e., insurance identification) on my side. Maybe I should point out to her that the customer is always right!

That's when I remembered the old "walk a mile in her shoes" adage. The drugstore chain wrote up the rules and expected her to follow them, whether the customer was sweet or sour, wrong or right. Which reminded me of Moses's no-nonsense "obey!" approach to those stone tablets...and the fact that it was the supreme sacrifice of *Jesus* that delivered grace unto us all.

Now my little dilemma seemed petty and ridiculous. I took a deep breath. I said a prayer for the poor girl—and whatever had put her into a foul mood—and set about helping her to believe that *she* was in the "right." Suddenly she was smiling, fingers click-clacking over the keyboard in a mad search to get me "reinstated." In no time I was home, happily chasing my first dose of antibiotic with a tall glass of water.

Sadly (pun intended), that's life, isn't it? At the end of every day, if we can count up more good things than bad, we're happy. Or at least satisfied.

And that beats "being right" all the way to the drugstore and back! * *LL*

A Life of His Presence

I am God Almighty. Live in My presence.

GENESIS 17:1 HCSB

My parents had given us land overlooking the Arkansas River, and my husband and I had saved our money for years, looking forward to the moment when we could build our dream home and raise our growing family. After renting, scrimping, working, and planning, finally that moment had come. We had survived the building phase and the moving in—and, finally, we were home.

It was fall, and I'd just finished unpacking the last box. The lights in the cabinets were shimmering, the wood floor was freshly polished, and I was sitting on my couch admiring the natural stone of the fireplace in front of me and the oak mantel I designed. It was a Martha Stewart moment! Taking a sip of hot chocolate, I looked out the window at our deck and the majestic Arkansas River flowing far beneath me, carving its way through the Ozark Mountains bursting with color. A feeling of satisfaction flooded my soul. It's true what the Bible says: "Hope deferred makes the heart sick, but a longing fulfilled is a tree of life" (Proverbs 13:12).

I closed my eyes, breathing in the sweetness of that ful-fillment and thanking the Lord for making our dream come true. My heart was filled to the brim with joy. And there in the stillness of my living room, I felt Him speak softly to my heart.

It was not an audible voice, but His meaning was very clear: *"This home is a place for you to live a beautiful life before Me. I have freely given it to you to enjoy, but you must always remember that the beauty of your life and home has nothing to do with what you can see. It is My presence—and My presence alone—that makes something beautiful."*

I've seen that principle operate over and over in my life and home. After several years, the wood floor is no longer freshly polished, and most days it desperately needs to be swept. The mantel usually wants to be dusted, and the deck is littered with my children's toys. My house is a lot like my body, I suppose—it doesn't always get the care it requires in order to look its best. But it's a beautiful place. Whether we're hosting a group of friends, bowing our heads at the dinner table, or tucking our kids into bed—Jesus is here. And His presence makes all of the difference. * *GF*

You Can't Argue Alone

Do not answer a fool according to his folly, or you will be like him yourself.

PROVERBS 26:4

Are you big on arguing? Combativeness can be contagious. I was at my most argumentative when I dated a man who was practically a caricature of a "fiery Latino." He argued passionately about everything from who was the best pickup basketball player (after *every single game* he played) to which restaurant made the best shrimp scampi. It was exhausting.

One thing I've noticed as I've aged is that I don't get into arguments as easily as I used to, despite the strengthening of my core beliefs (about important things, not basketball and shrimp). When I was younger, it seemed so important that my points were at least understood, if not embraced. I was infected with last-word-itis.

After I became a Christian, an unsaved friend of mine constantly instigated arguments with me about a particular moral issue. She knew where Christians generally stood on the issue, so she assumed (correctly) that I stood there as well. She, of course, stood on the other side of the matter. She was forever sending me newspaper articles to back up her argument and turning our otherwise-entertaining conversations to the debate.

I felt an obligation, as a Christian, to engage her when she did this—to help her understand the truth. I didn't think she was a fool, but because of the Lord's Word, I knew that her stance was worldly folly. It wasn't until I asked one of my pastors for advice about a particular point that he adjusted my view of the problem.

"I don't mean to belittle your friend," he said, "but you know that verse about not casting pearls before swine? It sounds as if your friend isn't seeking clarity about your Christian stance on this matter. She's just trying to denigrate your beliefs. She's not seeking understanding; she's seeking to destroy."

I knew what I believed and what she believed. My friend knew the same. What were we accomplishing by constantly rehashing an argument neither of us would concede? I chose to refuse further debate with her on the subject. Proving myself right wasn't important, and God was going to have to convince her of the truth since I couldn't.

She wasn't happy about it, but she had to drop the assault because I was unwilling to play "my role." Sometimes it's best to just step away from the argument, ma'am. Just step away and pray. I like this anonymous saying: "When you're arguing with a fool, make sure he isn't doing the same thing." * TP

Facing Forward

Forget the former things; do not dwell on the past.

ISAIAH 43:18

It happens whether you're in a canoe or a station wagon. If you face backward, you'll have a view. It just won't help you on your journey.

In my childhood, at a time when my four siblings and I fought epic battles for the primo window seats, we were thrilled when our parents bought a station wagon, offering that wide panoramic view from the back-facing seat. We called it the "way very back." It could hold three of us across.

"Can I sit in the way very back?"

"Me too?"

"Me too?"

"Me— Aww! I get dibs next time."

"Me too!"

What was so fascinating about facing backward, having no clue where we were going but a clear vision of where we'd been?

Why does that still capture our attention?

A friend of the family made several visits to the local prison…as an inmate. He was given multiple opportunities for a fresh start. But he was pointing backward, his attention captivated by where he'd been, the mistakes he'd made, the shame and misery he'd known, the misery he'd caused.

God's grace being what it is, our friend's been given another opportunity for a fresh start. This time feels different to him and to us. Why? He's facing forward this time.

He has a clear view of the future, a plan for how to navigate the obstacles ahead—obstacles he would have backed into and tripped over if he'd been facing the other direction.

My husband and I have canoed the complicated web of lakes and rivers in the Canadian wilderness several times. Not recently, though. I told him I could only manage a trip like that once a decade. It's been eighteen years. One of these days he's bound to do the math.

When paddling past small granite islands and long stretches of northwoods forest in the wilderness, we'd get into serious trouble if we tried to find our way facing backward. Could we see interesting scenery that way? Oh, sure. But we'd bash the canoe into rocks, get caught by rogue waves, hit the rapids at the wrong angle, miss our put-in points for portages or a place to camp, and risk remaining constantly lost.

As a child, I soon found that facing backward was a good way to invite car sickness too. I relinquished my dibs on the way very back. I needed to face where we were heading to keep my equilibrium.

I don't think I'm alone.

Making every dance move backward and in heels might have worked for Ginger Rogers when she danced with Fred Astaire, but it's a clumsy way to try to navigate life.

We need to *know* where we've been. But *facing* that direction can invite life sickness. * CR

Monsters in the Shadows

Have I not commanded you? Be strong and of good courage; do not be afraid,
nor be dismayed, for the LORD your God is with you wherever you go.

JOSHUA 1:9 NKJV

I had a part-time job for a while at the children's photography studio of a department store. It was a great job. I loved working with the kids, and I quickly developed a reputation as the only photographer on staff who could get the really young babies to smile. I'd set them in place, talk to them while I prepped the camera, and then make some funny noises to snag their wide-eyed attention.

The studio faced out into the mall, and I'd often draw a crowd of onlookers with those ridiculous noises when working a later shift. Sometimes I would even notice a couple of the same faces back to watch the action.

One night, I decided to go out for coffee with a friend after work, and I returned home fairly late. My upstairs neighbor trotted down the stairs to meet me at my door.

"Hey, listen," he said, "I just wanted to let you know that there was a very strange guy outside your back door earlier."

Dennis had come across the stranger and asked him what he was doing behind the condo building where I lived. He said he was looking for the woman who worked at the photography studio—and he didn't use my name.

"I told him you weren't home," Dennis explained, "and that he would have to come back another time. He was kind of creepy, wearing this battered army jacket with patches on the arm."

I immediately thought of one of those returning faces in the crowd outside of the studio. I'd seen him there at least three times that week, and *creepy* was a perfect word to describe him.

A week later, I was watching the local news when they aired footage of a serial rapist who had just been captured. The dark-haired man being led into a police cruiser was wearing a torn T-shirt beneath a very familiar army jacket.

"What if I hadn't decided to go out for coffee?" I asked Dennis afterward. "I would have been home that night."

"Somebody was looking out for you, that's for sure," he replied. I just smiled, knowing full well who that Somebody was. * SDB

Unwanted Hair

For the waywardness of the simple will kill them, and the complacency of fools will destroy them; but whoever listens to me will live in safety and be at ease, without fear of harm.

PROVERBS 1:32–33

I don't like to be told what to do.

If you know me, you're laughing out loud right now. "Really? You?"

It's a lifelong, recurring theme in my life. If you tell me what to do, I will almost always do the opposite, just to show you how utterly brilliant I am. It's not a positive character trait in any way, shape, or form. And it's much worse in my children, who seem to have caught this antiestablishment gene with vigor.

People like me, people who don't listen to advice, can be annoying, and they're often in need of rescuing. There are simply times (probably most times) when we don't have the whole picture, only a fragment of it, even though we think we do—and that's why God's laws are here for us, set in place for those who will hear. The operative word: WILL. I know it's pride, pure and simple. The Bible says that pride (haughty eyes—*ugh, the description!*) is one of those ugly sins, the kind that God hates. In fact, He uses it to describe the way he felt about hairy Esau.

Unwanted hair—I so get that. It's hateful! (I'm Italian.) And it is painful to remove, just like the sins we're not willing to part with. That's what pride is like to God: *unwanted body hair*. So why do I do it? Time and time again, why do I look up and say, "But wait! I think I have a better idea!"

The thing about unwanted hair (and sin) is that it comes back if you're not diligent. Sometimes I look back at those moments and see God there, shaking His head and saying to His angels, "Get out the hot wax and muslin strips. She's at it again."

So when you think you have way too much to do in a day, when there's just not enough time to drag out the wax and get serious about removing what shouldn't be there...that's the day to get on your knees. Do the work and remove the unwanted from your life.

Imagine the world we'd have if we all did as we were told. It would be a much nicer place to live. * KB

The Great Round Tuit

Thus, by their fruit you will recognize them.
MATTHEW 7:20

I took one of those silly online quizzes this morning, titled "Are You a Procrastinator?" I'll share my score…later.

For now, if I hope to avoid procrastination, I guess I'd better figure out what it is.

The first example of procrastination that comes to mind is Scarlett O'Hara, with her "I'll worry about that tomorrow" mantra. Remember how, as the movie begins, she's *working* toward arriving late to her neighbors' fancy shindig…because she was afraid that without the grand entrance, Ashley wouldn't notice her?

According to today's psychiatrists, that very type of fear causes more procrastination than anything else. We can't fail at something if we never get around to it, right?

The pros also say that procrastinators are made, not born. Which means that if we grew up watching our mothers and fathers trying to avoid getting things done, it's a pretty sure bet we'll walk that slow mile in their shoes.

We can blame distraction for our procrastination too.

And while we're at it, let's add perfectionism to the list, because, hey, it takes a lot of time to dot every *i* and cross every *t*!

Experts also claim that most of us don't take procrastination seriously enough. A little "there but by the grace of God," maybe?

If so, I'm in good company, since 20 percent of Americans call themselves procrastinators. We're late paying bills. Late to work. Late in sending birthday cards. Unfortunately,

that's when procrastination leads to prevarication. Can't just waltz in late for Thanksgiving dinner without a believable *lie* to explain things, now can we?

Now about my score: 32 out of 100 (the higher the number, the bigger the procrastinator) means I'm not much of a putter-offer after all. I have a feeling that if the good Lord had graded the test, He'd quickly point out that procrastination can be a major setback to my reaching the goals He has set for me. And He'd probably say that, with a score of 32, I have plenty of room for improvement. Because seriously? If I'm all wrapped up in finding ways to get *out* of doing His will, how will anyone recognize me as a child of God?

Which reminds me of the time when my eldest daughter was about three and she colored a picture of the family: Dad, Mom, herself, and little sister, the cat and dog…and a big round ball, smack in the middle, that she'd colored black.

"What's that?" I asked as I taped the drawing to the fridge.

"Why, a round tuit, of course."

"But…what's a round tuit?"

"It's what you and Daddy say *all the time.*"

And then I remembered the dozens of times my husband and I had said, "Not now, sweetie, but we'll get around to it soon, okay?"

Procrastination comes in many shapes and forms, and sometimes it comes in rainbow colors too. * *LL*

What Did I Miss?

*So we fix our eyes not on what is seen, but on what is unseen, since
what is seen is temporary, but what is unseen is eternal.*

2 CORINTHIANS 4:18

I'm a bookaholic, so one of my favorite things to do is to listen to recorded versions of novels while I drive. I got into the habit after reading Stephen King's *On Writing*. He encourages novelists to read as much fiction as possible, and he says a large percentage of his own reading happens while he travels or jogs, thanks to recorded books. I'm totally onboard with that now, and I no longer mind long drives or traffic jams (not much, anyway), because I know I'll get deep into the world of the novel while I'm on the road.

Although I've never found it difficult to pay attention to my driving while I listen, I have noticed on occasion that my mind will wander from the story. When that happens, I'm forced to rewind and refocus. When I do that, I'm often shocked at how much storyline I missed. It passed me by while I drove and thought about my grocery list or something minor that happened recently or even some tangent triggered by something the book "said."

The other day, the heroine wrote a letter to a soldier who'd said he wanted to marry her, but she didn't hear back from him. Before I realized it, my mind had trailed off to the movie I watched several nights prior, *The Notebook*, because of the hidden-letters facet of that story, which made me think about the star, Ryan Gosling. By the time I finished remembering the crime drama he had made with Sir Anthony Hopkins, my recorded book had moved far into the heroine's story, even referring to people whose introductions I had missed.

Now, there was nothing wrong with my mental wanderings. They were temporary, harmless bits of cerebral fluff. And I still had the book 132 on disc and was able to backtrack and absorb what was permanently etched there. But it occurred to me that I sometimes do the same thing on a spiritual level.

My heavenly Father is so gracious, He makes himself available to me twenty-four hours a day. Whenever I think of Him and His love and guidance and promises, or when I go to Him with praises and petitions, He's there for me, despite everything He has on His plate. While the things of this world will come and go, He'll *always* be there for me. Is that why I sometimes take my mind off Him for long stretches of time?

Is that why I give inordinate attention to what is seen—what is worldly—and sometimes far too little of my attention to what is eternal? Sometimes I catch myself getting all wrapped up in something that honestly doesn't matter in the grand, eternal scheme of things. Sometimes I need to stop, rewind, and refocus—on Him. * *TP*

A Life of Thankfulness

Give thanks unto the LORD; for he is good.

PSALM 106:1 KJV

As the expression goes, I turned thirty-six this year. *Turned*, like a leaf turns colors, like one turns the pages of a book or turns down a new road. The road out of my thirties is one I'd like to take slowly, but as someone rather rudely reminded me, "Thirty-six rounds off to forty." I can already see forty around the bend, and even fifty and sixty don't appear too far away.

This "turning" has been a time of reflection for me. Route thirty-six has many good places to stop and ponder over the years of my life and to consider what they have meant, what my life has been. This pondering has been a most rewarding experience.

Of course, when I look in the mirror there is the realization that I don't look just the same as I did in my twenties, and when I play with my children at the park I see that even my relatively young body is not as young as it once was. (I got stuck on the monkey bars and fell flat when I tried to jump out of a swing.) These things are undeniable. But are they real losses at age thirty-six? No. My seventy-two-year-old aunt would laugh me to shame at any other answer.

Naturally, taking another honest look—a little deeper—reveals a few regrets. Have I made all of the best choices? Spent all of my time wisely and with the most enriching or worthy people? No. Have I gone to all the right places? Said all the right things? Have I always given my utmost to and for the God I love? No, no, no. Sadly but truly, no. Again, these facts are unfortunate and as undeniable as the crow's feet I see in the mirror.

However, as I walk down this new road called thirty-six, the view I see behind me is overwhelmingly beautiful. Marred though the landscape may be with what are thankfully few regrets, it is a breathtaking sight. Pausing, pondering, its loveliness envelops me, fills me, warms me, rises up in me, and catches like a sob in my throat.

I see all the people who have shared my journey…my parents, my brother, my grandparents, and other family. Their faces beam at me as I look back. A fresh-faced couple with newborn me as their prize, a baby brother to cuddle and love, a man in a straw hat with pride glowing in his big brown eyes, a woman who made the best homemade rolls ever.

I see others who loved me and helped me find the way… school teachers, Sunday school teachers, music teachers, friends. College professors, my husband and babies, my inlaws, colleagues at work. These are the ones who shine like stars on the horizon of my life. They are the gleaming, resounding answers to the questions of what my journey has been. They rise above any regrets I have and soar like eagles on the wings of joy.

I am grateful for the life I've lived so far. It has not been perfect—but it has been a blessed, wonderful, extraordinary life. The experiences afforded, lessons learned, goals accomplished, and most of all the relationship with God and others, can only be defined as abundant. The theme of my thirty-sixth year, and I pray to the end of my road here on earth, is thankfulness. * *GF*

First Things First

Finish your outdoor work and get your fields ready; after that, build your house.
PROVERBS 24:27

I've been dreaming of owning my own home for a very long time. I came close when I was living in California, but when I made the move to Florida and started over, it looked like a faraway dream that might never come to fruition.

I muddled through a disheartening season where it seemed like everyone I knew went house-hunting and ended up buying something. I made offers on three different homes and someone beat me to the punch every time. It bordered on the ridiculous when a longtime friend phoned to tell me that her brother had purchased a home *for her.*

Finding a home of my own finally wrangled my full focus: I researched the best mortgage brokers; talked to Realtors; looked into lenders and loans for first-time buyers; Googled neighborhoods within a fifteen-mile radius and explored them thoroughly.

During that period, I also sold a couple more books and accepted a promotion at my day job. The added income lined my fledgling savings account, earmarked "Future Home." Meanwhile, I became so tired of the whole "future" concept that some nights I would cry while praying and ask the Lord why it was taking so long to have what every other adult in America seemed to have acquired long ago.

And then one day I found it: a sunny little yellow house in a great neighborhood just a few minutes from my office. When I phoned my Realtor, I learned that the homeowners were facing personal issues and wanted to move as soon as possible. The broker found me a fantastic loan where I wouldn't have to put down any money at all; in fact, at closing, I came away with a check! The movers charged me less than they quoted. I came across a handyman so reasonable and fair that a move-in-ready home welcomed me within a week of closing. And the icing on the cake? I slid in under the velvet rope with eligibility for the federal tax credit for first-time buyers just a couple of weeks before the offer expired.

I'm often asked if I'm sorry I had to wait such a long time. My reply: "Are you joking?"

In the spirit of the Scripture that says to prepare your life first and then build your home, I am confident, humbled, and thankful. When I walk through my house early in the morning or sit and look out the window just before sunset, I am inspired *every time* to thank the Lord for holding up the works. My heart's desire rolled out before me like a choreographed production with a very happy ending. * *SDB*

This One Is for Keeps

And so after waiting patiently, Abraham received what was promised.

HEBREWS 6:15

When my son was in grade school I was big on volunteering with any school- or church-sponsored activity in which he participated. I hadn't been able to stay at home from work when my daughter was little, so I wanted to take advantage of the opportunity to be a more obvious presence in my boy's life while I could.

So it was I found myself herding a large number of fifth graders during a breakout session at Vacation Bible School. All week the kids had been taking part in crafts that spelled out something wonderful about Jesus and salvation. Every morning my group and a couple hundred other kids enjoyed raucous, funny, uplifting songs about the Lord. Even the obstacle-course-type activities held some kind of symbolism about God and the redemptive sacrifice of His beloved Son.

It was salvation, all morning, every morning, for five days. And now, as we neared the end of the week, we teachers were afforded the opportunity to simply talk with our charges and see if they had any questions or had the desire to turn their hearts over to the Lord.

Since I had the oldest group—and since most of them had been attending my church since infancy—there weren't many kids in the group who hadn't already taken that big step into eternity. My job was simple.

But I felt a little tweaking in my mind and asked the group, "Are there any of you who worry about losing your salvation?"

I was floored by the number of hands that went up. It broke my heart.

Maybe it had something to do with the fact that sometimes parents' well-meaning promises end up broken for one unfortunate reason or another. Maybe it was because of the unfathomable nature of salvation and how Christ's sacrifice makes it possible; perhaps that's hard for kids to fully grasp. Or maybe those kids who raised their hands simply hadn't been assured enough that God doesn't break His promises, that by His nature He is *unable* to break His promises.

The "patient waiting" in today's verse refers to the twenty-five-plus years Abraham waited for a son after God promised him he would have one. Yes, Abraham slipped in his patience, which resulted in Ishmael's birth. Still, God's promise was fulfilled.

God's promises are forever. None of us means to lie by breaking our promises, but that's essentially what we do. God doesn't lie. He can't.

I assured those kids that their salvation was there to stay. God had made a promise to them—to all of us—that, if we made the decision to accept salvation as a free gift from Christ, we would *never* lose that salvation. "We're saved," I told them, "not because of what we do, but because of what He did. And that's a promise that will never change." * *TP*

Whether Vain

As God's coworkers we urge you not to receive God's grace in vain.

2 CORINTHIANS 6:1

Something in me rattled like a rock in the clothes dryer when I heard that a school system several states away had decided to eliminate cursive writing from its curriculum. The reason?

"Our students' time can be better spent learning computer skills rather than cursive."

It's not that I'd argue the point. But do I want to walk into a museum and hear the curator say, "And in this exhibit, a quaint and at one time artistic form of written communication called *cursive*. In its declining years, it served a purpose for signatures until the discovery that a squiggly line would work just as well. A real find for our museum, in this glass case is a rare, perfectly preserved antiquity—a handwritten note."

My fingers spend an inordinate amount of time on a computer keyboard and very little gripping a pen or pencil. But I remember learning cursive in school. The rhythm. The angles. The loops and swirls and careful placement of the dot above an *i* and the cross member of a lowercase *t*.

One of my most cursive-conscious teachers (some would call her obsessed) seemed determined to create a room of students with identical signatures. She insisted we purchase special pens that forced us to conform to her idea of the ideal grip. I wonder how she'd feel about people who talk with their thumbs? *R u cmg 2 prty? C u.*

What was I thinking when creating that texting example? No one uses capital letters anymore.

In her classroom, Mrs. Strictandproudofit's students learned new vocabulary words every week. Important words like *omnibus. Phrontistery. Logorrhea.*

We also were required to keep one notebook of "Homonyms" and another for "Palindromes." I capitalized those two titles because they were written in cursive on the front covers of our notebooks. Fascinating stuff. No, really, it was…for word nerds like me.

I have that teacher to thank for helping me create future magazine article, book, and devotional titles using homonyms. *The Rain of the King. Knot on My Watch. Be Stings.*

Subtle regional differences in the way we pronounce words open new possibilities. *Weather vane. Weather vain. Weather vein. Whether vain.*

A few months ago, I took a serious look at a Scripture verse I'd skimmed past. "We urge you not to receive God's grace in vain." A "whether vain" verse.

What does it mean to receive God's grace in vain? To waste it?

I know some people like that. They heard about the grace God offers through His Son Jesus, expressed momentary appreciation—at an altar, kneeling beside their bed, bent over a Bible—but then abused that gift of grace. Some neglected to feed their faith and it starved to death. Some neglected to protect it and it was battered by winds of circumstance. Some ignored it, thinking it was fine for that moment in time but not for the long haul.

The price was the same for Jesus no matter how the gift was handled later. Lord, I want to treat it with the respect and honor it deserves. * CR

Sharing Blessings

*The generous will themselves be blessed,
for they share their food with the poor.*

PROVERBS 22:9

It's been a few decades since I worked in Washington, DC, and there are so many things about being in the city that I miss. I truly love my current status, which enables me to work from home sweet home, but I also loved the active, noisy, bustling environment inherent in working "a good job in the city," as Tina Turner would say.

I'm sure the situation is worse today than it was twenty years ago, but one of the constants of my time in the city was the appearance of homeless people on the streets. Workers dashed from place to place and became jaded to the sight and smell of scraggly men wearing cocoons of dingy gray blankets, huddling over grates in the sidewalk, seeking warmth. On occasion, the homeless panhandle. As often as not, though, they simply sit there, thinking who knows what. Many are mentally challenged, many are addicts, all are a little scary at first and sad always.

Because of the "scary" part, I tended to be one of those people rushing by. I was busy, and I was usually only on the street to grab some lunch to take back to the office. One weekend, though, I worked overtime with a coworker. We got to the office early and neither of us had had breakfast, so we crossed the street to pick up some MacSomethings. We walked past the obligatory homeless man on the way, and neither of us said anything about that.

But when my friend ordered her breakfast, she ordered a second one as well. She answered my teasing by saying, "Oh, no, this is for the man outside." I was immediately convicted. That thought had never occurred to me. I'd always been cautioned not to give money to the homeless, because chances were likely they'd spend it on whatever substance they were addicted to, so I was furthering their demise. But this was genius.

My friend allowed me to split the cost of the man's breakfast, and I couldn't believe how joyful it felt to be a tiny part of making his day just a little less horrible.

The catch was that I wasn't always on the way to buying food when I passed homeless people. Finally, the Lord convicted me further: it's really not my business what a poor man does with what I give him. That's between him and God.

So I developed the habit of carrying a few dollars in my pocket whenever I left the office. Again, I felt immediate and amazing joy with the simple gesture of handing a bill or two to someone, whether he asked for it or not, and saying "God bless you." When someone from the office accompanied me, my action often sparked conversations about charity, the homeless, and God. I don't know how many people the Lord touched through those conversations, but they were conversations we wouldn't have had if I hadn't given away a few measly dollars. And my actions came about from my coworker's sharing food with the poor. Blessings grow like that. * *TP*

Act Now!

Dear children, let us not love with words or tongue,
but with actions and in truth.

1 JOHN 3:18

This verse reminds us that God's action, God's truth, is always given as a side dish to love.

A famous Christian recently came out and said she was leaving the church. Not Christianity, not Jesus, but the church. She said she didn't fit in and couldn't find a connection with God's people. After a heated argument among a group of Christians, she was cast off, dismissed, as not a real believer. Someone who denied God's commands could not be a Christian.

What bothered me about this conversation was that it was so easy for a group of solid Christians to cast off this person, though she was still a young Christian. For her, the church hadn't been a warm place. I wonder how many have that same truth…and yet we condemn them, as if there's no truth in their statements. But if we're honest with ourselves, have we welcomed everyone who walks through our church doors? Have we made it a point to *make* everyone welcome there, rather than to *say* that everyone is welcome there?

What ended up being a scriptural argument that ended in self-satisfaction did not (to me, anyway) take into account that a woman who claimed to love Jesus and called Him her Savior had been summarily shut out because she had not lived up to their ideals of a Christian. If that were my son or daughter, could I so easily dismiss them? Could I decide that their walk with the Lord was over because they'd broken this "rule"?

Christ laid down His life for her…for me. Don't we owe it to Jesus to look into the matter within our own hearts before we condemn another? Where this woman's faith is, I can't be sure—it's not for me to know. Those who obey His commands live in Him and He in them. I don't know about you, but there are times during each and every day when I couldn't claim this. It's why I continually struggle to listen to that still, small voice even when it feels overwhelmingly impossible.

To be famous while becoming a Christian must be incredibly difficult. I remember all the idiotic things I said in my youthful zeal of becoming a Christian. What would it be like to have all that recorded for YouTube history?

Before you decide someone else's walk, will you take the time to look at your own? Will you treat that person with love and not hate—which, by the way, God calls murder, and He goes on to say that no murderer has eternal life in Him (1 John 3:15). It's not a small matter. * *KB*

Are We There Yet?

Evildoers do not understand what is right, but those who seek the LORD understand it fully.

PROVERBS 28:5

You know that old adage about there being a joy in the journey? I've never really been a fan of the journey, myself. I'm the girl who wants to take the expressway rather than the side streets. Even if the scenery is staggering, I almost always want to get to my destination as quickly as possible. I'm known for being impulsive, for making decisions quickly. But since it's in our weaknesses that God becomes strong, it is no surprise that, through testing my general impatience, the Lord has presented the greatest teachable moments of my life.

"It's not about the destination," my friend Carol used to tell me. "It's about the journey along the way."

I don't think I realized how wise her words really were. In fact, I remember thinking at the time that she should write greeting cards. But despite the fact that God does sometimes work suddenly, immediately, or instantly, He most often delivers the deepest truths through a process— a series of twists and turns, mountaintops and deep valleys that lead—often slowly—to the end result.

I've had more than a few broken hearts in my life, and I suppose there was a time when I wished I could erase every instance of a bad relationship or poor choice. One particular person comes immediately to mind. He was that one guy—the one in every woman's life—where I lost sight of myself in his shadow, where I behaved in ways I never could have imagined. It took me several years of heartache and craziness, praying for God to transform him, before I finally saw the light. God wasn't going to change him because he didn't want to be changed. At last, I understood the role that free will plays in the realities of life.

I'm smarter about relationships because of him. I haven't had my heart broken again, at least not to that degree. I can spot a lie more easily now, and I'm much quicker to listen to that still, small voice when it tells me to run like the wind. And the thing is…none of those lessons would have been learned without *Him*.

Whether a wound to the heart, disease to the body, or agony of the mind, it's always a bit of a journey toward ultimate healing, and God's grace is most certainly always involved. How else would we bear the process; how else could we make it through to the end where the lesson is finally counted as learned?

Okay, so I, Sandie Bricker, do hereby admit that there really is a joy to the journey. Maybe it's even more about the journey than about the destination. I don't like it, just to be clear. But I have at least learned something. * *SDB*

Mercy Me!

Surely your goodness and love will follow me all the days of my life,
and I will dwell in the house of the LORD forever.

PSALM 23:6

Every now and then, when I'm home alone or wandering the house in the middle of the night, I get that creepy-crawly, "somebody's following me" sensation. Especially when climbing stairs. (When I use the phrase "tuck and run," you can bet I know what I'm talking about!)

The other day, in a mad rush to outrun the…what*ever* it was…I thought of my friend's daughter, recently diagnosed with SAD (Seasonal Affective Disorder). Poor Barbie! Rainy days really get the poor kid down. As part of her treatment, Barbie's mom had to buy a goose-necked lamp and a pricey bulb that mimics sunlight. Yet even when coupled with psychotherapy and medication, cloudy weather and the creepy-crawlies go hand in hand for Barbie.

By contrast, I often joke that I squint because, like Clint Eastwood, I'm sensitive to bright light. See, I really *like* the hush that falls over the land at night, wrapping around me like a soft shadow. Then why, you ask, do I try to outrun it?

Maybe for the same reason so many of us have trouble knowing when to say "The End." Songwriters, poets, authors—we all face this little life dilemma from time to time: Barbie, when the sun hides behind the clouds; high-school sweethearts, when one has outgrown the other; me, when I'm alone, on the stairs, in the darkened house.

It hasn't been all that long since my full-blooded Italian aunt faced the end of her life. Just weeks after she'd blown out the candles on her seventieth birthday cake, the doctors said "terminal." Chemo, radiation, pills, they insisted, would give her a year or so to get her affairs in order.

"Thanks to my lawyer, my accountant, and my financial advisor," she announced, "my affairs couldn't *be* in better order. And," she went on to say, "I've already hired the harpist who'll pluck out 'Amazing Grace' at the funeral and the piper who'll play my favorite Irish ballads at the 'after dinner.'"

Friends and family rallied round, trying to change her mind. "We'll miss you!" they insisted, and "You've got to fight this!" "God will heal you," they cried, "if only you ask Him to."

Her face lit up with the joy of acceptance as she drew them close. "I won't become one of those people who live like they're being chased by the shadow of death. I've lived a good, long life, and soon, I'll live for eternity in paradise!"

So next time I'm alone, on the stairs, in the dark, and that "somebody's following me" sensation tempts me to tuck and run, I'll face and embrace it and call it by name:

Dear, sweet Mercy, my 100 percent Italian auntie. * *LL*

When We Think No One Is Watching

Even small children are known by their actions, so is their conduct really pure and upright?

PROVERBS 20:11

My adult daughter is my best friend and someone I hold in great admiration. But for the first ten years of her life, she didn't have the benefit of parents who followed Christ and His teachings. When I gave my heart to the Lord, it wasn't clear to my ten-year-old girl that she should do the same. As a matter of fact, it was another eight years before she made that decision.

As a consequence of my early negligence, we had some catching up to do in the discipline-and-teaching department. Although my daughter always had a sweet heart, she gave me a run for my money during her tween and teen years. I tried to be a good example of honest living for her, but I was working against some mighty powerful influences in her life, and she was forever getting into trouble. Sometimes I wondered how so many other parents managed to get their kids to follow the rules. It seemed as if my efforts were futile.

With more than a small degree of trepidation, I allowed her to participate in a two-week foreign exchange program through her high school when she was seventeen. During the trip she lived with a family in Scotland, as did about twenty of her classmates. It wasn't until they returned home that we parents heard about some trouble stirred up across the pond. I learned that my girl and her best friend—or as I called her, her partner in crime—were the only two students who didn't get drunk and carouse around the village, bringing shame upon themselves, their school, and their parents. Every student but my daughter and her partner in crime were suspended from school for a week once they returned to the States.

My daughter's theory was that all of the other students went as wild as they truly were as soon as they were free from their parents' close watch. That could have explained their bad behavior, but it didn't explain my daughter's good behavior (not that I was complaining). As that year progressed, I saw other changes in the choices my daughter made. It didn't all happen at once, but eventually her conduct reflected more than maturity. It reflected a changing heart.

Maybe my efforts weren't so futile after all. And certainly God wasn't ignoring what was going on.

Despite the seemingly upright behavior of my daughter's classmates while they were home and strictly supervised, they became infamous—for a while, at least—because of their unruly actions when left to their actual lack of self-discipline. While I feared my daughter would never clean up her act, she was actually learning through consequences how best to live once she was on her own.

We can profess to be pure and upright, but what do our actions say? * *TP*

An Elephant Never Forgets!

Brethren, I do not count myself to have apprehended; but one thing I do,
forgetting those things which are behind and reaching forward to those things which are ahead,
I press toward the goal for the prize of the upward call of God in Christ Jesus.

PHILIPPIANS 3:13–14 NKJV

Michael was just about the cutest boy I'd ever seen. He had dark, floppy, Hugh Grant kind of hair that still does me in to this day…and crystal-blue eyes that peered right through the window to my soul. The moment I laid eyes on him, I fell in love.

Fifteen-year-old kind of love, anyway.

And the worst part was…he was the boyfriend of one of my closest friends. I saw them together at dances and parties and barbecues. It was enough to shatter my teenage heart into a million tiny pieces.

One night at a swim party, Michael brought me a glass of soda. Just as he handed it to me, he leaned in and kissed me. My heart soared, my knees grew weak, and my equilibrium fell right over. And then I looked up to find my friend, his girlfriend, standing in the doorway and watching us in horror.

She never spoke to me again after that incident. When I ran into her again ten years later, after she was married with two children, it turned out that she still wasn't speaking to me.

"It's kind of water under the bridge, isn't it?" I asked, trying to get her to communicate with me. "Neither one of us ended up with Michael, and we were just teenagers anyway."

"An elephant never forgets," she finally said.

"But…you're not…an elephant," I replied.

It didn't matter that her nose was small and upturned and not shaped like a trunk. She turned on her heel, grabbed her daughter's hand, and marched out of the shop with that nose right up in the air—and without another word to me.

It just broke my heart that something done out of teen-aged ignorance had pierced my old friend so deeply that she'd been carrying it with her all those years. I thought about calling her, urging her to listen to reason, but something within me warned against it. Going forward is almost always the better choice, even if someone else seems stuck in the past. * SDB

A Life of Light

Godliness with contentment is great gain.

1 TIMOTHY 6:6 KJV

This is the story of my friend Charlene Lessin in her own words.

I grew up on a farm in a small community in Minnesota, where I had a wonderful childhood. My parents were committed Christians who planted Bible truths into my life. I was a "good girl" who knew a lot about the Lord, but I'd never come to know Him personally.

When classes began my first year of college, I would go to one class and hear, "Jesus loves you. He not only loves the world, but He loves you." I knew He had died for the world, but I began to understand more and more His love for me personally! In another class, the teacher would say, "Being good is not enough; you need Jesus."

One day I heard someone read the Bible verse that says all of our righteousness is as filthy rags (Isaiah 64:6). I realized that all of my efforts to *be* good and to *do* good could not save me and could not impress God for my salvation. Shortly after hearing that verse, during one of our classes, I felt the guilt of sin heavy within me.

I had experienced a tug at my heart similar to this while I was in high school. My dad took me to a Billy Graham film geared for young people. As I heard parts of the story and singing, I sensed deep within that what I needed was what the film was sharing about the gospel of Jesus. But I did not respond at that time. Now I knew clearly, without a doubt, what I needed to do to get rid of the nagging fears and guilt of sin. All my trying to be good was not enough. I was a sinner, and I needed Jesus.

By this time I had become part of a girls' trio, and we sang at a Sunday night service. After the sermon that night, the preacher asked if anyone had a need and would like prayer. I knew what I had to do. I went to the front. I wept, knowing I was a sinner, and I repented of my sin and cried to the Lord to save me and to come into my heart and life.

In that moment it was like a ton of bricks fell off my shoulders, and I knew that Jesus had accepted me and come into my life! All the songs that I had sung about Jesus's love for me throughout my childhood became very real in that moment. I had a lot to learn in my new walk, but I had such peace and joy, knowing for sure that I was right with God.

How could it happen that this girl who was raised in such a good home, with wonderful parents and raised in church, did not understand these things earlier? I don't know, except I do know that whoever we are, black is black, and I was in the blackness.

I remember being a young teenager lying on my bed and trying to pray to God, but my words bounced back to me like the ceiling was made of thick iron. I remember going to the pasture to fetch the cows for milking one day and looking up into the sky, wondering if God knew I existed. I felt sure He didn't!

Everybody else had a purpose, but I didn't. God knew everyone else, but maybe He didn't know me.

To answer my earlier question in all honesty, I would have to say it was no one's fault but mine that I didn't understand. I was inwardly a proud person, and I couldn't clearly hear the Lord's voice for many years. It was not that I had robbed a bank to realize this, but the Lord showed me that my own way, my pride and my selfishness, kept me from knowing Him.

I thank the Lord over and over that He revealed to my blind eyes my need and He was the answer! I have learned through the years that even though people loved me, there was a need for God's love in my heart and life, and only He could fill that with Himself. Religion can't fill it; traditions can't fill it; good works can't fill it. Only Jesus can fill it.

Wow, what a joy to be able to walk around each day with that load of bricks gone! To walk each day in the Light!
* *GF*

Taking It to the Top

*If my people who are called by My name will humble themselves,
and pray and seek My face, and turn from their wicked ways,
then I will hear from heaven, and will forgive their sin and heal their land.*

2 CHRONICLES 7:14 NKJV

Last week I kissed my twenty-seven-year-old son good-bye. I won't see him for a whole year. He and his wife both serve in the Army National Guard. They boarded a plane for Texas. From there they'll ship off to Iraq.

My mother's heart is breaking. This is Brian's second tour overseas.

War. I hate it. In fact, I wouldn't allow my sons to play with guns and GI Joe action figures when they were little boys. The violence of war runs against the grain of my very nature. But here's my "baby," leaving the country with the Army National Guard.

My mother's heart breaks just a little more, although I'm the first to declare that our troops are heroes and I do respect what they're doing overseas. I'm a supporter of the United States military. It might seem oxymoronic; however, somehow I've been able to separate and rationalize. What's more, I call myself a patriot even though I still buy into that old 1960s saying that "war is not healthy for children and other living things." Perhaps you could say I'm for it while being against it.

Oh, brother! Now I sound like a politician!

Okay, well, I'll admit there are things in the political arena that I feel strongly about, but I'm not a political activist, and yet God calls me to speak out against that which I feel is unjust. However, He doesn't lead me, personally, to protest and carry picket signs, although He might lead others to do so. No, the Lord calls me to activism on my knees. God says if I humble myself and pray and seek His face, He will hear me from heaven and heal my land.

You know, much can be accomplished when we bow the knee. Abraham pleaded with the Lord to spare his nephew Lot's life before God destroyed Sodom and Gomorrah. God heard Abraham's prayer and sent His angels to rescue Lot (Genesis 19).

Jesus Himself tells of how God can be persuaded by persistent prayer. He said we should pray and not lose heart; God will bring about justice (Luke 18).

So what's troubling you today? Global issues? Our country's state of affairs? A family crisis? Whatever it is, the Lord is waiting for you—and for me—to get on our knees, seek His face, and pray. * *AKB*

When She Spoke, We Listened

Reckless words pierce like a sword, but the tongue of the wise brings healing.

PROVERBS 12:18

Someone once said, "The only difference between you now and you five years from now is the books you read and the people you meet."

No doubt about it, other people influence us and we influence other people—in good *and* bad ways. The people who come to mind first for me when thinking of influencers are teachers.

We've all had our share of good and bad teachers, though maybe we judge the good and the bad of it by different criteria—she didn't teach well, she yelled all the time, and so on.

I had a third-grade teacher whom I well remember to this day. And let me just say for the record, I'm not yet on Social Security, but I am past menopause, just so you know. In other words, *third grade* was a long *time* ago.

The thing that struck me most about Mrs. Burton, aka *Teacher Extraordinaire*, was her soft voice. I don't ever remember her raising her voice. There were days when we tested her patience, I'm sure. Maybe, if I tried real hard, I could remember a frown or two when we were a tad too energetic. But I never, ever remember her raising her voice.

Anytime she walked past my desk, she may as well have been Mother Teresa. Yes, I thought that much of her. She was my hero. I loved just being around her because she was kind and gentle. Her presence brought comfort and inner happiness to me.

There could have been any number of reasons for her soft voice, of course. A yearlong bout with laryngitis. A determination to set an example so we would keep our voices down. But somehow my little third-grade brain knew it was much more than that.

Turns out, I was right.

Later, when I reached high school, I visited a church with my friend…and who do you suppose was a regular member? That's right, Mrs. Burton. No wonder I'd sensed something extra special about her. It was her love for the Lord that shone through and opened the eyes of this third grader to a tenderness I'd rarely seen in others. Her gentle, encouraging words impacted my life in ways I can hardly quantify. Without even knowing it, she challenged me to make a difference with my words in my corner of the world.

How about you? At day's end, if you played back the words you used on any given day, would they be words that build up or tear down? Let's pray that God will use our words to bring healing and encouragement in the heart of another today. * *DH*

Change of Heart

My heart is changed within me; all my compassion is aroused.

HOSEA 11:8

I had a change of heart.

My girlfriend and I sat at a local restaurant sipping iced tea and waiting for our taco salads. Conversation never waned between the two of us when we met for lunch. Happy talk. Intriguing ideas. Always a celebration of what the Lord had been doing in our lives lately.

As we chatted, a young family entered the restaurant. I watched them cross the room: a too-young mom, a too-young dad (I wondered if they were married), two toddlers, and an infant. Writers are trained to be observant, so I didn't for a minute think myself judgmental in noticing that their clothes were probably from the thrift shop's clearance rack. They took a table near our booth. I could watch without staring.

They sat the toddlers in booster seats and plopped the baby into a high chair.

Three children already. At their age.

The dad wore ratty jeans and an almost-white T-shirt with…with a pack of cigarettes rolled into the sleeve.

I caught myself before a *tsk* escaped my mouth. Maybe it was a product of that writer-imagination thing, but I pictured those poor babies sucking secondhand cigarette smoke into their fragile little lungs. And could the parents afford better shoes for those children if Dad quit the habit? What other bad habits threatened their family's ability to pay their bills? Did he even have a job?

The waitress took their order while I reined my attention to the discussion around my own table.

But then, the young dad reached for the pack in his sleeve. Right there in the restaurant! I didn't realize I even had any ire, but there it was, popping out as I watched him pull the pack free from his T-shirt sleeve.

A pack of crayons.

He flipped the kids' paper placemats over to the blank side and set a handful of crayons before each of his toddler daughters. Then he picked a marine-blue crayon and began to color a corner of one daughter's sky.

I was so wrong about him. All the ill feelings I'd had about that young man turned into compassion for him and appreciation for a dad who colored with his girls, a dad who told stories, who loved them, who got involved in child care, and who smiled at their mother while he did so.

My compassion kicked in, tardy and finicky as it was, when I saw the man doing something right.

Where would I be if the Lord acted the way I did? God's compassion for me is constant, not fickle, and kicks in even when my choices turn His stomach.

The Hosea verse that sparked these thoughts says, "All my compassion is aroused" in context with His people consistently choosing to ignore what He told them and reject what He offered. Even *then* His compassion is stirred. Unlike mine.

Remembering that day in the restaurant humbles me. A pack of crayons showed me how far I have to go in understanding what it means to live a life of grace. * *CR*

My Cross to Bear?

Therefore, in order to keep me from becoming conceited, I was given a thorn in my flesh,
a messenger of Satan, to torment me. Three times I pleaded with the Lord to take it away from me.
But he said to me, "My grace is sufficient for you, for my power is made perfect in weakness."

2 CORINTHIANS 12:7–9

I was almost ten pounds when I was born (so sorry, Mom). By the third grade, I'd developed a weight problem, and I've been struggling with it ever since. I've tried every diet known to mankind, every pill, juice, shake, bar, vitamin, and injection.... I've bought treadmills, bicycles, thigh masters, butt masters, balance balls, weights, bands, and workout DVDs.... I've talked to therapists, priests, reverends, personal trainers, nutrition experts, and hypnotists. At the age of fifty-*cough*-years-old, I am still overweight. What's up with that?!

If I had a nickel for every prayer in which I'd pleaded with the Lord to show me, lead me, or just miraculously heal me, I would be writing this from that Pacific Ocean beach house I dream about so frequently! The thing that's really strange to me about this lifelong struggle is that I'm a true believer. I have faith for things that other people laugh off. I believe in the promises of God, and I call upon them often. So why is this *one issue* so unattainable?

Someone I love and respect very much told me something not so long ago that's really stayed with me. "You know, Sandie, you have to stop second-guessing God's will. All you can do is the best you can. Beyond that, you have to remember that everything about you was planned before you were even a twinkle in your birth dad's eye. Nothing about you is an accident. You were created with a specific purpose, and what you consider to be your greatest weakness could turn out to be the thing that God uses to drive you forward."

That night, I received a message with today's Scripture verse typed into the body of the e-mail. Nothing else, just the verse, and it really made me take a serious look over my life and the many successes and failures I've had with my weight. Although I'm certainly not willing to accept defeat, I do perceive a certain wisdom in what my friend had to say.

I still have a clear vision of myself in skinny jeans and stiletto boots one day (Hey! Don't judge. I've been carrying this picture since the eleventh grade). And I'm not letting it go until about twenty minutes after I take my final breath. But if I don't manage to attain it before then, there are three things I know for certain: (1) His grace is sufficient for me; (2) in my weakness, He becomes even stronger; and (3) the grapefruit diet wasn't meant to be followed for more than a week. It does unpleasant things to the digestive system beyond that. I'm just sayin'. * *SDB*

Singles Only!

There is surely a future hope for you, and your hope will not be cut off.
PROVERBS 23:18

I have a friend whose husband is sharp and hardworking, who gave his all for the company for which he used to work. He loved his job, and it showed in his dedication to an organization that has since grown to be a huge conglomerate.

There was one catch, though. The founder was relatively young, single, and highly successful, which may have influenced corporate policy. Social events, like company-sponsored trips to Hawaii and elaborate company dinners, while designed purely for pleasure rather than business, were *verboten* for spouses. Married employees were expected to attend as singles at all events.

I would imagine that every one of us knows someone who has been touched by an illicit workplace "romance." They come about strictly as a result of men and women working long hours in close proximity and letting their guards down. Imagine the additional stress in company-sponsored social interaction—sometimes involving several consecutive days of celebrating, vacationing, most assuredly drinking, all away from spouses. Plenty of questionable hijinks went on, as one would imagine. Yes, marriages endure and survive, but would you want yours to have to suffer that temptation?

My friend's husband tended to go along with most of the events, but never comfortably. He was less enthused than others, and in some rare instances, he didn't attend at all.

He probably would have seen a more rapid rise within the company had he been a more willing player, but he had his wife and children in mind, and sometimes he simply had to risk his political corporate status in order to uphold honor for his family and his Christian principle.

Today's verse in Proverbs is surrounded by other verses about why one might envy others who seem to do brilliantly well, even though they don't give thought to God or His tenets. We can all fall prey to that kind of envy, especially if we notice the success of nonbelieving people in the same field we're in: *Oh, sure, it's easy for her to do that well! She caters to all the worldly {employers, clients, readers, enterprises}.*

Maybe so, but God's Word, above, encourages us by turning our thoughts to future hope. Our hope will not be severed simply because others seem to do so well.

There may be only so many corporate positions to fill, so many awards to win, so many promotions to achieve, or so many readers to gain, but the promises God has in mind specifically for me will be fulfilled regardless of what goes on around me. My part in that plan is to remain hopeful and trust Him to bring about everything that must happen to make that hope a reality.

My friend's husband eventually took a position at another corporation. Better pay, family-friendly, and less stressful. This hope-and-promise stuff is for real! * *TP*

Busy, Busy, Busy

In the beginning God created the heavens and the earth.

GENESIS 1:1

I have so much to do today," I whined to my husband one morning. "I have three loads of laundry to wash, dry, and fold. Then I have to write at least one chapter, or I won't make my deadline, and I have to write an article."

"Yeah, I'm busy too." My husband paused for a couple of seconds by the door then glanced at his watch. "I have a client coming in first thing this morning, and I have to prepare for him. But I have a feeling I'm forgetting something." He nodded toward a file he'd placed on the kitchen island. "Oh, there it is. Would you mind getting that for me? My hands are full."

I grabbed his file and followed him out to his car. After he got situated with his files, coffee, and lunch bag, he headed off to work while I went inside to toss some clothes into the washing machine before sitting down at my computer.

Wally and I have become so busy with all our "work," we often feel like we're forgetting something. Busy, busy, busy. That night, we sat down to eat dinner in silence, too exhausted to talk.

As I consider the things I do each day and how much importance I place on each little task, I realize it's nothing compared to what God did in one single day. God created the heavens and the earth in the time it took me to write a chapter of a book and do laundry. If I skipped laundry that day, the worst thing that would have happened is we'd have to wear clothes stuck in the back of the drawer. Imagine what would have happened if God had skipped creating either heaven or earth. I obviously wouldn't be worried about laundry, would I?

If we held up our tasks next to what God has done for us, we'd always feel insignificant, but He doesn't see it that way. He knows each of us, and we're all important to him. Our laundry? Not so much. Finishing a chapter of a book? Nah. But our souls matter. God's power is humongous. He prepared a place for us to live and learn about Him. He gave us the work we do, but the stress we feel is self-imposed. I can only imagine how Wally and I would freak out if we were assigned God's to-do list. *Create heavens—check. Create earth—check.* By the time we finished with that, we'd have to live in total darkness for a very long time before we summoned the energy to move on to creating light. * *DM*

A Life of Childlikeness

Now faith is the substance of things hoped for, the evidence of things not seen.
HEBREWS 11:1 NKJV

In the early hours of yesterday morning, the world lost a beautiful person. Ron Core, the music teacher at my kids' school and my daughter's piano teacher, passed away unexpectedly after what he'd called a minor foot surgery. He was in his fifties.

Mr. Core was the best elementary music teacher I've ever seen—phenomenally talented. What's even more important, though, is that I knew he loved my kids. I felt safer, somehow, sending them to school and knowing he was there. The news of his death hit me like the proverbial ton of bricks.

My first impulse was to drive over to the school and get my daughter. I knew she would be deeply affected, and I wasn't sure she needed to be told at school. I first called Mrs. Jones, the principal, to find out how they were handling it.

"We had to tell the kids," she explained in a voice veiled with sorrow. "The story was spreading and we knew we had to manage it, to tell them the truth and help them deal with it."

Along with the counselor and school-based therapist, Mrs. Jones had gone from room to room, assisting the teachers and talking to the kids. My kindergartner, Harper, told me that she cried when she visited their class. "She really loved him," he'd said, obviously moved by his principal's tears.

Grace, in second grade, said Mrs. Jones talked to her class about Mr. Core's faith and how he was in heaven. "His foot isn't hurting anymore, and he can dance all around,"

Grace exulted, twirling across the room. "Mrs. Jones said he's probably constructing a choir of angels right now!" She waved her arms like a music director, meaning that he was conducting. I was struck by the delight in her eyes as she pondered these things. Grace was sad that her friend was gone, yes, but her focus was on heaven.

That night, after tucking the kids into bed and saying prayers for Mr. Core's family, my husband and I talked about the situation. We both had been melancholy all day, and I was even a little angry. What good could come out of a loss like this? It just didn't make sense. Mr. Core had been a light for Jesus in the school, his community, and all our lives.

Grace's reaction had surprised me somewhat. She's very emotional and deep, and I guess I expected her to cry a lot and be as sad as we were. *Maybe she's just too young to fully understand what's going on,* I decided, and I know there's a level of truth in that. But, later, I felt like the Lord spoke to my heart. He said, *"You know, she's the one who really understands better than you. To understand My kingdom, you have to become like a little child."*

It's raining today, and the kids have gone to school, where the music that so blessed their lives has fallen silent. Looking out my window into the gray, it appears that the world is crying. But faith says there's something more going on here—a kingdom beyond what my eyes can see. I'm choosing to receive that kingdom by faith and to walk as a child, even in the rain. * *GF*

What's Wrong with Being Jill the Admin?

*Judge not, that you be not judged. For with what judgment you judge,
you will be judged; and with the measure you use, it will be measured back to you.*

MATTHEW 7:1–2 NKJV

When I first entered college, I assumed it would be my golden ticket to the job of my dreams. Was I in for a surprise when I graduated! Not only did I get HR doors slammed in my face, I was told I wasn't qualified for anything other than a clerical position—something I could have done without a degree.

After I worked for a temp agency and eventually accepted an admin job, I got into the groove of my daily tasks. I learned that I actually enjoyed being someone's assistant. It enabled me to earn a living and then go home at the end of the day without worrying about work-related problems, unlike those higher on the corporate ladder.

Then one day I heard from a social service agency where I had applied for a director's position. They needed someone who could start right away, and I was next on their list of prospective candidates. After a couple of long interviews with the executive director and the board members, I was offered what I always thought I wanted. Since it was a social service agency, the pay was only so-so, but my title sounded good. People were impressed that someone so young could be in such a position. For a while I actually enjoyed my work—but mostly the prestige of the title.

My assistant was so good and vital to our programs that I leaned on her as much as she allowed, which was quite a bit. Occasionally someone would demand to speak to a supervisor, so she'd calmly put them through to me. That made me feel bad for her, so one day I asked her if she'd like a new title. The board of my agency was made up of an understanding group of women, so I was pretty sure they'd go along with my request. My assistant tilted her head, gave me a questioning look, and said, "Why? What's wrong with being an administrative assistant?"

Wow! What an eye-opener! And she was right! What was wrong with being an assistant? Every admin assistant I knew was smart, efficient, and respected.

Judging people by their title or pay range is wrong. A good administrative assistant is one of the most valuable people in any company. * *DM*

Jacob's God

May the LORD answer you when you are in distress;
may the name of the God of Jacob protect you.

PSALM 20:1

Most of us remember life before cell phones. Travel back in time with me, children, *way* back to the days of disco. I was young, single, living paycheck-to-paycheck, and enjoying life. After a long night of dancing the bump and the hustle, I was headed home when my car broke down.

To this day, I notice how dark some roads would be at night if it weren't for our headlights. I do that because of the night in question. My car died on an unlit road with no traffic. I became frighteningly aware of how stranded I was. I was an hour's walk from my apartment, dressed in a sparkly disco minidress and heels, surrounded on either side by black, dense woods. And to make matters especially bad, there had been a number of assaults on local women that month.

Distressed? You betcha. These days, a damsel in distress would whip out her cell phone and summon help right away. I didn't have time to wait for the invention of the cell phone. I turned immediately to God. I wasn't yet a Christian, but I believed in God…and it didn't take brilliance to understand I wasn't going to get help anywhere else. I was terrified and crying, but I started walking home and prayed out loud all the while.

A carload of young men pulled up beside me, and they offered me a ride home. None of them looked like they could be Jack the Ripper, but I was savvy enough not to take comfort in that. Still, I didn't know what else to do. I was willing to walk all the way home; I just didn't know if I'd make it before falling prey to someone dangerous. And I didn't know if that someone dangerous was sitting right there in that car.

Are you thinking these men were God's answer to my prayers? Nope. That answer came when yet another car pulled up behind the first. Despite the late hour and the fact that I knew few people in town, the couple who lived right next door to me were in the second car. They didn't recognize me until they felt led to pull over. Even they were amazed by the "coincidence" and curious about how matters might have evolved had they not happened down the road when they did.

The God of Jacob…. You know, Jacob wasn't exactly the poster boy for the fine, upstanding Christian believer. Yet God protected him the way He protected me that night. May the Lord answer your prayers of distress in the same way.
* *TP*

It Takes More Than Chocolate

All the days of the oppressed are wretched, but the cheerful heart has a continual feast.

PROVERBS 15:15

When I'm in a good mood, I feel festive, energetic, ready to meet my day's goals. When my mood goes south, I want to go to bed—and all those around me want me to go to bed too.

Let's face it. We don't *feel* happy every minute of the day. Sometimes we have bad hair days (or in my case, bad wig days). And what woman doesn't get in a bad mood when she's having a bad hair day?

It's true that we don't live in a constant Pollyanna attitude. But we can choose to make the best of our days. As Christians, regardless of how we *feel*, we can have inner joy that holds us steady when life throws chaos our way. It's a joy that says, "Regardless of the circumstances, I choose to trust God to get me through this."

When the doctor told me I had ovarian cancer, it took a-while for that to sink in. I didn't immediately fall apart or get depressed. I was in a state of shock and disbelief. Once the news did sink in (as I was getting my hair shaved off), everything and everyone I looked at had a clock on them. For instance, I'd look at my grandkids and wonder if I'd see them grow up. I looked at my husband and wondered if I'd

make it to retirement with him. Those thoughts threatened to oppress my spirit.

However, as I released my fears and future to God, He anointed me with His hope and assurance that He would walk every step with me, come what may. After all the many blessings He'd given me, did I think He couldn't take care of my family if I weren't here? Of course He could handle it.

My joy has been in place since. Does that mean I'm happy about the cancer? No, I can't say that I am. Do I think God can use it for good? Most definitely. Is my heart full of cheer? You bet it is! I love my life with my family and friends, but the thing is, it only gets better from here. One day I will be with my Lord for all eternity. The knowledge of where I am and where I'm going gives my heart a continual feast.

The next time you feel grumpy, remember that God is there, ready to help you through whatever struggle you're facing. Sorry to break it to you, but although chocolate is good, it's just not enough. * LL

Love Covers a Multitude of Sins

*The LORD bestows favor and honor; no good thing does he withhold
from those whose walk is blameless.*

PSALM 84:11

Before her untimely death, I'd known Roanne since we were kids. She played such an integral and life-altering role in the person I am now. For instance, she was the first person to believe in me as a writer. And she introduced me to several of the great loves in my life, such as English Breakfast tea, Cary Grant movies, and the difference between Taco Bell and *authentic* Mexican cuisine. That being said, she and I couldn't possibly have been more different.

Very much a Renaissance woman, Roanne's diverse interests included a passion for needlework. She embroidered some of the most stunning canvases, and I often marveled at her ability to sit in a chair for hours on end, focusing on one teeny little stitch after another—especially in contrast with her complete *inability* to focus on any other area of her life in order to complete a task from beginning to end! Eventually those little specks of thread blended together to create something exquisite and astonishing.

My one and only embroidery experience dated back to the summer (and fall and winter) of 1971 when I made a truly awful piece for my mother that she later displayed proudly. But watching Roanne inspired the ridiculous idea that I wanted to give it another go. Roanne threw her enviable enthusiasm and patience into the task of teaching me, and it didn't take long to discover that time had not developed any new skills in me. I still had absolutely no talent whatsoever for embroidery.

After countless hours of work on a Scripture sampler, I threw the canvas down on the ottoman and exclaimed, "I'm so over this!" Roanne set down her own project and encouraged me to pick it up again. "Look at it!" I cried. "It's a mess. There's a whole line of stitches in the wrong color, and look at this one right here!"

Holding it a few feet away, she said, "Now look at it. Do you see the mistakes from there?" I had to admit that I didn't. "There isn't a single wrong stitch that ruins the overall picture," she pointed out. "The only thing that can do that is if you give up and don't finish. It's kinda like how your sins are covered over by what the Lord has already done. The only thing that messes up grace is if you fail to reach out for it."

Roanne always said things like that. But in this particular case, I didn't roll my eyes because she'd actually reached me. Success!

I finished that project after all, quoting her grace reference in my head the whole way to completion. I framed it and hung it on the wall, and I often gazed at it from across the room, knowing full well where to find each mistake but unable to actually see them…and feeling really, really blessed that, in God's perspective, I looked like that sampler. * *SDB*

Too Much of a Good Thing

It is not good to eat too much honey, nor is it honorable to seek one's own honor.

PROVERBS 25:27

After I grew tired of scrimping and pinching pennies, I got a part-time job as a merchandising sales representative for a candy company about twenty years ago. My boss sent me home with a huge stash of candy at the end of my first day of training. Until then, my kids rarely had sugar—mostly only for special occasions. I walked through the door and placed it on the kitchen counter without a second thought before going upstairs to do some chores while my kids watched a movie.

When I came back down, my older daughter, Alison, who was seven or eight at the time, lay on the couch clutching her stomach. "I ate too much Laffy Taffy," she moaned. I went into the kitchen and glanced at the counter. At least a third of the candy was missing.

I looked over at my other daughter, Lauren, who smiled and said, "I'm not sick. I didn't eat too much." That was a relief, because having one sick little girl was enough.

Although Proverbs 25:27 isn't speaking directly to eating too much Laffy Taffy, it does relate in a symbolic sort of way. A little bit of a good thing is…well, good. Too much can be nauseating and take our focus away from God. It can also create an extreme dislike of whatever was overdone. To this day, I bet Alison would be perfectly happy if she never saw another piece of purple Laffy Taffy again. Even the reminder of that day twenty years ago elicits a groan.

In this world of overindulgence, it's easy to overdo anything—from food and personal possessions to ambition. A little bit of career ambition is fine because it generally brings an income for the family and respect from peers. However, too much often leads to greed and contempt. Climbing the corporate ladder has provided many people with fat wallets and empty lives. Then there's athletic ambition. We've all heard of those overachievers who are determined to win at all costs and willing to abuse their bodies, their friends, and their spiritual lives to have that moment of glory. But once they step down off that pedestal, it's over. What then?

As a Christian, I'm working hard at not wanting more of what I already have. It's so easy to fall into the trap of craving "one more" of anything because one more leads to another, and it never seems to stop until it harms us. Scripture is very clear that the only thing we can't get too much of is time with Him in His Word. * DM

Walking with Grandpa

"I the LORD do not change."
MALACHI 3:6

On the day my Italian grandfather became a US citizen, he bought himself a pocket watch. As he was a foreman at a mattress factory, it came in handy, timing his team's productivity to ensure a few extra dollars in their pay envelopes. Mostly, every *tick-tock* reminded him that he was now a free man. He timed our walks using that watch too, a tradition that never altered, even on cold, snowy days.

Once, as we maneuvered the slanting, cracked sidewalks of his neighborhood, he told me about his papa's bull. Everyone walked a wide berth around the monster that even brawny men agreed was the stuff children's nightmares are made of. But the animal worked hard, dutifully pulling heavy wagons, grinding wheat and corn to help fill the Citeroni family coffers. Grandpa was twelve—my age—when he got distracted while pouring feed into the beast's trough...and it gored him. Lifting his shirtsleeve, Grandpa showed me the ropelike scar that crisscrossed a hollow of still-missing muscle.

Not long after he told me that story, Grandpa had a stroke. He called me from the hospital and struggled to say, "I won't be home for a while, so will you do me a favor and wind my watch?"

I was proud that he'd trust me with it and only too happy to agree.

"Promise me something?"

"Anything," I said, meaning it.

"Don't ever change, and always remember...you are my heart, *cara mia*."

I pretended not to understand that he was saying good-bye, and I spent the next week focused on homework, my crush-of-the-week, Jimmy Cicotti, and caring for the precious timepiece. I loved the job. And I hated it. Because I wanted Grandpa to come home and wind it *himself*!

The following Sunday after services, the hospital called: Grandpa was gone. During those next days, the house filled with friends and family, pies and casseroles, plants and favorite "Frank stories." The days became weeks, and the weeks turned into months, yet I didn't cry for my best friend, my hero, my beloved Grandpa; if that first tear fell, would it be like Noah's ark all over again?

Like Grandpa's dependable watch, life ticked on. I moved east, fell in love, got married, and had kids. Then, recently, on a sunny spring afternoon, the mailman delivered a brown-wrapped package. Inside, nestled on a cloud of tissue paper, was his watch. "Your grandpa would want you to have it," Nonna wrote, days before her own passing.

Of all the treasures I've collected, Grandpa's watch is my most prized possession—despite its $50 appraisal—for it's a reminder of his love and loyalty that inspired such affection that, thirty years after his death, Nonna went to her grave still his devoted widow.

Someday, he will greet me in paradise, but until then, when life is bleak and burdensome, I need only to see that familiar shimmer of gold and hear the dependable *tick-tock* and I'm an innocent girl again...walking with Grandpa.
* LL

I Approve This Message

*Your word is a lamp to my feet and a light to my path. I have sworn
and confirmed that I will keep Your righteous judgments.*

PSALM 119:105–106 NKJV

How many times during presidential campaigns do we hear the phrase "I approve this message"? In the context of a presidential race, everyone understands that the candidate is simply confirming that he or she has the final say before a commercial is aired. But if we think about the significance of those same words in another situation, they could mean something completely different.

As a product information writer for a major television retailer, my job was to write copy for the Web, for call-center representatives, and for show hosts. Before I wrote the first word, each item had passed through the hands of the buyer, quality assurance, and, if necessary, the legal department. By the time I had the silk blouse or leather handbag in my queue, I was fairly certain that the spec sheets were accurate.

When I hit the final button on my computer to post the description on the Web, I was essentially saying "I approve this message" for everyone at the company. If the customer received the item and discovered that any of my words were untrue, someone could lose his or her job—so I was always extremely careful to check or double-check anything that didn't seem accurate. Occasionally an error would slip through in one of the early stages of the process, and the spec sheets would need to be changed. Anyone in the lineup could question the information, so by the time it hit the air or the Web, it had passed the approval of several people.

In another circumstance, the same statement could have still a different meaning. Think about how children rely on a parent's approval. While one child may have permission to walk to the store alone, another might not. When my children were little, they weren't allowed to watch PG-13 movies unless I'd either prescreened them or I was right there beside them with my finger on the remote control FAST-FORWARD button. One day my older daughter came home and said she was the only kid in the entire world whose mother did this. Although I doubt this was accurate, I suspect that there were quite a few parents who gave their children free rein with movies and TV.

Early in my Christian life, even before the WWJD bracelet rage, I heard someone in my church comment that he made his decisions based on what he thought Jesus would want him to do. That stuck in my head, and I still hear that voice when I'm tempted to stray, no matter how right it feels.

Knowing that God is constantly watching can be disconcerting sometimes—particularly when I look with longing at something I know I shouldn't have, see, hear, or do. And that happens way more often than I would like. However, it also gives me a peaceful spirit, knowing that a moment of giving in to something He doesn't approve of, no matter how wonderful it seems at the moment, isn't anything compared to the heavenly treasures He promises. And even when we fail to please Him, His mercy and grace endure with the ultimate approval of our faith in Jesus. * *DM*

With All My Heart

My brothers who went up with me made the hearts of the people melt with fear.
I, however, followed the LORD my God wholeheartedly.

JOSHUA 14:8

"Wholeheartedly" means without reserve, without reservation, with all your heart. Society shines with examples of wholehearted living. These dedicated individuals come from all career fields and walks of life—from pop superstars to missionaries to the soldiers defending our freedom. Maybe you know one of these stellar folks. They excel in politics and in medicine, in the church and in Little League. Students, teachers, janitors, truck drivers, parents, and grandparents are all part of the wholehearted who strive for their best in their work and for the people in their lives.

Living with full engagement, committing targeted energy to your assignment, is a deliberate choice. Living with all your heart takes commitment to a passion bigger than yourself. It means knowing what matters deeply to you and sticking with that in the storms and challenges of life. It means following your course even when your closest friends go another way.

In the pause of this moment, consider your life today. Imagine living it wholeheartedly. Imagine following God without fear, confident in His faithfulness. Feel the freedom. God urges His people to follow Him wholeheartedly because in living without reservation there is freedom. And in that freedom, you're truly alive. * SGES

Chocolate

*Wherefore do ye spend money for that which is not bread? and your labour
for that which satisfieth not? hearken diligently unto me, and eat ye that
which is good, and let your soul delight itself in fatness.*

ISAIAH 55:2 KJV

Mel Gibson once said, "After about twenty years of marriage, I'm finally starting to scratch the surface of what women want, and I think the answer lies somewhere between conversation…and chocolate." (These days, I'll bet he and his wife wish he'd talked less…and bought more chocolate!) Still, the quote makes me wish politicians would draft a new law requiring every husband, boyfriend, father, brother, and son to recite Mel's quote at least once a year!

It's no secret that I love chocolate. Always have, always will. My first memory of the slippery-when-soft substance was the Easter before my fourth birthday, when Nonna hid Hershey's Kisses (my all-time-favorite form of the stuff) all around her cozy dining room. In no time, the cotton candy–pink dress I'd worn to church bore streaky evidence of my finds.

Nowadays, when my too-busy life threatens to overwhelm me, I'm assured a moment of calm and comfort… if I stop and spend a quiet moment unwrapping a Hershey's Kiss. I pop it onto my tongue and wait as it melts with deliberate, delicious slowness, spreading choco-joy throughout my mouth.

It's as I unwrap those foil-shrouded delights that I'm reminded how, all around me, God has provided sweet reminders…proof that life isn't just about work, deadlines, and racing around like a madwoman to cross every item off today's to-do list. He uses the lure of chocolate to force me to stop, and as I'm enjoying the delectable delicacies, I notice robins and finches splashing in the birdbath outside my window. I spy a bright new bud on one of my rosebushes. Or I catch the expression of unconditional love emanating from the furry face of my faithful mutt.

Without my tiny treats, would I notice meaningful lyrics lilting from the radio in my office? Would I acknowledge camera-captured images of my lovely daughters and their families, smiling from the shelf above my desk?

Probably.

But each moment is sweeter and lasts longer when I'm feasting on my favorite candy. As I toss wrappers into the trash, I'm acutely aware that God has used those moments to awaken my senses, broaden my imagination, and exercise my "thank you for the little things!" muscles.

Because there are days when not even the most soothing symphony can stir my soul the way chocolate can. The sweet treat is capable of turning me from a pessimist into an optimist who believes that if no one witnesses my consumption, the calories don't count. If I had proof that there's chocolate in heaven, would I try even harder to live by the Golden Rule!

I think I'll pop a handful of Kisses into my pocket, so I can say "God bless you!" and hand them out to the strangers I meet today! * *LL*

A Life of Truth

For the word of God is living and active. Sharper than any double-edged sword,
it penetrates even to dividing soul and spirit, joints and marrow;
it judges the thoughts and attitudes of the heart.

Hebrews 4:12

One Sunday morning on the way to church I stopped by my brother's house to deliver something. Leaving my two small children in the van, I went up to the door for just a moment then dashed back down the steps to where my van was running. As I slid into my seat, I shivered. Something cold, thin, and hard was pressed against my neck. Without moving my head, I strained my eyes downward to see that there was a silver blade poking through the space between the headrest and seat. Someone sinister was holding it to my throat. "I've got you now!" he bellowed in a cruel voice.

With a shriek of terror, I turned around to face my attacker. He stared long and hard into my eyes, the blade unflinching, as I begged him to spare my life. With his teeth gnashing, he finally relented. I burst into laughter. My then-three-year-old son, Harper, reluctantly pulled his sword back into his car seat scabbard, and away we went down the hill.

You will rarely catch Harper without his sword. It's the first thing he grabs in the morning (after a sippy cup of milk), and the last thing he relinquishes at night. He carts it everywhere with him, brandished high, as he gallops around on his trusty stick horse. When he's not the villain, chasing his sister with his sword and delighting in her fearful screams, he becomes a handsome prince and bravely declares he will protect her from "robbers...croco-diles...pirates...mooses..." or whatever the enemy of the moment may be. He challenges us all to fencing matches. As he swings his plastic sword, he yells, "Ya! Ya!" and "Get back, you scoundrel!" Or my personal favorite, a quote from Peter Pan: "Take that, you codfish!" When we pretend to fall down wounded, the dark marauder kisses us back to life. Oh, the joy of having a little boy!

It occurs to me as I watch Harper play with his sword that I have a sword of a different kind that means so much to me. I first came to love it as a little girl growing up at home. It is far more powerful, sharper, and of course more beautiful than any toy. I can take it with me wherever I go, by literally carrying a copy or just by hiding it in my heart. Knowledge of it protects me from enemies of any form—doubt, discouragement, anger, bitterness, jealousy, condemnation, hurt...and I can also use it to speak life into the hearts of those around me.

I am challenged by the fervor of my son for his make-believe sword. I pray that one day he will have the same passion for God's Word. May I reach for my sword, the real sword of the Spirit, each morning and meditate on it day and night. May it never gather dust in my home or heart. May its truth shine so brightly in my life that others will want to read it, learn it, and cherish it and always carry it as their guide through life. * *GF*

His Word

Then the woman said to Elijah, "Now I know that you are a man of God and that the word of the LORD from your mouth is the truth."

1 KINGS 17:24

Lately I've intently sought God's guidance regarding some decisions that will significantly impact my future security. I haven't yet heard His answer, so I vented to a couple of my girlfriends the other night. "God knows I'm wide-open to whatever path He wants me to take with this. I just wish there wasn't all this *mystery* to it! I'm listening as hard as I can. Why doesn't He just *tell* me what He wants me to do?"

Even though both friends nodded in empathy, one of them said, "That's just not the way He works, is it? He's a 'lamp unto our feet.' No farther than that."

We decided God knows our wayward hearts. He knows that if we see too far ahead, we'll cast Him a jaunty salute, say a quick thanks, and turn our backs to get on with our business. By only granting us a lamp unto our feet, He keeps us looking up for more light all through the journey, which is exactly what we faulty creatures need to do to stay on the straight and narrow. In that way He's truly a light unto our path.

Today's verse highlights a point in time when the prophet Elijah followed the lamp at his feet. During a drought he followed it into a ravine, where he had water for a time and God had ravens bring him food. *Ravens*. You don't plan something like that. But God did.

Then Elijah followed the lamp to a widow making a final loaf of bread for her son and herself, after which she expected to die of starvation. The last thing she needed was another dinner guest. You *certainly* don't plan that kind of visit (if you have manners). But God did. Elijah assured the widow that God would work it out. And with God's provision, the three of them had bread every day.

Then the widow's son became ill and died. She blamed Elijah and his God. Elijah saw no lamp for his feet to follow. Still, he took the boy from her, expressed his utter frustration to God, and lay across the boy. Why? Maybe after following the lamp for a while, we start to understand what we need to do even when the path isn't well-lit. Elijah's desperate prayer on the boy's behalf led to his resurrection.

So I'll keep watching that lamp at my feet and trust that, if things become so desperate I just lay myself before Him and pray, He'll very likely breathe new life and light unto my path. * *TP*

This Is Grace

In him we have redemption through his blood, the forgiveness of sins,
in accordance with the riches of God's grace that he lavished on us.

EPHESIANS 1:7–8

My first grandchild entered life on a tsunami of pain. A devastating wave of emotional and spiritual concerns accompanied what should have been a joy-filled announcement—"Mom, we're pregnant."

The words were couched with shame and embarrassment. My son and his girlfriend weren't married and faced far more challenges than the fact that she craved fish sticks and Funyuns. They both knew they'd made bad decisions. One of those "what were we thinking?" decisions meant that now, rather than ironing out their relationship issues and dealing with a 747-worth of baggage, they—and we—prepared for a baby in the house.

As with most parents of young people in trouble, we were heartbroken over their choice to bypass the divine plan for a husband and wife to bring children into the world in God's glorious timing. It's not that we didn't understand how a thing like that could happen. But my husband and I and everyone else concerned knew that the path my son and his girlfriend chose came laced with difficulties and complications they weren't prepared to handle, challenges the Lord never intended them to experience.

The young woman was homeless, and a legal issue kept them from getting married right away. My son had a home of his own a few miles from ours, but the expectant mom lived at our house. As her belly grew, we tamped our disappointment and chose to love and forgive, taking our cue from the mercy that floods the pages of Scripture. Together we walked through morning sickness and fatigue and community stares and whispers. We traversed a path of embarrassment and concern and faced challenges that only happened to "other people." We felt every bit of the baby weight on our own frames and somehow adopted the waves of nausea and the clenching of false labor in our own bodies.

But through it all, we counted on the wonder of the Lord's forgiveness, His redemptive heart, His ability to turn what started out as distressing into something of great beauty. It's what He does. He molds rough clay to make art. He recycles pain to make a place for His joy to land.

As expected, He did just that.

At four thirty in the morning one day in September, my son came to get us from the waiting room to lead us into the birthing center, where a new life had entered the world moments before. Warm and bright-eyed and rose-petal pink, the child was laid into my eager Grammie arms.

"Mom," my humbled but glowing son said, as if a formal introduction were necessary, "this is Grace."

I drew that darling baby to my heart, as I imagine the Lord drew me, and answered, "Yes, it is. *This* is grace." * *CR*

He Crowns the Year

You crown the year with your bounty, and your carts overflow with abundance.

PSALM 65:11

Not long after I was diagnosed with ovarian cancer, reality began to set in…and fear followed. Disability insurance would provide only half of my regular income over the period of time away from work for surgeries and treatment. Would I be able to keep the lights on, the telephone at the ready? Would there be food in the refrigerator?

A local friend in whom I'd confided sent me a card with today's Scripture in it, and she scribbled a note on the bottom. "He promises. You can count on it."

But how? The hysterectomy took its toll, and recovery was excruciatingly slow over the next six weeks. As I prepared to begin five weeks of daily radiation therapy, my slashed income started to catch up to me. I looked up at my friend's card where I'd placed it in my office, and I shook my head. "You promised, Lord," I reminded Him.

Back then, author Loree Lough was a valued writer bud whom I'd only met via the Internet. She and I frequently chatted on IM, and we'd developed quite a budding friendship. She e-mailed and called me many times during my recovery. Then one afternoon in the mail came an envelope from her address, and inside was a check for $100.

But wait! There were three more envelopes in the stack of mail, each of them from longtime friends in different states across the country: $100, $75, $50. The next day it was more of the same. It turned out that the friend who'd given me that Scripture card had privately contacted ten of the friends she'd most often heard me speak about and asked them to help in any way they were led to keep me above water until I came out on the other side, cancer-free. As a result, each and every time I flipped a switch, lo and behold, the lights went on. With the push of a button, *voilà!* A dial tone. And my refrigerator stayed stocked throughout my treatment and beyond with whatever bland food I could manage to keep down.

Ever since that time, whenever I come across today's Scripture, I smile and think of that first envelope I opened from Loree. Since that time, Loree and I have collaborated on one book and brainstormed on I don't know how many others, and we've finally met in person. Our friendship has morphed into a sort of sisterhood that began with the arrival of that first check and the sweet little note she attached about how much she had come to love me. Loree and my other friends who came through for me at that time were God's hands to crown my year with His goodness, and I'll never forget them (or Him!) for it. * *SDB*

Word Up!

Whoever of you loves life and desires to see many good days,
keep your tongue from evil and your lips from speaking lies.

PSALM 34:12–13

It's scientifically proven that positive words have a positive effect on us as humans. In fact, using negative words has been shown to lead to immediate negative results on the body and our overall mood. If we continually use negative words, they can zap our spirit, our emotional strength, and our self-confidence.

When reading books about abused women for a novel I wrote, I was astonished to find that emotional abuse leaves a deeper scar than physical abuse. Why? Because emotional abuse goes to the very heart of what makes up the essence of that person. It tells them they're unworthy and of no value.

Sticks and stones may break your bones, but words can destroy you. Don't underestimate the value of what a kind word can do for someone today.

This morning, my daughter had horseback riding camp. She begged me not to get coffee first. "Mom, no! We'll be late!"

"I won't go to Starbucks," I told her. "I'll go the local shop. It won't take so long."

Naturally, I got to talking to the owner, and my daughter was soon yanking me by the arm.

"See? You have to talk to everyone!" she exclaimed as we left.

And I do.

The owner told me the business was having trouble with the city and may be closed by the end of this year. How could I not offer words of encouragement and my own experience in dealing with the city?

My daughter made it on time, incidentally. I've developed the ability to account for my chatty nature and leave early. But when you talk as much as I do, it isn't always positive.

Sometimes I blow it. Trust me, it's harder to make up for harsh words than it is to say something kind. They say that a bad experience will be shared seven times, but a good one is only conveyed to someone else once. Now, with Twitter and Facebook, I imagine that number is multiplied! I like to think of our words as echoing to the world. Are we sending a pretty, uplifting echo?

Consider the way you use words. God promises us more good days and a longer life if we keep our tongue from evil. That's a pretty big reward for something that might come naturally to us as we practice, but the Bible tells us that the tongue is a fire, a world of evil among the parts of the body, so we must constantly check ourselves and be mindful of our words. * KB

Heavenly Music

*The LORD your God is with you, the Mighty Warrior who saves. He will take great delight
in you; in his love he will no longer rebuke you but will rejoice over you with singing.*

ZEPHANIAH 3:17

The crowd scrunched shoulder-to-shoulder in the pews, each person eager to catch a glimpse of his or her child in the children's program. With the cameras and videos charged and ready, the children trudged toward the platform, a child here and there stopping the flow to wave wildly at a relative in the audience.

Dressed in their Sunday-best and giving eager smiles, the children belted out tunes of praise to their God. Some stared at their shoes. Some hid behind the person in front of them. Some scratched, nodded, waved, or stared at their neighbors. Yet nothing diminished the audience's adoration for the young performers.

Off-key melodies brought smiles and apparent pride to the listeners. Spellbound and enraptured with the budding artists, the audience's adulation escalated with every number, and by concert's end an uproarious applause broke out in their midst.

As I ponder those moments where my husband and I sat in awe and delight of our own children's musical offerings, I can't help but think of today's Scripture and how we live our lives in much the same way.

The melody of our lives is a little off-key. Fears assail. We try to hide our failures, making one excuse after another.

Sometimes life's challenges make us wonder how we will get through another day. We wave at God for assurance that He is there. We question how He can love us when we are unlovable. We struggle to understand how He can meet our needs when they are so great—when we feel certain there is no way out or that all is lost.

Life bulldozes pain into our tranquil world. Life turns things upside down. Life brings questions and doubts. Life brings fear.

Ah, but God is in control. Much like a parent watching a child in a church program, He watches over our lives with a love we can't begin to comprehend. He loves us when we mess up, sing off-key, get distracted, or forget our words. He understands our pain, our fears, our questions, and our doubts. And you know what? He loves us still. Like the warm embrace of a mother holding her baby, His love wraps around us and carries us through the good and the bad days of life. *He never leaves us.*

Did you get that? Never. Leaves. Us.

So the next time you're faced with a challenging day, know that our Father longs to quiet you with His love and rejoice over you with singing! * DH

Furry Wings and Fuzzy Halos

Charm is deceptive, and beauty is fleeting; but a woman who fears the LORD is to be praised.
PROVERBS 31:30

When my daughters were young, we lived in Maryland farm country, far from the nearest…anything. Once, while driving home from the grocery store, my trusty Nova conked out. In the center lane of a highway. Miles from the nearest exit. With night falling. And snow in the forecast. And three hungry and yawning kids in the back seat. I pumped the gas pedal, but it was no use. The motor refused to turn over.

I ran down my short list of options: hike to the nearest gas station with the girls in tow or hike to my husband's office just past the next exit. "Please, Lord," I whispered, "get us home safely…and get us there *soon*."

At that precise moment, a little red sports car pulled up behind us. Its driver, a flashy middle-aged woman in a long fur coat, jogged closer, holding tight to a thick, fuzzy hat as she squinted into the icy wind. "Oh, sweet Jesus," she exclaimed. "Car trouble?"

The TV news was full of scary stories about carjackings, roadside muggings, missing persons…and in one case, the suspect was *<gasp> a woman!* I cranked down the window, but only an inch. "Yes," I squeaked out.

"Dear Lord…do you park your car outside at night?"

"Yes."

"Probably just a little water in the line," she said. "My husband's a mechanic, and I think I have just what you need in my glove box."

A knife? Maybe even a pistol? I wondered. But before I could speculate on other weapons, she was back and hoisting a can of Drygas. "I'll just pour this into your gas tank and you'll be on your way in no time."

She didn't give me time to object, and when she returned to the window with the empty can, the lady peeked into the backseat and, smiling, waved at the kids. "I can follow you home," she said, "and make sure you all get there safely."

I rooted in my purse and withdrew a five-dollar bill. "No. Thanks. You've done so much alre—"

"You don't owe me a penny. My husband's a mechanic, remember? I get this stuff for free!" She giggled and then added, "Now, crank 'er up. I said a prayer for you while I was dumping this stuff into the tank. I just know God is watching over you and those beautiful babies of yours."

One turn of the key had the Nova purring like a kitten. Tears of relief filled my eyes as I laughed. "Thank you," I said.

But when I turned, she was gone.

And so was her car.

"Mommy," my youngest said, "I didn't know angels drove tiny red convertibles."

Was the fur-clad woman an angel? Or just a wonderful coincidence?

I won't know until I reach heaven's gates, but I know this: the woman in the matching fur hat and coat will be praised by my family every time it snows! * *LL*

Honoring Veterans of Life

Rise in the presence of the aged, show respect
for the elderly and revere your God. I am the LORD.
LEVITICUS 19:32 NIV

While reading Scripture, you'll notice a distinct contrast in the way God venerates the aged and the way that our culture treats them. We applaud and celebrate veterans of war, but what about veterans of life? Don't we owe honor and respect to those who have survived the ravages of living?

God retains the aged among us to teach us the kind of wisdom that only comes with time and experience. It is a generous act of mercy that allows us the privilege of age, and living among the elderly community brings out certain virtues in us that need to be nurtured.

Take the time to contemplate in prayer what a difference dealing with the aged could make in your character. For instance, you will cultivate humility as you learn to listen to those who have lived through the things you are currently experiencing. You stand to learn a great deal about sacrifice in dealing with the weakness and feebleness of the aged. And furthermore, God nurtures tenderness within the community when you take the time to dignify the elderly by taking care of their needs.

Honoring the aged with compassion will enrich your life, deepen your character, bless the elderly, and please the Lord. * SGES

A Life of Brokenness

Though He slay me, yet will I trust Him.

JOB 13:15 NKJV

My friend and fellow writer Holley Gerth sent me something she wrote the other day that ministered to me. She's going through a period of brokenness in her life that, among other things, involves the desire to have a baby.

Holley and her husband, Mark, have been happily married for eight years; both have flourishing careers, a lovely home—everything in place, it seems, to start a family. They've done everything they can to make it happen, and many of their friends and family have prayed for years that Holley and Mark could become parents. But so far the Lord has said no.

Here's what Holley writes:

Lord,
Life can be so hard.
We are so fragile…
all of us one breath away from eternity.
We forget until tragedy comes
and we are reminded
how we are all like flowers of the field.
And yet You love us.
You value us.
You gave Your life for us.
But You also allow us to be broken.
How do we make sense of that?
Where is the beauty in the shattered pieces?
We want You to make

something lovely of our lives
but more often it is more like a mosaic—
beauty out of a million broken pieces—
than the flawless work of art we imagine.
So help us, Lord.
Give us strength in our brokenness.
Let us say with Job,
"Though He slay me,
yet will I trust Him."
Is there a harder prayer to pray?
I do not know of one.
Come to us, take our pieces,
use them for Your purposes
until we see, as You do,
the beauty in the brokenness.

Although I am a mother of three and my story is not the same as Holley's, I have my own broken pieces. We all do. Shards of dreams that have been shattered like glass, broken relationships we can't fix, jagged edges of our lives that cut us till we bleed. Holley writes that it's those very things—our deepest hurts—that become our ministry. God picks up the pieces and helps us turn them into an altar—a place we can offer sweet, beautiful sacrifices to Him. It's a place where He meets us and blesses us so that, in our brokenness, we can be a blessing to others. * *GF*

Flying under the Radar

A thousand may fall at your side, and ten thousand at your
right hand; but it shall not come near you.

PSALM 91:7 NKJV

Have you ever heard the old adage, "You don't know what you've got till it's gone"? Well, I'd worked at a particular company for three years, and despite the fact that I was deeply grateful for the job, I was never particularly fond of it. Over time, it became more and more challenging to think of new ways to motivate myself to keep at it. And then one day the rumor we'd been hearing for several months was standing at the door waiting for us when we clocked in. The Tampa office would be closing in just sixty days.

I'd been praying that this wouldn't happen, citing God's scriptural promise that ten thousand might fall right beside me but it wouldn't come near me. However, it had not only come near me but I'd been slapped by the reality of just what I dreaded the most: unemployment.

As those first days wore on, I started recognizing clear patterns among my coworkers. Many of them began making plans to live off their severance for as long as possible for a little paid vacation; others decided unemployment benefits would get them by and the severance funds would be better used toward a new stereo system or computer. Others, like me, started preparing for job hunting within the first hours after the news.

Because I'd been miserable in my line of work for three years, I immediately began to wonder about changing fields. I redesigned my resume and collected letters of recommendation that targeted a new direction, and I applied for a "dream job," one that appealed to me more than any of the others on the job boards. You can imagine my surprise when that very job, the first one for which I'd applied, was the first offer I received.

Weeks passed, and the mood in the office began to change. A sense of desperation ensued and then panic that seemed to permeate every conversation between coworkers. Because I already had something to go to, I was able to relax and comfort my friends, even help them by redesigning their resumes and making suggestions about how to target jobs that might be a good fit for them.

On the day that the doors closed at our company for the final time, one of my coworkers gave me a hug and thanked me for helping her through those last days.

"It was encouraging to watch you," she commented. "It was like everything was falling around you but it didn't touch you at all."

My prayers and that foundational Scripture sprang to mind, and I grinned at her. "Thank you," I said. "You just reminded me who is really in charge here."

The Lord knew all along that the company was going to close. He knew that I would be looking for a change, and He prepared the ground ahead of me so that I could survive the thousand falling at my side. He walked me right through so that I would be in a position to be a blessing to those around me. * *SDB*

You Are What You Think

Therefore I say unto you, what things soever ye desire,
when ye pray, believe that ye receive them, and ye shall have them.
MARK 11:24 KJV

A pessimist, it's said, sees the difficulty in opportunity, while an optimist sees opportunity in every difficulty. Oh, that we could all think like optimists all the time! Our thoughts, much too often, turn into words. And if what we're thinking is negative stuff, we're bound to say things that will turn others' smiles upside down, in addition to our own.

What we see and hear—and how we react to it—is directly connected to everything we are and do. For centuries, the sages have said that the tongue is the most difficult part of the body to control. The Bible has a lot to say about this human peculiarity. It strongly urges believers to renew their minds and change their attitudes to ensure that their actions are as upbeat as the rest of their lives.

Some mind-body experts have compared the "mind over matter" dilemma to medical studies that separate pill-testing patients into two groups: One group receives the real thing while the other gets a placebo, but neither is told which is which. Doctors dole out pills along with a list of possible side effects, and they're always amazed at the results, because the fake stuff can cause drowsiness, nausea, palpitations, headaches, and vomiting...just like the actual medication. Just as amazingly, every miserable symptom disappears the instant patients stop taking the placebo!

Positive thinking, they say, is a very real and powerful thing. And guess what? It's every bit as contagious as the illnesses, diseases, and disorders those researchers are trying to cure by comparing real meds to placebos.

So the next time you wake up in a truly bummy mood, remember that your attitude is not something you must accept. Nor do you have to allow it to shadow you for the entire day. And it needn't invade your conversation and relationships as you go about your business, either.

The Swiss have a great attitude about attitude. "Fear less, hope more; eat less, chew more; whine less, breathe more; talk less, say more; love more, and good things will be yours." Some might say that's a tad cheesy, but I say there are no "holes" in that quote!

Bottom line? If you ask the Lord to blanket you with happy thoughts and an upbeat mind-set, that's exactly what you'll get.

And on those days when it seems you just can't shake that bad mood, remember what the comedian/philosopher Herm Albright said: "A positive attitude might not solve all your problems, but it will annoy enough people to make it worth the effort." * *LL*

My Secret

*Indeed He says, "It is too small a thing that You should be My Servant to raise
up the tribes of Jacob, and to restore the preserved ones of Israel; I will also give You
as a light to the Gentiles, that You should be My salvation to the ends of the earth."*

ISAIAH 49:6 NKJV

*B*ack when I was in college, I worked at a health club that had quite a few wealthy members. I was one of a half-dozen exercise and fitness instructors who catered to folks with maids, gardeners, and assorted other servants at home. I often thought about how nice it would be to walk in their shoes, and I dreamed of the day when I would graduate, find a high-paying job, and live the life I assumed my clients led. (Although my boss told me that I'd never make a lot of money doing what I did, but I'd find some satisfaction from helping others.)

A couple of years after I started, one of my favorite clients invited me to lunch. My boss gave me the go-ahead (I didn't want to do anything unethical), so I accepted. I was excited to have even a slight taste of this woman's endlessly glorious life. But I was shocked to learn that she was miserable.

We spent the first half hour ordering and chatting about mostly insignificant things. Then she fidgeted for a moment, gulped, and reached out her hand. "Debby," she said softly, "what's your secret?"

I tilted my head and gave her one of those clueless looks. *What secret?*

"You always seem so happy. I never see you without a smile. I want what you have."

I was stunned into silence. She wanted what I had?

"But you have everything you could possibly want," I squeaked.

A smile slowly crept over her face as she shook her head. "It might look that way, but I'm miserable. I spend most of my days trying to fight depression. I go to the health club every day hoping that some of your joy will rub off on me."

That was a major eye-opener. I really was a happy person, and it certainly wasn't because I had a lot of external things to keep me that way. Between tight quarters in my dorm room and a car that I prayed would start every time I got in it, there was always something that could be improved.

My joy came from within—that feeling of knowing Christ was always with me. I wasn't sure how I'd be received, but I took a chance and told my client the source of my happiness. To my surprise, she teared up and said, "I thought that might be the case, but I wasn't sure. I haven't been to church in years. Do you think it would be okay if I went sometime? With you?"

Of course I said I would love it! * *DM*

Seeing the Truth in Time

*At the name of Jesus every knee should bow, in heaven and on earth and under
the earth, and every tongue acknowledge that Jesus Christ is Lord, to the glory of God the Father.*

PHILIPPIANS 2:10–11

When I was a fine young chickadee, full of romantic notions and all kinds of misconceptions about real life and my own capabilities, I fell for a young man with a natural talent for honing in on every vulnerable aspect of my personality. He played the romance card beautifully, and I was sucked right in, regardless of some pretty horrible behavior on his part. With my starry-eyed, naive blessing, he distracted me from accomplishments and goals of which I was fully capable. I pretty much made him my everything.

After a year of this relationship, I was one insecure, confused, mistreated mess. I sought professional counseling and was advised that I had invested far too much of myself in this fellow. I needed to pursue activities and ambitions that had nothing to do with my devotion to him and everything to do with my own independence. "Take some college courses," the counselor said. "Consider hobbies for your own personal enjoyment! Spend time with girlfriends, apart from him, once in a while."

Of course, at the time, I thought the counselor would have given me different advice had she but known what a catch this guy was. I couldn't risk losing him to another girl by turning my attentions elsewhere.

But the day finally dawned when I realized I had been duped all along. Despite solid, truthful advice, I had carried on my shallow existence, not realizing how much better my life could be. I accepted that the counselor had been right. I had been wrong.

I think of that humble realization when I read today's verse. As a believer in the Lord's gracious gift of salvation, I crave that day when we will enthusiastically kneel right there in His physical presence and acknowledge that He is Lord. Imagine that!

I don't want to be a woman who hears about His grace but chooses to ignore it—who carries on in a shallow life, unaware of how much better life could be. And worst of all, to be kneeling on that day, at the name of Jesus, for sad reasons rather than joyous ones. I look forward to falling to my knees because I'm thrilled, as a believer. Not kneeling in the worst, most painful kind of humiliation possible, knowing I've been wrong all along and have left it too late.

I want that day to be a celebration for everyone I know. I remember the pigheaded young woman I was when very little sound advice got through to me, when I was certain I knew better, even though the truth was buried deep in my heart. If I hope to influence others about the joy, blessing, and absolute necessity of recognizing Jesus for who He is and what He offers, I need to ask for all the help I can get.
* TP

What's That Smell?

*Perfume and incense bring joy to the heart, and the pleasantness
of a friend springs from their heartfelt advice.*

PROVERBS 27:9

"What is that smell?"

It wasn't asked with the lighthearted voice of a shopper lured into a candle store by the scent of—*what is that?*—pumpkin-pie spice or cinnamon-apple crisp or brown-sugar pound cake. It wasn't said with a smile and a soul-satisfying deep breath on the edge of an orange grove in full bloom. The scene wasn't a late spring deck where the fragrance of lilacs wafted on one breeze and lily-of-the-valley on the next.

The "fragrance" came from the heat duct in the family room.

Dead mouse?

I know what a dead mouse smells like. You can't live in a hundred-year-old house in the country without developing a nose for that smell. This was different.

A furtive search for the source of the odor turned futile. My beloved and I looked everywhere—on the canning shelves, inside the furnace, under the water heater, in the dark corners of the fieldstone basement that I only venture into if I have no other option. None.

We never did find the culprit. It…and the smell…eventually dissolved or disappeared or, oh, I don't really want to know. I'm just glad it's gone. If it comes back again, we're moving.

While we waited for the odor to dissipate, I thought about my mom. That sounds incredibly rude, and I apologize to moms everywhere. What I mean is that the ability to smell is a gift I don't always appreciate. My mom did…after it was gone.

Congestive heart failure stole her strength, but a bizarre reaction to a medical procedure stole her ability to taste and smell. She missed the smell of lemons and lily-of-the valley and Baby Magic lotion on a newborn. She missed knowing when the turkey was done by the aroma. When we visited her apartment, she'd pull a quart of milk from her fridge and ask, "Would you sniff this? I can't tell if it's still good." She missed knowing when something had soured.

"Perfume and incense bring joy to the heart," reads Proverbs 27:9. The ability to smell is one of life's great, though underappreciated, joys.

I may whine about the "gift" when an unidentified stink wrinkles my nose. But when I slice into a lemon, I think of how much Mom would have enjoyed that scent.

Buttered popcorn. The air between snowflakes. Fresh basil. Sun-dried pillowcases. Warm brownies. Toasted coconut. Campfire. Jasmine tea. Joy to the heart. Sticky toffee buns.

I can smell. Eucalyptus. That's a grace-gift (hazelnut coffee) I've taken for granted (lavender) too long. Strawberries.
* CR

The Value of Time

The LORD God is my strength; He will make my feet like deer's feet,
and He will make me walk on my high hills.

HABAKKUK 3:19 NKJV

Back in college, Maureen was one of my closest friends. When I discovered her in the parking lot, slumped over the wheel of her car and crying, I opened the door and climbed in beside her.

"What did he do?"

Blaming her on-again, off-again boyfriend, Craig, was always the first response.

"It's not Craig," she told me. "It's my parents."

A week before Thanksgiving break, Maureen's parents had sent her a gift certificate to an elegant local restaurant. It seemed they had decided to go away on a cruise over the holiday, and they'd sent her a certificate to have Thanksgiving dinner on them. Alone. Maureen came from a dairy farm dynasty. Eggs, milk, that kind of thing. Okay, so calling it a *dynasty* might not be accurate, but, all things being relative, my middle-class upbringing would likely appear as a scene out of *Oliver Twist*, in comparison. Despite that, I couldn't see my friend eating turkey at a table for one, so I invited her to come home with me.

If there is one thing memorable about my family, it's that there was always room at our table for a few more. If there were more than six of us eating at a given time, well, we just moved in a chair or two from the kitchen. So what if the plates didn't match or the drinking glasses had yellow sunflowers etched on some and American flags on others.

Our dining room table was the gathering place, a melting pot of friends, family, and assorted strays.

The turkey was perfect, even if there was too much sage in the stuffing. My mom knew how to lay out a spread! There was a variety of vegetables, a dozen different starches, and desserts that crowded the large table in the kitchen. Mom lit bright blue candles that didn't match anything, and our neighbor's grandson spilled milk from one end of the dining room table to the other.

When I drove Maureen back to campus that night, I half expected her to say something like, "That was, uh, very special. Thanks."

Instead, the minute we got into my car, she burst into tears.

"I know. The stuffing was heartbreaking," I said.

"What a beautiful family you have," she exclaimed. "Thank you so much for letting me be part of your holiday."

We didn't say much more in the car that night, but I've never forgotten my moment of realization. Maureen didn't care about the menu for the Thanksgiving meal. She cared about being part of something. And now that I'm grown and my parents are gone, I often feel as if I'm walking in Maureen's shoes—grateful when friends open up their homes, allowing me to share in their celebrations, and happy to be a part of something again. * *SDB*

Clueless Comfort 101

*All of you, live in harmony with one another; be sympathetic,
love as brothers, be compassionate and humble.*

1 PETER 3:8

Don't get me wrong here—I'm not claiming to have figured out all the answers after twenty-three years on this side of salvation. But I'm better than I used to be.

Years ago, when I was taking my first stumbling baby steps in my walk with Jesus, I loved hanging out with one of my more eccentric friends. Gina was a good old gal from North Dakota. She was feminine but tough; she was flirtatious but independent; and she always spoke her mind. In fact, sometimes she embarrassed the living daylights out of me with her blunt comments to me and others. But Gina always made me laugh, and she had a 24-karat-gold heart, which was one of the things I loved most about her. Certainly not a woman of means, she was nonetheless generous with what she had, including her affection. She cared far more about others than about herself.

So it was with confusion that I listened to her complaints one day, when she faced a number of significant disappointments in her life. We stood in her apartment, and I listened as she unloaded the list of events that had brought her down. She started to cry as she spoke. I looked at my normally strong, upbeat friend with what I assumed she recognized as concern. I wanted to be there for her as a good friend and as a Christian. I tried to think of what I was going to say to make her feel better and hopeful.

Finally, she stopped talking, heaved a sigh of exasperation, and spoke to me as if I were frustratingly clueless (which I was). "Oh, *Trish*! Will you just give me a *hug*?"

I blinked stupidly a few times and then stepped forward and hugged the poor girl. That's all she wanted from me. That's why she was kvetching about her lot in life. She needed nothing more than a hug. A shoulder to cry on. No pithy comments, just a physical demonstration that someone cared. I was so used to watching Gina show sympathy to others (and to me), I'd lost sight of the fact that she probably needed someone to return the favor on occasion.

I remember that moment whenever someone chooses me as their sounding board. They're not always asking for a solution. Yes, I've hugged a few people who rebuffed the gesture, which was a little awkward. But, hey, that's where the "humble" part of Peter's verse comes in, right? * *TP*

A Life of Rest

Come to me, all you who are weary and burdened, and I will give you rest.

MATTHEW 11:28 NIV

Robin was a "good girl" who grew up in a good home. Her family went to church, and she became a Christian at a fairly young age. Through the years she wanted to stay "pure." She didn't go through much rebellion as a teenager, unless you count the time she chose to date a certain boy against her parents' wishes.

When Robin was fifteen, she was babysitting for some friends. Her boyfriend came to the door, and she let him in.

They had a good visit, drinking a soda and talking while the children played. That's all she remembers, though. Apparently he drugged her during that time, because when she awakened later she found she'd been raped.

Before the rape Robin was a virgin. Imagine her surprise the next month when she found out she was pregnant. In shock and fear, she told her parents everything, and they took her directly to a clinic, where a doctor performed an abortion. She relates that it all happened very fast.

That bad situation—and Robin's role in it—would define the next several years of her life. After high school, she married and began to build a life that from the outside appeared very happy and successful. But on the inside Robin still struggled. Her heart, always haunted by the past, was never fully at rest.

Robin wanted to believe that God forgave her, but the enemy pelted her with lies. "I thought God might hate me for having an abortion. I believed the rape was His way of punishing me for disobeying my parents and that I was a murderer who wasn't worthy to be forgiven."

Robin filled her life with good things in order to dull the pain. She was active in her community, took care of her home, and tried to be the perfect mother. She searched for answers—as well as absolution—by being involved in her church. Through all of these things, she did find a measure of happiness, but they were like putting a Band-Aid over a wound. After all, she thought she deserved it.

But God had other plans for Robin. As time passed, He used many circumstances to speak to Robin's heart. Through prayer, Bible study, and the love of a few real friends, Robin began to understand the true meaning of forgiveness.

One day Robin prayed a simple prayer: *Lord, I receive Your mercy and grace in my life. I know You forgive me for disobeying my parents. Even though that choice had horrific consequences, I know it's not true that You punished me when I was raped. I know it grieved You. Your heart for me is love and not hate.*

I receive Your forgiveness for my abortion. Even though to me it is the greatest possible sin, I believe Your forgiveness is greater. Through the blood of Jesus You have blotted it out. Yes, even this sin.

Through You, I choose to forgive the man who raped me, my parents, the doctor, and myself. I place the burden of my shame at Your feet. I claim the rest that You offer me, Jesus. From now on, I will rest in Your mercy, and Your love for me. Thank You.

When the Lord takes away our pain, He replaces it with His rest. When He takes away our shame, He gives us joy in return. In Robin's case, when she gave the Lord her past regrets, He restored something in her life beyond what she had ever dreamed possible.

Robin heard about a young girl in her community who was struggling. Her father was dead and her mother had abandoned her. The girl was working her way through college and barely had enough money to cover her basic needs.

Robin relates: "As soon as I saw her, I felt this overwhelming love—mother love. I knew, somehow, that the Lord had brought her into my life to allow me to love the child I never had."

Robin and her husband now have a beautiful bond with the girl and Robin has found healing and a restoration. * GF

Boggled Minds

Set your minds on things above, not on earthly things.

COLOSSIANS 3:2

Sometimes it seems as though clutter begets clutter—whether it's a piece of paper I lay on a table or a thought that muddles my mind. There are so many examples of clutter, it's not possible to mention all of them…so I'll start with my dining room table. We seldom use it for its intended purpose, and it's become a catchall for stuff we're not sure what to do with. On my way to my bedroom, sometimes I plop something on the table with the intention of handling it later—but later may be a day from now or even the next time I dust, which isn't all that often anymore. It starts with one small sheet of paper, and by day's end, like a magnet, it has attracted what seems like a mountain of paperwork.

Then there's the mental clutter that bogs me down so much I don't know where to begin. It wakes me up some mornings, creating a sense of panic that I'll never get through what needs to be done. And it keeps me awake at night as I worry about how I can accomplish all I need to do. The more I think about my concerns, the more scrambled they become, until I have a huge mess in my mind that has me tossing and turning all night…and snapping at people who slow me down during the day.

So what happens if we don't deal with any of that mess—from the physical clutter to the mental bog? Oh, there are some things you should handle, or you'll have a bigger problem later. If there's a bill involved, you'd better pay it. Some big decisions such as buying a new house or trading a car need careful consideration. Or if it's an invitation from someone you care about, you need to RSVP. If your child needs you, be there. And instead of letting your daily concerns clutter your mind or your dining room table, handle them once so you can file them away.

Other than those few things, not much else is important enough to clutter our lives. Our focus should be on God and His plan for us. Worry never serves any purpose, except to take our eyes, hearts, and minds off Him.

Every thought that enters our minds needs to be filtered by our faith in Jesus and what He's called us to do. Instead of shuffling along with too much clutter that is ultimately meaningless, focus on the big picture. It's impossible to truly put Jesus first in your life and still worry about insignificant things. * DM

Sew Blessed

We do not make requests of you because we are righteous, but because of your great mercy. Lord, listen! Lord, forgive! Lord, hear and act! For your sake, my God, do not delay, because your city and your people bear your Name.

DANIEL 9:18–19

New friends might find it curious or even a bit disturbing that I used to sew my family's clothes. I still have pictures of the matching calico granny dresses I made for my daughter and me. If she'd been older than three at the time, she might have objected more strenuously.

What was my first sewing project? I don't remember. That might be a merciful memory loss. I bonded with a sewing machine in fifth grade. Some projects turned out admirably. If I hadn't sewn the sleeves in backward, the kelly-green wool dress I made for 4-H could have warranted at least an honorable-mention ribbon.

After years of practice with patterns and pins and whatever fabric was on sale, I made my own wedding dress, my bridesmaids' dresses, and the miniature version for the flower girl. Long, flowing sleeves were "in" back in 1972. Who knew it would be 100 degrees with 4000 percent humidity on our wedding day? I'm not sure my bridesmaids are ready to forgive me yet.

Budget-conscious by necessity, as a newlywed I also tried my hand at sewing clothes for my husband. The results hovered between unnerving and disturbing. Wouldn't you be unnerved by the idea of a homemade sky-blue polyester leisure suit? If I ever wonder whether my husband is a good sport, I think of that fashionless statement and swallow my wondering.

Did I mention that I attached the sleeves of my wedding dress backward too? I ripped them out and reattached them the correct way before the wedding. No one knew they'd been sewn twice.

"You made your own wedding gown?"

"I did. Not flawlessly, but…"

It occurs to me that no matter how hard I try or how practiced I am, my best righteousness is sleeves-sewn-in-backward.

I don't pray because I deserve God's attention, but because He offers it. I love Him because He first loved me (1 John 4:19). I don't follow Jesus because I was bright enough to realize that was a smart move, but because He said, "Come. Follow Me."

"Not because of righteous things we had done, but because of his mercy. He saved us." Same message in the New Testament book of Titus (3:5) as in the Old Testament book of Daniel. Sounds like a theme, doesn't it?

The Lord responds not because I frame my prayer perfectly—oh, the pressure!—but because I belong to Him. I bear His Name.

How freeing!

What do I deserve? If I didn't have this propensity for sewing sleeves in backward, maybe honorable mention. What am I offered? Everything.

Sewing update: These days I'd rather stitch words together than French-seam a silk shirt, which, for the record, is not as hard as it sounds. Making a French seam, that is. * *CR*

Black (Friday) Fat Pants

*Take heed to yourselves, lest at any time your hearts be overcharged
with surfeiting, and drunkenness.*

LUKE 21:34 KJV

Department and discount stores call the day after Thanksgiving "Black Friday" in the hope that their cash drawers will overflow. That's what I call it, too...because it's the day I draw the drapes, bolt the doors, take the phone off the hook, and run around the house in a black leotard, working off the turkey, stuffing, mashed potatoes and gravy, and pumpkin pie and whipped cream I've recently devoured.

I'm big on holiday dinners. And I'm more than happy to carve time from my hectic schedule to prepare meals so large I'm forced to add every leaf to the dining table *and* a card table at each end to make room for centerpieces, main courses, side dishes, assorted breads, and the good china.

I have to snicker, saying that, because the only "good" thing about my china was the $69.95 I plunked down for twelve five-piece place settings of faux Blue Willow. Ditto the Bohemian crystal water goblets and Paul Revere–styled flatware. If somebody chips one of those cups or loses a fork in the trash as we scrape plates...? No big deal!

I've been told that my "Don't worry about it!" attitude is why not one of the dozens gathered 'round the Lough table complains about squeezing in, shoulder-to-shoulder, between old codgers and damp toddlers, good friends and total strangers. But I don't suppose it hurts that every bowl and platter overflows with tried-and-true recipes...and a few Weight Watchers concoctions, snuck onto the table for good (waist) measure...

I'm no scholar, but I've learned how to make folks believe *mi casa es su casa.* I'm not related to Amy Vanderbilt or Emily Post, but I'll treat you like royalty. And while I'm far from wealthy, I pray you'll leave here richer than when you arrived...in good times and laughter, memories and friendship...and bloated bellies!

Did we need that cornucopia of appetizers and desserts, or Nonna's linen tablecloth and napkins on the table? Were scented candles on the mantel and a glowing fire in the woodstove necessary? Nah, but even those finger-pointin' mamas who taught us to avoid overindulgence look the other way on holidays at my house, as they sneak a second helping of ham or a third slice of homemade pie.

Makes you wonder, doesn't it, how many of *them* wriggle into "fat pants" on Black Friday so they'll be more comfortable on the treadmill or the Exercycle while working off that bowl of Jell-O piled high with whipped cream.

Um...pass the cheesecake, will ya? * *LL*

A Life of Unity

Behold, how good and how pleasant it is for brethren to dwell together in unity!
PSALM 133:1 KJV

Thinking about the beauty of unity takes me back to an experience I had a few years ago with believers from a different denomination than my own. I was asked by a friend to help out with a Christmas musical at her church. I had no experience directing a choir, but I do read music, which was what she said they needed. So I said I'd give it a try.

I showed up the next week at the Bread of Life Fellowship for practice. It was quite intimidating. I stood in front of about twenty people, mostly adults who were older than me, as they sang the songs. I read along in the book, trying hard to keep up.

I had a nagging fear they would see that I didn't really know what I was doing. I remembered from my drum major days in junior high band how to mark time, so I started waving my arms to the beat. I sang along. By about halfway through the program, I was completely swept away by the music. The kind and eager faces of the singers looking out at me won my heart and gave me courage. I began to have *fun*!

Each week I looked forward to the practices. When I entered the church I was greeted with smiles and encouragement. I learned the names of the singers and felt a sweet camaraderie with each one. They were so patient with me and open to my instructions. The sound man was always there to stop and do it over, stop and do it over—every time I yelled "Cut!" We had lots of laughs and did a lot of hard work. Every night after practice I left mentally and physically tired but also strangely energized and fulfilled.

There were two performances. When the time for the first one came, we met early to pray and warm up our voices. It was pouring down rain and cold outside, but in that little church on those dark nights there was a warm fire glowing in us. When the music began, our spirits started to soar and I forgot everything else around me except for the lovely faces of those singers and the hearts behind them. They sang like angels and I, their lowly director, being ushered into the meaning of Christmas, lifted my hands and truly worshiped Christ, the newborn King.

I am hesitant to make the statement, as some will about different things, "That's what Christmas is all about." How can we, as finite beings, ever comprehend what it is all about? But I have the distinct impression that one thing Christmas is about is unity. What a beautiful thing it was for me to stand in unity with other believers—not of my same denomination, but of the same Lord. A choir of different voices blended together in perfect harmony. How sweet the sound! I believe with all my heart that it was music to His ears. * *GF*

Cheap Runs Deep

*Give portions to seven, yes to eight, for you do not know
what disaster may come upon the land.*

ECCLESIASTES 11:2

There are few things in life that can ruin one's witness as a Christian faster than being cheap. Some call it *frugal*, but think about it. You had a friend, somewhere in your history—you know the one—where you all planned to put in an extra couple of bucks because her "portion" wouldn't cover the tax and tip in a restaurant. And it wasn't because she couldn't afford it. *That* friend.

I grew up with a very generous family, but neither my grandparents nor my parents possessed a lot of money when I was a child. One of the biggest "outings" in our family was when my cousins and I went to see my grandfather's bridge in Menlo Park, California. Grandpa had made a bridge with curved wood at the local civic center. He'd tell us about all the engineering and work that went into building a "curve" into wood, and we'd listen patiently because he'd take us to Foster's Freeze for ice cream cones once we were done. Kids will endure a lot for ice cream.

Although I can't ever remember him spending more than twenty dollars on me at any time, Grandpa would treat me to lunch at Burger King when I was in high school. The most expensive thing I recall is a dress he bought me at J.C. Penney's for kindergarten. We fought over the color.

My grandfather is ninety-four now, living in the lap of luxury at a gorgeous retirement home, where his biggest trouble is trying to get the coveted seat in the sunshine after lunchtime…or if he doesn't like the soup of the day. His money lasted because he saved; he scrimped, but he was never cheap. And if my grandfather ever did run out of money before he ran out of life, there would be countless loved ones there to rescue him from his fate…because he invested in what really mattered.

When I think of today's verse, I think of my grandpa and grandma: always careful, always aware of the future, never cheap. When you invest your money, are you thoughtful of where it goes? Do you deny yourself rather than someone else? Is someone else's tip a place where you find savings? If so, think of God's promise to care for you and what true value means. * KB

BFFs

The LORD your God will be with you wherever you go.

JOSHUA 1:9

One of the beauty parts of living alone is that I have developed a very tight relationship with Jesus Christ, so I'm never really by myself. When I'm making breakfast in the morning, I talk to Him about the day ahead, and on the drive to work I often sing to Him at the top of my key-challenged voice; He doesn't even seem to mind the klunker notes! When coworkers get the best of me, when the salad I order has wilted lettuce, when some Joe cuts in front of me in line at Starbucks…He's the Friend to whom I turn. There's nothing I can't say to Him. He knows my darkest secrets as well as my deepest desires.

Yep, me and the Lord, *we're like this.*

In fact, He's such a comfortable, familiar Companion in my everyday life that I can sometimes forget that He is the awesome Maker of the universe, the Holy One of Israel, the Anointed One, the Author of our very faith. There is nothing He doesn't know, no place on earth we can go where He can't find us; He knew all our days before even one of them passed, and He numbers every hair on our heads.

I was watching one of those entertainment shows a few days ago, and they were interviewing an A-List movie star. She spoke about her children. Her youngest is around two years old, so she's lived all her life with the paparazzi following the family everywhere they go; however, her older daughter, a teenager, had a relatively normal childhood until the last couple of years. So when Mom was suddenly surrounded on the red carpet or followed down every inch of Melrose while shopping, the teenager was appalled.

"Sometimes I think she forgets that there's this whole other side to Mom now," the actress explained. "I'm not just the person she baked cookies with on Saturday…or who scrubbed the grape jelly off her backpack. I'm also someone who makes movies, and with that comes this sort of celebrity. Sharing me with her little sister was hard enough, but sharing me with the rest of the world isn't something she'd ever considered before."

That resonated in me. God has numbered the hairs on your head as well as mine; and my Jehovah-Jireh provides for you too. Despite the deeply personal relationship we share, it's important for me to acknowledge the enormity of this personal Savior of mine and to take time to bow down before Him to worship the awesome God that He is. Beyond being my closest Friend, He is so much more.
* SDB

Kick Me When I'm Down

God is our refuge and strength, an ever-present help in trouble.
PSALM 46:1

When my husband walked through the door at noon on a weekday more than a couple of decades ago, I didn't have to ask if something was wrong. Instead, my question was, "What happened?" He tipped his head toward our two daughters, our unspoken language for letting me know we'd discuss whatever it was later.

Once the kids had finished their lunch and were outside playing, my husband and I sat down at the kitchen table. "I lost my job," he said. "The company cleaned house, and they got rid of most of the people in my position." My shoulders sagged. We'd only been in our house for a year—not enough time to build equity to pay a real-estate commission, so we couldn't sell. And just a few months earlier my mother's health had failed, and she was two states over, living in a persistent vegetative state. I felt as though someone had kicked me after I'd already fallen.

My husband and I discussed options. He'd always been a good provider, but the economy was in a downturn and options were limited. I was a stay-at-home mom of two toddlers. I didn't want to put my children into day care, but I was willing to do whatever was needed to help the family. For a time, I had to scrape money from the spare-change jar to keep food on the table while my husband got another job

and worked an obscene number of hours to pay the mortgage. It was never easy, but when one of us got down, the other was able to rise up and do a little extra.

There's no doubt in my mind that the Lord was the source of our strength during that very difficult time. We had many sleepless nights, wondering how we'd be able to provide for our children without losing our sanity or some of the precious moments of their childhood. My wonderful mother-in-law, Bobbie, stepped in and traveled with me to visit my mother until my mother died. If it weren't for Bobbie, making the trip to see my mom would have been nearly impossible with two toddlers who didn't understand what was going on.

I can't say *anything* during that time was easy, but with His strength, we persevered. During the times we felt as though we might fall, He scooped us up. If it weren't for our faith in the Lord, our family might have wound up being a statistic. He didn't promise that we'd be able to keep our house, but somehow we managed to live there until we were ready to move. Life has been smoother lately, but after that rough time, I know that with God's strength, I can face whatever challenges come before me. * *DM*

Trying Not to Limp

Like a broken tooth or a lame foot is reliance on the unfaithful in a time of trouble.

PROVERBS 25:19

I'm way too young to need a knee replacement. Waaaaaay too young. Decades too young. But along with crooked teeth and stick-straight hair that actually resists even industrial-strength curling irons, my siblings and I inherited bad right knees. One sister got her knee replacement a few years ago, brave woman. The rest of us are lined up like marine recruits waiting to get our heads shaved. Or knees, rather.

I blame it on the jump rope. Not the jump roping I did as a kid, but that resurgence of interest a couple of years ago when I thought jumping rope on my deck was a better idea than other forms of Dread Exercise. It wasn't pretty, but it elevated my heart rate more than leaning across my desk to grab a reference book.

Apparently my knees were just waiting for a reason to go on strike. The paint on their picket signs had dried long ago. They awaited the call: *She's gone and done it. Spread the word. She's jumping rope.*

My current schedule won't accommodate knee surgery and months of rehab until three cycles of leap years have come and gone. So I'm coping. And trying not to limp.

Well-practiced now, I can sometimes pull off a nearly normal gait, although it takes concentration and the use of muscles designed for other purposes. There's a downside to walking without a limp. It sometimes lulls me into thinking my knee is reliable.

I'm not a farm-tractor kind of person, but once in a while my husband the hobby farmer needs a hired hand to help him with a project that involves someone to run the levers and whatever those other knobs are on a tractor.

"Just climb on up there, honey, and lower the bucket while I slide this metal plate under it."

The blankest of stares washes over me. So Bill tries a new tactic. "Lower the bucket. The lever to the right of the steering wheel."

Still blank.

"Steering wheel. The round thing."

I know what a steering wheel is. I was stopped by, "Climb on up there." It's not so easy with a bum knee. It's either the good one or the bad one that has to go first for a successful climb. I can never remember which one until after I've tried it. Climbing down from the tractor is worse. I can't be sure my knee will hold me.

That's the truth that tops my list of blessings today. Not that my knee can't be counted on, but that the Lord always can. I never have to wonder if His love is going to give out, if I'm putting too much pressure on His patience, if leaning that hard on His grace will make it collapse and send me tumbling awkwardly to the ground. He is always and ever reliable.

No matter how hard I work not to limp, the fragility of my knee remains. But I never have to wonder if His grace can hold me. * *CR*

Mirror, Mirror on the Wall

Therefore we do not lose heart. Though outwardly we are wasting away,
yet inwardly we are being renewed day by day.

2 CORINTHIANS 4:16

When I look in the mirror, the following Scripture almost always comes to mind: "Charm is deceptive, and beauty is fleeting; but a woman who fears the Lord is to be praised" (Proverbs 31:30). Now why do I hear that in my head when I look in the mirror?

It's a rhetorical question, just so you know.

My daughter is a photographer. When she takes a picture of me, she fixes it. You know, she uses all her fancy know-how to ease the wrinkles and give me a flawless complexion. She thickens my hair and whitens my teeth. In short, when all is said and done, the picture doesn't look like me at all. And I'm okay with that.

Then I take a look in my mirror, and reality hits. The real me in living Technicolor. And if I really want to punish myself, I pick up the mirror that magnifies a hundred times. That one always drives me to chocolate.

Just once I would like for my mirror to lie to me.

So I buy into all the creams, foundations, age-spot reducers—anything short of cosmetic surgery (there's just something very frightening about having a knife near my face; I grow wrinkles just thinking about it)—in hopes of keeping my grandma's age-worn face from looking back at me in the mirror.

The bottom line? I'm growing older. So what? There are worse things, right? Say, like root canals, espionage torture, and a chocolate strike.

My body may be wasting away, but the more time I spend with the Lord, the more my inner self is being renewed. That's why there are so many sweet little grandmas spreading joy in our world—they've spent plenty of time in His presence.

Now, don't get me wrong. I think it's perfectly fine to look our best. After all, we represent Jesus, and we want to look and be our best for His glory. So go ahead and use your creams or whatever makes you feel better about yourself. Just remember, the world is all about making money, so they try to get you to buy those things to fill their pockets. I finally came to the conclusion that there's not enough cold cream on the face of this earth to get rid of all my wrinkles. I buy some, yes, but I'm learning self-control. I don't go out and buy the next thing that comes out on the market. In short, I'm learning to be at peace with who I am at this age. Besides, there is comfort in knowing that true beauty shines from the inside out.

So spend more time with Jesus. Your face will thank you, and so will everyone in your corner of the world. * *DH*

Who, Me?

At this, she bowed down with her face to the ground. She asked him,
"Why have I found such favor in your eyes that you notice me—a foreigner?"

RUTH 2:10

I adore Ruth! She's one of my favorite Bible friends, for so many reasons, but I really identify with that unassuming, somewhat clueless nature of hers. There she is, extending so much unselfish grace toward Naomi; yet when the Lord touched the heart of Boaz to bless her, Ruth immediately wondered why she'd found favor with him.

Why do we do that?

I love Proverbs 3:4. It says we find favor with both God and man. In fact, it's one of several Scriptures that I've placed where I can see it every day. So you wouldn't think I'd always be so astonished when God's grace glides me through; but like Ruth, despite what I know about the character of God, I'm often taken by complete surprise!

When I was just barely out of my teens, I had a terrible accident and my car was completely demolished. I pried open the door and walked away without a scratch on me. I asked myself so many times: why had my life been spared that way?

I've recently been dealing with a leg problem that has affected my mobility in sudden and profound ways. During the ordeal, I discovered that I had overlooked the expiration of my driver's license by several months, and the only way to renew it was a trip to the DMV. I made two treks there before I was able to collect all the paperwork they needed for renewal, and both times it was excruciatingly painful for me to stand and wait in the inevitable lines.

On that third and final trip, I sat in my car outside for about ten minutes before going in, praying that I would somehow find the strength to do it one more time. I finally took a deep breath, braced myself for another ordeal, grabbed my cane, and slowly hobbled toward the front door.

A man inside left his place in line to hurry and open the door for me. The woman behind the counter called me directly up to her desk to inspect my paperwork. When she sent me to another area and it was announced that they'd encountered a computer problem and we would have to stand in line until it was resolved, the young man in front of me suddenly broke away, fetched a chair, dragged it toward me, and softly said, "This might be easier for you." I left the DMV less than an hour later with my new license in hand.

I thought of Ruth that morning on the drive home, and I wondered how many times God's favor glides me through a situation and I never have the insight to acknowledge Him. His promises await all His children, and yet so often we fail to recognize the manifestation of His love when it's laid out right before our eyes. * SDB

Gotta Stay Sharp!

As iron sharpens iron, so one person sharpens another.

PROVERBS 27:17

Writing is a solitary profession. Typically an author spends a good part of her day on her own, sitting before a computer. And if she's a novelist, she mostly interacts with people who exist only in her imagination.

I'm a novelist, and I'm also single, *and* I'm an empty nester. These three facets of my current life weren't always so, but they've all settled in at once and I expect this relative "aloneness" to be the case for the foreseeable future.

And I couldn't be more thrilled.

Don't get me wrong. I thoroughly loved raising my kids and having them running around me in all stages of their formative years. They were—and still are—the best part of my life. Moving into the grandparenting stage of child-rearing has been yet another blessing, but that's an entirely different, less-demanding situation altogether.

And I don't regret having been married, despite the sad path my marriage took. I know myself well. Had I not gone through the experience, I would always wonder what I had missed, and I wouldn't have so many of the fantastic people in my life that I do today.

But I absolutely love my alone time. Always have. There's something to be said for reaching a stage in life when you can call your own shots without stepping on anyone else's schedule, needs, or toes.

Still. Today's verse provides such a valid comment that I know I need to take it to heart. When you live alone, it can become very easy to let your involvement with other people take too low a position on the to-do list. Not good. The concept of relationship is so important that God is *three persons*! There's no denying His intention for us to be relational creatures.

Not only do we need others for the joy of friendship, love, and fun, but we need each other to stay sharp. As a writer, I make a point of passing everything I write before my critique partners, because I miss so much otherwise. I don't notice where I've made mistakes in form or logic or where I could have made something better. Our lives, and especially our faith, need the same kind of sharpening.

I need to be a part of a church body in order to hear good teaching on His Word rather than simply lean on my own interpretation. I need to spend time in friendship with other Christian women so I grow and remain empathetic to others rather than focus on my own wishes, needs, and struggles. I have things to contribute to the lives of others as well. God didn't design me and give me whatever gifts I have just to have me hide them under a bushel (or in front of a computer). * *TP*

A Life of Simplicity

It is the Spirit that gives life. The flesh doesn't give life.
The words I told you are Spirit, and they give life.

1 PETER 3:4 NCV

A beautiful life doesn't require lots of money or fancy clothes. It's not a life of ease and extravagance, nor is it a life of striving for success. A beautiful life can be lived by any ordinary person in any ordinary place.

I know this to be true because one of the most beautiful lives I've ever encountered was shared with me in my hometown of about three thousand people, in a normal house on a normal street. I used to go there once a week for piano lessons.

When I met Gail, I was in the first grade, and I was shorter than her dog Anheuser. He was a St. Bernard who would greet me at the back door, sliming me on the face with his enormous pink tongue as I ran past, trying to dodge him on my way to the piano.

Gail would meet me in the living room. For thirty minutes or so she'd sit beside me in a beige chair and listen as I tried to play whatever songs she'd assigned me the previous week. Sometimes she'd take over the piano, demonstrating a difficult section of the music or sharing something new with me that she was practicing herself. She was our church pianist, and she made magic out of ordinary hymns. Her hands shook from a neurological condition, but the shaking never seemed to affect her amazing skill and tone.

I can still see her sitting in that chair beside the piano, watching me through her dark-framed glasses. What she must have thought sometimes of my lack of practice or the strange phases I went through as a teenager… Her lessons were a balance between tough and tender—a wise teacher's effort to push a student, but not too hard.

As the years passed, so eventually did Anheuser, and I grew up. Spending thirty minutes with Gail each week playing the piano was one of the few things in my routine that never changed. By opening her life to me, she taught me many lessons that go beyond the piano. The most important was what it means to live by the Spirit.

Gail's life hasn't been easy. In fact, if you looked at her condition from its outward appearance, you might never see the beauty inside. Her only son was struck and killed by lightning. Her husband, whom she adored, fought with demons that sought to destroy them both. Even now she lies in a bed at home, where for years she's been dealing with cancer and unable to stand or even sit for more than a few minutes at a time.

Through everything, Gail remains faithful. She chooses to draw life from the Spirit instead of dwelling on what's wrong with the flesh. I visited her not long ago and had to ask, "How do you handle having to lie in bed all day long?"

"Well, I don't like it," she grinned, spunky as ever. "But I know the Lord is in control. I trust Him to take care of me." She quickly changed the subject to intercessory prayer and how I might join her in praying for someone she knew who was in need.

This response, so typical of her, is one that challenges and inspires me, just as her life always has. Gail's journey is one of cultivating deep inner beauty in herself and those around her. Just as she did with me all those years, thirty minutes at a time. * *GF*

Love, Hope, and Faith

Not only so, but we also rejoice in our sufferings, because we know that suffering produces perseverance; perseverance, character; and character, hope. And hope does not disappoint us, because God has poured out his love into our hearts by the Holy Spirit, whom he has given us.

ROMANS 5:3–5

Do you remember the first time your heart was broken? I had to dig through the old memory to remember getting dumped the first time, but I found the little gem hiding in a far-off corner. I can't dredge up the pain I felt back then, but I remember feeling it. It was devastating. The truly odd thing is that the pain of that first heartbreak seemed more searing than the pain of having a marriage pulled out from under me after nearly two decades. Was I really that cold about my marriage?

Quite the opposite. I didn't rejoice about the end of my marriage— but after a life's worth of romance and breakup, my devastation has been replaced by hope. Not necessarily hope for more romance, mind you. Simply hope. Because after suffering through multiple heartbreaks, I discovered I could *survive* them, I could persevere. And learning to persevere built my character. Part of my character today is the result of experiencing heartbreak and surviving it. And surviving loss. And surviving failure. And surviving…[fill in the blank]. God designed us to develop multifaceted characters. Knowing He cares enough to improve my character gives me hope.

So it is with all suffering. Regardless of how Paul phrased it, he surely wasn't saying that "real" Christians dance for joy when they learn they have serious illnesses or they lose loved ones or they get laid off or any number of awful turns our lives can take. But the longer we live, the greater the opportunity we have to develop hindsight and wisdom… and hope.

So often we hear people say things like, "I would never have asked for this to happen to me, but I wouldn't change a thing because it made me who I am today." That might sound trite, but the insinuation is that the person *appreciates* who she is today. For a Christian, that means she sees God's hand in her life. She has hope for a God-ordained future.

That kind of hope won't disappoint us. It eventually rises to the surface, despite any suffering we experience, if we persevere and allow our sufferings to build our strength and character.

What does it take for us to believe that hope won't disappoint us? To believe that hope will arrive, and to believe it so strongly that we'll eventually rejoice in our sufferings? Well, it takes faith. When you think of it, that's really the only gift we can give the Lord. It's all He's ever asked of us.
* TP

Wham, Bam, and Done!

A man's wisdom gives him patience; it is to his glory to overlook an offense.
PROVERBS 19:11

I have a secret nickname for one of my friends. I've never said it out loud; it's just something that pops into my head whenever she calls me.

Wham-Bam is a great girl. She's very funny, and she can be so compassionate. But at least once a week, I receive a phone call from her that goes something like this:

ME: Hello?

W-B: Hi, how are you doing?

ME: I'm okay, I guess. Just very tired. I—

W-B: I was up all night three nights in a row because the kids…

She talks about 80 miles per hour as she tells me all about her own life, moving directly into why she called, and then why she has to run.

After about a year of keeping a mental accounting of these calls, I started to take offense. I often pictured that cartoon character that whirled into view and mowed down anyone who came across his path before moving on without looking back at the poor Joe sitting on his duff in the middle of the road, dazed and wondering what had just happened. *Wham-Bam is the Tasmanian Devil!*

More often than not, I've had to really fight the temptation to speak up: "Why do you even call me? You never listen to what I have to say! Am I just the dumping ground when you need to vent?" One evening I turned to the Lord with the questions instead. In that instant, I had what Oprah calls a "lightbulb moment."

How many times had I done the same thing to the Lord during prayer? How many times had I clamped my eyes shut and started a dissertation somewhere in the middle without taking the time to enter into relationship with Him, without thanking Him for the many blessings He had bestowed? At least once a week, I'm certain. Probably more often still.

I started to pray for Wham-Bam that night. I prayed that she would find peace, that her frantic life of carpools and family illness and veterinary bills wouldn't overtake her, and that somewhere in the midst of the chaos, she would find the time to be still before the Lord and trust Him to take care of her every concern.

The next time I received a call from her, I empathized with her predicament, and I told her that I'd been praying for her. Her response? She burst into tears and thanked me. "You know, that's just what I need," she told me. "To know someone is hearing me and praying for me." * *SDB*

Broken Things

For God did not send His Son into the world to condemn the world,
but that the world through Him might be saved.

JOHN 3:17 NKJV

I have watched with a saddened heart as several Christians gave up on their faith. They stumbled in their walks, got lost in the darkness, and figured there was no way back to Jesus. Worse, they believed that God didn't want them back because of their blemished pasts. After all, friends and family—even former church family members—didn't want them back.

But the truth is, God will take us and our hurtful pasts and use them all together for His good (Romans 8:28). Of course, repentance is involved with restoration. But if we confess our sins, He is faithful and just to forgive us and cleanse us from all unrighteousness (1 John 1:9). Once restored, our hearts can't even condemn us, because God is greater than our guilt-ridden, broken hearts.

This magnificent truth in no way gives us a license to sin, but I have seen God take the pieces of a broken life, put them back together, and create a thing of extraordinary beauty—and one that's of great service to Him.

God really does use broken things. * AKB

A Life of Grace

For of His fullness we have all received, and grace upon grace.

JOHN 1:16 NASB

I teach a class called Introduction to American Literature at a local university. This semester my class examined several slave narratives and discussed them in the context of freedom as an American ideal. At the conclusion of this part of the semester, I invited my students over to my house to watch a movie called *Amazing Grace*. It is the story of William Wilberforce and his fight to abolish the slave trade in Great Britain. The character of Olaudah Equiano, an American slave writer and former slave himself, appears in the movie as a huge influence on Wilberforce's life.

Another major character, portrayed in the movie as the religious figure who shaped Wilberforce's passion for the cause of freedom, is John Newton. He is the former slave trader who, after his conversion to Christianity, denounced slavery and wrote the famous hymn "Amazing Grace." My daughter got her name from that song.

So there we all were, the class and I spread out like old friends around my living room. They range in age from twenty to seventy-two and seemed to be having a good time eating nachos and strawberries with chocolate fondue. My family, who had gone to Granny's for dinner, came in about the time the movie started. Harper and Grace love these occasions and settled in with their bowls of strawberries to watch the movie with us. Grace crawled up in the recliner in one student's lap, and Harper joined me on the couch with another. They were soon enthralled by the movie—we all were.

As a class we had already talked about the implications of the movie as it related to our readings. Grace and Harper weren't in on any of that. But a few days later, I was riding with my mom and sister-in-law and all our kids, who were packed in the back seats of René's Suburban. I was eavesdropping on my kids, as I often do in these situations, and I heard Harper say to his sister:

"Hey, Grace, you know that movie we watched with Mom's class? I just thought about that song 'Amazing Grace,' and I think I figured out something. You know when he sings 'I once was lost, but now am found, was blind but now I see'?"

Grace says, "Yes."

"Well, he wasn't really blind. But I think what that means is that when he was doing those bad things, he was lost and it was like he was blind and in total darkness. But then when God found him and showed him what he was doing, it was like light came and he could see the truth. Isn't that cool?"

Grace says, "Yes, Harper, that's cool. Now hand me my lip gloss."

I was a little more touched in that moment than Grace was by the magnitude of what Harper had just said. Not only was it so neat to me that he "got it," but as I listened to his wonderful revelation, the truth of what he said opened my eyes again so I could see.

Even though I've never been a slave owner, I know what it's like to walk in darkness. I know—we all do—how it feels to wear chains in different areas of our lives. I love teaching and seeing minds open up and stretch. It's wonderful when I get to help a student gain new freedoms through education. But the message of that song goes much deeper than education. Truth sets us free in our hearts. It *is* cool, Harper! It's amazing!

No wonder I named my kid *Grace*—I need a lot of it. Good thing God never runs out. * *GF*

Shame, Shame, Go Away

No one whose hope is in you will ever be put to shame.

PSALM 25:3

When I read this verse, the image of the biblical Noah comes to me. Noah, in the middle of the desert, building a giant boat, bringing in his own petting zoo two by two (or by seven, if you count the "clean" animals), then packing up what would be the equivalent of a massive Costco run onboard. Can you imagine what the neighbors said? Can you imagine their mocking laughter and pointing fingers? What was it like to be his family during this time? How did they explain God's still, small voice in their father's ear?

The short answer is, they didn't. How could they? If Noah lived today, he'd probably be under psychiatric care and on some pretty heavy doses of medication.

The Bible, however, doesn't talk about the neighbors, except to say that the earth was corrupt and filled with violence. We're told that Noah was a righteous man, blameless among the people of his time, and he simply did *all that God commanded him.*

I'm sure that when the rains started, those folks left on earth had a different view of the odd man building an ark in the desert. Something tells me Noah took no pleasure in being right, but he had to be grateful for his obedience.

I have a special-needs child. One day, we were in Target and that child threw a fit the size of Montana. My other three kids looked on in horror as I tried to calm my child and get out of the store without any major damage. Looking into my other kids' eyes, I saw the shame and humiliation—and I saw the way they stepped back, not wanting to be associated with their sibling.

Through their eyes, I saw myself as a child watching my mother handle my handicapped brother in some overwhelmingly embarrassing situation, and a light came on for me that day. My mother was not ashamed because she loved my brother, and she was focused on the moment and his needs. I felt the same about my child at that moment. There was no shame because I was focused in love.

God did not give me this child by accident. There are many days when I could have easily been put to shame but chose to focus instead on the incredible gift of this child. I've watched my kid blossom and overcome disabilities I didn't think possible to overcome. That is God's grace. That is God saying, "Kristin, build the ark and don't worry about what the neighbors are saying. Your walk isn't theirs."

Someday, my kids will learn this lesson for themselves. There is never any shame in obedience. * KB

All That and Toilet Paper?

Then he climbed into the boat with them, and the wind died down.
They were completely amazed, for they had not understood about
the loaves; their hearts were hardened.

MARK 6:51–52

Like many newlyweds, we struggled financially when we were first married. Six months into wedded bliss, we found ourselves needing groceries. Being young and full of faith, we decided we would tell no one…but God.

Several days into this, as our stomachs growled and the food cabinet grew bare, I got a call from a friend wanting to know if I would go shopping with her. The last thing I wanted to do was go shopping. We barely had enough to put a meal together; shoes were the last thing on my mind. Yet, not wanting to spoil her enthusiasm and also not wanting to let on that there was a problem, I quickly agreed.

Once I hung up the phone, I asked God for strength and grace to go shopping with my friend—and for help to keep our need from her. We wanted to rely totally upon God for this need.

So I got dressed and ready to go. My spirits perked as I thought about spending some time with my friend and enjoying our day.

When she showed up at the front door, she had a paper sack filled with groceries in her hands. I opened the door and she walked inside, heading straight for my table. She plunked the groceries on the table and turned to me. "I know this seems crazy, but during my quiet time this morning, the Lord told me you needed this." Then she marched back to her car and brought in several more bags of groceries—right down to paper towels and toilet paper!

God had thought of everything.

I'll never forget that day. We hadn't told a soul of our need. We were careful to not let on to anyone that we had a problem. I don't know if we were putting God to the test or just plain trusting, but He came through for us. The thing that I hadn't expected was how surprised we were. We say we trust Him, so why is it we are amazed when He comes through for us?

God met our need that day—and has every day since then.

Do you have a need? Have you given it over to Him? God uses His people to reach out to others. It doesn't hurt to share your need—unless He tells you to do otherwise. But no matter how you handle it, He is there for you. Trust Him. He's a *BIG* God. * *DH*

Bing! The Light Bulb Goes On

*I now send you, to open their eyes, in order to turn them from darkness to light,
and from the power of Satan to God, that they may receive forgiveness of sins
and an inheritance among those who are sanctified by faith in Me.*

ACTS 26:17–18 NKJV

One sunny winter morning as we drove to church, my husband, Daniel, reminisced about how we had taught third-grade Sunday school. We taught the same grade together for almost five years. I used to dislike all the preparation that went into it and the follow-up, but Daniel enjoyed each minute of it. He's got a gift with children.

One year a little girl began to cry when she learned that Daniel was her teacher. At first glance my husband looks like a big, stern guy, but he's really a gentle giant with a huge heart and lots of patience. A month later, the same little girl came to trust and admire "Mr. Boeshaar" and even made him homemade Christmas ornaments that we hang on our tree to this day. Now that little girl is a young woman attending a Christian college!

"You sure are an old man," I teased Daniel. Then I saw the grin form under his mustache.

As we passed farm fields blanketed in snow, Daniel remarked how much he enjoyed seeing "the light go on" when children in our class understood the biblical concept he was presenting. "Their eyes lit up," he said. "It was so rewarding for me when I reached them like that."

"You impacted a lot of lives."

"Well, so did you."

I think about some of the kids in my classes, too. Even now when I see "my kids," all grown up in the hallways at church, I can tell that they remember I was once their fun-loving Sunday school teacher.

As much as I thought it was a pain to get ready for class, teaching Sunday school was a rewarding experience for me, too. I remember when I taught a lesson on baptism. One little girl in my class caught the meaning and wanted to be baptized. Her parents were so happy, and one Sunday night Naomi was baptized while I watched from a pew inside the sanctuary. I'll never forget how awed I felt that God would use me to reach a little girl with His truth. I guess I took the power of teaching for granted—when in actuality it's a privilege!
* AKB

Snow Wonder

*Like a snow-cooled drink at harvest time is a trustworthy messenger
to the one who sends him; he refreshes the spirit of his master.*

PROVERBS 25:13

It's snowing as I write this. What month is it? Doesn't really matter. Here in northern Wisconsin, you could flip a calendar to any month of the year and it's likely there's been snow on that date somewhere in history. With the possible exception of July.

Our furnace has been called into action many times when it thought it was on summer vacation. The conversation it conducts with the air-conditioning unit goes something like this:

"Tag. You're it."

"I thought you had it."

"That was yesterday. Your turn."

The first snowfall in a season fascinates and intrigues, as if we conveniently don't remember the batch that finally melted a few months previously.

"Look! It's snowing!"

We rush to the windows of our offices and family rooms, mesmerized by the glitter falling from the sky.

Glitter loses some of its luster toward the end of winter. A sigh follows the words, "It's snowing again." Where the sound of the snowplow once comforted—a reassuring reminder that the county guys care about our personal safety—when winter should have quit long ago, it grates like fingernails on asphalt.

But, oh, that first snowfall! Rain's fluffy but surprisingly-light-on-her-feet cousin. Angora shawls for the pine trees. An unstitched quilt for the tired lawn. A drink of once tepid air now chilled by shaved ice.

Kids and husbands beg to go out into the white. They ask for the privilege of shoveling or firing up the snowblower.

Yeah.

Those first flakes of snow make me dance too, but not because I'm enamored with a snowblower. They signal the end of canning season. Hallelujah.

Some years, the tomato crop doesn't know enough to come in out of the...snow. Though the vines had sense enough to shrivel on schedule, the tomatoes continue to ripen, spotting the garden plot more thoroughly than acne the day before prom.

Frugal enough not to waste a harvest, I'll haul in the produce with a bushel basket again, take it into the house again, dip the orbs in boiling water to remove the skins again, stuff the tomatoes into jars again, fit the jars with flats and rings again, process the jars in a hot-water bath again, cool the jars again, label them again...

"It's snowing!"

What a relief. The snow means I can put a lid on any false guilt and declare I'm done canning for another year. Grateful for the harvest and for the ability to make chili or venison stew midwinter, I'm also blessed when the snow signals the end of canning season.

Snow at the end of harvest—sweet relief.

Am I? Am I a relief for others?

When I show up on the scene, do I refresh others like an invigorating, relief-bringing first snowfall? What would have to change in my understanding and application of God's grace for that to happen? * CR

Just Kidding!

Like a maniac shooting flaming arrows of death is one who deceives
their neighbor and says, "I was only joking!"
PROVERBS 26:18–19

Recently, I watched another news story about a child who was bullied to the point of attempting suicide. When I see such things, I want to cradle the poor victim in my arms and hug him up. I also want to grab hold of the bullies and throttle them.

I was never the victim of bullying as a child, other than the occasional mean girl who muttered insults under her breath. I never suffered at the hands of a group of kids, which can even take the shape of just one bully and a roomful of silent bystanders.

I'm glad celebrities have taken up the cause of the underdog. There have been anti-bullying movements in the past in the schools and on the news, but what I've seen lately has been focused on the victims, with emphatic assurance that life gets better. And messages of conviction urge bystanders to step in to defend victims whenever they can.

That can be a scary thing to do. I remember, as a painfully shy little girl, riding the school bus and seeing a pushy girl make a big show of pretending she was in love with the heavyset boy across the aisle. She did it strictly to make fun of him. How absurd, her joke insinuated, that she would ever consider falling for someone like him. And I just sat there, staring at the ground, afraid to step in and defend him. The shame of remaining silent still burns today.

But there's another kind of bullying that's far less obvious and in many ways more devious. I've experienced it, and I've seen it between Christian husbands and wives. It's heartbreaking in its unfairness. In front of others, a husband makes a snide comment to his wife about some flaw and she's forced to either "grin and bear it" as if she doesn't care or confront him about the jab. If she does confront him, he chuckles—he might even grab her and give her a cuddle—and he says something like, "I was only joking, honey!" Or a wife might do the same about some perceived shortcoming on her husband's part, only to laugh and claim that he's being overly sensitive if he calls her on it.

That kind of bully hides behind jocularity and pretends that he or she has been misunderstood when confronted by the victim. Bystanders almost *always* notice the tension behind the so-called teasing. How often have you witnessed that kind of attack and felt comfortable to step up to defend the victim? Most of us stare at the ground like that frightened little girl on the bus. Or we smile and hope the moment will pass.

There's a place for grace in these circumstances. God's grace can shield us against words with deceitful motives. And His grace can provide us with words of encouragement for victims of such "joking." * TP

Enough Already!

*But my God shall supply all your need according
to his riches in glory by Christ Jesus.*

PHILIPPIANS 4:19 KJV

I visited a friend's new house today and happily joined the tour of oohing and ahhing partygoers. Some drooled over Italian marble floors; others wished aloud for their very own room-sized closets, big-as-a-boat spa tubs, or state-of-the-art media centers.

I like to think I'm more practical than that. The objects of my desire nestled quietly in her expansive laundry room. *Whoa,* I thought, gawking at her pearly blue front-load washer and dryer, *think what quick work I could make of dirty clothes mountains if I had those! If I earn a few extra dollars here, gave a little less of myself there, maybe—*

Then the Lord reminded me of the prior weekend, when I'd babysat my six-year-old "grandtwins" and we'd watched some cartoons and children's movies on TV. Dozens of advertisements had hit their target audience and inspired the intended "I want that!" responses. "But you already have three talking Elmos!" and "You don't even play the piano you have!" I was quick to point out.

And in a flash of insight, I realized that what I and my friend's other guests had oohed about during our house tour and the things we'd ahhed about while watching made-for-grown-ups commercials for gadget-laden cars, high-def TVs, and computers capable of controlling the lights while balancing the checkbook and sending messages to friends from Toledo to Timbuktu—that was the same thing!

Constant exposure to such products and materials just tweaks our desire to acquire more, bigger, better. Almost from the moment we set our greedy, envious eyes on Things We Don't Yet Have, we set about devising ways to replace the Just Fine devices humming in our laundry rooms, making music in our parlors, and shining in our garages.

As I prayed about this, the Lord also reminded me of all those times when my mom—flustered by her kids' never-ending need for more—shouted, "Enough, already!" I wonder if our Father ever feels like bellowing a similar line at His children....

He's blessed us so richly, with so many gifts, that maybe in being surrounded by such surplus, we overlook what—and who—is truly important.

So I hope you won't think I've gone completely nuts when you see me at the mall shouting "Enough, already!" at my own reflection in store windows! * *LL*

A Life of Giving

God loves a cheerful giver.
2 CORINTHIANS 9:7 NKJV

Before I ever met Cheryl, she gave me something. It was my husband's first year to teach and her son's last year of high school. There was an instant chemistry between Ruston and Stone and me, and we got close to him. He was smart, funny, and mature for his age. We had him in our home several times.

At Christmastime, Ruston came for a visit and brought a little bag. In it was an ornament—pewter angels—and a hand towel embroidered with a dove. "My mom wants to thank you," he said shyly, "for being my friends."

Not long after that Cheryl invited us over. We sat on striped chairs in her living room in front of the fire and bonded with her and her husband, Steve. I don't know if they were testing us—these new people in their son's life—but I guess if they were, we passed. They became some of the best friends we would ever have.

We moved to Gentry shortly after that to be closer to Stone's job. Cheryl had a rental house she offered us, and we planned to move into it until she called us. "I've found something better for you," she said. "You can't move into my little house when there's a nicer one down the street." I began to recognize this selfless sort of giving as a pattern in my new friend. She came and decorated my house, hauling in pillows she'd made, curtains she'd bought, trinkets she'd found here and there. The delight I felt as I saw my "nest" taking shape around me was second only to the delight I saw in Cheryl—the sheer joy she seemed to get out of giving.

And it wasn't only me. The more time I spent with her, the more I realized she did things like this for everybody, at least everybody who would let her. Shopping with her became a lesson in gift buying. Christmas, new babies, friends' birthdays, the weather—she was always looking for an opportunity to give.

One time we were out to lunch. We had just been to our favorite store, TJ Maxx, where she'd picked up an assortment of odds and ends. "I know you'll think I'm crazy," Cheryl told me with a surreptitious grin, "but I believe God leads me to things He wants me to give other people. Just look at this great stuff I found!" She dug in her bag, showing me what was for whom and explaining how each thing was the perfect fit for a need she'd seen.

"I don't think you're crazy." I smiled at her. "I believe you have the gift of giving."

Cheryl's gift has been poured out in my life so many times I could never list them all. And while she's blessed my family with countless material things, it's her heart that she's given most of all. In phone calls, e-mails, a road trip to a friend's "just to be together," Cheryl gives away her heart like my baby, Adelaide, gives kisses—free and with abandon.

"How can you give so much?" I've asked her before, knowing there are times her generosity has met with painful rejection and, what's maybe worse, others taking advantage of her. It makes me angry when I see this happen, and I'm amazed sometimes at the way she keeps on giving.

"I can't help it," Cheryl says, like we're talking about resisting chocolate. "God's blessed me, and I just feel it's the right way to live." * *GF*

Missing the Point

It is a trap to dedicate something rashly and only later to consider one's vows.
PROVERBS 20:25

You really want to help, and so you impulsively blurt out your plans. "I can lend you the money, Sarah. It will take care of the immediate situation. Just pay me back whenever you can." And then reality sets in.

Yes, you have the money in your savings account, but what if Sarah doesn't repay the debt before the taxes come due? What if the circumstance is part of God's plan for Sarah's life? Have you stolen the teaching opportunity by rashly swooping in to help?

My father was a strong and resolute man, an influence over our family's life that loomed large and cast an imposing shadow. If a decision needed to be made, he made it without flinching. I can't tell you how many times I found myself in a tight spot only to be rescued by my father. I learned early what a hero is made of.

The upside: I had someone in my life that I could always count on. The downside: *I had someone in my life that I could always count on.*

I never learned until long after my father died how to problem solve or weigh the details of a situation and make an independent, well-informed decision all on my own. I also learned far too late that having a strong male figure in your immediate sphere does *not* mean he will be heroic. In fact, those expectations can put a lot of added pressure on a relationship in the real world—the world where retired Marine Corps Officer Dad no longer exists and mere mortal men are trying, just like you, to figure things out for themselves.

I have come to believe that part of the grace that God extends to us includes the lessons we learn through the really tough times. In many cases, He's not going to prevent us from falling into unexpected trouble, but He will be there to walk through it with us. So jumping into something impulsively, even with the best of intentions to help someone, might just be a "trap," as the proverb says—a trap to the sav*er* as well as the sav*ee*.

When no one has been there to pick me up, put me back on my feet, and tell me which way to go in order to find safety, I've had to figure it out. Not always gracefully, and certainly not always without consequence or even regret, but always with a Silent Partner at my side to help me to keep going when strength fails…and to help me learn a valuable lesson.

You know that saying, "Give a man a fish, feed him for a day; teach a man to fish, feed him for a lifetime"? I always thought that was well and good, until it came down to it. I'd much rather order the salmon at my favorite restaurant than have to catch it, clean it, and cook it! But isn't it nice to know that you can if you have to? *SDB*

I Want What I Want

The LORD is my shepherd, I shall not be in want.

PSALM 23:1

"Take what's yours before someone else gets it." "You deserve the best of everything." "Be tough and stand up for yourself." "Whoever amasses the most toys wins." "Be assertive." With thinking like this, who needs God? We can make our own destiny by following the rules of the rich and famous. All we have to do is watch a few reality shows on TV, take notes, and do what they do.

I have to admit that I've been guilty of watching some of these shows. I'm amazed by the sheer opulence I see. I'm also appalled by the train-wreck lives some of them have and how they are rewarded for misbehavior. (Shh! Don't tell anyone—that's part of what draws me.) Sure, everyone knows it's important to behave—at least when people are looking. Or if we have a good reason and a TV camera captures the moment, it's okay to misbehave. According to the laws of the land, we're good citizens if we don't murder, steal, or cheat. Some of the older rules included marital fidelity and respect toward others, but as nonbelievers take over, the rules change.

Following God's plan seems to be an outdated way to live, based on what we see on TV. We're challenged to follow a format that seems attractive and exciting on the outside, but beneath the outward appeal is a sinful motive of self-indulgence in whatever feels good. I think it's obvious that, deep down, most people feel empty with this type of thinking.

As people ridicule the Bible and God's Word, I'm deeply saddened by the bitterness their lack of belief in the Savior has caused. On the surface, their point seems valid. They look at Christ and how He's described: humble servant; always loving; never sinned; born in a stable to outcast parents; filled with sorrow; a crown of thorns. So they ask, "Huh? This is the King we're supposed to follow?" They wonder what happened to the glorious splendor befitting royalty: purple robes and golden sashes; an ornate throne; a crown with gemstones so heavy a common person would get a headache from it; promises of special favors if we suck up; power; prestige; famous people on speed dial. In their world, God's Word is falling on deaf ears to anyone who isn't willing to look past the shell of righteousness.

Occasionally, I think about how fun it would be to trade places with people who live the trendy lifestyle of shallow perfection. But as I look closer, I see that the joy of knowing Christ is missing. * DM

A Pfennig for Your Thoughts

Hear, O Israel: The LORD our God, the LORD is one.

DEUTERONOMY 6:4

The shelf above my computer is filled with photos of my husband, kids, grandkids, and deceased pets (including Keith, the county fair–won goldfish that lived to the ripe old age of eleven). And the wall behind the pictures is papered with dozens of old saws, adages, parables, and proverbs.

The two I quote most often are, "Do or do not; there *is* no try" and "Good enough never is." (Just ask my kids!) The message is threefold:

Commitment ignites action; your word is your bond; practice your beliefs consistently.

"Stand for something," I've said a hundred times if I've said it once, "or you'll fall for anything." After speeches like that, my kids had every right to expect that, as their mother, I would set a proper example. Self-confidence, integrity, a willingness to dig in and perform the same jobs I'd asked them to do was, of course, important. But so was supporting them—especially when "slipshod" seemed to be their modus operandi—and giving them a chance to prove that maybe, just maybe, they really *could* find faster, easier, more effective ways of getting things accomplished.

I'm reasonably certain that long before Ferdinand Porsche built his first automobile, *his* mama bounced her fair share of *pfennigs* off his blankets, which no doubt led to his success. (Remember the now-clichéd response he gave the reporter who asked which was his favorite Porsche?

"Why, I haven't built it yet!")

And how could I expect my girls to improve in mind, body, and spirit if they didn't see improvements in me too? Seeking a better, easier way of doing things, in my honest opinion, proves personal growth. Equally important? A willingness to take a risk now and then, instead of merely insisting that things get done *my* way.

Motivating our kids to do the right thing isn't easy, particularly when we're asking them to perform difficult or boring tasks. But as Epicurus taught his young'uns way back when, "A captain earns his reputation during storms." We all want smooth-sailing in our children's future, so why not test their navigation skills while they're still in the boat with us, rather than let them flounder all alone on life's turbulent seas?

Our Father promised always to be there, lifeline at the ready, any time we need Him. If we add "faith in Him" to the lessons we teach our children, they'll have the strength to stand up against those who'd try to steer them off course. If they learn to rely on God with every cell He set pulsing inside them, they'll recognize the grace that can be theirs just by asking for it.

And you know, I can't think of any greater gift to give them than that! * *LL*

Times Not Meant for the Faint of Heart

*Do not fear, for you will not be ashamed; neither be disgraced, for you will
not be put to shame; for you will forget the shame of your youth, and will not remember the reproach
of your widowhood anymore. For your Maker is your husband, the LORD of hosts is His name;
and your Redeemer is the Holy One of Israel; He is called the God of the whole earth.*

ISAIAH 54:4–5 NKJV

I was sixteen when I met Marian for the first time. She was a couple of years older than I was, a barrel of fun, and so pretty. All the boys' heads turned when Marian walked across a room, and I felt *cooler* just being around her. We've been through some roller-coaster years together, but now, at fifty-*cough* years old, Marian is still one of my favorite people. She still turns heads, she can still make me laugh in a nanosecond, and I still feel a little bit cooler just by being in her company.

When I met Stan for the first time, I remember scratching my head. This wasn't the husband I had pictured for Marian! He was a cowboy, and she was a social butterfly. But over the many years since they'd found one another, I was able to get to know him better—his humor, his wit, his enormous heart—and I started to see the beauty in the pairing. It simply worked for them.

Stan died on my birthday this year. I was heartbroken not just at losing him, but in knowing that, for the rest of her life, my dearest friend would remember my birthday as the day she lost her partner in life.

I expected her to fall apart; after all, that's what I did when my first love died. I closed myself away from everyone who loved me, rejecting any offered comfort, reminding myself several dozen times a day that I would never love anyone like that again and no one would ever love me. But Marian's strength and grace in the absolute worst of times, and her ability to take such joy in the memory of her dear husband as she simultaneously dealt with his loss, was astonishing.

I'd watched her faith blossom over the decades that we'd known each other, but it occurred to me on the morning of Stan's memorial service that, rather than losing herself in fears about the future or misgivings about how to live without her husband, Marian was leaning hard on the God she knew she could rely upon. She knew that secret only believers know; she was held up by the promise that her Maker was her husband now.

Times such as these are not recommended to the faint of heart; however, with deep and abiding faith also comes strength. And wearing the godly strength that she's grown into makes me feel far more secure—and just a little bit *cooler*!—when basking in the illuminated light of my friend's faith. * *SDB*

Sweet Words

Gracious words are a honeycomb, sweet to the soul and healing to the bones.
PROVERBS 16:24

One Christmas, a middle-aged relative—we'll name him Ted—gave everyone in the family the DVD of a stand-up comic's live performance. He loved the comedian's routine and wanted to share it with everyone.

I'm no prude. I was grown up, with a lifetime's worth of worldly experiences, by the time I found Christ. So I've heard and seen what "the world" finds humorous. I can handle bawdy humor, and I love wry, satirical storytelling.

But this guy's words were far from honeycomb sweetness. He wasn't even funny, just foul and juvenile.

Later I heard that Ted lost his temper with my aging mom after he played the same DVD in front of her and she reacted with confused shock at the content. That didn't sit well with me.

So at the next family gathering, when we all sat down to a meal and Ted started to talk about this same comic, I interrupted. "Ugh! I *hate* that guy!"

That news didn't sit well with Ted. Especially not delivered as it was, in front of everyone to whom he had given the DVD. He seethed during our before-meal prayer, uttering expletives and breathing heavily. Then he wolfed down his meal and stormed out of the room.

This paints a harsh picture of Ted—there's no other way to paint him in this instance. But the point of this story isn't to focus on Ted or the vulgar comedian. It is to focus on *moi*.

"Ugh! I *hate* that guy!" Not exactly sweet words. No images of honey spring to mind, do they? I felt justified in taking a stance against the comedian's words and in squelching a rehash of his humor in mixed company. But my method was far from pleasant.

Clearly, Ted felt that a part of his identity was connected to this DVD because he had made it a gift to others. What he probably heard was, "Ugh! I hate *you*." I'm not saying that's a healthy or mature reaction on his part. I'm saying it's the likely one.

Had I taken the time to find a kinder way to express my thoughts, Ted might still have taken it personally. But that really isn't the issue here. My role as a Christian is to find words that fall sweetly on the ears of others, whenever I can.

I often picture the stereotypical, sweet-talking Christian woman whose voice is as soft as bunny tails, whose delivery is what you'd expect from a cuddly lamb, if it could talk. She is *so* not me, and I sometimes think of women like that as kind of…weak.

My voice is often more like a crow's, my delivery like a snapping turtle's. I'd have to work hard to sound that pleasant, which is probably what those "weak" women have already figured out. * *TP*

A Life of Confidence

Then Mary said, Behold, I am the handmaiden of the Lord;
let it be done to me according to what you have said.

LUKE 1:83 AMP

Mary was a teenager when the angel visited her and announced that she was to be the mother of God. Her response, one of total trust, is something that amazes me. She's dazzling in her simplicity, her purity. On the written page of the gospel of Luke, her words of submission seem to flow without any effort or struggle. And yet, I wonder, what was really going on with Mary, on the inside?

A few verses before this, we find a hint. Luke writes that when Mary first saw the angel and was greeted by him, "She was greatly troubled and disturbed and confused." These feelings seem to dissipate only when the angel says, "Do not be afraid, Mary, for you have found grace with God" (Luke 1:29–30 AMP).

It seems there was a principle for Mary in the angel's words, one she would carry with her throughout her life. "Do not be afraid…for you have found grace." It's God's grace that would calm her fears in that moment and motivate her to trust Him…God's grace that would carry her this time, through a scandalous pregnancy, and also later, through every phase of her Son's life. His grace became her confidence.

We're not given a lot of details about Jesus's childhood. There's the blessing of the baby by Simeon, when Mary is told that a sword will pierce through her own soul (Luke 2:35 AMP). And after that, a time when Jesus stayed behind in the temple in Jerusalem after His parents left town.

When Mary and Joseph found their son and scolded him for worrying them, he said, "Did you not know that I must be about My Father's business?" (Luke 2:49 NKJV). After that, the Bible says "Mary kept and…guarded all these things in her heart" (Luke 2:51 AMP). Though we don't know everything it entailed, there's a sense that Mary is actively engaged, participating in the will of God—and the destiny of her Son Jesus—all along.

What must it have been like to be there, to see Him beaten and hung on a cross? As a mother, this is where Mary's story touches me the deepest. I'm sure everything in her flesh cried out against the soldiers to save him from such pain. What would it take for a mother to stand there and watch her Son die, offering every grain of strength she had in her to support Him in His mission?

Trust. That's what it would take—confidence in the grace of God.

Mary was not superhuman. She was not pure or strong in herself, nor did she hold herself up as a model for others to worship. Her beauty was not in her glowing résumé, but something much deeper.

She is an example of a real woman who chose to put her confidence in God's character, no matter what it cost. She did not give in to fear because she'd found His grace. And God's grace enabled her to trust Him, even at the cross.
*GF

Reality Does Bite!

May the LORD answer you in the day of trouble; may the name of the God of Jacob defend you; may He send you help from the sanctuary, and strengthen you out of Zion; may He remember all your offerings, and accept your burnt sacrifice. Selah. May He grant you according to your heart's desire, and fulfill all your purpose.

PSALM 20:1–4 NKJV

Some days take a real nip at your joy, don't they?

I always try to start my mornings with a little bit of Jesus—maybe a few minutes reading the Word or having a nice chat with Him while I'm putting on my makeup. And then each day, I walk out the door with the same words on my lips: "This is the day the Lord has made. I will rejoice and be glad in it!"

And I mean it, too. I'm determined. After all, my God has given me a pretty great life. I've survived cancer; I have great friends and a personable dog; and I'm surrounded with a lot of love. Best of all, despite the fact that I still work a "day job," I've finally begun to realize my dream of becoming a writer after a lifetime of hoping and trying. So when I walk out that door, proclaiming my intention to rejoice and be glad in the day the Lord has made just for me, I mean it. I'm going to do my job, try to bless someone along the way, and then head home for some time in front of the computer to work on my latest novel!

Ah, I'm such a very good planner. It's a gift, really.

Then comes the commute to work and the guy who cuts me off in traffic and makes me spill my coffee. This fun is almost always followed by my painstakingly organized calendar of duties getting shot with meeting requests, ringing phones, project emergencies, and coworkers who need a hand.

And so, by lunchtime, all those early morning thoughts of a nice dinner and a few writing hours at home after work begin to shred beneath the grinding, biting teeth of Reality.

I'm the type of person who can really be thrown off track by a few days like that in a row. Things start to back up on me, my calendar becomes a bit of a joke, and I find myself missing the breathtaking view of the forest for all the trees standing tall in front of me. In fact, I am often overwhelmed by those tall trees, and my methodical plans and godly purpose end up scattered and broken, roadkill on the shoulder of the highway that is my life.

I once had a friend ask me, "When is my life going to calm down?"

I had a moment of sheer clarity when I smiled and said, "It's not."

The truth is that this is the stuff life is made of. Interruptions and challenges, obstacles to overcome and mountains to climb: It all acts like iron against iron to grow us stronger throughout our lives. The best we can do is bounce back every now and then, remind ourselves what's most important, and take a deep breath and let it out slowly before we head out the door with words of assurance on our lips once again:

"This is the day the Lord has made. I will rejoice and be glad in it!" * *SDB*

Step Away from the Sack!

Return to the LORD your God, for he is gracious and compassionate,
slow to anger and abounding in love.

JOEL 2:13

Okay. All right. So I get it: we all get mad from time to time. It's normal. In some cases, it's healthy. At the very least, it's *human.* Why, even Jesus lost His temper in the temple.

And therein lies the rub: if you're gonna go ballistic, you'd best have a justifiable reason. If only the <*ahem*> gentleman ahead of me at the airport last week had lived by those words.

There are rules posted here and there in the airport—not many, but since they change like the weather, everybody knows it's mostly monkey-see-monkey-do once you enter the terminal:

Check in at the ticket counter (even if you've done so online) and release your suitcase to the agent. Put your ID and boarding pass where they're easy to get to, and when you reach the security lanes, remove your shoes, coat, metal-buckled belt, bracelet, watch, and whatever else might go *beep* in the X-ray tunnel.

Empty your pockets of coins, cell phone, throat lozenges, and tissues—even used ones—then open your briefcase and purse and place them, with your laptop and everything else listed above, into an ugly gray plastic bin. Now wait your turn at shoving the works down the conveyor belt, and then wait your turn *again* as the guards randomly select which passengers will walk through the metal detector and which they'll put into the we-can-see-all-of-you-and-we-do-mean-all-of-you booth.

I'm sure you've watched old Westerns where cattle are herded into a corral. Take your behavioral cues from the bovines, my friends, and just moo-o-ove quietly along, because trying to buck the system will only clog the chute. And nobody wants that, because on The Other Side...freedom, wonderful freedom awaits!

So anyway, although this so-called seasoned traveler-guy in front of me knew all of this, he *still* blew a gasket when a guard said he had to dispose of his fast-food sack. Mr. Not-so-Cool waved his arms. Stomped his blue-socked feet. Hollered and cursed and made hit-and-miss threats until he was hoarse and his face went purple and sweaty.

Was he justified, losing his temper? Mmm...nah.

Did anyone in the line show pity? Mmm...yeah, but his red-faced wife wasn't among them.

Safe on The Other Side, I prayed for the guy whose conduct made me wonder if he had a relationship with God. I prayed that if he didn't, he'd *find* God, and soon, so that he could learn firsthand what it's like to be loved by a being who is slow to anger, gracious and compassionate, abounding in love...even when the behavior of His children tempt *Him* to go ballistic.

I prayed for the rest of the people in line too, and for the flight crew and myself. Because let's face it...there but by the grace of God... * *LL*

For When You Go Batty

Commit to the LORD whatever you do, and your plans will succeed.

PROVERBS 16:3

How do you know when you're following God's plan for you?

When the UPS man handed me the first copy of my first published book, you'd have thought I'd jump up and down with joy, wouldn't you? Not this girlfriend! Rather, I stood there, holding that book, and experienced a momentary flood of freak-out.

What am I doing? What if my loved ones and friends read this novel and think I stink on ice? What if I never get another book idea? Who am I fooling? Did I misunderstand God's plan for me? How will I know if I'm getting it wrong? Will He use mean reviews and a public shunning to communicate His message? Will He smite me thusly? I don't want to be smote! I don't do well with smiting!

After all these years, I know to stop and pray whenever I go batty like that. I'm telling you, you'll never go wrong with prayer. Like Jell-O, there's always room for it. And in this particular situation, He gave me immediate peace. This time He blessed me with this thought:

"If you commit to Me whatever you do, I will never stomp on your efforts to honor Me. I'm not saying there won't be bumps in the road, but if you commit to Me whatever you do, and I want you to do something else—no worries, dear—I'll lovingly guide you to that something else. I'll lift up in you a desire to do that something else. I love that you want to honor Me. So commit to Me whatever you do, pay attention to what drives you, and then go for it!"

The comforting aspect of such a thought is that, yes, my plans will succeed because eventually He'll make my plans the same as His.

Do you find yourself in flux about decisions, big and small, immediate and long-term? Are you trying to live the life He planned for you but feeling confused about what that entails? Do you struggle to know whether something in your life is God's guidance or simply the hard knocks of life? Or the blessings of life? If you'll take the time each morning to commit to God everything you do that day, you can rest in His promise. Your plans might change. Or they might not unfold exactly as you expected. But they will most definitely succeed. * *TP*

True Fulfillment

*A man can do nothing better than to eat and drink
and find satisfaction in his work.*

ECCLESIASTES 2:24

Wealth is flaunted in front of us every day. As an advertising major in college and a marketing director before becoming a writer, my job was to sell people the dream.

As I've gotten older, I realize how ridiculous that dream is. One doesn't have to look far to see empty lives in gilded cages. Everyone on this earth needs a purpose, and looking half your age is not really a purpose. It's a nice gift but, ultimately, it makes your life no richer. Without purpose, we search to be filled; but without a mission, we are merely wanderers in the desert, hoping in vain to find the elusive oasis and drink heartily from its pool.

Living through the dot-com bust, I watched friends become multimillionaires...but lives didn't really change that much. People's houses got bigger, maybe their kids went to better schools, but in the end, what was important to them was important to all of us. Money made no difference in their quality of life at all. They had more, but they had more to worry about.

When you know what you're about, making the right choices becomes easier and you can't be sold a bill of goods by a skilled marketing magnate. Once, I wrote a book born out of passion and zeal for a subject close to my heart. I partnered with a publisher on the project, and it didn't work out. Our missions did not coincide. In the end, after trying to make a square peg fit into a round hole, we mutually decided the book belonged elsewhere.

It was a costly decision, not only in time, which I didn't have to lose, but also in finances, which I also didn't have. But because of my purpose, my passion for the book, it was easy to walk away and do the right thing. I answer to Him, and I thought that answer would be compromised if the book was written the way this publisher's mission required. I notice that when I look around me to see what everyone else is doing and compare myself, it's a lot more difficult to do what God is calling me to do.

In the end, God will replace the years the locusts have eaten. He has proven that time and time again. I can look upon the time as wasted, or I can look upon it as a lesson learned, a reminder to stay on the path God has ordained for me. At the end of it, there is nothing better than to be in His will and find satisfaction in my work. The cherry on top is fellowship and food. * *KB*

Wait Is a Four-Letter Word

Be still, and know that I am God.

PSALM 46:10 NKJV

The neighborhood luminaria was a tradition. Every Christmas Eve before the big family dinner, my dad and I would go into the garage and fill paper bags with sand. Then we carried them out to the street and, measuring out five big teenage-sized steps between them, plopped down the bags along the edge of our property line. Then it was my job to carefully plant one candle into each bag. After dinner, right at dusk, we'd go outside, bundled up with coats and gloves and scarves, and light the candles with the neighbors so that the entire neighborhood was outlined with a magical Christmas Eve luminaria. It's my favorite Christmas memory.

For several years, it was just about all I could do to get through dinner. I wanted to light those candles so badly!

"You don't want to light them too early," my mom explained. "You want them to blend in with the rest of the neighborhood. That's why everyone lights them at the same time."

But I didn't care about blending or the neighborhood, and certainly not about waiting! I just wanted to see those beautiful lights flickering along the bottom of the hill next to our road.

One year, I was able to talk my dad into letting me light the candles before dinner. It was going to snow, I reasoned. It made sense to light the candles beforehand. When my father finally agreed, I was jubilant and ran out of the house without a coat, flicking the lighter before I ever reached the bottom of the drive.

But the truth is…it was a bit of a letdown. Ours was the only house flanked by the luminaria lights, and although it was lovely, I was really struck by the difference later that night when our neighbors joined in and the unbroken trail of lights circled the entire block and curved around the steep hill at the edge of our neighborhood. I admitted that night that I wished I'd waited. I think it must have been music to my mother's ears.

Waiting is such a difficult thing, especially when the prize is well within our sight. But I've learned over the years that there is actually a joy in learning to wait. There is delicious anticipation, never knowing what God might do at the last minute to surprise you.

"Be still, and know that I am God," His Word tells us. But today He might say to us, "Be still and put your feet up. Think about something else. Let your nail polish dry! Be still and wait to see how I'm going to dazzle you."
* SDB

Looking for a Refund

*Her husband Joseph was an honorable man and did not
want to disgrace her publicly. So he decided to break
the marriage agreement with her secretly.*

MATTHEW 1:19 GWT

Today the Christmas story conjures up images of shepherds and angels, a baby in a manger, wise men kneeling with expensive gifts. We hear "Silent Night" in our imagination and smile as we think of snowflakes softly falling and gifts wrapped neatly with a bow.

But it didn't start out that way. It started out with Joseph, an honorable young man, receiving the heart-wrenching news that Mary, the woman he intended to marry, was pregnant with someone else's child. No explanation could cover the facts. The law and custom of the day gave him two choices: have her stoned for prostitution, or quietly break off the engagement.

As we unwrap the gift of life, sometimes we see things we didn't expect. In panic, we want to rush back to the store with the receipt and demand an exchange. Nothing makes sense. God must have it wrong. Life dealt us the wrong set of cards. The beauty of Joseph's story and our own is this: As we enter God's presence to ponder our choices, a whole new way of looking at things opens up before us. Our tragedy is erased. In its place is the wonder of God's perfect plan.
* SGES

Christian Is as Christian Does

You, however, must teach what is appropriate to sound doctrine.

TITUS 2:1

Not too long ago, I wrote an e-mail to my daughter about a family member with whom I was frustrated. It was angry. It was even snarky. My daughter was a safe person to vent to because she and I both love this family member and nothing I said in frustration would shake that love. I just needed to blow off steam.

The only problem was that, in my emotional distraction, I didn't enter my daughter's e-mail address. I entered the family member's address—the one about whom I was rudely complaining—and pushed SEND.

I didn't discover my mistake for hours, and I nearly went into shock when I did. I think the only time I've sweated more was when I was in labor with my kids.

Never has an apology—a profuse apology, I should add—come easier. It killed me that I had inflicted such hurt on a loved one. I'm blessed that she has such a forgiving spirit.

The memory of my embarrassing error arose when I looked into today's verse. I had always thought that "sound doctrine" meant sensible, reasonable, well-substantiated doctrine. So it sounds as if the verse means "make sure what you teach is biblically based." Certainly that's always true. But apparently, for purposes of this verse, the meaning is that we must teach doctrine that conforms to the Lord's Word and results in encouraging Christlike behavior.

Certainly we see that quality in the teaching we receive on Sunday morning from our pastor, who wants his words to motivate us to live as Christ wants us to. And Sunday school teachers have that result in mind when they find creative ways to instill God's tenets in the hearts of our little ones. Our Bible-study groups are all about an end result that includes behavior so attractive that others will be drawn to what we have in our hearts. We should mirror Christ in our attractive behavior.

Ahem.

I think it's safe to say that my behavior—my nasty, ranting little e-mail—didn't exactly fall within the parameters of "sound doctrine." Because, when you think about it, if we profess to be followers of Christ, our actions and words teach the world about how Christ affects lives and choices. What we do is a picture of what we are. And what I was at that moment wasn't just distracted. It was mean and horribly hurtful. I'm sure I didn't just break my loved one's heart. I know I broke my own. And I surely broke His. Look at me! I'm the good little Christian, and look how I show it! Yeesh.

As beaten to death as the phrase is, "What Would Jesus Do" is still a smart thought to review before taking emotional action. If Jesus had had access to e-mail, something tells me that He would have written something my loved one would have absolutely cherished. * *TP*

Dangerous

But grow in the grace and knowledge of our Lord and Savior Jesus Christ.
To him be glory both now and forever! Amen.

2 PETER 3:18

Too young. He was too young to die. She was too young to become a widow. Their children were too young to sit in the front row at a funeral, too young to squeeze out a smile and say "Thank you for coming" as the mourners filed past.

Condolences and casseroles sustained them for those first intense, swirling, numb days of grief. Reality followed on the heels of the casseroles and cakes. As it often happens, single parenting was accompanied by financial desperation. She breathed only because she knew she had to and dove into God's Word the way a sobbing child might bury herself in her father's shoulder.

I didn't meet her until years later, long after her path changed again with a corporate job that more than met their financial needs and an outpouring of God's grace that met every cry of their hearts. Comfortable suburban life settled around their family. Her children graduated, married, and blessed her with grandchildren. And then God spoke.

When she prayed for the Lord to send someone to work with the homeless and destitute in the inner city, He said, *"You go."*

"Me, Lord? I'm about to retire. I don't feel confident driving through the inner city, much less living there. I know what it's like to be poor and hurting, but You brought me out of that. Thanks again, by the way. A silver-haired Caucasian suburban grandmother? I'm the unlikeliest candidate."

Despite the shocked expressions of...well, everyone... she moved from hard-won comfort to the graffitied heart of one of the poorest neighborhoods in the country, into the heart of danger.

Today she claims she moved out of danger to a place of safety.

"Complacency is dangerous," she says. "I left complacency and took up residence where my heavenly Father is responsible for my safety. I was in danger of growing indifferent because I was comfortable."

Her eyes shine with reflections from the poverty-stricken and spiritually troubled to whom she's shown God's love, those whose lives she's seen transformed by His grace. "I can't be indifferent anymore. I can only live by grace."

Grace applied to the fatherless. Grace lavished on the homeless. Grace poured out for those whose pupils are perpetually dilated from who-knows-what, and whose clothes—both sets—smell rancid with the sludge of life. Grace offered freely with no hope of "You can pay me back later." Grace the way God designed it.

I have a lot of growing to do. * *CR*

Weighting

Wait for the Lord; be strong and take heart and wait for the Lord.
PSALM 27:14

I sent a quick e-mail to a friend: "I haven't heard from you in ages. What are you up to?"

Her reply came the next day. "Same as always. Just weighting."

Weighting? Was she being cryptic? I had to pick up the phone and find out. When I pointed out the incorrect spelling in Kelly's e-mail, it turned out (at least in her mind) to be an honest mistake. Her story convinced me, however, that it may have been a bit Freudian.

For almost a year, Kelly played the role of the silent brokenhearted wife, knowing full well that the man she'd married now had another woman in his life. Then one afternoon, she returned from the office to find her home devoid of every last trace of her husband of thirteen years. Jason had taken his clothes, electronics, stacks of opened mail, the framed photos of his parents, even the blue toothbrush that stood next to Kelly's red one. On the kitchen counter was a note scribbled on the back of a takeout menu. "I can't do this anymore. Sorry."

When I reached her that day, I found Kelly curled up in a ball on the bedroom floor, crying like a baby. An hour later, she was still sobbing and I was on the floor too, my arms around my friend, struggling to find some speck of comfort to offer her. So when she later told me that her future plans revolved around waiting for Jason to come to his senses and return to her, I was the one who wanted to cry.

But wait Kelly did. Week after week, month after month, she waited, praying every day that God would reward her with the return of her husband. The misspelling in her e-mail reminded me what a heavy burden she'd been carrying. "Waiting on the Lord" had been an enormous "weight" on Kelly. She sounded exhausted, weary from the battle, but not so weary that she might give up.

"I still believe Jason will come home," she told me. "I know God put us together for a reason. Until He changes my heart, I have no choice. I'm waiting on the Lord."

Despite my own lack of faith in Jason's redemption, I really admire my friend for hanging on the way that she has. Her own devotion to the promises of God inspire me to question how many times in my life I may have missed out on something because I didn't have the fortitude to hang on and see how the Lord might turn the situation around.
* SDB

A Life of Prayer

Now there was one, Anna, a prophetess, the daughter of Phanuel,
of the tribe of Asher. She was of a great age, and had lived with a husband seven years
from her virginity; and this woman was a widow of about eighty-four years,
who did not depart from the temple, but served God with fastings and prayers night
and day. And coming in that instant she gave thanks to the Lord, and spoke
of Him to all those who looked for redemption in Jerusalem.

LUKE 2:36–38 NKJV

Anna is mentioned only once in the Bible, in the Gospel account of Luke, when Mary and Joseph take baby Jesus to the temple to dedicate Him to the Lord. Simeon is there, a righteous man who was led by the Spirit to the temple, and Luke writes that *in that instant* Anna also shows up and gives thanks to the Lord. She testifies that Jesus is the Messiah (v. 38) to everyone who is looking for redemption. Anna is over one hundred years old.

I can learn a lot from this woman about timing, thankfulness, evangelism, and even aging gracefully. But all of those things branch out from a deeper central stream: The basis for everything Anna is and does is prayer. The Bible says she served God with prayer *night and day* (v. 37).

Imagine this older woman, a widow for eighty-four years, praying every day without ceasing at the temple. She fasted and told God everything that was on her heart.

She probably confessed sin and thanked the Lord for His goodness. I'm sure she interceded for others and listened for God's voice.

This day was, in many ways, like all the others. She was doing her job. Except today the Messiah would appear in the temple in the form of a baby in His mother's arms. And Anna, who had faithfully yielded her heart in prayer for a lifetime, would be there. She got to see Jesus.

What happens when we pray? It's not so different from Anna's experience. We pour out our thoughts. We confess our sin and offer thanksgiving. We intercede for others; God speaks to our hearts. Most of us could probably benefit from more fasting. But the greatest thing that happens when we yield ourselves to God in prayer is this: Like Anna that day at the temple, the Messiah comes to us. We see Jesus. * *GF*

Critics, Schmitics

He mocks proud mockers but shows favor to the humble and oppressed.

PROVERBS 3:34

I love the way Jesus ignored the critics. So self-assured of His mission, even at a very young age, He traveled the path from manger to cross with enviable laser vision.

In the weeks leading up to the release of a novel, the reviews start to hit the forums. To a large extent, most of the reviewers of my books for the inspirational market have been Christians themselves. Somewhere within the pages of my novels, they've been able to find someone or something with which to identify, so they've warmed up to the characters and their challenges.

Recently, publishers have been hooking up with Amazon to provide free downloads of certain books for Kindle customers. These promotions have the benefit of supporting the relatively new idea of e-books as well as getting the work of various writers into hands they might otherwise never reach.

On the downside, however, people really love getting something for free. Often it doesn't matter in the least whether it's something they would normally purchase—*it's free!* So people who don't gravitate toward romantic fiction, particularly geared for the Christian market, download our books and are surprised by the content. In response, they hurry over to the Web site and post one-star reviews because they don't like that the author "pushed Jesus" on them or they feel like romance is a waste of text.

But…*it's Christian romantic comedy.* So a little Jesus and a lot of romance are kind of required, aren't they? And now the one-star reviews have pulled all those other four- and five-star ratings out of their happy heights. With those first few bad reviews, I had visions of tracking them down, explaining my point of view and…. But, of course, that wouldn't be wise. I worried about those one-stars just the same. They gave me queasy stomachs and pounding headaches, and I started wishing I could put a stop to those free downloads altogether.

Cut to: Sandie, growing up.

There are always going to be critics. There will be people who genuinely don't appreciate my writing alongside haters who simply don't like overweight, sarcastic redheads with the arrogance to believe that God has called them to do something in life. I get that. In fact, I'm annoyed by myself all the time.

Proverbs 4:25–27 admonishes us to keep our eyes fixed on the road ahead without swerving to the right or the left. I think that's the secret. Don't get pulled into battles you can't win; they will drain your energy in their futility. Just press on, staying humble about the mission God has given you; maintain your focus and don't get distracted by the haters (or the one-star givers). As today's verse promises, He will provide the grace needed to carry you through. In the bigger picture, isn't that really all you need? * *SDB*

Seeking Intimacy with God

Set your mind and heart to seek the LORD your God.

1 CHRONICLES 22:19 NRSV

Those of us who have goals quickly discover that setting the goal is only the beginning. The diligence required to reach your goal is the most demanding part of the journey. For example, deciding to be a professional golfer is the easier part. The determination to make it a reality will consume the better part of your life.

What about goals that are of a more private and personal nature? For instance, how do you reach the goal of becoming a friend of God? Just as is true in any friendship, to become intimate with God you must learn to engage with Him with your intellect and your emotions. And since you can't meet with Him face to face you must seek Him where He can be found.

First, discover God with your mind. Seek Him by reading about Him in the Bible, inspirational books, stories, and testimonials. Listen to godly teachers and preachers. Ask family and friends about their experiences with God.

The more you know about Him, the more you will experience God with your heart. Speak to Him in prayer and wait for the quiet impression of His Spirit speaking to your heart. Don't be afraid to talk to Him about anything. He already knows you inside and out. * SGES

Ellie Claire® Gift & Paper Expressions
Brentwood, TN 37027
EllieClaire.com

Be Still...and Let Your Nail Polish Dry: A 365-Day Devotional Journal
© 2014 by Ellie Claire
Ellie Claire is registered trademark of Worthy Media, Inc.

ISBN 978-1-60936-956-9

Stock or custom editions of Ellie Claire titles may be purchased in bulk for educational, business, ministry, fundraising, or sales promotional use. For information, please e-mail info@EllieClaire.com.

Devotions by: Kristin Billerbeck (KB), Andrea Boeshaar (AKB), Sandra D. Bricker (SDB), Gwen Faulkenberry (GF), Diann Hunt (DH), Loree Lough (LL), Debby Mayne (DM), Trish Perry (TP), Cynthia Ruchti (CR), Snapdragon Group Editorial Services (SGES)

Cover and interior design by Thinkpen Design | thinkpendesign.com
Typesetting by Scott Williams | Richmond & Williams

Printed in China

1 2 3 4 5 6 7 8 9 – 19 18 17 16 15 14